Twelve to Sixteen: Early Adolescence

Essays by

J. M. Tanner
Chad Gordon
Peter Blos
David Bakan
Jerome Kagan
Joseph Adelson
Lawrence Kohlberg / Carol Gilligan
Edward C. Martin
John Janeway Conger
John H. Gagnon
Robert Coles
Phyllis La Farge
Thomas J. Cottle
Tina deVaron

Twelve to Sixteen: Early Adolescence

Edited by JEROME KAGAN *and* ROBERT COLES

 W · W · NORTON & COMPANY · INC · *New York*

Library of Congress Cataloging in Publication Data
Kagan, Jerome.
  Twelve to sixteen.

  Includes bibliographical references.
  1. Adolescence. I. Coles, Robert, joint
author. II. Tanner, James Mourilyan. III. Title.
HQ796.K16   301.43′15   72–4446
ISBN 0–393–01092–9

1 2 3 4 5 6 7 8 9 0

CONTENTS

JEROME KAGAN

Introduction

IT IS a paradox that adolescence should be the period of greatest concern to parents and youth and the era least well comprehended by psychologists. Our understanding of the human infant has been enhanced enormously during the last decade as elegant methodology and rich theory were simultaneously focused on the first year. But no comparable wisdom has been accumulated for early adolescence. There are several reasons for this intellectual frustration.

In the first place, the questions of priority seek answers to affective and motivational phenomena, especially the experiences surrounding sexuality, anger, and ambivalent independence. Since the adolescent has impermeable defenses against simple probes into his motivational world and since psychologists do not possess more powerful methods of inquiry, most of our knowledge is limited to what the adolescent is willing to tell us in an interview or questionnaire. The answers are helpful guides to the region but far from a detailed map.

Further, we do not possess a coherent theoretical view of this developmental period and, as a result, must use monetary concerns of the community and hunch when problems are selected.

Finally, we have often been misled into culs-de-sac by focusing too narrowly on urban middle-class adolescents and assumed too quickly that alienation, rebellion, drugs, and whole earth catalogs are characteristic of all adolescents. We have relied too often on our personal memories of this period and the easy availability of adolescents. Since most of us know a few of them moderately well, we make the presumptuous leap to omniscience and generate maxims without restraint. It is not that personal recollections or quiet conversations are without value, but that they offer only partial access to the mosaic of cognitive and motivational phenomena we want to understand. Moreover, these sources of information inevitably lead to an exaggeration of the superficial structure of local issues and obstruct a vision of the deep structure that is more likely to be characteristic of youth in varied cultural settings.

The editors appreciate the lacunae in our knowledge of early adolescence and hope that this volume adds perspective to this most dynamic of growth periods and poses a new set of questions while answering or discarding old ones.

ROBERT COLES

Introduction

As I WENT THROUGH the various essays in this volume I found myself
remembering some words of advice (and warning) I received in
1960, when I was beginning to talk with the much harrassed black
children who pioneered school desegregation in New Orleans. I had
gone to see the psychologist Dr. Kenneth Clark, who at that time
headed a child guidance clinic in Harlem. I had just finished years
of training in medicine, psychiatry, and child psychiatry—and now
I wanted to put all that knowledge to work. Dr. Clark listened and
listened as I told him what I hoped to do, what I was already beginning to observe. Then he spoke. He gave me much encouragement,
but he also said something (and repeated it in a letter to me) I was
not at the moment able to appreciate as enormously important—
only later, much later: "Watch out. You've been in a groove all these
years, burrowing in deeper and deeper. You've probably paid a lot
for what you've gained. So try to find a vantage point for yourself.
Try to get a broader look."

I know from my own experience working with troubled adolescents at the Children's Hospital in Boston how dangerous it can be
for anyone, from any discipline, to bring to bear in a singleminded
way his or her particular point of view; so often the complexity of the
growing youth's life is thereby forsaken—all because a pediatrician
or child psychiatrist happens to want things made unequivocally
clear and precise. Especially with adolescents, that kind of un-
qualified clarity and precision turns out to be, again and again, sheer
illusion. As Anna Freud has insisted, both with respect to children
and adolescents, the best initial posture for a therapist (maybe the
best *continuing* posture) is that of the tactful and interested observer
who allows in himself or herself (and acknowledges to others) more
than a little wonder, if not awe. Yet, it is just such a response that
frightens so many of us, hence the resort to dogmatic theories of one
sort or another: adolescence is *this* or *that*, requires one or another

theoretical explanation—and conversely, has been poorly described or analyzed in book X or book Y, and on and on. Meanwhile, of course, children grow up, and in different countries or continents find their way to adulthood. Even within countries the variation is enormous, as anyone knows who bothers to leave the upper-middle-class suburbs of cities like Boston, New York, Los Angeles, or San Francisco (where so many of our social scientists live and work and write up their observations) for other towns, villages, "spots," which is what I have heard a relatively populated area sometimes called by rural people in Kentucky or West Virginia.

In any event, Dr. Clark was right; for me to understand how boys and girls grow up in those rural areas was not to be easy. Especially when I tried to work with young adolescents were my assumptions and preconceptions and outright prejudices challenged. All one need do is spend time with an Appalachian family, or a young migrant farmer (of, say, ten or twelve years of age) or a sharecropper youth—and soon one begins to wonder *which* adolescence all those textbooks mean to portray. Nor is the issue only one of class or caste. As David Bakan has explicitly emphasized in his essay, as others in this volume also point out more implicitly, we have to look at the very word "adolescence" and try to fit it into a historical perspective. Even the notion that certain years (twelve to sixteen or eighteen) have special social and psychological significance requires attention and analysis.

I think it fair to say that for many readers the essays to follow will give not one but many perspectives. The biologist is here. The psychoanalyst speaks. There are some shrewd and extensive sociological observations. Historians and political scientists will not find their point of view and their exceedingly important interests ignored. Educators will find pages that speak to their concerns. Developmental and social psychologists, still up against man's stubborn refusal to reveal his own secrets even as he reaches out for those nature possesses, are once again heard from—and Professors Kohlberg and Kagan are among the very best of those psychologists, the most flexible and wise, the least given to outlandish and shaky, if temporarily "exciting," generalizations. And finally, there are the "human documents," so to speak, the moving but also carefully deliberate efforts of a man and a woman to go back in time and capture for themselves and us, their readers, a measure of what they, two middle-class American youths, once experienced in the course of growing up.

No doubt this volume is a mere beginning. One wonders, for instance, what a group of similar "experts" from Asia or Africa, let alone Europe, might come up with. Still, I believe the tone that consistently characterizes these essays and the ecumenical spirit the volume as a whole offers are as edifying and valuable as the many bits of information or speculation to be found by the reader as he works his way through the observations and conclusions of a group of writers who have struggled with the idea (and the driving reality of) adolescence. It may now be harder than ever for any one formulation about adolescence to capture the minds of students going into fields like education, medicine, or any of the social sciences—fields whose members have traditionally demonstrated an interest in the vicissitudes of young people. It may be even harder than ever for us who claim an interest in "youth" to come forward with ideas and formulations which in their sum do scant justice to the complexities and ambiguities human beings, no matter how young or old, keep on presenting to those who choose to observe them, listen to them, and write up what has been seen and heard.

ACKNOWLEDGMENTS

The Ford Foundation is thanked by the Editors for its generous support of this study. Its grant to the American Academy of Arts and Sciences to support interdisciplinary research has been very helpful in making this book possible.

J. M. TANNER

Sequence, Tempo, and Individual Variation in Growth and Development of Boys and Girls Aged Twelve to Sixteen

FOR THE majority of young persons, the years from twelve to sixteen are the most eventful ones of their lives so far as their growth and development is concerned. Admittedly during fetal life and the first year or two after birth developments occurred still faster, and a sympathetic environment was probably even more crucial, but the subject himself was not the fascinated, charmed, or horrified spectator that watches the developments, or lack of developments, of adolescence. Growth is a very regular and highly regulated process, and from birth onward the growth rate of most bodily tissues decreases steadily, the fall being swift at first and slower from about three years. Body shape changes gradually since the rate of growth of some parts, such as the arms and legs, is greater than the rate of growth of others, such as the trunk. But the change is a steady one, a smoothly continuous development rather than any passage through a series of separate stages.

Then at puberty, a very considerable alteration in growth rate occurs. There is a swift increase in body size, a change in the shape and body composition, and a rapid development of the gonads, the reproductive organs, and the characters signaling sexual maturity. Some of these changes are common to both sexes, but most are sex-specific. Boys have a great increase in muscle size and strength, together with a series of physiological changes, making them more capable than girls of doing heavy physical work and running faster and longer. The changes specifically adapt the male to his primitive primate role of dominating, fighting, and foraging. Such adolescent changes occur generally in primates, but are more marked in some species than in others. Male, female, and prepubescent gibbons are hard to distinguish when they are together, let alone apart. No such problem arises with gorillas or Rhesus monkeys. Man lies at about the middle of the primate range, both in adolescent size increase and degree of sexual differentiation.

The adolescent changes are brought about by hormones, either secreted for the first time, or secreted in much higher amounts than previously. Each hormone acts on a set of targets or receptors, but these are often not concentrated in a single organ, nor in a single type of tissue. Testosterone, for example, acts on receptors in the cells of the penis, the skin of the face, the cartilages of the shoulder joints, and certain parts of the brain. Whether all these cells respond by virtue of having the same enzyme system, or whether different enzymes are involved at different sites is not yet clear. The systems have developed through natural selection, producing a functional response of obvious biological usefulness in societies of hunter gatherers, but of less certain benefit in the culture of invoice clerk and shop assistant. Evolutionary adaptations of bodily structure usually carry with them an increased proclivity for using those structures in behavior, and there is no reason to suppose this principle suddenly stops short at twentieth-century man. There is no need to take sides in the current debate on the origins of aggression to realize that a major task of any culture is the channeling of this less specifically sexual adolescent energy into creative and playful activity.

The adolescent changes have not altered in the last fifteen years, or the last fifty, or probably the last five thousand. Girls still develop two years earlier than boys; some boys still have completed their whole bodily adolescent development before other boys of the same chronological age have begun theirs. These are perhaps the two major biological facts to be borne in mind when thinking of the adolescent's view of himself in relation to his society. The sequence of the biological events remains the same. But there has been one considerable change; the events occur now at an earlier age than formerly. Forty years ago the average British girl had her first menstrual period (menarche) at about her fifteenth birthday; nowadays it is shortly before her thirteenth. Fifty years ago in Britain social class differences played a considerable part in causing the variation of age of menarche in the population, the less well-off growing up more slowly. Nowadays, age at menarche is almost the same in different classes and most of the variation is due to genetical factors.

In this essay, I shall discuss (1) the growth of the body at adolescence and its changes in size, shape, and tissue composition, (2) sex dimorphism and the development of the reproductive system, (3) the concept of developmental age and the interaction of physical and behavioral advancement, (4) the interaction of genetic and environmental influences on the age of occurrence of puberty and the secular trend toward earlier maturation.

Growth of the Body at Adolescence

The extent of the adolescent spurt in height is shown in figure 1. For a year or more the velocity of growth approximately doubles; a boy is likely to be growing again at the rate he last experienced about age two. The peak velocity of height (PHV, a point much used in growth studies) averages about 10.5 centimeters a year (cm/yr) in boys and 9.0 cm/yr in girls (with a standard deviation of about 1.0 cm/yr) but this is the "instantaneous" peak given by a smooth curve drawn through the observations. The velocity over the whole year encompassing the six months before and after the peak is naturally somewhat less. During this year a boy usually grows between 7 and 12 cm and a girl between 6 and 11 cm. Children who have their peak early reach a somewhat higher peak than those who have it late.

The average age at which the peak is reached depends on the nature and circumstances of the group studied more, probably, than does the height of the peak. In moderately well-off British or North American children at present the peak occurs on average at about 14.0 years in boys and 12.0 years in girls. The standard deviations are about 0.9 years in each instance. Though the absolute average ages differ from series to series the two-year sex difference is invariant.

The adolescent spurt is at least partly under different hormonal control from growth in the period before. Probably as a consequence of this the amount of height added during the spurt is to a considerable degree independent of the amount attained prior to it. Most children who have grown steadily up, say, the 30th centile line on a height chart till adolescence end up at the 30th centile as adults, it is true; but a number end as high as the 50th or as low as the 10th, and a very few at the 55th or 5th. The correlation between adult height and height just before the spurt starts is about 0.8. This leaves some 30 per cent of the variability in adult height as due to differences in the magnitude of the adolescent spurt. So some ado-

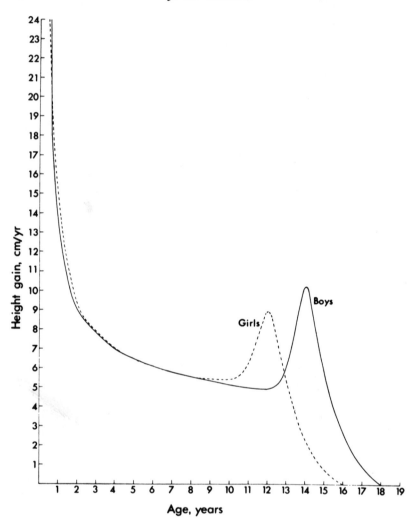

Figure 1. Typical individual velocity curves for supine length or height in boys and girls. These curves represent the velocity of the typical boy and girl at any given instant. (From J. M. Tanner, R. H. Whitehouse, and M. Takaishi, "Standards from Birth to Maturity for Height, Weight Height Velocity and Weight Velocity; British Children, 1965," *Archives of the Diseases of Childhood,* 41 [1966], 455-471.)

lescents get a nasty and unavoidable shock; though probably the effects of early and late maturing (see below) almost totally confuse the issue of final height during the years we are considering.

Practically all skeletal and muscular dimensions take part in the spurt, though not to an equal degree. Most of the spurt in height is due to acceleration of trunk length rather than length of legs. There is a fairly regular order in which the dimensions accelerate; leg length as a rule reaches its peak first, followed by the body breadths, with shoulder width last. Thus a boy stops growing out of his trousers (at least in length) a year before he stops growing out of his jackets. The earliest structures to reach their adult status are the head, hands, and feet. At adolescence, children, particularly girls, sometimes complain of having large hands and feet. They can be reassured that by the time they are fully grown their hands and feet will be a little smaller in proportion to their arms and legs, and considerably smaller in proportion to their trunk.

The spurt in muscle, both of limbs and heart, coincides with the spurt in skeletal growth, for both are caused by the same hormones. Boys' muscle widths reach a peak velocity of growth considerably greater than those reached by girls. But since girls have their spurt earlier, there is actually a period, from about twelve and a half to thirteen and a half, when girls on the average have larger muscles than boys of the same age.

Simultaneously with the spurt in muscle there is a loss of fat in boys, particularly on the limbs. Girls have a velocity curve of fat identical in shape to that of boys; that is to say, their fat accumulation (going on in both sexes from about age six) decelerates. But the decrease in velocity in girls is not sufficiently great to carry the average velocity below zero, that is to give an absolute loss. Most girls have to content themselves with a temporary go-slow in fat accumulation. As the adolescent growth spurt draws to an end, fat tends to accumulate again in both sexes.

The marked increase in muscle size in boys at adolescence leads to an increase in strength, illustrated in figure 2. Before adolescence, boys and girls are similar in strength for a given body size and shape; after, boys are much stronger, probably due to developing more force per gram of muscle as well as absolutely larger muscles. They also develop larger hearts and lungs relative to their size, a higher systolic blood pressure, a lower resting heart rate, a greater capacity for carrying oxygen in the blood, and a greater power for neutralizing the chemical products of muscular exercise such as lactic acid.[1] In short, the male becomes at adolescence more adapted for the tasks of hunting, fighting, and manipulating all sorts of heavy objects, as is necessary in some forms of food-gathering.

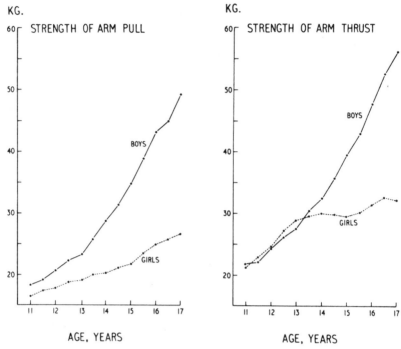

Figure 2. Strength of arm pull and arm thrust from age eleven to seventeen. Mixed longitudinal data, sixty-five to ninety-five boys and sixty-six to ninety-three girls in each age group. (From J. M. Tanner, *Growth at Adolescence,* 2d ed. [Oxford: Blackwell Scientific Publications, 1962]; data from H. E. Jones, *Motor Performance and Growth* [Berkeley: University of California Press, 1949].)

The increase in hemoglobin, associated with a parallel increase in the number of red blood cells, is illustrated in figure 3.[2] The hemoglobin concentration is plotted in relation to the development of secondary sex characters instead of chronological age, to obviate the spread due to early and late maturing (see below). Girls lack the rise in red cells and hemoglobin, which is brought about by the action of testosterone.

It is as a direct result of these anatomical and physiological changes that athletic ability increases so much in boys at adolescence. The popular notion of a boy "outgrowing his strength" at this time has little scientific support. It is true that the peak velocity of strength is reached a year or so later than that of height, so that a short period may exist when the adolescent, having completed his skeletal and probably also muscular growth, still does not have the

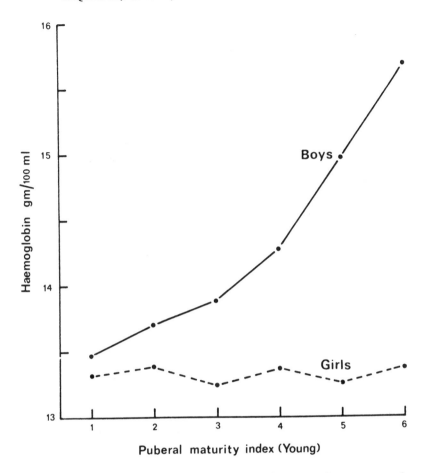

Figure 3. Blood hemoglobin level in girls and boys according to stage of puberty; cross-sectional data. (From H. B. Young, "Ageing and Adolescence," *Developmental Medicine and Child Neurology,* 5 (1963), 451-460, cited in J. M. Tanner, "Growth and Endocrinology of the Adolescent," in L. Gardner, ed., *Endocrine and Genetic Diseases of Childhood* [Philadelphia and London: Saunders, 1969].)

strength of a young adult of the same body size and shape. But this is a temporary phase; considered absolutely, power, athletic skill, and physical endurance all increase progressively and rapidly throughout adolescence. It is certainly not true that the changes accompanying adolescence enfeeble, even temporarily. If the adolescent becomes weak and easily exhausted it is for psychological reasons and not physiological ones.

Sex Dimorphism and the Development of the Reproductive System

The adolescent spurt in skeletal and muscular dimensions is closely related to the rapid development of the reproductive system which takes place at this time. The course of this development is outlined diagrammatically in figure 4. The solid areas marked "breast" in the girls and "penis" and "testis" in the boys represent the period of accelerated growth of these organs and the horizontal lines and the rating numbers marked "pubic hair" stand for its advent and development.[3] The sequences and timings given represent in each case average values for British boys and girls; the North American average is within two or three months of this. To give an idea of the individual departures from the average, figures for the range of age at which the various events begin and end are inserted under the first and last point of the bars. The acceleration of penis growth, for example, begins on the average at about age twelve and a half, but sometimes as early as ten and a half and sometimes as late as fourteen and a half. The completion of penis development usually occurs at about age fourteen and a half but in some boys is at twelve and a half and in others at sixteen and a half. There are a few boys, it will be noticed, who do not begin their spurts in height or penis development until the earliest maturers have entirely completed theirs. At age thirteen, fourteen, and fifteen there is an enormous variability among any group of boys, who range all the way from practically complete maturity to absolute preadolescence. The same is true of girls aged eleven, twelve, and thirteen.

In figure 5 three boys are illustrated, all aged exactly 14.75 years and three girls all aged exactly 12.75. All are entirely normal and healthy, yet the first boy could be mistaken easily for a twelve-year-old and the third for a young man of seventeen or eighteen. Manifestly it is ridiculous to consider all three boys or all three girls as equally grown up either physically, or, since much behavior at this age is conditioned by physical status, in their social relations. The statement that a boy is fourteen is in most contexts hopelessly vague; all depends, morphologically, physiologically, and to a considerable extent sociologically too, on whether he is preadolescent, midadolescent, or postadolescent.

The psychological and social importance of this difference in the tempo of development, as it has been called, is very great, par-

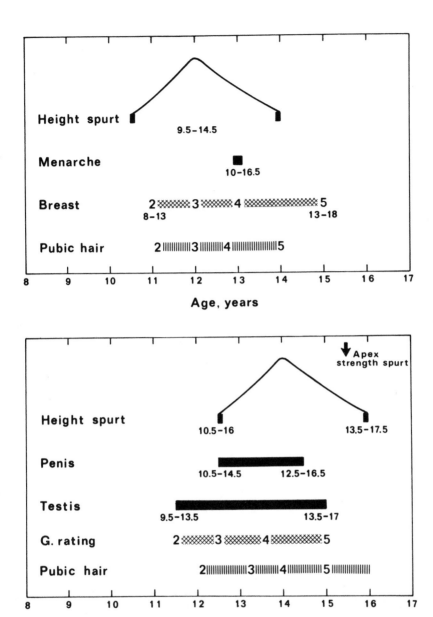

Figure 4. Diagram of sequence of events at adolescence in boys and girls. The average boy and girl are represented. The range of ages within which each event charted may begin and end is given by the figures placed directly below its start and finish. (From W. A. Marshall and J. M. Tanner, "Variations in the Pattern of Pubertal Changes in Boys," *Archives of the Diseases of Childhood,* 45 [1970], 13.)

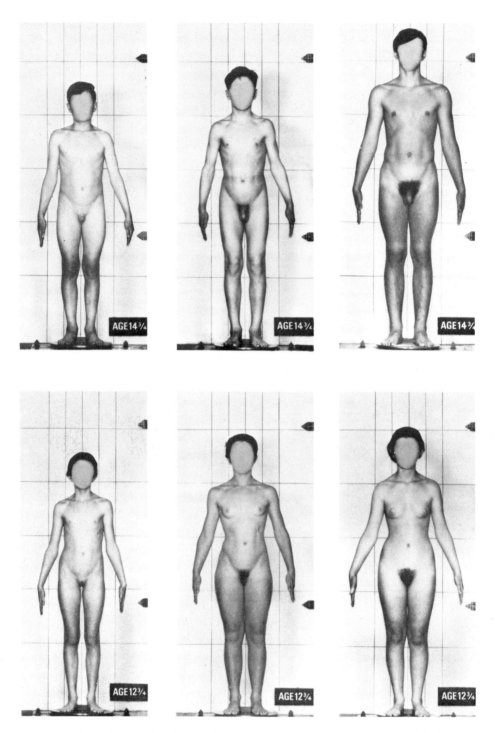

Figure 5. Differing degrees of pubertal development at the same chronological age. Upper row three boys all aged 14.75 years. Lower row three girls all aged 12.75 years. (From Tanner, "Growth and Endocrinology of the Adolescent.")

ticularly in boys. Boys who are advanced in development are likely to dominate their contemporaries in athletic achievement and sexual interest alike. Conversely the late developer is the one who all too often loses out in the rough and tumble of the adolescent world; and he may begin to wonder whether he will ever develop his body properly or be as well endowed sexually as those others he has seen developing around him. A very important part of the educationist's and the doctor's task at this time is to provide information about growth and its variability to preadolescents and adolescents and to give sympathetic support and reassurance to those who need it.

The *sequence* of events, though not exactly the same for each boy or girl, is much less variable than the age at which the events occur. The first sign of puberty in the boy is usually an acceleration of the growth of the testes and scrotum with reddening and wrinkling of the scrotal skin. Slight growth of pubic hair may begin about the same time, but is usually a trifle later. The spurts in height and penis growth begin on average about a year after the first testicular acceleration. Concomitantly with the growth of the penis, and under the same stimulus, the seminal vesicles and the prostate and bulbo-urethral glands enlarge and develop. The time of the first ejaculation of seminal fluid is to some extent culturally as well as biologically determined, but as a rule is during adolescence, and about a year after the beginning of accelerated penis growth.

Axillary hair appears on the average some two years after the beginning of pubic hair growth—that is, when pubic hair is reaching stage 4. However, there is enough variability and dissociation in these events that a very few children's axillary hair actually appears first. In boys, facial hair begins to grow at about the time the axillary hair appears. There is a definite order in which the hairs of moustache and beard appear; first at the corners of the upper lip, then over all the upper lip, then at the upper part of the cheeks in the mid-line below the lower lip, and finally along the sides and lower border of the chin. The remainder of the body hair appears from about the time of first axillary hair development until a considerable time after puberty. The ultimate amount of body hair an individual develops seems to depend largely on heredity, though whether because of the kinds and amounts of hormones secreted or because of the reactivity of the end-organs is not known.

Breaking of the voice occurs relatively late in adolescence; it is often a gradual process and so not suitable as a criterion of puberty.

The change in pitch accompanies enlargement of the larynx and lengthening of the vocal cords, caused by the action of testosterone on the laryngeal cartilages. During the period of breaking, the pitch is variable, and the true adult pitch associated with full growth of the larynx may not be established until late adolescence. In addition to change in pitch, there is also a change in quality or timbre which distinguishes the voice (more particularly the vowel sounds) of both male and female adults from that of children. This is dependent on the enlargement of the resonating spaces above the larynx, due to the rapid growth of the mouth, nose, and maxilla which occurs during adolescence.

In the skin the sebaceous and apocrine sweat glands, particularly of the axillae and genital and anal regions, develop rapidly during puberty and give rise to a characteristic odor; the changes occur in both sexes but are more marked in the male. Enlargement of the pores at the root of the nose and the appearance of comedones and acne, though liable to occur in either sex, are considerably commoner in adolescent boys than girls, since the underlying skin changes are the result of androgenic activity. A roughening of the skin, particularly over the outer aspects of the thighs and upper arms, may be seen in both sexes during adolescence, but again is commoner in boys than girls.

During adolescence the male breast undergoes changes, some temporary and some permanent. The diameter of the areola, which is equal in both sexes before puberty, increases considerably, though less than it does in girls. Representative figures are 12.5 millimeters before puberty, 21.5 millimeters in mature men, and 35.5 millimeters in mature women. In some boys (between a fifth and a third of most groups studied) there is a distinct enlargement of the breast (sometimes unilaterally) about midway through adolescence. This usually regresses again after about one year.

In girls the appearance of the "breast bud" is as a rule the first sign of puberty, though the appearance of pubic hair precedes it in about one in three. The uterus and vagina develop simultaneously with the breast. The labia and clitoris also enlarge. Menarche, the first menstrual period, is a late event in the sequence. It occurs almost invariably after the peak of the height spurt has been passed. Though it marks a definitive and probably mature stage of uterine development, it does not usually signify the attainment of full reproductive function. The early cycles may be more irregular than later ones and are in some girls, but by no means all, accompanied by dysmenorrhea. They are often anovulatory, that is unaccompanied by the shedding of an egg. Thus there is frequently a period of adolescent sterility lasting a year to eighteen months after menarche; but it cannot be relied on in the individual case. Similar considerations may apply to the male, but there is no reliable information about this. On the average, girls grow about 6 cm more after menarche, though gains of up to twice this amount may occur. The gain is practically independent of whether menarche occurs early or late.

Normal Variations in Pubertal Development

The diagram of figure 4 must not be allowed to obscure the fact that children vary a great deal both in the rapidity with which they pass through the various stages of puberty and in the closeness with which the various events are linked together. At one extreme one may find a perfectly healthy girl who has not yet menstruated though she has reached adult breast and pubic hair ratings and is already two years past her peak height velocity; at the other a girl who has passed all the stages of puberty within the space of two years. Details of the limits of what may be considered normal can be found in the articles of Marshall and Tanner.[4]

In girls the interval from the first sign of puberty to complete maturity varies from one and a half to six years. From the moment when the breast bud first appears to menarche averages two and a half years but may be as little as six months or as much as five and a half years. The rapidity with which a child passes through puberty seems to be independent of whether puberty is occurring early or late. There is some independence between breast and pubic hair developments, as one might expect on endocrinological grounds. A few girls reach pubic hair stage 3 (see figure 4) before any breast development starts; conversely breast stage 3 may be reached before any pubic hair appears. At breast stage 5, however, pubic hair is always present in girls. Menarche usually occurs in breast stage 4 and pubic hair stage 4, but in about 10 per cent of girls occurs in stage 5 for both, and occasionally may occur in stage 2 or even 1 of pubic hair. Menarche invariably occurs after peak height velocity is passed, so the tall girl can be reassured about future growth if her periods have begun.

In boys a similar variability occurs. The genitalia may take any time between two and five years to pass from G2 to G5, and some boys complete the whole process while others have still not gone from G2 to G3. Pubic hair growth in the absence of genital development is very unusual in normal boys, but in a small percentage of boys the genitalia develop as far as stage 4 before the pubic hair starts to grow.

The height spurt occurs relatively later in boys than in girls. Thus there is a difference between the average boy and girl of two years in age of peak height velocity, but of only one year in the first appearance of pubic hair. The PHV occurs in very few boys before genital stage 4, whereas 75 per cent of girls reach PHV before breast stage 4. Indeed in some girls the acceleration in height is the first sign of puberty; this is never so in boys. A small boy whose genitalia are just beginning to develop can be unequivocally reassured that an acceleration in height is soon to take place, but a girl in the corresponding situation may already have had her height spurt.

The basis of some children having loose and some tight linkages between pubertal events is not known. Probably the linkage reflects the degree of integration of various processes in the hypothalamus and the pituitary gland, for breast growth is controlled by one group of hormones, pubic hair growth by another, and the height spurt probably by a third. In rare pathological instances the events may become widely divorced.

The Development of Sex Dimorphism

The differential effects on the growth of bone, muscle, and fat at puberty increase considerably the difference in body composition between the sexes. Boys have a greater increase not only in the length of bones but in the thickness of cortex, and girls have a smaller loss of fat. The most striking dimorphism, however, are the man's greater stature and breadth of shoulders and the woman's wider hips. These are produced chiefly by the changes and timing of puberty but it is important to remember that sex dimorphisms do not arise only at that time. Many appear much earlier. Some, like the external genital difference itself, develop during fetal life. Others develop continuously throughout the whole growth period by a sustained differential growth rate. An example of this is the greater relative length and breadth of the forearm in the male when compared with whole arm length or whole body length.

Part of the sex difference in pelvic shape antedates puberty.

Girls at birth already have a wider pelvic outlet. Thus the adaptation for child bearing is present from a very early age. The changes at puberty are concerned more with widening the pelvic inlet and broadening the much more noticeable hips. It seems likely that these changes are more important in attracting the male's attention than in dealing with its ultimate product.

These sex-differentiated morphological characters arising at puberty—to which we can add the corresponding physiological and perhaps psychological ones as well—are secondary sex characters in the straightforward sense that they are caused by sex hormone or sex-differential hormone secretion and serve reproductive activity. The penis is directly concerned in copulation, the mammary gland in lactation. The wide shoulders and muscular power of the male, together with the canine teeth and brow ridges in man's ancestors, developed probably for driving away other males and insuring peace, an adaptation which soon becomes social.

A number of traits persist, perhaps through another mechanism known to the ethologists as ritualization. In the course of evolution a morphological character or a piece of behavior may lose its original function and, becoming further elaborated, complicated, or simplified, may serve as a sign stimulus to other members of the same species, releasing behavior that is in some ways advantageous to the spread or survival of the species. It requires little insight into human erotics to suppose that the shoulders, the hips and buttocks, and the breasts (at least in a number of widespread cultures) serve as releasers of mating behavior. The pubic hair (about whose function the textbooks have always preserved a cautious silence) probably survives as a ritualized stimulus for sexual activity, developed by simplification from the hair remaining in the inguinal and axillary regions for the infant to cling to when still transported, as in present apes and monkeys, under the mother's body. Similar considerations may apply to axillary hair, which is associated with special apocrine glands which themselves only develop at puberty and are related histologically to scent glands in other mammals. The beard, on the other hand, may still be more frightening to other males than enticing to females. At least ritual use in past communities suggests this is the case; but perhaps there are two sorts of beards.

The Initiation of Puberty

The manner in which puberty is initiated has a general importance for the clarification of developmental mechanisms. Certain children develop all the changes of puberty, up to and including spermatogenesis and ovulation, at a very early age, either as the result of a brain lesion or as an isolated developmental, sometimes genetic defect. The youngest mother on record was such a case, and gave birth to a full-term healthy infant by Caesarian section at the age of five years, eight months. The existence of precocious puberty and the results of accidental ingestion by small children of male or female sex hormones indicate that breasts, uterus, and penis will respond to hormonal stimulation long before puberty. Evidently an increased end-organ sensitivity plays at most a minor part in pubertal events.

The signal to start the sequence of events is given by the brain, not the pituitary. Just as the brain holds the information on sex, so it holds information on maturity. The pituitary of a newborn rat successfully grafted in place of an adult pituitary begins at once to function in an adult fashion, and does not have to wait till its normal age of maturation has been reached. It is the hypothalamus, not the pituitary, which has to mature before puberty begins.

Maturation, however, does not come out of the blue and at least in rats a little more is known about this mechanism. In these animals small amounts of sex hormones circulate from the time of birth and these appear to inhibit the prepubertal hypothalamus from producing gonadotrophin releasers. At puberty it is supposed that the hypothalamic cells become less sensitive to sex hormone. The small amount of sex hormones circulating then fails to inhibit the hypothalamus and gonadotrophins are released; these stimulate the production of testosterone by the testis or estrogen by the ovary. The level of the sex hormone rises until the same feedback circuit is reestablished, but now at a higher level of gonadotrophins and sex hormones. The sex hormones are now high enough to stimulate the growth of secondary sex characters and support mating behavior.

Developmental Age and the Interaction of Physical and Behavioral Advancement

Children vary greatly in their tempo of growth. The effects are most dramatically seen at adolescence, as illustrated in figure 5, but they are present at all ages from birth and even before. Girls, for example, do not suddenly become two years ahead of boys at adolescence; on the contrary they are born with slightly more mature skeletons and nervous systems, and gradually increase their developmental lead (in absolute terms) throughout childhood.

Clearly, the concept of *developmental* age, as opposed to *chronological* age, is a very important one. To measure developmental age we need some way of determining the percentage of the child's growth process which has been attained at any time. In retrospective research studies, the per cent of final adult height may be very effectively used; but in the clinic we need something that is immediate in its application. The difficulty about using height, for example, is that different children end up at different heights, so that a tall-for-his-age twelve-year-old may either be a tall adult in the making with average maturational tempo, or an average adult in the making with an accelerated tempo. Precisely the same applies to the child who scores above average on most tests of mental ability.

To measure developmental age we need something which ends up the same for everyone and is applicable throughout the whole period of growth. Many physiological measures meet these criteria, in whole or in part. They range from the number of erupted teeth to the percentage of water in muscle cells. The various developmental "age" scales do not necessarily coincide, and each has its particular use. By far the most generally useful, however, is skeletal maturity or *bone* age. A less important one is dental maturity.

Skeletal maturity is usually measured by taking a radiograph of the hand and wrist (using the same radiation exposure that a child inevitably gets, and to more sensitive areas, by spending a week on vacation in the mountains). The appearances of the developing bones can be rated and formed into a scale; the scale is applicable to boys and girls of all genetic backgrounds, though girls on the average reach any given score at a younger age than boys, and blacks on the average, at least in the first few years after birth, reach a given score younger than do whites. Other areas of the body may be used if required. Skeletal maturity is closely related to the age at which adolescence occurs, that is to maturity measured by secondary sex character development. Thus the range of *chronological* age within which menarche may normally fall is about ten to sixteen and a half, but the corresponding range of *skeletal* age for menarche is only twelve to fourteen and a half. Evidently the physiological processes controlling progression of skeletal development are in most instances closely linked with those which initiate the events of adolescence. Furthermore children tend to be consistently advanced or retarded during their whole growth period, or at any rate after about age three.

Dental maturity partly shares in this general skeletal and bodily maturation. At all ages from six to thirteen children who are advanced skeletally have on the average more erupted teeth than those who are skeletally retarded. Likewise those who have an early adolescence on the average erupt their teeth early. Girls usually have more erupted teeth than boys. But this relationship is not a very close one, and quantitatively speaking, it is the relative independence of teeth and general skeletal development which should be emphasized. There is some general factor of bodily maturity creating a tendency for a child to be advanced or retarded as a whole: in his skeletal ossification, in the percentage attained of his eventual size, in his permanent dentition, doubtless in his physiological reactions, and possibly in the results of his tests of ability. But not too much should be made of this general factor; and especially it should be noted how very limited is the loading, so to speak, of brain growth in it. There is little justification in the facts of physical growth and development for the concept of "organismic age" in which almost wholly disparate measures of developmental maturity are lumped together.

Physical Maturation, Mental Ability, and Emotional Development

Clearly the occurrence of tempo differences in human growth has profound implications for educational theory and practice. This would especially be so if advancement in physical growth were linked to any significant degree with advancement in intellectual ability and in emotional maturity.

There is good evidence that in the European and North American school systems children who are physically advanced toward maturity score on the average slightly higher in most tests of mental ability than children of the same age who are physically less mature. The difference is not great, but it is consistent and it occurs at all ages that have been studied—that is, back as far as six and a half years. Similarly the intelligence test score of postmenarcheal girls is higher than the score of premenarcheal girls of the same age.[5] Thus in age-linked examinations physically fast-maturing children have a significantly better chance than slow-maturing.

It is also true that physically large children score higher than small ones, at all ages from six onward. In a random sample of all Scottish eleven-year-old children, for example, comprising 6,440 pupils, the correlation between height and score in the Moray House group test was 0.25 ± 0.01 which leads to an average increase of one and a half points Terman-Merrill I.Q. per inch of stature. A similar correlation was found in London children. The effects can be very significant for individual children. In ten-year-old girls there was nine points difference in I.Q. between those whose height was above the 75th percentile and those whose height was below the 15th. This is two-thirds of the standard deviation of the test score.

It was usually thought that both the relationships between test score and height and between test score and early maturing would disappear in adulthood. If the correlations represented only the effects of co-advancement both of mental ability and physical growth this might be expected to happen. There is no difference in height between early and late maturing boys when both have finished growing. But it is now clear that, curiously, at least part of the height-I.Q. correlation persists in adults.[6] It is not clear in what proportion genetic and environmental factors are responsible for this.

There is little doubt that being an early or a late maturer may have repercussions on behavior, and that in some children these repercussions may be considerable. There is little enough solid information on the relation between emotional and physiological development, but what there is supports the common sense notion that emotional attitudes are clearly related to physiological events.

The boy's world is one where physical powers bring prestige as well as success, where the body is very much an instrument of the person. Boys who are advanced in development, not only at puberty, but before as well, are more likely than others to be leaders. Indeed, this is reinforced by the fact that muscular, powerful boys on the average mature earlier than others and have an early adolescent growth spurt. The athletically-built boy not only tends to dominate his fellows before puberty, but also by getting an early start he is in a good position to continue that domination. The unathletic, lanky boy, unable, perhaps, to hold his own in the preadolescent rough and tumble, gets still further pushed to the wall at adolescence, as he sees others shoot up while he remains nearly stationary in growth. Even boys several years younger now suddenly surpass him in size, athletic skill, and perhaps, too, in social graces. Figure 6 shows the height curves of two boys, the first an early-maturing muscular boy, the other a late-maturing lanky one. Though

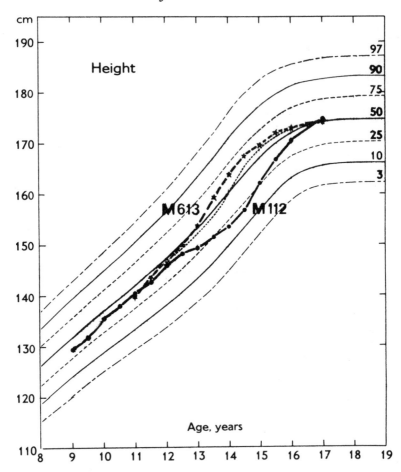

Figure 6. Height attained of two boys, one with an early and the other with a late adolescent spurt. Note how at age eleven and again at age seventeen the boys are the same height. (From J. M. Tanner, *Education and Physical Growth: Implications of the Study of Children's Growth for Educational Theory and Practice* [London: University of London Press, 1961].)

both boys are of average height at age eleven, and together again at average height at seventeen, the early maturer is four inches taller during the peak of adolescence.

At a much deeper level the late developer at adolescence may sometimes have doubts about whether he will ever develop his body properly and whether he will be as well endowed sexually as those others he has seen developing around him. The lack of events of adolescence may act as a trigger to reverberate fears accumulated deep in the mind during the early years of life.

It may seem as though the early maturers have things all their own way. It is indeed true that most studies of the later personalities of children whose growth history is known do show early maturers as more stable, more sociable, less neurotic, and more successful in society, at least in the United States.[7] But early maturers have their difficulties also, particularly the girls in some societies. Though some glory in their new possessions, others are embarrassed by them. The early maturer, too, has a longer period of frustration of sex drive and of drive toward independence and the establishment of vocational orientation.

Little can be done to reduce the individual differences in children's tempo of growth, for they are biologically rooted and not significantly reducible by any social steps we may take. It, therefore, behooves all teachers, psychologists, and pediatricians to be fully aware of the facts and alert to the individual problems they raise.

Trend Toward Large Size and Earlier Maturation

The rate of maturing and the age at onset of puberty are dependent, naturally, on a complex interaction of genetic and environmental factors. Where the environment is good, most of the variability in age at menarche in a population is due to genetic differences. In France in the 1950's the mean difference between identical twins was two months, while that between nonidentical twin sisters was eight months.[8] In many societies puberty occurs later in the poorly-off, and in most societies investigated children with many siblings grow less fast than children with few.

Recent investigations in Northeast England showed that social class differences are now only those associated with different sizes of family. The median age of menarche for only girls was 13.0 years, for girls with one sibling 13.2, two siblings 13.4, three siblings and over 13.7. For a given number of siblings the social class as indicated by father's occupation was unrelated to menarcheal age.[9] Environment is still clearly a factor in control of menarcheal age, but in England at least occupation is a less effective indication of poor housing, poor expenditure on food, and poor child care than is the number of children in the family.

During the last hundred years there has been a striking tendency for children to become progressively larger at all ages.[10] This is known as the "secular trend." The magnitude of the trend in Europe and America is such that it dwarfs the differences between socioeconomic classes.

The data from Europe and America agree well: from about 1900, or a little earlier, to the present, children in average economic circumstances have increased in height at age five to seven by about 1 to 2 cm each decade, and at ten to fourteen by 2 to 3 cm each decade. Preschool data show that the trend starts directly after birth and may, indeed, be relatively greater from age two to five than subsequently. The trend started, at least in Britain, a considerable time ago, because Roberts, a factory physician, writing in 1876 said that "a factory child of the present day at the age of nine years weighs as much as one of 10 years did in 1833 . . . each age has gained one year in forty years."[11] The trend in Europe is still continuing at the time of writing but there is some evidence to show that in the United States the best-off sections of the population are now growing up at something approaching the fastest possible speed.

During the same period there has been an upward trend in adult height, but to a considerably lower degree. In earlier times final height was not reached till twenty-five years or later, whereas now it is reached in men at eighteen or nineteen. Data exist, however, which enable us to compare fully grown men at different periods. They lead to the conclusion that in Western Europe men increased in adult height little if at all from 1760 to 1830, about 0.3 cm per decade from 1830 to 1880, and about 0.6 cm per decade from 1880 to 1960. The trend is apparently still continuing in Europe, though not in the best-off section of American society.

Most of the trend toward greater size in children reflects a more rapid maturation; only a minor part reflects a greater ultimate size. The trend toward earlier maturing is best shown in the statistics on age at menarche. A selection of the best data is illustrated in figure 7. The trend is between three and four months per decade since 1850 in average sections of Western European populations. Well-off persons show a trend of about half this magnitude, having never been so retarded in menarche as the worse-off.[12]

Most, though not all, of the differences between populations are probably due to nutritional factors, operating during the whole of the growth period, from conception onward. The well-nourished Western populations have median menarcheal ages of about 12.8

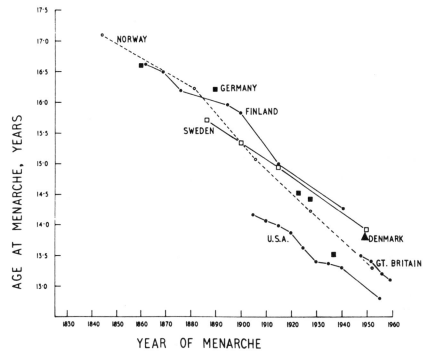

Figure 7. Secular trend in age at menarche, 1830-1960. (Sources of data and method of plotting detailed in Tanner, *Growth at Adolescence.*)

to 13.2 years; the latest recorded ages, by contrast, are 18 years in the Highlands of New Guinea, 17 years in Central Africa, and 15.5 years in poorly-off Bantu in the South African Transkei. Well-nourished Africans have a median age of 13.4 (Kampala upper classes) or less, comparable with Europeans. Asians at the same nutritional level as Europeans probably have an earlier menarche, the figure for well-off Chinese in Hong Kong being 12.5 years.

The causes of the secular trend are probably multiple. Certainly better nutrition is a major one, and perhaps in particular more protein and calories in early infancy. A lessening of disease may also have contributed. Hot climates used to be cited as a potent cause of early menarche, but it seems now that their effect, if any, is considerably less than that of nutrition. The annual mean world temperature rose from 1850 to about 1940 (when it began to fall again); the polar ice caps have been melting and the glaciers retreating, but on present evidence it seems unlikely that this general warming up has contributed significantly to the earlier menarche of girls.

Some authors have supposed that the increased psychosexual stimulation consequent on modern urban living has contributed, but there is no positive evidence for this. Girls in single-sex schools have menarche at exactly the same age as girls in coeducational schools, but whether this is a fair test of difference in psychosexual stimulation is hard to say.

REFERENCES

1. J. M. Tanner, *Growth at Adolescence,* 2d ed. (Oxford: Blackwell Scientific Publications, 1962), p. 168.

2. H. B. Young, "Ageing and Adolescence," *Developmental Medicine and Child Neurology,* 5 (1963), 451-460.

3. Details of ratings are in Tanner, *Growth at Adolescence.*

4. W. A. Marshall and J. M. Tanner, "Variations in the Pattern of Pubertal Changes in Girls," *Archives of the Diseases of Childhood,* 44 (1969), 291, and "Variations in the Pattern of Pubertal Changes in Boys," *Archives of the Diseases of Childhood,* 45 (1970), 13.

5. See references in Tanner, *Growth at Adolescence,* and Tanner, "Galtonian Eugenics and the Study of Growth, *The Eugenics Review,* 58 (1966), 122-135.

6. Tanner, "Galtonian Eugenics."

7. P. H. Mussen and M. C. Jones, "Self-Concepting Motivations and Interpersonal Attitudes of Late- and Early-Maturing Boys," *Child Development,* 28 (1957), 243-256.

8. M. Tisserand-Perrier, "Etude comparative de certains processus de croissance chez les jeuneaux," *Journal de génétique humaine,* 2 (1953), 87-102, as cited in Tanner, *Growth at Adolescence.*

9. D. F. Roberts, L. M. Rozner, and A. V. Swan, "Age at Menarche, Physique and Environment in Industrial North-East England," *Acta Paediatrica Scandinavica,* 60 (1971), 158-164.

10. J. M. Tanner, "Earlier Maturation in Man," *Scientific American,* 218 (1968), 21-27.

11. Tanner, *Growth at Adolescence.*

12. Details on average age of menarche of various populations and the methods for collecting these statistics will be found in Tanner, "Galtonian Eugenics."

CHAD GORDON

Social Characteristics of Early Adolescence

I. Orienting Concerns

OF ALL the ten or more reasonably clear stages of the ideal-typical middle-class life cycle in contemporary urbanized and industrialized societies, early adolescence is one of the least studied and least understood. The period from the onset of puberty (now around eleven for girls and twelve for boys) until the legally defined changes of status concerning driving and leaving school at one's own discretion (typically at age sixteen) contains some of the life cycle's most important developments in value, aspiration, role, identity, and interaction patterns, but comprehensive theory and solid empirical research on this period of early adolescence are both in short supply.

Table 1 presents an overview of the developmental model I have been using to order a wide range of research and theory on the life cycle. The patterns of age ranges, most significant others, and major dilemmas of value-theme differentiation and integration are expressly intended to represent some of the life cycle dynamics of contemporary urban, white, middle-class persons in the United States. It is explicitly recognized that different subgroups having different ethnic, social class, family structure, and subcultural configurations will have somewhat different patterns of socialization and development, especially where counterculture themes are strong. The dual concerns of this essay are to outline the major sociological parameters of early adolescence in contemporary America, and then to marshall some of the existing literature so as to document what I feel is one of the core value dilemmas of this developmental stage: the problem of integrating the partially contradictory value themes of social *acceptance* and social *achievement*.

II. Selected Social Characteristics of Early Adolescence in the United States

While the twelve to fifteen age range is a reasonably good ap-

Table 1. Stage developmental model of the ideal-typical life cycle
in contemporary urban, middle-class America.

Life cycle stage	Approximate ages	Most significant others	Major dilemma of value-theme differentiation and integration security/challenge
I. Infancy	0–12 months	mother	AFFECTIVE GRATIFICATION/ SENSORIMOTOR EXPERIENCING
II. Early childhood	1–2 years	mother, father	COMPLIANCE/SELF-CONTROL
III. Oedipal period	3–5 years	father, mother, siblings, play-mates	EXPRESSIVITY/INSTRUMENTALITY
IV. Later childhood	6–11 years	parents, same sex peers, teachers	PEER RELATIONSHIPS/ EVALUATED ABILITIES
V. Early adolescence	12–15 years	parents, same sex peers, opposite sex peers, teachers	ACCEPTANCE/ACHIEVEMENT
VI. Later adolescence	16–20 years	same sex peers, opposite sex peers, parents, teachers, loved one, wife or husband	INTIMACY/AUTONOMY
VII. Young adulthood	21–29 years	loved one, husband or wife, children, employers, friends	CONNECTION/SELF-DETERMINATION
VIII. Early maturity	30–44 years	wife or husband, children, superiors, colleagues, friends, parents	STABILITY/ ACCOMPLISHMENT
IX. Full maturity	45 to retirement age	wife or husband, children, colleagues, friends, younger associates	DIGNITY/CONTROL
X. Old age	Retirement age to death	remaining family, long-term friends, neighbors	MEANINGFUL INTEGRATION/ AUTONOMY

SOURCE: Chad Gordon, "Socialization Across the Life-Cycle: A Stage Developmental Model," Department of Social Relations, Harvard University, 1969, and "Role and Value Development Across the Life-Cycle," in a symposium on role theory edited by John Jackson, Sociological Studies IV: Role (London: Cambridge University Press, forthcoming 1971).

proximation of the period of early adolescence, major sources of data
on the social characteristics of young people do not generally use
this particular age categorization. Since persons in these early teen
years are no longer considered a major component of the labor
force, Labor Department documents rarely deal with early adoles-

cents at all, or use only such gross categories as "under eighteen" or "under sixteen." The United States census contains by far the most comprehensive and complete information, but the 1970 materials are just being tabulated and will be released slowly over the next several years. The following discussion will draw upon these 1970 census materials where they were available as this essay was being prepared, but a number of sections will have to be based on the most recent information obtainable from sources other than the census.[1]

The most useful of the new census documents (1971) is "Characteristics of American Youth: 1970," which presents many important demographic features of the nation's youthful population, but its major age categorizations are fourteen to seventeen and eighteen to twenty-one. In terms of length, these groupings correspond fairly well to the conceptualization of early and late adolescence in the developmental model proposed in table 1, but they are two years "late." This will affect some of the interpretations of the census data, but at least in terms of simple numbers of adolescents, use of these age categories will give quite good approximations to the actual number of early adolescents aged twelve to fifteen and later adolescents aged sixteen to twenty.

Current Size of the Adolescent Population and Trends Over the Past Fifty Years

Figure 1 presents in graphic form the number of Americans in the fourteen to seventeen and eighteen to twenty-one age ranges at the time of the census in each decade since 1920, and shows the relation of these numbers to the total United States population at each of the census years. The over-all pattern of very dramatic increase in absolute numbers is clear, especially since 1950. The census estimates that in 1970 there were approximately 15,730,000 Americans aged fourteen to seventeen, and 14,330,000 aged eighteen to twenty-one. These figures are approximately double the numbers found in the 1920 census, but it should be noted that the total population also has nearly doubled, leaping from approximately 106 million to over 204 million in 1970. From 1920 through 1940, the early adolescent age group (fourteen to seventeen) stayed at approximately 7.5 per cent of the total population, but the sharply lowered birth rate of the depression reduced this segment's relative size to only 5.6 per cent of the total in 1950. Since 1950, the early

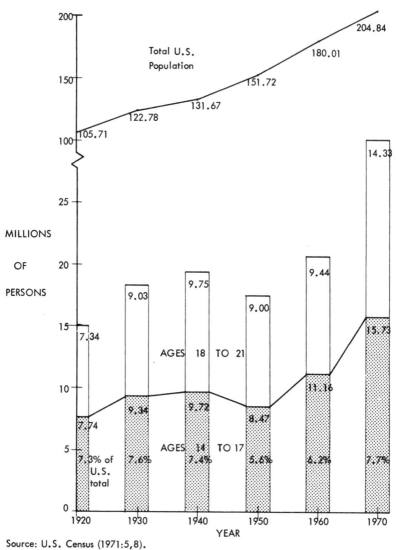

Source: U.S. Census (1971:5,8).

Figure 1. Numbers of early and later adolescents in the United States over the past fifty years.

adolescent group grew much faster than the total population (al-most +32 per cent from 1950 to 1960, and then +41 per cent on the larger 1960 base by the time of the 1970 census). These children of the postwar "baby boom" reached their early adolescence period in such numbers that they comprised 6.2 per cent of the total population in 1960 and 7.7 per cent in 1970, thus regaining the proportion that the fourteen to seventeen age group had maintained in the decades before the depression of the 1930's.

This important increase in the number of Americans in the fourteen to seventeen and also in the eighteen to twenty-one age categories over the last twenty years has resulted in an appreciable lowering of the median age of the entire population even though the same period also has seen a very substantial rise in the number of persons over sixty-five. Figure 2 presents the median age of the population at each census since 1910, and reveals that we are now

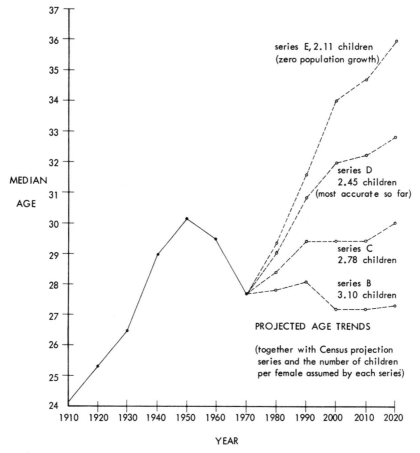

Source: U.S. Census, 1971: Table 2; 1970; Table 2.

Figure 2. Actual and predicted median ages for the total United States population, 1910 to 2020.

back to the youthful average age (27.6 years) that was the case somewhere between 1930 and 1940. It should be noted, however, that all but the very "most fertile" curve projecting fertility, death rates, and net migration for the United States through the year 2020 show an increasing rather than decreasing median age for at least the next fifty years (U. S. Census, 1970, table 2). Thus both "death control" *and* birth control will probably work together to produce an older rather than a younger total population. Projection series D on figure 2 (assuming an average of 2.45 children per female) has been the most accurate predictor so far, and its predicted median age of 32.8 by 2020 would have wide social and political implications.

The 1970 census figure of 15.73 million Americans aged fourteen to seventeen is also the best available estimate of the number of persons aged twelve to fifteen, although the series D curve of the Census Bureau indicates that this twelve to fifteen figure might be as high as 16.37 million. This series predicts a decline to 14.73 million by 1980, then an increase to 18.80 million by the year 2000 (1970, table 2). This essay will try to outline some of the major social characteristics of these approximately 16 million early adolescents and their late adolescent brothers and sisters now in the stage toward which the younger ones are moving.

Race and Sex Composition of the Adolescent Population

A recent Labor Department report[2] provides a rather comprehensive body of information on the race, sex, and employment characteristics of those who were in the sixteen to nineteen age range in 1970. Figure 3 presents selected aspects of this information in a form that allows simultaneous inferences concerning the over-all racial composition and detailed sex ratios within the races, as well as inspection of the rather wide differentials in labor force participation and unemployment as these are affected by the interaction of race and sex.

The total number of young people in the sixteen to nineteen age range was estimated by the Labor Department to be approximately 14,909,000, of whom some 86.4 per cent were white and 13.6 per cent were "Negro and other races" (including a rather small number of Orientals, American Indians, and "others," representing a total of only about 5 per cent of the nonwhite category). This 13.6 per cent share of nonwhite adolescents represents an appreciable increase

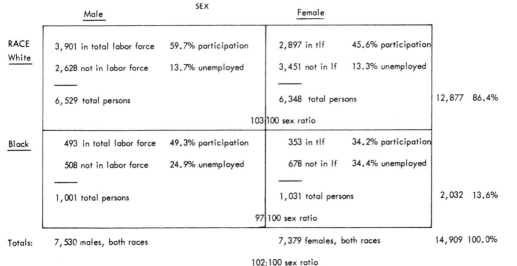

	Male		Female			
RACE **White**	3,901 in total labor force	59.7% participation	2,897 in tlf	45.6% participation		
	2,628 not in labor force	13.7% unemployed	3,451 not in lf	13.3% unemployed		
	6,529 total persons		6,348 total persons		12,877	86.4%
		103|100 sex ratio				
Black	493 in total labor force	49.3% participation	353 in tlf	34.2% participation		
	508 not in labor force	24.9% unemployed	678 not in lf	34.4% unemployed		
	1,001 total persons		1,031 total persons		2,032	13.6%
		97|100 sex ratio				
Totals:	7,530 males, both races		7,379 females, both races		14,909	100.0%
		102:100 sex ratio				

Source: U.S. Department of Labor (1971: Tables A-2, A-3).

Figure 3. Race and sex composition of the noninstitutionalized population aged sixteen to nineteen in 1970 (numbers in thousands of persons).

from the approximately 12 per cent at the time of the 1960 census. The increase in the sixteen to nineteen age range reflects the fact that while blacks now make up approximately 11.2 per cent of the total population, they have a higher birth rate and thus are over-represented in the younger age groups. For all ages, blacks represented only 9.8 per cent of the population in 1940, then rose to 10.5 per cent by 1960; the 11.2 per cent segment in 1970 represented some 22,672,570 persons, for a growth rate between 1960 and 1970 of 20 per cent as opposed to 12 per cent for whites.[3]

The over-all sex ratio for the sixteen to nineteen age group is shown at the bottom of figure 3 as 102 males for every 100 females, but this conceals a substantial difference between whites and blacks. Whites have a sex ratio of 103, reflecting the typical pattern in which approximately 104 boys are born for every 100 girls. Then the weaker boys begin to succumb to the childhood diseases that more girls survive. Black adolescents, however, show a sex ratio of only 97 males for every 100 females. In part this may be explained by the facts that black boys are exposed to even more childhood hazards than are white boys, and that black males of this age are often very hard to find in a census survey. Yet it also should be noted that the data in figure 3 concern only the noninstitutionalized population, and it is quite probable that the low number of black males recorded as either in or out of the total labor force reflects their higher proportion of members who have been sent to various "correctional" institutions.

Labor Force Participation and Unemployment Rates of Teenagers

The totals in each box of figure 3 are the sum of those of a particular race and sex who were counted as being in the "total labor force" plus those who were counted as "not in labor force," that is, neither employed nor actively seeking work. This "total labor force" is larger than the more commonly used figure for the "civilian labor force" because it adds on those serving in the military, an important segment of the population in this sixteen to nineteen range (some 300,000 males and 9,000 females). At the upper right corner of each box is rate of participation in this total labor force, meaning the percentage who are either working or who are unemployed but looking for work, as opposed to "keeping house, going to school, unable to work, or other reasons." Beneath these labor force participation rates are the unemployment rates given for each race and sex combination, expressed as a percentage of the civilian (not total) labor force who are actively seeking work.

Close examination of these participation and unemployment rates reveals that the blacks have much lower participation rates than their white counterparts and very much higher unemployment rates even when they do attempt to get work. Of course, it would be desirable to introduce the factor of differing levels of education into these comparisons, but those data are not yet available. In any case, the unemployment rates are very high for the whites (13.7 per cent for males and 13.3 per cent for females), but they are astronomical for blacks (24.9 per cent for males and 34.4 per cent for females). All these teenage unemployment rates have risen sharply just since 1969, when they were 10.7 for whites and 24.0 for blacks. Even the newer figures understate the great magnitude of the problem because the rates apply to an ever-larger base number of adolescents, and furthermore ignore the very large number of young people who are so discouraged or confused that they simply do not actively seek work and are thus classified as not in the labor force rather than unemployed. In particular cities the problem of unemployment for poor black (and poor white) teenagers may be aggravated by the unusually large fraction of the total inner-city population that they constitute. The situation in Houston is a case in point, as described by Barbara Phillips of the Southwest Center for Urban Research in one of the analytic papers coming from our Model Cities Evaluation Project.[4]

It is very hard to estimate how many of these "discourageds" are among the Labor Department's breakdowns of reasons for there being 50 per cent of the sixteen to nineteen group not in the labor force: 37 per cent in school, 0.5 per cent disabled, 5.5 per cent with home responsibilities, 0.8 per cent overtly expressing their thought that they could not get a job, and 6.7 per cent giving other reasons.[5] In any case, this form of social dynamite will become ever more menacing as new school-leavers meet returning young veterans in the search for the shrinking number of entry-level jobs. Even when they do find work, young employees are concentrated in low paying, sporadic, or seasonal jobs. Among the 1,362,000 employees aged fourteen to fifteen in 1970, the major occupations for boys were nonfarm labor (36 per cent), sales clerk (28 per cent), farm labor (18 per cent), and service work (18 per cent). Among these young girls, the order was service work (mostly in private households, 79 per cent), sales or clerical (12 per cent), farm work (6 per cent), and nonfarm operative (4 per cent).[6]

School Enrollment Across the Adolescent Years

Data on school enrollment from the 1970 census have not yet been released, but figure 4 shows the 1960 census estimate of the proportion of each racial group who was still enrolled in some kind of school program (full- or part-time) at the various age levels.

The over-all proportions enrolled in school is doubtless a good deal higher now for the seventeen to twenty age group, but it is probable that the racial groups still show similar relative patterns. The enrollment curves show that orientals consistently have the highest proportion enrolled as students, across all the teen years. White students come next in every age, but among older adolescents whites fall far behind orientals (about 35 per cent in school at age twenty, as compared to an amazing 51 per cent for orientals).

The large increases in school-leaving occur at age seventeen for whites and at age sixteen for blacks, while the Indian group showed substantial reductions in the proportion enrolled even from age twelve.

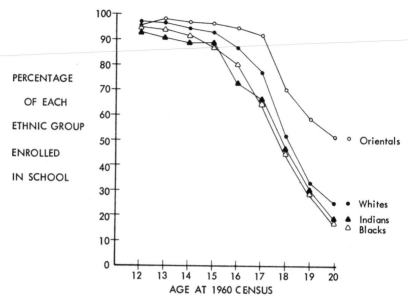

Source: U.S. Census, PC(2) 5A, 1960: Table 1.

Figure 4. School enrollment at each age, by ethnic group.

Family Structure

The Moynihan report[7] triggered a reexamination of many re-search traditions concerning the probable effects of father absence on young children, especially on adolescent boys. More recent work has borne out the seriousness and scope of the problem of absent or economically insufficient fathers for economically disadvantaged whites as well as blacks.[8] Table 2 shows the proportion of house-holds in urban areas with incomes under $3,000 that were headed by females to be 38 per cent for whites and 47 per cent for blacks.

Table 2. Female-headed families with children, by race, income, and residence, 1960.

Residence	Income	Blacks (per cent)	Whites (per cent)
Urban	under $3,000	47	38
	$3,000 and over	8	4
Rural	under $3,000	18	12
	$3,000 and over	5	2

SOURCE: U. S. Census of Population, 1960, P(1) D, table 225; adapted from Hans Sebald, *Adolescence: A Sociological Analysis* (New York: Appleton-Century-Crofts, 1968), p. 276.

Where incomes were above the $3,000 level, the proportion of urban families that were headed by females was much lower for both races (4 per cent for whites and 8 per cent for blacks). However, it should be noted that the *number* of female-headed white families with very low incomes is actually much larger than the number of black female-headed families, since the somewhat lower rate is applied to the much larger base of all white families. In fact, it is important to recognize that of the approximately 29.7 million Americans that were living below the Social Security Administration's 1965 poverty level of $3,335 per year for an urban family of four, approximately 20.3 million or 68 per cent were whites.[9] More recent data (1966) on the relative frequency of female-headed families (without regard to income level and place of residence) show rates of 25 per cent for blacks and 9 per cent for whites, and a much higher absolute level but smaller differential when only those families earning under $3,000 are considered: 42 per cent for blacks and 23 per cent for whites.[10]

The comparative proportions of female-headed black and white families was seen in 1965 data to be very similar to the 1960 census data. In my reanalysis of the Coleman (1966) data on ninth grade urban black and white students (whose modal age was fourteen), 52 per cent of the lower-class blacks and 37 per cent of the lower-class white students reported father absence, which matches very well with the 47 per cent and 38 per cent found in the 1960 census material.[11] The other ethnic groups that are disproportionately poor also have high rates of female-headed families: Indians (16 per cent), Puerto Ricans (15 per cent), and Mexican-Americans (12 per cent).[12]

It should be noted that even where black families have both husband and wife present, the median family income was still only 61 per cent of that received by white husband-wife families ($5,998 as compared to $9,794). This 61 per cent comparison is up appreciably from the 51 per cent of 1959, but still is very seriously low. Black families that are relatively young do somewhat better because of higher education levels, earning 66 per cent of the comparable figure for whites. Those living in the North and West do much better than those in the South (73 per cent of white income as against 57 per cent in the South). But about 52 per cent of black husband-wife families still live in the South, and black husband-wife families as a percentage of all black families has dropped from 75 per cent in 1960 to only 67 per cent in 1970.[13]

The number of children in the nonwhite families having any children at all (averaging 2.96) is substantially larger than the corresponding figure for whites (2.33), and the gap is even wider in rural farm families (averaging 2.67 children for whites, 3.91 for nonwhites) (U. S. Census, 1963, table 5). This larger number of children and very difficult role for the father coupled with much lower income puts a great strain on black families that must have impact on the socialization of their children.

Table 3 shows that while only a small fraction of early adoles-

Table 3. Per cent ever married, by age: United States, 1920, 1940, 1960.

	Age at census	Census year			Increase 1940 to 1960
		1920	1940	1960	
Early	14	0.6	0.3	1.1	+0.8 points
adolescence	15	1.4	1.2	2.3	+1.1
Later	16	4.3	3.9	5.8	+1.9
adolescence	17	10.1	9.0	12.2	+3.2
	18	20.9	17.7	24.4	+6.7
	19	29.7	27.0	40.3	+13.3
	20	40.0	37.2	54.0	+16.8

SOURCE: Adapted from Clyde V. Kiser, Wilson H. Grabill, and Arthur A. Campbell, *Trends and Variations in Fertility in the United States* (Cambridge, Mass.: Harvard University Press, 1968), p. 113.

cents were married at the time of the 1960 census (under 6 per cent at any age), the proportion married has increased substantially since 1940. More important, the median age at first marriage has been lowering in recent years. The proportion of first marriages in which the wife was between fourteen and seventeen years old had been dropping from approximately 20 per cent in 1925-1929 to 15 per cent in 1940-1944, but rose again to over 20 per cent by 1955-1959. This pattern of early marriage (median age 20.6 for females and 22.8 for males in 1965, down from 22.0 and 26.1 in 1890) has important effects on the socialization and value-theme developments in early and later adolescence.[14]

The young-bride pattern is also important because these young married women tend to have children very soon. Burchinal's study in Iowa reported in 1960 that 87 per cent of high school marriages were forced by pregnancy,[15] and brides even at age sixteen are very likely to have a child in the first year of marriage (69 per cent of whites, 83 per cent of blacks). Illegitimacy rates are exceptionally high among adolescent girls: Department of Health, Education and Welfare data for 1964 showed that unmarried females under age twenty then accounted for over 40 per cent of the total number of illegitimate births. This proportion has increased markedly since 1940 and has probably increased even more since the 1964 reports— a result of the greater *number* of teenage girls as well as the increasing *rate* of illegitimate births. Race and social class again are important considerations, although rarely do official statistics display both characteristics at once. Thus the data of table 4 indicate

Table 4. Rate of illegitimate births per 1,000 unmarried women, by race and age.

	Age	1940	1965	
White	15–19	3.3	7.9	+4.6 points or +139%
Nonwhite	15–19	42.5	75.8	+33.3 points or +78%

SOURCE: Adapted from Kiser, Grabill, and Campbell, *Trends and Variations in Fertility in the United States*, p. 141, from data of the National Center for Health Statistics.

that nonwhite females age fifteen to nineteen in 1965 had nearly ten times as high an illegitimacy rate as did white females of the same age, but this does not take the necessary social class factor into account. Any differences in illegitimacy rates would not be nearly so striking if the comparison could be made between non-white females and white females of the same social class level.

In any case, the increasing frequency of father-absent homes, premarital pregnancy, early marriage, and having children very soon after marriage must of necessity force vital issues of intimacy and autonomy earlier and earlier in the adolescent years, and these in turn put increasing pressure on two of the core concerns of the twelve to sixteen age group: acceptance and achievement.

III. The Acceptance/Achievement Dilemma in Early Adolescence[16]

A rush of biological maturation brings childhood to a close and socially patterned expectations soon provide both problems and solutions, centering mainly around the paradoxically contradictory value themes of acceptance and achievement. Early adolescence is usually thought to begin with the "growth spurt" that produces marked development of the primary and then secondary sex characteristics, a rapid change in the nature of the hormonal secretions.

Of perhaps greater importance, the growth spurt signals the start of the adolescent's social metamorphosis into a fully sexualized person, capable of producing serious harm as well as significant pleasure. In girls, this rapid growth produces breast buds at about ten and a half and first menstruation about a year or so later; in boys, rapid testicular growth starts about eleven and a half, with the development of secondary sex characteristics coming approximately one year later.[17] For both sexes, these first major changes are followed by extremely rapid growth in height and weight, which causes many girls to tower over boys (who always seem about one and a half years behind), and makes both sexes awkward and concerned with the uncertain arts of impression management.

One of the main social contexts of the early adolescent period is the shift from the neighborhood elementary school to the more distant junior high school and eventually (in urban areas) to a relatively remote high school. The effects of the family's social class, ethnicity, and more directly interactional patterns can be seen in relation to the early adolescent's level of self-esteem.[18] Parents and siblings are still of very great importance, but now some of the main roles are changing and a new component of *responsibility* is being added.[19] The "child" component of the "son" and "daughter" roles is disappearing, and the young adolescent boy may become furious if his sister introduces him as her "little brother."

Own-sex peer groups drawn from the school now become very engrossing, so that the role of "member" becomes elaborated. The same-sex best-friend pattern provides emotional security as a basis for more extensive relations involving the issue of social acceptance.[20] Since parents and peers alike invest all sorts of sexual activity with moral meaning, it can be hypothesized that the sense of moral worth will be related to the interpretation of his sexual status made by the adolescent's significant others.

High schools and junior high schools are also significant social contexts in that their official culture embodies the value theme of social achievement in addition to the continuing stress upon valued qualities such as ethnicity, social class, and gender-role attributes such as sexual attractiveness.[21] Thus the role of student takes on special meaning as a qualitative attribute (since some peers have already chosen or been forced to do other things), and as a performance dimension (in the sense of "good" student and "poor" student).[22]

Acceptance, or *symbolically validated membership and wel-*

comed participation in a group's important interaction patterns can refer to the family, to the peer crowd or clique, to official school groups, or to the wider world of social class, socioeconomic status, and ethnic subcultures. Likewise, *achievement,* or *symbolically validated performance against a socially defined standard of excellence or competition* can take place in any of these social arenas.

There is inherent contradiction between acceptance and achievement in that some of the most visible forms of achievement (such as making high grades in school) rank quite low as grounds for popularity, and peer group and dating activities (beginning at around thirteen or earlier) that engender and maintain popularity take large segments of time and attention away from studying. Coleman's study of some 7,000 Illinois high school students in 1957 does show, however, that certain kinds of achievement can form important grounds for increased popularity, especially for boys. Having high grades was ranked quite low by the students as a basis for popularity for boys and even lower for girls. Being an athlete, being in the "leading crowd," and being a leader in activities were the most important criteria for boys; being in the leading crowd, being a leader in activities, and having nice clothes were most important for girls.[23]

While the value priorities found by Coleman in 1957 have doubtless altered in recent years as counterculture norms have spread, it is quite probable that newer evidence would still document the continuation of cultural emphasis on value-theme dispositions established in the oedipal period.[24] That is to say, during early adolescence boys show an increasing devotion of energy to the instrumental area (achievement and independence) receiving in return approval to support the sense of competence and response to support the sense of self-determination. Girls are increasingly directed toward the expressive area, especially development of interpersonal skills, which yield approval and also the acceptance that increases the sense of unity.[25]

Thus recognition for performances and qualities that are valued in both official and peer cultures can resolve the paradox and dilemma of achievement and acceptance. Furthermore, the period of early adolescence represents a series of attempts by these twelve- to fifteen-year-olds to gain some autonomy from their parents while gaining peer support through conformity to the teenage or youth culture norms.[26] However, the totality of commitment to acceptance in this peer society has been greatly overstated, to the near exclusion of the personal ambitions that make themselves very strongly evident in later adolescence. Turner has supplied a better perspective:

> In sum, the youth subculture is a segmental and ritual pattern which many youth enact in the spirit of a game while still retaining private standards and goals at variance with it. On the one hand, the pattern provides a ready identity for the individual in an otherwise amorphous situation and protects the individual by imposing controls on his peer environment. On the other hand, the special youth interests provide a basis for sociable enjoyment and a considerable degree of fellow-feeling. The ritual forms of interaction and subjects of communication provide a means for ready communication in casual and fleeting interpersonal relations. The declarations against success in fields of serious accomplishment are hardly to be taken other than as public disavowals to protect the individual's pride in the face of possible failure in highly valued pursuits.[27]

The following sections will attempt to trace some of the broad patterns of the interrelation of acceptance and achievement themes in the contexts of the family and the unofficial peer world. Again it should be noted that this discussion intentionally excludes those adolescents who get labeled "seriously delinquent," since their patterns of coping with law enforcement and correctional institutions would require an entire separate study. Also, no attempt will be made to deal with moral development.[28] The main focus of the analysis will follow my initial orienting objective: tracing the impact of social class and ethnicity on the interrelations of social acceptance and social achievement.

IV. Family Influences on Early Adolescent Acceptance and Achievement Themes[29]

Social Class Aspects

Many of the existing studies of the family as a socializing institution have been conducted from a theoretical orientation quite heavily influenced by Freudian conceptions of psychosexual development. Therefore, where social class or status factors were considered at all, the research concentrated on class differences in modesty, toilet training, feeding, and weaning practices. Although this type of study has been conducted for many years, there is no convincing evidence of any effects on the individual's conception of himself or on his view of the stratification system and very little concerning such generalized personality traits as aggressive drive for achievement or status insecurity, even though the patterns of so-called permissive and strict child-rearing practices do seem to be associated with the middle and the working class, respectively.[30]

More enlightening for our purposes is a study by Kohn of parental values held desirable in their children's conduct (and which would bring on punishment if violated) among a Washington, D. C., sample of two hundred white middle-class and two hundred white skilled working-class parents.[31] Hollingshead's criteria of class placement were used. Kohn found that although there was a large ground of agreement and shared values (happiness, honesty, consideration, dependability), the middle-class parents were much more likely to report that they desired to instill values of inner control and concern for others while the working-class parents put greater emphasis on obedience and neatness. This difference Kohn found to be reflected in punishment patterns: the middle-class parents were more likely to consider the *intent* of the infringing action with a view to the child's development of internalized standards of conduct—for example, "did he really *mean* to do it?"—while working-class parents saw children's behavior in terms of *respectability*, so that desirable behavior consisted in not breaking rules. With some stretching, these findings can be interpreted to mean that the differentially placed families were attempting to instill different motivations (observation of situational rules versus action in accordance with internalized principles). Conceivably this difference might be carried over to differences of generalized achievement motivation, but the connection is admittedly weak. Coopersmith's more recent work, however, underlines the effectiveness of firm parental standards in developing positive self-esteem and strong achievement orientations in middle-class boys.[32]

This question of achievement motivation is a thorny one, and the entrance of middle-class bias is extremely easy. First, is the child of low socioeconomic status in fact likely to be less motivated toward achievement of the core culture or middle-class values? And if so, is this lower motivation a reaction to the frustration of failure after attempt, or is it the function of internalizing an entirely different set of values in the first place?

Allison Davis suggested that in times of economic crises, lower- and working-class families are under such pressure for survival (food, shelter, and so on) that the children do not learn ambition or the drive for education and higher skills because they are too submerged in the daily battle. Ambition is held to be a kind of luxury requiring a minimum of physical security which is not present in lower- or working-class life. Davis asserted that children brought up under such conditions were taught that their standard of living is natural for people of their class, and thus they become accustomed to it. They were not trained or encouraged to plan ahead or defer whatever current gratifications may be available in order to prepare for elevation in status and living conditions.[33]

Other writers have also maintained that the "deferred gratification pattern" is a middle-class phenomenon and not often found in lower socioeconomic status groups.[34] Schneider and Lysgaard, in one of the few empirical studies of this pattern (and its reverse, which they call "impulse following"), give direct support to the argument that lower-class gratification patterns show very little deferment.[35] These patterns are characterized by relative readiness to engage in physical violence, free sexual expression (also documented by Kinsey), minimum pursuit of education, free spending of available resources, and a short time of dependence upon parents. Of particular interest for our inquiry are the results of Schneider and Lysgaard's national poll of 2,500 students (held to be representative of the high school population but underrepresentative of lower-class adolescents because of dropouts). After these students were categorized by their father's occupation (four levels based on degree of independence, supervision of others, and skill) and by their own subjective class identification (upper, middle, working, and lower), a scale designed to tap the deferred gratification pattern found it (and especially the high value on long education) to be clearly directly related to both subjective and objective class placement.

A more sophisticated approach to the study of class differences in the motivations of young people has been developed by Rosen. He not only provides further documentation to the fact that achievement motivation varies by class position of the child, but also introduces a valuable distinction between two elements of what he calls the achievement syndrome:

1. *achievement motivation* (a psychological, personality characteristic) and
2. *value orientations* defining and implementing achievement motivated behavior (a cultural factor).

By the use of thematic apperception tests on a sample of 125 high school sophomores classified according to Hollingshead's criteria, Rosen found that achievement motivation was clearly class-related, with Classes I and II rating more than five times as high in it as

Class V. But this alone, Rosen claims, would not produce mobility; there must also be a set of implementing value orientations which orient the individual for mobility-producing preparation such as increased education or skill development. Using Florence Kluckhohn's conceptualization of various possible major value orientations, Rosen found that the frequency and intensity of the most mobility-favorable orientation pattern (activistic, future-oriented, and individualistic) was also directly related to class position.[36]

A complete review of the literature on family and achievement patterns is not possible here because of space limitations.[37] The available evidence on the contribution of the family to development of interpreted status awareness, although skimpy and unconnected, may tentatively be said to be oriented along the following major dimensions:

1. *Differential inculcation of values* regarding internal motivation and the deferred gratification-achievement syndrome (accompanied by the requisite implementing values on education).

2. *Provision of different languages or sets of interpretative meaning categories* and vocabularies of motive which effectively structure the child's perception and evaluation of the social world and his place in it.

3. *Provision of logic or explanations of the nature of status differences,* particularly the negative contrast and, in the case of the lowers, shifting the axis of comparison to maintain favorable self-conception.

4. *Differential inculcation of strong and specific value on education* in order to "have the chance I didn't have."

5. *Differential provision of money* for peer activities and clothes.

In a recent analysis I attempted to interrelate self-conceptions, race, social class, family role structure, parental urgings, and the student's measured verbal ability into a single theoretical model of the factors shaping adolescent achievement orientations.[38] Data with which to construct and evaluate the model were drawn from the huge Equality of Educational Opportunity study, directed by James Coleman,[39] and I wish to express my appreciation for the opportunity to conduct a reanalysis of a portion of this rich mine or data. The following section presents a brief summary of the analysis of the above mentioned structural and personal factors in relation to educational aspiration, a particularly important aspect of social achievement among this sample of 1,684 urban northeast black and white ninth graders.

*Simplification Path Diagrams of an Achievement Orienta-
tion Model*

Figures 5 and 6 present the modified path diagrams summariz-
ing the major one-way causal effects estimates (path coefficients) of
race, social class, verbal ability, parental aspirations, and self-esteem
on educational aspiration. A family structure variable has been completely removed because of its nonlinear and nonadditive relations
with the other variables, and the arrow from social class to self-
esteem has been deleted due to its insufficient strength (.086 for
blacks and −.006 for whites). Because even one causal arrow has
been deleted, the path coefficients are no longer exactly equal conceptually or numerically to beta weights.

Among the black students, verbal ability is most important at
.349, with .242 direct into educational desire and .107 indirect,
mostly through parental aspiration (.082). Parental aspiration is
second in causal importance at .337, with only .022 indirect through
self-esteem. In third position quite a bit lower is social class at .215
via parental aspiration. In last place is self-esteem at .110, all direct.

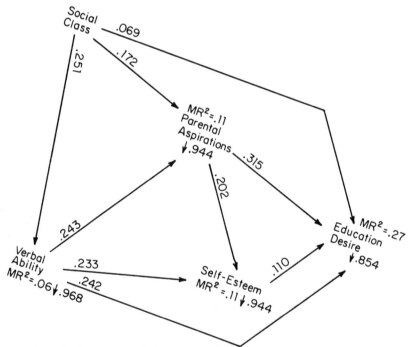

Figure 5. Simplified path diagram, black students only.

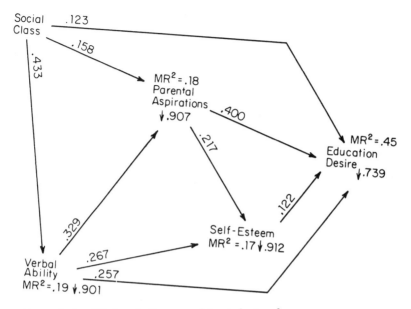

Figure 6. Simplified path diagram, white students only.

Together, the entire set of variables accounts for 27 per cent of the variance in educational desire among the black students, thus leaving plenty of room for addition of other factors in future research.

The total level of determination is much greater among the white students (45 per cent), but the ordering of the causal estimates is identical. Verbal ability here stands at .430 with .257 direct and .173 indirect, mainly through parental aspirations (.140). Parental aspirations is nearly as strong, at .426, having the most potent direct path (.400) and only .026 via self-esteem. Social class is quite close behind at .376, composed of .123 direct, plus .186 through verbal ability and .067 through parental aspirations. Finally, self-esteem has a .122 direct path into education desire, independent of the effects of the other causal variables and their correlates. Addition of a self-conception dimension thus helped in predicting educational aspirations for both blacks and whites, but much more work needs to be done on this important domain.[40]

V. Acceptance and Achievement in the School

As an on-going social system composed of a great many activities (each with a corresponding social subsystem) and acting upon the early adolescent for the greater part of his waking hours, the school has the opportunity and institutionalized arrangements both formal and informal to accomplish deep and extensive socialization. Attendance and the dropout or forceout phenomena have been found to be clearly related to social class in both early and more recent research.[41] College preparatory versus commercial, general, or vocation program enrollment is also strongly related to social class;[42] academic grades[43] and treatment of students by teachers also show strong class and race effects.[44]

We may return to Hollingshead's Elmtown for a look at the cliques and activity participations and their class relations. In athletics, all classes were represented, but the uppers snubbed the lowers; the school dances and parties were advocated and supported by the Class I's and II's and their families, while the IV's and V's objected on the grounds of cost and hardship on the students who could not afford the formal clothes. Class IV's and V's seldom went to these, anticipating snubs. Participation in the twenty-three available clubs and activities was also directly class-related, ranging from 100 per cent participation for Class I's to 27 per cent for Class V.[45]

Turning to informal student relationships we find that membership in cliques (small primary groups of friends, involving "going places and doing things," mutual exchange of ideas, and personality acceptance) was very clearly class restricted, there being usually only students of one class as members, or perhaps a few from an adjacent class. No cliques combined Class I or II with a Class V. These clique patterns were of special importance in Elmtown high school because they largely determined the prestige pattern within the school: a three category system comprised of "the elite" (leaders in activities), the "good kids" ("never this or that," two-thirds of the student body), and "the grubbies" (seen as nobodies, from unfortunate families and the wrong part of town). All this of course was very closely class related.

In both the Hollingshead study of Elmtown high school and West's Plainville work, it was found that teenagers felt very strong pressures from their parents against making social contacts across class lines. The development of more parent-independent subcultures oriented around drugs and folk, soul, or rock music may permit and in fact encourage cross-class contacts, but this should not simply be assumed without evidence.

Three more recent and more generalizable studies support the contention that social acceptance is a crucial dimension of early adolescence, but one which is sometimes facilitated and sometimes blocked by particular forms of achievement. In Coleman's *Adolescent Society* study it was found that those students who were members of cliques (and especially of the higher status or "leading crowd" cliques) were less likely than others to disparage themselves and admit to wanting to be someone else.[46] Further, self-disparagement was found to be more common even among those who had achieved recognition as one of Coleman's three major social value exemplars (athletic star, most popular, and brilliant student for boys; leader in activities, most popular, and brilliant student for girls) in schools where that particular form of achievement was not highly valued. Where these dimensions of achievement were not significantly rewarded, these students tended to turn toward heavier mass media usage as a form of escape.[47]

The Sherifs' observational study of adolescent boys' groups at working-, middle-, and upper-middle social class levels showed many interesting ways in which the members could attain greater acceptance and status through achievements in the realms of personal commitment to the group, ability to plan activities, and all kinds of recognized skills, especially in relation to sports, cars, girls, and obtaining illicit pleasures.[48]

The Douvan and Adelson study used a richer psychodynamic framework with which to illuminate important male/female differences in the handling of the acceptance/achievement dilemma. They argue that their sample of fourteen- to sixteen-year-old boys were typically wrapped up in working out problems of identity, eroticism, and autonomy (assertiveness and achievement), while the girls of the same age were typically concerned with issues of identity, eroticism, and the interpersonal sphere (security, support, and acceptance).[49]

Many social types in the informal pantheon of American high school cultures (whether straight or hip, square or cool) articulate the possible integration of the acceptance and achievement themes, such as "Big Wheel," "Gentleman Jock," or "Super Head." Figure 7 presents a collection of these common high school types (drawn from personal observations, interviews, and student papers concerning the types prevalent across the 1950's and 1960's), ordered in terms of the dimensions of achievement orientation, acceptance orientation, and orientation toward either "outside" values or institutionalized school values. Of course not all of these types would be

Orientation toward acceptance by the "leading crowd"

ACHIEVEMENT ORIENTATION	Low Outside Values	Low "Official" Values	Medium Outside Values	Medium "Official" Values	High Outside Values	High "Official" Values
High	Prudes Pilgrims	Brains Grinds Wonks Brown-nosers Weanies Curve-breakers Super Jocks			Lovers Hot dogs In-group Popular kids Soshes	Gentlemen Jocks Big Wheels Politicos Student council types Cheer leaders Colleeges
Medium	Fags Queers Pansies Fairies			Invisibles Losers Nebbishes Frumps Nerds Rednecks		
Low	Shop-boys Animals Surfers Goof-offs Heads Hoods Grubbies Goers Pigs Thugs		Heads Hippies Freaks Hodads Longhairs Swingers			Bible clubbers Service clubbers

Source: Student papers, interviews and personal observations

Figure 7. High school social types of the 1950's and 1960's.

operative in a given school especially given the recent development of counterculture patterns, including the stress on *not* relating to other persons in terms of stereotypical images. It is my contention, however, that these achievement and acceptance themes are still very important factors even in schools in which the prevailing ideology is extremely hip. The relevant criteria of good achievements and validated acceptances will in these cases have shifted to the "outside" value patterns. Perhaps there is also a kind of reverse or residual resolution of the acceptance/achievement problem: if (as football coaches are likely to assert) it is true that "nice guys finish last," is it also true that last guys finish nice?

VII. Conclusion

The importance of gender role modeling and differential situation/challenge/response/reward patterns for young males and females can hardly be overestimated.[50] Yet, as our friends in the Women's Liberation Movement rightfully remind us, these differences are not innate, could be removed or at least greatly reduced, and need not be structurally constraining to each succeeding generation.

Unless and until major changes in socialization patterns, reward structures, and societal expectations occur, it seems clear that females in our society will continue to be socialized to maximize and give primacy to the left-hand member of each of the value-theme dilemmas shown in table 1 at the outset of this paper.[51] The sequence of affectivity, compliance, expressivity, peer relationships, acceptance (in the early adolescence period now under consideration), then intimacy, connection, stability, dignity, and meaningful integration seems to me to be a processually related set of idealized value themes clustering around the central concept of security in interpersonal relations and quite firmly grounded in the social structure of family, peer, occupational, and then again family life in this country. Males, of course, also generally are socialized to pay consistent attention to activities that increase security. But much more than females in our contemporary, urban, middle-class society are males socialized to take on (and perhaps successfully respond to) a very wide range of value themes having to do with the core concept of challenge regarding individual performance. Under this concept of challenge can then be seen the various aspects stressed at the different stages in the male's life cycle. He is likely to be taught to give primacy to sensorimotor experiencing, self-control, instrumental activity, evaluated abilities, achievement (in the early adolescent phase now under consideration), then autonomy, self-determination, accomplishment, control, and again, personal autonomy. Changes in gender role socialization are definitely going on,[52] but the older pattern still predominates.

The value of these concepts and of the over-all theoretical formulation from which they are derived remains to be seen in the hard light of systematic empirical research across all the stages of the life cycle. On the basis of existing literature, it can be concluded at least that the acceptance/achievement dilemma asserted to be central to the stage of early adolescence has been shown to characterize the general run of major studies. From this basis, it should now be possible to design research to trace the mechanisms of this socialization, the variations found in different subcultures or structural positions, and some of the major implications of the particular resolutions attained for both male and female adolescents. Perhaps such research and theoretical work might even provide some guidance as to the kinds of activities and interaction patterns that could be expected to lead toward an increased integration and authentic resolution of the often clashing and self-defeating value themes of acceptance and achievement that give early adolescence much of its pain and bittersweet poignancy.

REFERENCES

1. The following census material was used: U. S. Bureau of the Census, *Families, 1960; Final Report PC(2)-4A* (Washington, D. C.: Government Printing Office, 1963); *School Enrollment, 1960; Final Report PC(2)-5A* (Washington, D. C.: Government Printing Office, 1964); "Projections of the Population of the United States, by Age and Sex (Interim Revisions): 1970 to 2020." *Current Population Reports*, Series P-25, no. 448 (Washington, D. C.: Government Printing Office, 1970); "Characteristics of American Youth: 1970," *Current Population Reports*, Series P-23, no. 34 (Washington, D. C.: Government Printing Office, 1971).

2. U. S. Department of Labor, "Employment and Unemployment in 1970," Special Labor Force Report, no. 129 (Washington, D. C.: Government Printing Office, 1971).

3. U. S. Department of Commerce, "Whites Account for Reversal of South's Historic Population Loss Through Migration, Census Shows," *U. S. Commerce Department News*, March 3, 1971.

4. Barbara R. Phillips, "Employment Problems in Houston: Dynamic Factors," Model Cities Monographs, no. 1 (Houston: Southwest Center for Urban Research, July 1971).

5. Department of Labor, "Employment and Unemployment in 1970," table A-28.

6. *Ibid.*, table A-27.

7. Daniel P. Moynihan, "The Negro Family: The Case for National Action," Office of Policy, Planning and Research, U. S. Department of Labor (1965).

8. Chad Gordon, *Looking Ahead: Self-Conceptions, Race and Family Factors as Determinants of Adolescent Achievement Orientations*, Arnold Rose and American Sociological Association Monograph Series, forthcoming.

9. National Advisory Commission on Civil Disorders, Report, also called "The

Kerner Commission Report" (New York: Bantam Books and The New York Times Co., 1968), p. 258.

10. President's Commission on Income Maintenance Programs, *Background Papers on Income Maintenance* (Washington, D. C.: Superintendent of Documents, 1970), p. 114.

11. Gordon, *Looking Ahead,* figure 6. James S. Coleman and others, *Equality of Educational Opportunity* (Washington, D. C.: Department of Health, Education and Welfare, 1966).

12. President's Commission on Income Maintenance Programs, *Background Papers,* p. 112.

13. U. S. Department of Commerce, "Differences Between Incomes of White and Negro Husband-Wife Families Are Relatively Small Outside the South," Commerce Department news release and supporting tables, February 18, 1971. Note the ideological implications of the title.

14. Clyde V. Kiser, Wilson H. Grabill, and Arthur A. Campbell, *Trends and Variations in Fertility in the United States* (Cambridge, Mass.: Harvard University Press, 1968), p. 267; Hans Sebald, *Adolescence: A Sociological Analysis* (New York: Appleton-Century-Crofts, 1968), p. 414.

15. Cited in Sebald, *Adolescence,* p. 422.

16. This section is adapted from my unpublished paper, "Socialization Across the Life-Cycle: A Stage Developmental Model," Department of Social Relations, Harvard University, 1969, pp. 42-47.

17. Elizabeth Douvan and Martin Gold, "Modal Patterns in American Adolescence," in Lois W. Hoffman and Martin L. Hoffman, eds., *Review of Child Development,* II (New York: Russell Sage Foundation, 1966), 469-528.

18. Morris Rosenberg, *Society and the Adolescent Self-Image* (Princeton, N. J.: Princeton University Press, 1965); Gordon, *Looking Ahead.*

19. Yehudi A. Cohen, *The Transition from Childhood to Adolescence* (Chicago: Aldine, 1964).

20. Ernest A. Smith, *American Youth Culture: Group Life in Teenage Society* (New York: The Free Press, 1962); Muzafer Sherif and Carolyn W. Sherif, *Reference Groups: Exploration into Conformity and Deviation of Adolescence* (New York: Harper and Row, 1964).

21. Talcott Parsons, "The School Class as a Social System: Some of Its Functions in American Society," *Harvard Educational Review,* 29 (Fall 1959), 297-318; Ralph H. Turner, "Sponsored and Contest Mobility and the School System," *American Sociological Review,* 25 (1960), 855-867.

22. The interrelations between acceptance and achievement can be seen throughout the literature on early adolescence, from August B. Hollingshead's *Elmtown's Youth* (New York: John Wiley and Sons, 1949) through

James S. Coleman's *The Adolescent Society* (New York: Free Press, 1961) and on into the broad range of recent material. See Paul Goodman, *Growing Up Absurd: Problems of Youth in the Organized Society* (New York: Random House Vintage Books, 1956); Edgar Z. Friedenberg, *The Vanishing Adolescent* (New York: Dell Publishing Company, 1959) and *Coming of Age in America: Growth and Acquiescence* (New York: Random House Vintage Books, 1967); Smith, *American Youth Culture;* Jerome M. Seidman, ed., *The Adolescent—A Book of Readings* (New York: Holt, Rinehart and Winston, 1960); Robert E. Grinder, ed., *Studies in Adolescence* (New York: Macmillan, 1963); E. Douvan and J. Adelson, *The Adolescent Experience* (New York: John Wiley and Sons, 1966); Bernard Goldstein, *Low Income Youth in Urban Areas: A Critical Review of the Literature* (New York: Holt, Rinehart and Winston, 1967); Sebald, *Adolescence;* Gerald Caplan and Serge Lebovici, eds., *Adolescence: Psychosocial Perspectives* (New York: Basic Books, 1969); Ernest Q. Campbell, "Adolescent Socialization," in David A. Goslin, ed., *Handbook of Socialization Theory and Research* (New York: Russell Sage Foundation, 1969), pp. 821-859. More general work on achievement can be found in David C. McClelland, J. W. Atkinson, R. Clark, and E. L. Lowell, *The Achievement Motive* (New York: Appleton-Century-Crofts, 1953); Bernard C. Rosen, Harry J. Crockett, Jr., and Clyde Z. Nunn, eds., *Achievement in American Society* (Cambridge, Mass.: Schenkman Publishing Company, 1969); and Rose Laub Coser, ed., *Life Cycle and Achievement in America* (New York: Harper Torchbooks, 1969).

23. Coleman, *The Adolescent Society,* pp. 43-50.

24. See table 1 above and Talcott Parsons, "Family Structure and the Socialization of the Child," in Talcott Parsons and Robert F. Bales, eds., *Family; Socialization and Interaction Process* (Glencoe, Ill.: The Free Press, 1955), pp. 35-131.

25. Douvan and Gold, "Modal Patterns in American Adolescence," pp. 494-495; Douvan and Adelson, *The Adolescent Experience,* chaps. 2, 7, 10; Chad Gordon, "Role and Value Development Across the Life-Cycle," in a symposium on role theory edited by John Jackson, Sociological Studies IV: Role (London: Cambridge University Press, forthcoming 1971).

26. See, for example, Coleman, *The Adolescent Society;* Smith, *American Youth Culture;* Douvan and Adelson, *The Adolescent Experience.*

27. Ralph H. Turner, *The Social Context of Ambition* (San Francisco: Chandler Publishing Company, 1964), p. 146.

28. See Lawrence Kohlberg, "Stage and Sequence: The Cognitive-Developmental Approach to Socialization," in David A. Goslin, ed., *Handbook of Socialization Theory and Research* (Chicago: Rand McNally & Co., 1969), chap. 6.

29. This section is adapted from portions of my unpublished paper, "Socialization to Interpreted Status Awareness."

30. See Urie Bronfenbrenner, "Socialization and Social Class Through Time and Space," in E. E. Maccoby, T. M. Newcomb, E. L. Hartley, eds., *Readings in Social Psychology*, 3d ed. (New York: Henry Holt & Co., 1958), pp. 400-425; H. Orlansky, "Infant Care and Personality," *Psychological Bulletin*, 46 (1949), 1-43; and the studies summarized by F. Elkin, *The Child and Society* (New York: Random House, 1960), pp. 78-87.

31. M. L. Kohn, "Social Class and Parental Authority," *American Sociological Review*, 24 (1959), 352-366, and "Social Class and Parental Values," *American Journal of Sociology*, 64 (1959), 337-351.

32. Stanley Coopersmith, *The Antecedents of Self-Esteem* (San Francisco: W. H. Freeman and Company, 1967).

33. A. Davis, "The Motivation of the Underprivileged Worker," in W. F. Whyte, ed., *Industry and Society* (New York: McGraw-Hill, 1946), pp. 86-106.

34. William B. Miller, "Lower Class Culture as a Generating Milieu of Gang Delinquency," *Journal of Social Issues*, 14 (1958), 5-19.

35. L. Schneider and S. Lysgaard, "The Deferred Gratification Pattern," *American Sociological Review*, 18 (1953), 142-149.

36. B. C. Rosen, "The Achievement Syndrome: A Psychocultural Dimension of Social Stratification," *American Sociological Review*, 21 (1956), 203-211.

37. Such a review would include such pioneer works as R. S. Lynd and Helen M. Lynd, *Middletown* (New York: Harcourt, Brace, 1956, first published 1929); James West, *Plainville, U.S.A.* (New York: Columbia University Press, 1945); Hollingshead, *Elmtown's Youth*; K. Eells and others, *Intelligence and Cultural Differences* (Chicago: University of Chicago Press, 1951); J. A. Kahl, "Educational and Occupational Aspirations of 'Common Man' Boys," *Harvard Educational Review*, 23 (1953), 186-203; W. H. Sewell and others, "Social Status and Educational and Occupational Aspiration," *American Sociological Review*, 22 (1957), 67-73; Miller, "Lower Class Culture"; Basil Bernstein, "Some Sociological Determinants of Perception: An Enquiry into Sub-Cultural Differences," *British Journal of Sociology*, 9 (1958), 159-174, and "Social Class and Linguistic Development: A Theory of Social Learning," in A. H. Halsey, Jean Floud, and C. Arnold Anderson, eds., *Education, Economy, and Society* (New York: The Free Press of Glencoe, 1961); and Turner, "Sponsored and Contest Mobility." More recent efforts are Martin Deutsch, Irwin Katz, and Arthur Jensen, *Social Class, Race, and Psychological Development* (New York: Holt, Rinehart and Winston, 1968); Rosen and others, *Achievement in American Society*; and Coser, *Life Cycle and Achievement in America*.

38. Gordon, *Looking Ahead*.

39. See note 11.

40. Chad Gordon, "Self-Conceptions: Configurations of Content," in Chad Gordon and Kenneth J. Gergen, eds., *The Self in Social Interaction*, vol.

1: *Classic and Contemporary Perspectives* (New York: John Wiley and Sons, 1968), pp. 115-136; "Systemic Senses of Self," *Sociological Inquiry*, 38 (Spring 1968), 161-178; "Self-Conceptions Methodologies," *Journal of Nervous and Mental Disease*, 148 (April 1969), 328-364.

41. Hollingshead, *Elmtown's Youth*, pp. 330ff; Daniel Schreiber, *Profile of a School Dropout* (New York: Random House, 1967).

42. Hollingshead, *Elmtown's Youth*, p. 168; Gordon, *Looking Ahead*.

43. R. J. Havighurst, "What Are the Cultural Differences Which May Affect Performance in Intelligence Tests?" in Eells and others, *Intelligence and Cultural Difference*, chap. 3.

44. See H. S. Becker, "Social Class Variation in the Teacher Pupil Relationships," *Journal of Educational Sociology*, 25 (1952), 451-465, for an early but solid theoretical statement.

45. Hollingshead, *Elmtown's Youth*, p. 201.

46. Coleman, *The Adolescent Society*, p. 223.

47. *Ibid.*, pp. 239-240.

48. Sherif and Sherif, *Reference Groups*.

49. Douvan and Adelson, *The Adolescent Experience*, pp. 193-194.

50. See Jerome Kagan and Howard A. Moss, *Birth to Maturity* (New York: John Wiley and Sons, 1962); Jerome Kagan, "Acquisition and Significance of Sex Typing and Sex Role Identity," in M. L. Hoffman and L. U. Hoffman, eds., *Review of Child Development Research*, I (New York: Russell Sage Foundation, 1964), 137-168; and Paul H. Mussen, John J. Conger, and Jerome Kagan, *Child Development and Personality*, 3d ed. (New York: Harper & Row, 1969).

51. Gordon, "Role and Value Development Across the Life-Cycle."

52. Margaret Mead, *Culture and Commitment* (Garden City, N.Y.: Doubleday & Co., 1970).

PETER BLOS

The Child Analyst Looks at the Young Adolescent

THE LITERATURE on adolescence has shown of late a distinctly new
trend: an increasing, even if only trickling, number of papers and
books have begun to deal with the early years of adolescence. This
trend is noteworthy because not so long ago most studies in adolescence had been devoted exclusively to the older age group. This
singular attention paid to the older adolescent, the spectacular
and tumultuous youth, appears in retrospect like myopic vision.
Would it not have been more obvious to bring first light into the
dawn of the adolescent process, instead of studying it in isolation
at high noon?

Two factors account for the rising interest in the young adolescent. In the first place, the young adolescent of late has become
increasingly similar in life style to that of the older boy and girl;
everything that is typical for middle or even late adolescence seems
to be happening at a younger and younger age. Secondly, research
in adolescence, especially in the field of psychoanalytic psychology,
has introduced a developmental differentiation of the adolescent
process as a whole. This research has afforded the opening stage
of adolescence (Preadolescence) the exclusiveness of a developmental phase.[1] My own work has aimed at the developmental deline-
ation of five adolescent phases,[2] each one defined in terms of drive
and ego positions as well as in terms of phase-specific conflicts and
their resolutions.* For some time I have emphasized the fact that
the initial stage of adolescence presents the most crucial period of
the adolescent process as a whole. Whatever follows later as, for
example, identity formation, personality consolidation, character
formation, or second individuation is augured favorably or un-

* Whenever I refer to a developmental phase, I use capital letters, for example, "Early Adolescence"; otherwise, the words are used in their colloquial
connotation, for example, "early adolescence," referring to the opening years
of adolescence.

55

favorably by the resolution of those particular developmental challenges that precede the unleashing of the adolescent turbulence of later years.

From our acquaintance with early child development we are used to thinking of a close and rather fixed proximity between age, maturation, and development. This does not hold true for adolescence. Menarche and first ejaculation do not occur at a chronological age as narrow as sitting or teething. This could hardly be different, if we acknowledge the fact that life during the first decade has brought about an increasing mutual disengagement, or a more specific correlation, between the somatic and the psychic systems of the organism. For example, performance expectancies, emanating from the social environment, rival more and more those triggered off by physical maturation alone. While pubertal maturation remains the biological initiator of adolescence, the advanced state of personality formation allows all kinds of transformatory influences to be brought to bear on the sexual drive. In fact, the monolithic cohesiveness between drive and behavior, so characteristic for the early years of life, is not in evidence any longer at puberty. With this reservation in mind, we can say that adolescence is the sum total of accommodations to the condition of puberty. The form this takes is dependent to a large extent on extrinsic, normative impingements.

The study of adolescents within a given age span (twelve to sixteen in this volume) involves several maturational and developmental stages. While there is, obviously, an orderly sequence of stages, their timing is, however, diverse as to onset and duration. As a child analyst I shall concern myself with psychological development or, in other words, with that process of psychic restructuring we call adolescence. The phenomenology of this process is dictated by the epochal characteristics of a given time and environment; consequently, it is legion and always changing in appearance. Yet, we assume that the attainment of sexual maturation and full body stature is given psychological form and content by social exigencies: social expectancies and taboos impose on the pubertal boy and girl, any time and everywhere, similar if not identical requirements for psychological modifications.

Preparation for Adolescence

It can be readily observed that the child, around the age of ten to twelve, loses some responsiveness to controls by adults, by the clock, by the routine of tasks, by the dictates of conscience. We witness the waning of the alliance between child and adult which, during middle childhood (Latency Period), had neutralized, by way of identification, the conflicts of earlier years. Emotional containment breaks out of its relatively narrow latitude with the first physiological signs of puberty (hormonal changes) and brings in its wake a growing intensity and uncontrollability of affective responses. Influences of the environment, communally and individually, turn these liabilities into either rebelliousness or inhibitions, dependent on the prevailing mores and pervasive ethos. Delays and restraints are, by no means, intrinsic impediments to the successful completion of the adolescent process. Any socially induced retardation or acceleration of adolescence is bound to reach a critical point, beyond which structural damage and maldevelopment are inflicted on the growing child. Damage derives equally from a "too much" as from a "too little," from a "too early" as from a "too late."

Another source of developmental injury lies in the essential incompleteness of the stage that precedes the one under consideration here. We are, therefore, well advised to foster latency development to the fullest as the precondition for a competent entry into adolescence. The psychological mastery of pubescent drive intensification--libidinal or aggressive—is determined by the level of ego differentiation and ego autonomy, both attained, in large measure, during the Latency Period. Among these consequences, the most significant one is, probably, the ego's distancing from the id. This forward move in ego autonomy during Latency results in the expansion and firm reliability of such ego function as cognition, memory, anticipation, tension tolerance, self-awareness, and the ability to make a distinction between reality and fantasy or between action and thought. Whenever these facilities remain critically underdeveloped, we speak of an incomplete or abortive Latency. Many disturbances of early adolescence are due to such developmental deficiencies. We search in vain for the signs of a transition into adolescence: what we find is an intensified revival of infantile modalities of drive discharge. This is not a regression, because no forward position had yet been reached.

The transition into adolescence can be effected only if drive tensions lead to phase-specific conflict formation and conflict resolution. This presupposes a capacity for internalization, as opposed to prolonged dependency on environmental adjustments to the needs of the child.[3] In such cases the conflict remains an external one, raging between child and environment, with the child expecting, even demanding, that the environment change; no other measure is in the child's reach by which he can control discomfort and anxiety, both arising from a sense of helplessness and a comparative paucity of inner resources. The crisis of the Latency Period has been well pinpointed by Erik Erikson's polarity of "industry versus inferiority,"[4] because these are the antagonistic foci around which middle childhood consolidates. The mastery of the world, concretely, symbolically, and conceptually, begins to serve as a self-regulatory source of self-esteem (instead of the earlier dependence on object love) and, beyond that, lifts the idiosyncratic childhood experiences onto the level of communicable and communal forms of expression. In saying this, we have already set foot onto that bridge which leads into the world of the young adolescent.

The Initial Stage of Adolescence: The Young Adolescent

It is common knowledge that instinctual tensions rise in the wake of pubertal maturation. The initial reaction of the young adolescent is a puzzling one, because infantile modalities of drive and ego positions are reactivated: he seems to be going backward instead of forward.

It has often been observed that the boy's latency achievements, the domestication and transformation of infantile drives, fall into shambles with the onset of puberty.[5] What we witness is a regression in the service of development,[6] manifested in oral greed, rapaciousness, smuttiness, oblivion to unkemptness, dirtiness and body odors, motoric restlessness, and experimentation in every direction of action and sensation (especially food and daring). Well-established ego functions suffer within this regressive turmoil, as is evidenced by the decline in concentration and neatness which boys display in school; girls seem to possess a greater sublimatory capacity which many a boy of this age takes as proof of her superiority. Hence he ridicules and derides her mercilessly and defensively.

Adolescent development progresses via the detour of regression. By coming into renewed contact with infantile positions, the older child is given a chance to overhaul, as it were, the defects, infirmities, and irrationalities of infancy by confronting these very conditions with an ego of advanced competency. This "work" is of the utmost importance and determines the entire course adolescence will take. It requires time and facilitation to accomplish this developmental task. In general terms it can be stated that the intensity of the regressive pull is proportional to the intensity with which "independence and freedom" are sought or, conversely, to the severity of inhibition and docility.

We have reached the point in our description where the similarity between male and female adolescence has come to an end. The boy's preadolescent regression is more massive than the girl's; it is action oriented and concretistic. In the first onrush of pubescence the boy turns away, with derision and contempt, from the opposite sex. The girl, by contrast, pushes romantic (heterosexual) thoughts or fantasies into the foreground, while regressive tendencies assert themselves peripherally and more secretively.

It is a striking fact that the boy upon approaching puberty—and for some years to follow—entertains an unusually unconflicted and, indeed, congenial relationship with his father. There is no sign of the awesome oedipus complex.[7] On the other hand, there is no doubt that he has little, or only conditional, or no use at all for mother and sisters, indeed, for the female sex generally. We must remember that pubertal drive intensification, in conjunction with strangely new and untested bodily sensations and affective states, invokes regulations along the body-mind continuum which hark back to the child's infantile training period. Here lies the first and momentous beginning of acquiring the ownership of one's body and experiencing the ecstasy of a "self." A similar ecstasy, yet far more complex, is reexperienced by the young adolescent when he enters the second individuation process at the dawn of puberty.[8] The fateful struggle of early body regulation remains permanently associated with the mother of early childhood. Her renewed assertion of power in taking over the guardianship of his growing body becomes anathema to the young adolescent boy. He resists the mother of his infancy to such a degree that he—easily and irrationally—attributes to her witchlike powers that soon are imputed to the entire world of the female.

It remains the psychological task of the boy at this stage to abandon the gratifications of early childhood as inappropriate aims of the pubertal drives. By so doing the boy prepares himself for the ultimate genital potency of a man. The side-stepping of this phase-specific task invites all kinds and degrees of sexual maldevelopment. With the rise of the boy's emotional self-control, there declines, proportionally, his irrational fear of the female; thus opens the road to his entry into the phase of Adolescence Proper. Before this can take its course, we witness the boy's relationship to his father undergoing a change. The closeness to him is resolved in the formation of the ego ideal.[*] [9]

The ego ideal constitutes a prerequisite for the later choice and pursuit of a vocational goal. Whenever the formation of the ego ideal is critically impaired, there ensues a sense of uncertainty, floundering, indecisiveness, restlessness, and low self-esteem. Under these conditions, whatever door flies open, promising a departure from this impasse, will give the adolescent a short-lived sense of direction and purpose.

It follows from what has been said, that the boy's emotional conflict during early adolescence centers primarily on the mother. The "mother" in this context is the internalized mother of infancy (the preoedipal mother), not the real mother of the present. This fact is responsible for much of the irrationality and misunderstandings between mother and adolescent child. To overcome this irrationality remains the challenge of this age. The emotional vulnerability of the young adolescent boy is twofold; both can be termed adolescent fixations. One aspect consists in an incomplete disengagement from the preoedipal mother with the consequence of marked ambivalence in later relationships and of an inordinate need for nurturing (Preadolescence). The other aspect lies in the perseverance of his emotional attachment to the father (Early Adolescence) with the consequence of divided loyalty to the sexes and being plagued, surreptitiously, by doubts about his masculinity.

A similar constellation holds for the girl, yet with a different resolution. Regressively, the girl seeks emotional closeness to the protective mother of early childhood. A very special relationship often develops in which the mother becomes the confidant of the girl ("I couldn't wait to get home and tell my mother") and the adviser in the bewildering emotional turmoil of this age. This partnership has a decisively positive influence on the girl's emerging femininity and, in addition, protects her against precocious emotional independence and sexual involvement. A widespread misconception interprets the young adolescent girl's emotional

[*] The definitive formation of the ego ideal during Early Adolescence is too complex a process to describe in this context. However, it could not be omitted altogether, since it influences profoundly the life of the young adolescent boy.

needs as an oedipal involvement with the father. Indeed, fathers often feel obliged to flirt with their daughter in order to enhance the girl's confidence in her femininity. The oedipal constellation belongs to a later stage. The misconception finds apparent support in the fact that, whenever the regressive pull to the mother of early childhood becomes too intense, feelings of oppositionalism, aversion, or estrangement take over, rendering the relationship to the mother highly ambivalent; in defensive flight the girl turns to the father or she becomes "boy-crazy." Should a proclivity to acting out already exist, it is not uncommon that the girl takes flight to the opposite sex as a countermeasure against the unduly severe regressive pull ("female sexual delinquency"[10]). Normally, however, the young adolescent of both sexes seems, for short stretches of time, to be comparatively unfettered by the dependency on, the search for, and the revival of infantile relationships. This subjective sense of freedom from childhood dependencies is constantly disrupted by passionate and ambivalent struggles with parents, siblings, and teachers, seeking closeness and distance at the same time.

From the beginning of her adolescence, the girl is far more preoccupied with the vicissitudes of object relations than the boy; his energies are directed outward toward the control of and dominance over the physical world. The girl, in contrast, turns—either in fact or fantasy—with deep-felt emotionality, mixed of romantic tenderness, possessiveness, and envy, to the boy. While the boy sets out to master the physical world, the girl endeavors to deal with relationships. Some girls unite in competitive coteries, sharing secrets and observations (who in the class has menstruated or what new eyeshade or hairdo the teacher wears and why), never tired of carrying on love affairs from afar. Other girls negate or postpone their female role through living the life of the tomboy or of the studious pupil. The strategy of delay which the girl employs at this age is supportive of normal female development. The girl's regressive escapades always remain counterbalanced by her turn to the other sex. She rarely loses herself as completely in regressive behavior as the boy. In fact, girls at this age are known to be better students than boys and their capacity for introspection is superior. Of course, what the girl at this stage has acquired is not genuine femininity; a more discerning look convinces us that it is aggression and possessiveness that dominate her relationship to the other sex. These infantile modes of object relation barely hide the narcissistic aspect of her yearnings—namely the need to find a sense of completeness through object possession.[11]

I have found that the emotional vulnerability of the young adolescent girl is twofold. Both are due to the perseverance ("getting stuck") in a normally transient position of development. One aspect consists in her incapacity to resist and overcome the regressive pull to the preoedipal mother (Preadolescence), thereby reinstituting permanently the primitive ambivalence of early object relations in the intimate affiliations of her life. The other aspect lies in her incapacity to relinquish the typical bisexual identity of Early Adolescence. Only in case the tomboy position becomes a lasting one, instead of being transient, is the girl's progression to femininity seriously imperiled. It should be evident that the developmental challenge for the girl at this phase consists in the successful resistance to the regressive pull to the preoedipal mother, in the renunciation of pregenital drive gratifications, such as infantile dependency or physical contact hunger in one form or another, and, last but not least, in the acceptance of her femaleness. Much of the maladaptive behavior which breaks out during Adolescence Proper and Late Adolescence shows clearly the insufficient relinquishment and, partial or total, failure to resolve the tasks and challenges as described above.

Under normal circumstances the young adolescent girl deals with the vicissitudes of emotional disengagement from the mother intrapsychically and she takes her time to harmonize her emotional and physical needs. This she cannot accomplish without the mother's help and protection. Not that the girl, necessarily, likes such interferences nor consciously wishes for it, but it remains the mother's prerogative and duty to pass judgment on this issue.

I have dwelled rather expansively on the opening stage of the adolescent process. This I did intentionally, because the importance of this stage is generally not appreciated sufficiently nor is its complexity defined succinctly enough in the literature. After the decline of the opening stage of adolescence there unfolds a wholly new and distinct stage, Adolescence Proper, which represents the proverbial adolescence. The resuscitation of oedipal conflicts dominate this stage in terms of drive progression; the ego, concomitantly, elaborates this forward movement in terms of higher levels of differentiation. The process of the second individuation[12] is vigorously pushed ahead with the result that character formation[13] lends enduring and irreversible structures to the adolescent personality.

I must confine the description of this stage to these few and general comments, because a detailed exposition of its course would exceed the format of this essay. Instead, I shall turn to a consideration of some broad concerns which have a bearing on adolescent development during the ages of twelve± to sixteen±.

From Theory to Practice

The spacious, yet condensed and abbreviated, exposition of psychological development during early adolescence was presented in order to demonstrate to the reader the enormous complexity of the adolescent process at its onset. Furthermore, it seemed necessary to emphasize the perils to later development that will take their toll whenever the phase-specific psychological tasks of early adolescence are given insufficient time to be fulfilled or are side-stepped altogether.

The Earlier Onset of Puberty

We are in a position to say—after about fifty years of observation—that pubescence starts about four months earlier every ten years. This changing schedule has been made responsible for the earlier display of adolescent behavior, such as the clamor for independence and the turn to genital sexuality. Since biology cannot be argued with, the simplistic conclusion has been drawn that, for example, family and school must provide accommodations for the earlier arousal of pubertal needs.

I intend to follow a different line of reasoning by pointing out, first of all, that the sexual drive constitutes a most extraordinarily moldable and transformable "instinct" as to object and aim. At the time when sexual functioning arrives (age thirteen±), the personality has acquired a complexity which can well accommodate delay, repression, transformation (sublimation) without endangering, but rather, aiding and solidifying the adolescent process. We must not forget that adolescence is a culturally determined transition from childhood to adulthood; it takes its cue from bodily changes (puberty), but puts the ensuing rise of drive tension to its own societal purpose.

The time required to prepare the pubertal child for adult functioning (vocation, citizenship, parenthood, and so forth) has been obtained by the prolongation of adolescence. The faculty for devoting energy, dedication, and perseverance to this process derived from a partial inhibition of the drives (sublimation) or, at least, from their delayed gratification and uncommitted state. In order for society and adolescence to fit together, the biological schedule was radically interfered with for the benefit of both. In this sense, we speak of prolonged adolescence as a necessary condition in an industrialized society. And even more so, an open, democratic society must, for its own survival, support educational upward mobility and accept the risks inherent in such accommodations. In this connection we must acknowledge the fact that without a high level of psychological differentiation, the adolescent is neither able nor fit to cope with the differential learning required of him. An ever increasing demand for advanced cognitive mastery is made on all those who desire to enter the complex vocations of an industrialized or technetronic society.

We have ample evidence to demonstrate that an acceptance of the young adolescent as a self-directing, sexually active "young person" interferes severely with the preparatory functions of this stage. We can say that ego building at this time augurs more promisingly for the attainment of maturity than premature id gratification. To extend adolescence downward will deprive adolescence of the psychic properties that will enable youth later to endure the period of that complex process of adaptation and prolonged dependency (schooling and financial support) which present-day society demands from an increasingly larger segment of youth. I submit that a prolongation, rather than an abbreviation of childhood is desirable if not, indeed, imperative. The young adolescent of thirteen—regardless of the status of his primary and secondary sex characteristics—is still, psychologically, a child. This fact should be acknowledged by family, by school, and by society at large. These institutions must continue to extend their containing and protective roles, rather than push the young adolescent ahead under the misleading banner of "the earlier and the faster, the bigger and the better."

What I am proposing, then, is the prolongation of childhood status, rather than the institutionalization of a downward extension of adolescence by blindly following a biological trend. In connection with this thesis I submit, furthermore, that the separation of the sexes in school during these early adolescent years is, psychologically and biologically, well advised. It is not necessary to recount here the well-known intellectual, physical, social, and psychological discrepancies that make boy and girl of this age ill fitting companions in work and play. We do not, by such a separation, deprive the sexes of their normal development; quite the contrary. It is the boy showing a precocious preference for girl playmates who is the one whose maleness proves in later years shakily established, while the young boy who keeps company with boys as a young adolescent tends to settle, later on, more firmly and lastingly in his masculine identity.[14]

The Young Adolescent in Relation to Social Class and Educational Philosophy

The general schema of psychic restructuring during initial adolescence, as outlined above, can be demonstrated in the most heterogeneous phenomenology of adolescence. Process and content need to be delineated, each in its own right, before both can be brought into a functional relationship to the social context where they find expression. Social class as referent in adolescence is no new concept. European working-class adolescents were studied in the thirties[15] and the "social locus" (ghetto, urban middle class, rural or regional environment, migrant worker, and so forth) is taken today for granted as an influence that molds decisively the course of adolescence. Unfortunately, we still lack sufficient data which help us to evaluate accurately the various forms and schedules of adolescence in relation to the attainment of social and emotional maturity.

Experience has impressed on me the fact that prolonged adolescence, especially prolonged early adolescence, enhances the capacity for complex cognitive functions ("stage of formal operations"; Piaget). The prolongation of childhood ("stage of concrete operations"; Piaget) allows additional time for the acquisition of that large body of factual knowledge (be this science, mathematics, language, geography, or history) which is later put to integrative use, when meaningfulness and relevancy of knowledge and of learning move into the forefront of the educational experience.

It is axiomatic that the prevailing educational philosophy exerts a decisive influence on the form maturation will take. Educational philosophies reflect values and ideologies held by the parent generation and projected on the young. The educated classes are most prone to be influenced by the treatises of the sophisticated experts whose expostulations and theories have given rise to all kinds of misunderstandings. One of them might be paraphrased by saying:

since sexual maldevelopment is implicit in every neurosis and considered, popularly, as "proof of parental failure," it follows, therefore, that emotional health is assured by not only accepting, but by actively fostering, heterosexual expression in early adolescence. Furthermore, I have observed a widespread fear which takes possession of many mothers at the time when their son arrives at early adolescence. They notice his typical prepubertal pudginess around the hips in conjunction with his disinterest in girls and his preference for male companionship; all this seems to foreshadow homosexuality. By shortcircuiting a developmental detour of utmost importance, the boy is forcefully yanked away from his normal course. This example should convince the expert (myself included) how much he has to remedy by way of public enlightenment. This brings me to what follows next.

Mass Media, Commercialism, and the Generation Gap

With the gradual, but radical, obsolescence of tradition in family life, reflected in child rearing, nutrition, manners, and moral stringencies, parent and child tend to rely more and more on the plethora of public advice which the mass media deliver into the home. Tradition has become replaced by the expert who offers answers to all of life's problems. Thus, the family has become, gradually, a laboratory for the application of all kinds of counsel which either fuse, contradict, or replace traditional patterns. Parents who reluctantly or eagerly put the bewildering jumble of advice into practice soon abdicate their personal responsibility in favor of the expert; thus, they are surrendering their own convictions rather than passing judgment on what has been offered them. This submission to the expert has drained parental actions or attitudes of consistency, integration, and integrity. In the face of such synthetic guidance, a child becomes unresponsive and confused. The "scientific" upbringing of children has turned out far more problematical than it seemed at first; indeed, many glorious expectations have come to dismal disappointments.

Of course, we must accept the fact that the mass media are with us for good and will continue to shape the minds of parents and children. Commercialism makes goods desirable to children through advertising and children, in turn, badger their parents to buy these goods. This turns into a particularly unsavory hucksHtery when the spontaneous innovations (especially in clothing) by the young become commercially exploited, namely, stylized and glamorized for mass consumption. The impact of this synthetic image, full of expectations and promises, has its special impact on the young adolescent. It is the age when opposition to family values and patterns starts to assert itself and parents, especially in urban areas, are hard pressed whenever they practice their parental privilege by setting limits and by affirming their personal values. Quickly, the exercise of parental authority becomes placated by the young as authoritarianism.

Opposition to parental guidance, silent or vocal, belongs to the stage of initial adolescence. What is new is the self-doubt of the adult, whether to grant the adolescent child his wishes and his freedom and, thus, speed up his "mature" independence, or to realize that tension and antagonism represent the essential conflicts of this period. Parents who are unable to tolerate this tension either leave the child to his own devices, or they support, explicitly and expectantly, his clamor for grown-up status. In both instances the phase-specific task (as outlined above) is aborted. The sequelae will become apparent at a time when the normative influences of parent or school have lost their impact and stringency. A misordered sense of timing has, in such instances, dealt with the budding conflict between the generations by pushing adolescence precociously ahead. As a consequence the syndrome of the generation gap emerges later on, as a self-protective rupture by which family dependencies and animosities are removed, in wholesale fashion, and fixed in the polarities of young versus old, of under versus over thirty, of "we" versus "they." It is my opinion that the subjective experience of the so-called generation gap is an indication of a developmental deficit, namely, a defensive avoidance of the painful and tortuous generational conflict.* [16]

This particular aspect of modern youth applies, almost exclusively, to middle-class families. There we see, upon close inspection, that the family unit of parent and child had prolonged an unusually close emotional involvement which neither one was able nor ready to relinquish when puberty had arrived. In order not to mislead the reader I must add that this closeness is not, necessarily, an idyllic and blissful bond; it is, more often than not, a tie racked with open or silent struggles. Be this as it may, such a predicament

---

* The generation gap experience of youth belongs to the normal course of disengagement from the past. I refer above to a specific type of the generation gap experience.

is aggravated by a habituation to incessant sensory stimulation (TV, radio, hi-fi). Both, in conjunction, reduce the faculty to be alone with oneself or, in psychological terms, to attend to internalization processes and to the use of fantasy. The process of internalization renders the demarcation between the inner and the outer world sharp and keen, with the result that acting out in later adolescence becomes dispensible as a means to problem solving. "Acting older" often turns out to be a mimicry adaptation which has its onset in early adolescence, whenever the environment has become insensitive to the developmental needs of the young. Despite the fact that the young adolescent has acquired sexual maturity, he still remains a child or, rather, stands on the threshold of leaving childhood behind for good. Physical stature and procreative capacity are the most unreliable indicators, at least in our society, of emotional maturity and independence from the parent generation.

The trend of the young adolescent to reach beyond his age, to be older by acting older, is complemented by the desire of the adult to be younger than his age. The fear of getting older has turned many an adult into a nostalgic expatriate from youth, who shuns neither ingenuity nor expense to stem the tides of aging. The young adolescent's violent rejection of his partial childhood status finds its complement in the adult's abhorrence of leaving his youth behind. In this sense the adolescent is right that adults want to appropriate "his thing."

Psychic Structure and Social Structure

Adolescence never occurs in a social vacuum. Society always bestows on the adolescent generation a unique and decisive impression which, so it seems, can obliterate many formative influences of the family. The collective integration by the young of whatever the epochal impact of society might be (conformity or oppositionalism), is subsumed under the concept of "youth culture," "peer culture," or "adolescent subculture." This social phenomenon can best be understood if we contemplate the adolescent task of psychological disengagement from the family as a simultaneous transition and entry into the wider context of society. The personal and intimate ties of love and hate which were the heartbeat of the child's social matrix become slowly replaced by the immersion into the anonymity of society, represented by its social institutions. Personal intimacy and emotional bonds become a matter of choice and private concern, thus complementing the impersonal, yet meaningful, affiliation and identification, disaffiliation and counteridentification, with social institutions and their executive functions.

During adolescence the child passes, gradually but persistently, from the highly personal family envelope to the eminently impersonal societal envelope. In this transition we witness the steady arousal of affective responses to social, moral, and spiritual issues. Should this response remain a direct displacement from childhood idealizations or grievances, then, and only then, can we speak of a miscarriage of psychic restructuring. Then we can say that the shadow of renewed childhood rage and blame has fallen on the environment.

On the basis of these observations and principles, I endeavor to make the point that no adolescent, at any station of his journey, can develop optimally without societal structures standing ready to receive him, offering him that authentic credibility with which he can identify or polarize. Whenever society lacks, to a critical degree, the quality of stable structure, then the maturing child turns, exclusively, to his contemporaries, his peers, in order to create for himself that social extrafamilial structure without which he cannot maintain his psychic integrity. As in most self-styled emergency and rescue actions which the child takes, the adolescent, similarly, protects himself against noxious environmental influences at the price of some measure of self-limitation. The extremism ("totalism") of adolescent attitudes and actions is by no means determined, exclusively, by the life history of the individual.[17] The chaotic condition of contemporary society is a decisive, contributing factor. According to the nature of trauma, the fateful juxtaposition of adolescent developmental urgencies, vis-à-vis societal resourcefulness and facilitation, will become the organizing experience from which the universal childhood complexes (what the kids call "hangups") take their form and expression.[18]

Observation and study of youth permits us to say that the psychic structure of the individual is critically affected, for better or worse, by the structure of society.[19] This is not a novel idea by any means; what I try to emphasize here is the fact that the successful course of adolescence depends intrinsically on the degree of intactness and cohesion which societal institutions obtain. It is not necessary to belabor here the fragmented, disoriented, antiquated, cynical, and corrupt state of many contemporary social institutions.

One might argue the point whether power has not always tainted the best of men. Be this as it may, one fact remains plain and obvious, namely, that the clever little boy in The Emperor's New Clothes can be found today almost everywhere and that his small voice has grown to a mighty chorus.

The increase of maladaptive behavior among the young cannot be related, solely, to their upbringing, to the laxity, severity of, or neglect by family, school, or church. Anomie is a decisive determinant. To call the "unconforming" adolescent "sick" is a meaningless attribution; the hope to stem the tide through individual or group counseling, through confrontation sessions or psychotherapy, must remain—in the light of what has been said—another labor of Sisyphus. Of course, there always were and are adolescents of any age who require therapeutic interventions of various kinds. But I speak here in terms of an epidemic-like "cop-out" and of an alarming rise in breakdowns (psychosis). There, the strategy for normalization lies, to a large extent, outside individual rehabilitation and, rather, in the restructuring of the environment, for example, the school, the juvenile court, and, above and beyond that, in the reform of the legislative and executive functions of government on all levels. This would constructively alter the attitudes of the young toward the adult.

In discussing the young adolescent I have described his psychological development in terms of psychic reorganization. I have traced the accommodations of the drives to the state of puberty and indicated the emergence of ego capacities that parallel physical maturation and changing social status. The conclusion was drawn that the beginning stage of adolescence decides critically the course which adolescence will take subsequently. Reasons for a prolongation, rather than an abbreviation, of early adolescence were set forth, despite the fact that physical maturation moves in the opposite direction. Societal structures in relation to individual psychic structures were afforded an eminent role in the transition from family dependencies to societal partnership.

My intention throughout was the explication of developmental principles and the localization of those critical conditions which either promote or impede the adolescent process. These considerations demanded that I pay explicit attention to the stage from which the young adolescent emerges as well as the one to which he is tending. The adolescent in mid-passage, the proverbial adolescent of the ages fourteen± to sixteen± (Adolescence Proper) was not given equal treatment. I elected to concentrate on early adolescence because this stage is the most crucial and least understood of all the stages that comprise the adolescent process as a whole. What I was aiming at, in essence, was the exposition of a developmental point of view which might serve as a reference point to the many specialists who work with the young adolescent.

REFERENCES

1. P. Blos, "Preadolescent Drive Organization," *Journal of the American Psychoanalytic Association,* 6 (1958); Blos, *The Young Adolescent: Clinical Studies* (New York: The Free Press—MacMillan, 1970).

2. P. Blos, *On Adolescence: A Psychoanalytic Interpretation* (New York: The Free Press of Glencoe, 1962).

3. *Ibid.*

4. E. H. Erikson, *Childhood and Society* (New York: Norton, 1950), p. 233.

5. A. Freud, *The Ego and the Mechanisms of Defence* (New York: International University Press, 1946; originally published 1936), pp. 158-159.

6. Blos, *On Adolescence.*

7. P. Blos, *The Initial Stage of Male Adolescence,* The Psychoanalytic Study of the Child, XX (New York: International University Press, 1965).

8. P. Blos, *The Second Individuation Process of Adolescence,* The Psychoanalytic Study of the Child, XXII (New York: International University Press, 1967).

9. Blos, *On Adolescence;* Blos, *The Initial Stage of Male Adolescence.*

10. P. Blos, *Preoedipal Factors in the Etiology of Female Delinquency,* The Psychoanalytic Study of the Child, XII (New York: International University Press, 1957); Blos, "Three Typical Constellations in Female Delinquency," in O. Pollak and A. S. Friedman, eds., *Family Dynamics and Female Delinquency* (Palo Alto: Science and Behavior Books, 1969).

11. Blos, *On Adolescence.*

12. Blos, *The Second Individuation Process of Adolescence.*

13. P. Blos, *Character Formation in Adolescence,* The Psychoanalytic Study of the Child, XXIII (New York: International University Press, 1968).

14. A. Freud, *Normality and Pathology in Childhood: Assessments of Development* (New York: International University Press, 1965), pp. 189-190.

15. S. Bernfield, "Über die einfache männliche Pubertät," *Zeitschrift für psychoanalytische Pädagogik,* 9 (1935).

16. P. Blos, "The Generation Gap: Fact and Fiction," in *Adolescent Psychiatry: Annals of the American Society for Adolescent Psychiatry,* 1 (New York: Basic Books, 1970).

17. Blos, *The Second Individuation Process of Adolescence.*

18. Blos, *On Adolescence,* pp. 132-140.

19. Blos, "The Generation Gap."

DAVID BAKAN

Adolescence in America: From Idea to Social Fact

The Idea of Adolescence

OFTEN A technical term is invented in order to create a social condition and a social fact; such has been true with respect to the term "adolescence." The idea of adolescence as an intermediary period in life starting at puberty and extending to some period in the life cycle unmarked by any conspicuous physical change but socially defined as "manhood" or "womanhood" is the product of modern times. The *Oxford English Dictionary* traces the term to the fifteenth century. Prior to that, if we follow the thought of Philip Aries,[1] the notion of childhood hardly existed, let alone the idea of the prolongation of childhood beyond puberty, as the term adolescence suggests.

Meaningful ascription of serious role characteristics for this period of life occurs, perhaps for the first time, in Rousseau's *Émile*, in which he characterized the period of adolescence as being beyond the earlier period of weakness of childhood and as a second birth. "We are born, so to speak, twice over; born into existence, and born into life; born a human being and born a man."[2] His aim was explicitly to prolong childhood, including the condition of innocence, as long as possible.

Although *Émile* has had considerable influence since its publication, the conversion of the idea of adolescence into a commonly accepted social reality was largely associated with modern urban-industrial life. Rousseau may have *invented* adolescence, as maintained by Musgrove,[3] but the notion as it is commonly understood in contemporary thought did not prevail prior to the last two decades of the nineteenth century and was "on the whole an American discovery."[4] The idea received an important stamp of reality from G. Stanley Hall in his monumental two-volume work on *Adoles-*

73

cence, which he proudly presented to the reader as "essentially the author's first book" in 1904.[5] In point of fact he had introduced the idea as a special stage of development earlier.[6] In *Adolescence* he complained that we in America, because of our history, "have had neither childhood nor youth, but have lost touch with these stages of life because we lack a normal developmental history . . . Our immigrants have often passed the best years of youth or leave it behind when they reach our shores, and their memories of it are in other lands. No country is so precociously old for its years."[7] The giving of social reality to adolescence would, as it were, youthen the nation.

By reviewing some of the history, I will attempt to show in this essay that the invention or discovery of adolescence in America was largely in response to the social changes that accompanied America's development in the latter half of the nineteenth and the early twentieth century, and that the principal reason was to prolong the years of childhood. Adolescence was added to childhood as a second childhood in order to fulfill the aims of the new urban-industrial society which developed so rapidly following the Civil War.

Historical Background

From the days of the early settlement of America to the second half of the nineteenth century, America suffered a chronic labor shortage. It sought to overcome this labor shortage through slavery, the encouragement of immigration, and industrialization. The incompatibility of slavery and industrialization plagued America during much of its early history, and that incompatibility remained until the Civil War, the Emancipation Proclamation, and the Thirteenth Amendment resolved it in favor of industrialization. But with the development of urban-industrial society, the nation became possessed of new contradictions characteristic of modern technological society, most serious among them the presence of a large number of persons who were mature by historical standards but immature in the new context.

The country changed dramatically during the second half of the nineteenth century. In 1880 the railroad network was completely integrated; there was no longer a frontier; the number of cities that had populations of more than 8,000 almost doubled in the decade from 1880 to 1890. By the year 1900 more than a third of the population was living in cities and more than half the population of the

North Atlantic area lived in cities of more than 8,000 persons. In 1890 more than a third of the American population were people of foreign parentage. The question of property was becoming increasingly salient, as testified to by the proliferation of criminal laws designed to protect property rights—a not unimportant fact when we consider the question of juvenile delinquency, because most juvenile crimes are crimes against property, such as burglary, larceny, robbery, and auto theft.

The low level of "morality" of the new occupants of the burgeoning cities was a matter of frequent comment. Drinking, sexual immorality, vagrancy, and crime were not only intrinsically threatening to orderliness, but were also particularly distressing influences on the young. The rapid breeding, the continuing threat of "street Arabs," evoked a strong cry that the state intercede in restraining and training the young. In an address before the American Social Science Association in 1875, the influential Mary Carpenter said that if the parents of the young fail in their duty, then the whole society suffers; it was therefore the duty of the state to intercede and "stand *in loco parentis* and do its duty to the child and to society, by seeing that he is properly brought up."[8] Not the least of the dangers was the presence of un-American ideas and ideologies brought by the new immigrants, which were considered threatening to the basic fiber of American life. Even private education, as compared with public education, was regarded as a threat, the fear being that the children would not be sufficiently socialized and "Americanized." The Ku Klux Klan, for example, took a firm stand against private education.

As a result of these conditions, three major social movements developed, all of which conspired to make a social fact out of adolescence: compulsory (and characteristically public) education, child labor legislation, and special legal procedures for "juveniles." By the explicit citation of a precise chronological age, the legislation associated with these three areas essentially removed the vagueness of all previous ideas of the time at which adolescence terminates. Thus adolescence became the period of time between pubescence, a concrete biological occurrence, and the ages specified by law for compulsory education, employment, and criminal procedure.

There is no doubt that these movements were strongly motivated, at least on the conscious level, by humanitarian considerations. The rhetoric in defense of these three types of law was always cast in terms of the benefit and the saving quality that they would have for the young. The presumption that the various child welfare laws were principally created for the benefit of youth must, however, be confronted with the fact that there has been only a small degree of legal attention to the serious problem of child abuse in our society. The so-called "battered child" was not discovered until the late 1940's and early 1950's, and to this day appropriate protective and social support legislation is still quite negligible in contrast to the magnitude of the problem and the frequency of cases of cruelty to children.[9] The confluence of humanitarian considerations with the major economic, social, and political forces in the society needs to be clearly recognized. Indeed, the recognition of these underlying forces may help us to understand some of the failures to fulfill humanitarian aims and the disabilities which currently prevail with respect to that period of life that we call adolescence.

Compulsory Education

In the late nineteenth century, public compulsory education for children between six and eighteen, characteristically to age sixteen, was introduced widely in the United States. English common law had given parents virtually complete control over the education of the child, a principle prevalent in colonial America and throughout most of our early history. However, the general legal position later became that: "The primary function of the public school . . . is not to confer benefits upon the individual as such." Rather "the school exists as a state institution because the very existence of civil society demands it. The education of youth is a matter of such vital importance to the democratic state and to the public weal that the state may do much, may go very far indeed, by way of limiting the control of the parent over the education of his child."[10]

In the case of a father who had violated the compulsory attendance law, the court stated in its opinion:

The course of study to be pursued in the public schools of our state is prescribed either by statute or by the school authorities in pursuance thereof. These schools include not only elementary schools, but high schools as well . . . A parent, therefore, is not at liberty to exercise a choice in that regard, but, where not exempt for some lawful reason, must send his child to the school where instruction is provided suitable to its attainments as the school authorities may determine.[11]

It has been held that even a competent parent may not engage in domestic education on the following grounds:

We have no doubt many parents are capable of instructing their own children, but to permit such parents to withdraw their children from the public schools without permission from the superintendent of schools, and to instruct them at home, would be to disrupt our common school system and destroy its value to the state.[12]

At the same time the school authorities have been granted virtually complete discretionary powers with respect to suspension, expulsion, and punishment.[13] Such power rests in the hands of school authorities even in cases where the pupil has violated no rules. In one case, for example, a pupil was expelled for general misbehavior. In holding that the board of education had power to expel the pupil, the court said:

> It matters not whether rules have been announced by either the directors or teachers. If the conduct of the pupil is such as reasonably to satisfy such school officers that the presence of that pupil is detrimental to the interests of the school, then the power of expulsion is conferred.[14]

Thus, it has turned out that the power of the state in America is such that it can, through its officials, not only compel school attendance, but also bar a pupil access to educational resources. Certainly there have been numerous legislative acts and court actions which would qualify particular cases. However, the total thrust of the various steps that have been taken since the middle of the nineteenth century has been in the direction of increasing the power of the state rather than protecting the rights of young people and their parents.

At the same time as the legal power of school authorities over pupils and their parents has been great, the schools have been derelict in the teaching of law—instruction which some regard as essential for people living in a democracy. In a society that is heavily dependent for its functioning on law, it is important that an appreciation of law, how it works, and its limits be taught in the public schools. One critic of this aspect of American education, in discussing the matter of education on due process, indicates that it is taught as though it applies only to criminals and that it fails to reflect itself in procedural fairness in school disciplinary matters. The idea of freedom of the press is characteristically not brought to bear in connection with school newspapers. "One of the difficult problems," he laconically comments, "is whether [proposed] law courses will be permitted to ventilate these issues, given the anxiety about them."[15]

Although from time to time there have been steps to increase the knowledge of law among educators, the emphasis has been on the kind of legal knowledge that an educator might require to deal with relationships of the school to outside institutions and individuals rather than on teaching law to students. One article along these lines, for example, deals with the legal structure of education, pupil personnel policies, control of pupil conduct, staff personnel policies, curricula, and liability. Illustrations are that: physical education coordinators should be expert in the law of liability for pupil injuries; guidance teachers should be familiar with compulsory education laws and their enforcement; curriculum coordinators should understand the legal position of parents in relation to school studies and activities; business administrators should understand contract law; personnel administrators should understand the legal aspects of employing and discharging teachers; and teachers of the history or philosophy of education should be acquainted with the relevant judicial opinions.[16]

Child Labor

The movement to restrict child labor in the United States also provided a definition of the termination of adolescence. Though there is a considerable amount of variation from state to state, the laws with respect to employment give specific minimum ages for definitions of maturity of different kinds: eighteen, minimum age for work in "hazardous occupations"; under eighteen, eight-hour day and forty-hour week; under eighteen, employment certificate required; under sixteen, limited hours of night work; sixteen, minimum age for factory work and employment during school hours; fourteen, minimum age for work outside of school hours. These are fairly typical laws governing age and employment.

The regulation of child labor has been one of the most controversial issues in this country since the nineteenth century. The harm to children from work in factories has been stridently declaimed. On the other hand, the virtues of work, the harm associated with idleness, and even the economic discriminatory effect of such legislation have also been consistently indicated. As an example, Senator Alexander Wiley, in questioning the representative of the American Federation of Labor before a Senate subcommittee to investigate juvenile delinquency said: "To me when I see the youth of this country in idleness, walking the streets of the cities, [I feel] we are meeting a challenge to our common sense because we know idleness breeds not only crime but everything else."[17] There have been repeated charges that the legal regulation of child labor is partly responsible for the widespread unemployment among young people, particularly Negroes.[18]

Adolescents in the labor force were a common occurrence throughout American history. In 1832 about 40 per cent of the factory workers in New England were children. Starting a few years after the Civil War the major historical trend of a chronic labor shortage began to reverse itself, with ever-increasing evidences of labor surplus. With the changes in the kinds of work needed in the growing cities in the second half of the nineteenth century, an increasing proportion of females sought gainful employment. Indeed, the possibility of a close relationship between the various movements in connection with "child saving" and female employment has been seriously suggested.[19] Labor began to organize. The Knights of Labor, the precursor of the American Federation of Labor, was founded in 1869. In 1885 it had a membership of 100,000; a year later it could boast a membership of 730,000. Virtually from its founding, the Knights of Labor began its campaign for the prohibition of child labor. In spite of its efforts, child labor increased. The participation rate of youth between the ages of ten and fifteen in the labor force increased until 1900 and then began to decline. Indeed, in the decade which ended in 1900, the number of child laborers in the canneries, glass industry, mines, and so forth in the South tripled. The effort to control the labor supply in the United States was evident also in legislation to restrict immigration. In 1882 the Chinese Exclusion Act, barring immigration of Chinese laborers, was passed and was followed by other laws which severely restricted immigration.

Among employers there was a polarization. On the one hand there were certainly those employers who were in favor of having access to the cheap labor of young people and new immigrants; on the other hand the nature of industrial requirements was changing rapidly in favor of more skilled, and especially more reliable, workers. One of the most serious interferences with the reliability of labor was alcohol, and the prohibition movement grew simultaneously with the efforts to remove young people from the labor market and to restrict immigration. The prohibition movement gained increasing support from industrial leaders, "who were not unaware of the economic implications of the trade in intoxicants."[20]

The belief, common during the early part of the nineteenth century, that the children of the poor should work and that education of the children of the poor was filled with social danger tended to decline in the course of the century. The enlightened leaders of industry, taking ever longer views of history, recognized the dependence of industry on the existence of a reasonably educated labor force, educated not only with respect to knowledge and skill, but also with respect to bureaucratic subordination and reliable work habits.[21] At the same time, organized labor sought not only reforms in the conditions of child labor, but also education for their own children, to increase the likelihood of vertical social mobility. The continuing interest of both industry and labor in the education of the young is evidenced by the clear agreement on this on the part of both the National Association of Manufacturers and organized labor.[22]

One of the classic conflicts in connection with child labor was that between the textile manufacturers of the North and those in the South. The northern manufacturers charged that the South had a competitive advantage from its greater use of young workers.[23] Among the factors that eventually led to a resolution of the conflict was the later discovery, resulting in part from the changed nature of manufacture and experience of some restrictive legislation, that, as the *Textile World Journal* in 1918 put it: "The labor of children under fourteen years of age is not only inefficient in itself, but tends to lower the efficiency of all departments in which they are employed; also children of fourteen to sixteen years, worked on a short time basis, are scarcely less efficient and have a disorganizing effect in the departments where they are utilized. Because of these facts, and entirely apart from humanitarian considerations, large numbers of southern mills will not re-employ children of these ages."[24]

Juvenile Delinquency

Quite analogous to the "invention of adolescence," as Musgrove put it, was the "invention of delinquency," as Anthony M. Platt puts it in his book on the history of the notion of delinquency in the United States.[25] The humane motivation associated with the development of the notion of the juvenile delinquent was the desire to remove young people from the rigidities and inexorabilities associated with criminal justice and to allow wider discretionary powers to authorities in dealing with juveniles. The new legal apparatus was intended to separate young offenders from older offenders, and to provide corrective rather than punitive treatment. The first Juvenile Court Act was passed by the Illinois legislature in 1899 and brought together for single consideration cases of dependency, neglect, and delinquency. The hearings under the act were to be informal, the records were to be confidential, the young people were to be detained separately from adults. The aims were to be investigation and prescription rather than the determination of guilt or innocence. Lawyers were to be unnecessary. The definition of the "juvenile delinquent" in the various laws which multiplied after the model legislation in Illinois now vary for the upper limit from sixteen to twenty-one. The United States Children's Bureau had recommended nineteen, and this has been followed in about two-thirds of the states.[26]

Although the juvenile acts tended to free the courts from the obligation of imposing punishments associated with the criminal codes, they also had the effect of suspending the fundamental principle of legality, that one may not be punished for an offense unless a definite law in effect at the time when the act in question was committed has been broken. Considerations of due process were not obligatory. Guilt did not have to be established beyond a reasonable doubt. Among the acts reported under the heading of juvenile delinquency may be found the following: immoral conduct around schools, association with vicious or immoral persons, patronizing public pool rooms, wandering about railroad yards, truancy, incorrigibility, absenting self from home without consent, smoking cigarettes in public places, begging or receiving alms (or in street for purposes of).[27] As Harvey Baker of the Boston juvenile court put it in 1910:

> The court does not confine its attention to just the particular offense which brought the child to its notice. For example, a boy who comes to court for such a trifle as failing to wear his badge when selling papers may be held on probation for months because of difficulties at school; and a boy who comes in for playing on the street may . . . be committed to a reform school because he is found to have habits of loafing, stealing or gambling which can not be corrected outside.[28]

Questions have been raised as to whether the procedures of such courts adequately protect the rights of young offenders and whether they are consistent with constitutional rights.[29] In some states corrective legislation has been attempted by providing for legal defense of persons who come under the jurisdiction of the juvenile courts. However, the evidence is that this is not common. Indeed, treatment by officials tends to be more kindly toward young persons who admit guilt and indicate that they will mend their ways than toward those who are defensive or those whose parents are defensive.[30] The failure of the juvenile court to achieve its avowed objectives is notorious.

Suggestions that the aim of the juvenile court is to introduce a middle-class child-rearing orientation to the courtroom are apparent in the opinion of Judge Ben Lindsey of Denver, one of the pioneers in the juvenile court movement, and in the findings of Melvin L. Kohn. In an introduction to a book called *Winning the Boy* by Lilburn Merrill, Lindsey stressed the importance of "character," rather than the act itself.

> You have not really a safe citizen until there comes into the boy's heart the desire to do right because it is right . . . I ask the boy why he will not steal again and he invariably replies, "Because I will get in jail." He is afraid of jail; he is not afraid to do wrong . . . Conscience is the moral director; without it character is impossible, and character is the greatest need, for it means that the pure in heart shall see and know and act the truth, as surely as they shall see God.[31]

Kohn has been able to show, on the basis of comparative data which he has collected, that there are differences in corrective actions between working-class and middle-class parents. Working-class parents tend to punish the external consequences of an action, as contrasted with middle-class parents who tend to punish on the basis of intention, rather than the action itself.[32] The latter mode is clearly suggested in Judge Lindsey's comment. Thus one way of interpreting the development of juvenile delinquency practices is as an effort to bring middle-class child-rearing practices into play, even when they involved the suspension of the principle of legality.

The legal disability of those who come under the juvenile laws is not limited to a small minority of youth in our society. "Statutes often define juvenile delinquency so broadly as to make virtually all youngsters delinquent . . . Rough estimates by the Children's Bureau, supported by independent studies, indicate that one in every nine youths—one in every six male youths—will be referred to juvenile court in connection with a delinquent act (excluding traffic offenses) before his 18th birthday."[33] As soon as the young person gains what may be called the animal sufficiency that comes with puberty, and may enter public places without an attendant, he becomes subject to extraordinary powers of the state until the legal definition of his maturity comes into being. This power of the state differs dramatically from the power of the state over adults in our society. The great discrepancy between adult justice and juvenile justice and the legal vulnerability of juveniles has been one of the major factors associated with the conversion of the idea of adolescence into the social fact of adolescence.

The Study of Adolescence

Starting with the work of G. Stanley Hall, adolescence became the subject of a considerable amount of investigation. There can be no doubt about the value of such investigation—indeed, this may be attested to by the essays in this volume. Nonetheless, this body of literature articulated with the cultural forces in the society at large. Although the intention of people like Hall to draw attention to an extremely important age period significant to the history of civilization generally, and the United States in particular, and thereby to create greater concern with proper development at that stage, was meritorious, there was another effect which needs to be pointed out. By stressing, for example, the presumptive emotional instability and unformed nature of people of that age—the work of Margaret Mead and others suggests that such phenomena of adolescence may be extrinsic rather than intrinsic[34]—Hall and others tended to put a gloss of psychopathology on this age period. Since it has long been a principle in our society that persons regarded as psychologically pathological are to be relieved of rights,[35] the effect of this literature has been to serve the general disability of persons under legal ages. In this way, the workers in the field of adolescence have tended to conspire, certainly unwittingly, with some of the forces depriving adolescents of their rights.

The Promise

A major factor which has sustained the social fact of adolescence in our society has been the belief, so pervasive in our success-oriented culture, in "the promise." The promise is that if a young person does all the things he is "supposed to do" during his adolescence, he will then realize success, status, income, power, and so forth in his adulthood.

A study by Arthur L. Stinchcombe[36] may help us to understand the operation of the promise. He studied the attitudes, behavior, and perceptions of the labor market among high school students, and found a direct and dramatic relationship between the images of the future that the students have and their rebellious attitudes and behavior. His data bear out the hypothesis "that high school rebellion, and expressive alienation, are most common among students who do not see themselves as gaining an increment in future status from conformity in high school."[37] In elaborating on the dynamics of the hypothesis, he writes: "When a student realizes that he does not achieve status increment from improved current performance, current performance loses meaning. The student becomes hedonistic because he does not visualize achievement of long-run goals through current self-restraint. He reacts negatively to a conformity that offers nothing concrete. He claims autonomy from adults because their authority does not promise him a satisfactory future."[38] Stinchcombe's hypothesis is derived from considerations of the legitimacy of bureaucratic authority as developed by Max Weber. Among the interesting derivations Stinchcombe makes from the hypothesis is an explanation of the difference between the sexes in various categories of expressive alienation. Girls are less likely to be rebellious because they perceive at least the possibility of marriage as a viable "career." He points out that the relatively high delinquency rate among Negroes is associated with the perception of the employment discrimination against Negro adult males.

As the credibility of the promise declines, the willingness of young people to accept the varieties of disabilities of adolescence equally declines. The profoundly pervasive metaphor of appropriate behavior in adolescence as a form of capital investment for the realization of returns in the future necessarily falters in cogency as the likelihood of such returns declines. The problems of order in the schools, juvenile delinquency, and other forms of expressive alienation cannot readily be solved by making small changes in the schools, Stinchcombe says.[39] It would appear that the schools cannot promise much because the society cannot promise much.

A study by William Westley and Frederick Elkin[40] of young people in an upper-class suburb of Montreal in 1951 attempted to explode the notion of the adolescent period as being one of storm and stress, nonconformity, gang formation, struggle for emancipation, and the like. The data collected in that place and time indicated considerably greater harmony and positive social adjustment by conventional standards than one might expect. However, the characterization of these young people would clearly indicate that they expected that the promise would be fulfilled. The typical youth in the study "internalizes aspirations for a professional or business career; he learns the expected patterns of language and breeding; he learns to resolve disputes by peaceable means; he learns to defer many immediate gratifications for the sake of future gains."[41]

The major question in our society today is whether, for youth of *all* social classes, the promise has continued credibility. Unemployment among manual workers is increasingly patent. The public service advertisements directed at potential drop-outs to remain in school in order to get better jobs later are met with increasing cynicism.[42] The poor acceptance rates of college students into the labor market predicted in the early sixties[43] are rapidly materializing. Even for scientists with Ph.D.'s the possibilities for employment are extremely dismal.[44] And few young people are ignorant of the fact that a career in "free enterprise" is virtually impossible without access to capital.[45] The idyllic vision of Erik Erikson that adolescence "can be viewed as a *psychosocial moratorium* during which the individual through free role experimentation may find a niche in some section of his society, a niche which is firmly defined and yet seems to be uniquely made for him,"[46] must increasingly be viewed cynically if that niche in life is contingent upon an appropriate niche in the labor force.

One of the likely consequences of these trends will be a strong move on the part of youth and their parents to dissolve the social fact of adolescence and to remove the historical disabilities which have been created by the state and sustained by the promise. Albert K. Cohen, in 1965, indicated that he thought it was sad that youth accepted their disabilities without protest.[47] The picture soon changed. Jerry Farber's critique of what he calls America's "Auschwitz" educational system, "The Student as Nigger," originally published in 1967 in the Los Angeles *Free Press*, quickly became one of the most widely distributed underground documents in history—reprinted, reduplicated, recopied many times by student groups all over America and Canada.[48] A national clearing house of anti-public school thought has been formed in Washington, D.C., which puts out a regular biweekly newsletter called *FPS* (*the letters don't stand for anything*). Ellen Lurie has written what is fast becoming a standard manual for parents seeking to reduce state control over their children's education in the public schools.[49] This book is consistent with the United Nations Universal Declaration of Human Rights, adopted in 1948, that "Parents have a prior right to choose the kind of education that shall be given to their children."[50] The crime statistics mount at an exponential rate. Demonstrations become ever more strident. The "underground revolution"[51] gets new recruits daily.

The future? My assignment was to discuss history. The future must be left to time and other occasions.[52]

REFERENCES

1. P. Aries, *Centuries of Childhood* (New York: Knopf, 1962).

2. Jean Jacques Rousseau, *Émile,* trans. Barbara Foxley (New York: Dutton, 1966; originally published 1762), pp. 128, 172.

3. F. Musgrove, *Youth and the Social Order* (Bloomington, Ind.: Indiana University Press, 1964). Musgrove titles one of his chapters "The Invention of the Adolescent," pp. 33-57.

4. John Demos and Virginia Demos, "Adolescence in Historical Perspective," *Journal of Marriage and the Family,* 31 (1969), 632-638, 632.

5. G. Stanley Hall, *Adolescence: Its Psychology and Its Relations to Physiology, Anthropology, Sociology, Sex, Crime, Religion, and Education* (New York: D. Appleton and Company, 1904).

6. G. Stanley Hall, "The Moral and Religious Training of Children," *Princeton Review* (January 1882), pp. 26-48.

7. Hall, *Adolescence,* p. xvi.

8. As cited in Grace Abbot, ed., *The Child and the State* (Chicago: University of Chicago Press, 1938), II, 372.

9. See M. G. Paulsen, "The Law and Abused Children," in R. E. Helfer and C. H. Kempe, *The Battered Child* (Chicago: University of Chicago Press, 1968), pp. 175-207; and D. Bakan, *Slaughter of the Innocents: A Study of the Battered Child Phenomenon* (San Francisco: Jossey-Bass, 1971; Toronto: Canadian Broadcasting Corp., 1971).

10. Newton Edwards, *The Courts and the Public Schools: The Legal Basis of School Organization and Administration,* rev. ed. (Chicago: University of Chicago Press, 1955), p. 24.

11. *Miller* v. *State,* 77 Ind. App. 611, 134 N. E. 209, as cited by Edwards, *The Courts and the Public Schools,* p. 524.

12. *State* v. *Counort,* 69 Wash. 361, 124 Pac. 910, 41 L.R.A. (N.S.) 95, as cited by Edwards, *The Courts and the Public Schools,* p. 522.

13. Edwards, *The Courts and the Public Schools,* pp. 601ff.

14. *State* v. *Hamilton,* 42 Mo. App. 24, as cited by Edwards, *The Courts and the Public Schools,* p. 603.

15. Alex Elson, "General Education in Law for Non-Lawyers," in The Amer-

ican Assembly, Columbia University, *Law in a Changing America* (Englewood Cliffs, N.J.: Prentice-Hall, 1968), pp. 183-191, 189.

16. E. E. Reutter, Jr., "Essentials of School Law for Educators," in Harold J. Carter, ed., *Intellectual Foundations of American Education* (New York: Pitman Publishing Corporation, 1965), pp. 216-225.

17. *Juvenile Delinquency: Hearings before the Subcommittee to Investigate Juvenile Delinquency*, Senate, 1955 (New York: Greenwood Press, 1968), p. 86.

18. See, for example, the effort to counter these charges by H. M. Haisch of the U.S. Department of Labor: H. M. Haisch, "Do Child Labor Laws Prevent Youth Employment?" *Journal of Negro Education*, 33 (1964), 182-185.

19. "Although child saving had important symbolic functions for preserving the prestige of middle-class women in a rapidly changing society, it also had considerable instrumental significance for legitimizing new career openings for women. The new role of social worker combined elements of an old and partly fictitious role—defender of family life—and elements of a new role—social servant. Social work and philanthropy were thus an affirmation of cherished values and an instrumentality for women's emancipation." Anthony M. Platt, *The Child Savers: The Invention of Delinquency* (Chicago: University of Chicago Press, 1969), p. 98.

20. John Allen Krout, *The Origins of Prohibition* (New York: Russell and Russell, 1967), p. 302.

21. For an analysis of relations between education and industry see John Galbraith, *The New Industrial State* (Boston: Houghton Mifflin, 1967).

22. See Charles R. Sligh, Jr., "Views on Curriculum," *Harvard Educational Review*, 4 (1957), 239-245; Walter P. Reuther, "What the Public Schools Should Teach," *Harvard Educational Review*, 4 (1957), 246-250.

23. Stephen B. Wood, *Constitutional Politics in the Progressive Era: Child Labor and the Law* (Chicago: University of Chicago Press, 1968), p. 9.

24. Cited by Wood, *Constitutional Politics*, p. 172.

25. Anthony M. Platt, *The Child Savers: The Invention of Delinquency* (Chicago: University of Chicago Press, 1969).

26. Robert W. Winslow, ed., *Juvenile Delinquency in a Free Society: Selections from the President's Commission on Law Enforcement and Administration of Justice* (Belmont, Calif.: Dickenson Publishing Company, 1968), pp. 119-120.

27. Winslow, *Juvenile Delinquency*, pp. 166-167.

28. Cited in Platt, *The Child Savers*, p. 142.

29. See Lewis Mayer, *The American Legal System* (New York: Harper and Row, 1964), pp. 146-149.

30. Winslow, *Juvenile Delinquency*, pp. 140, 150.

31. Cited in Bernard Wishy, *The Child and the Republic: The Dawn of Modern American Child Nurture* (Philadelphia: University of Pennsylvania Press, 1968), p. 134.

32. M. L. Kohn, "Social Class and Parent-Child Relationships: An Interpretation," *American Journal of Sociology*, 68 (1963), 471-480; M. L. Kohn, "Social Class and the Exercise of Parental Authority," *American Sociological Review*, 24 (1959), 352-366; M. L. Kohn, *Class and Conformity: A Study in Values* (Homewood, Ill.: Dorsey Press, 1969).

33. Winslow, *Juvenile Delinquency*, p. 2.

34. Margaret Mead, *Coming of Age in Samoa* (New York: W. Morrow and Co., 1928).

35. See Thomas S. Szasz, *Law, Liberty and Psychiatry* (New York: Macmillan, 1963).

36. Arthur L. Stinchcombe, *Rebellion in a High School* (Chicago: Quadrangle Books, 1964).

37. *Ibid.*, p. 49; see especially chaps. 3 and 4, pp. 49-102, titled "The Labor Market and Rebellion I; II."

38. *Ibid.*, pp. 5-6.

39. *Ibid.*, passim.

40. William A. Westley and Frederick Elkin, "The Protective Environment and Adolescent Socialization," in Martin Gold and Elizabeth Douvan, eds., *Adolescent Development: Readings in Research and Theory* (Boston: Allyn and Bacon, 1969), pp. 158-164; reprinted from *Social Forces*, 35 (1957), 243-249.

41. *Ibid.*, p. 158.

42. See, for example, the stress on the employment advantages of school in the *National Stay-in-School Campaign Handbook for Communities* (Washington, D.C.: Government Printing Office, 1957). The campaign was sponsored jointly by the Department of Labor, Department of Health, Education and Welfare, and Department of Defense.

43. J. Folger and C. Nam, "Trends in Education in Relation to the Occupational Structure," *Sociology of Education*, 38 (1964), 19-33; R. Havighurst and B. Neugarten, *Society and Education*, 2d ed. (Boston: Allyn and Bacon, 1962).

44. Allan Cartter, "Scientific Manpower for 1970-1985," *Science*, 172 (1971), 132-140.

45. Such has been the case at least since 1885 when Andrew Carnegie, the great exponent of the idea that any able and energetic young man could "rise to the top," told a group of students that "There is no doubt that it

is becoming harder and harder as business gravitates more and more to im-
mense concerns for a young man without capital to get a start for himself."
Cited in H. J. Perkinson, *The Imperfect Panacea: American Faith in Education, 1865-1965* (New York: Random House, 1968), p. 120. Ironically,
one of the few spheres in which "free enterprise," with relatively little
capital and high returns on investment, is still possible is in the illegal
merchandising of drugs.

46. Erik H. Erikson, "The Problem of Ego Identity," in Gold and Douvan,
    Adolescent Development, p. 19; reprinted from *Identity and the Life
    Cycle* (New York: International Universities Press, 1959).

47. In his foreword to Musgrove, *Youth and the Social Order*, p. xix: "Do they
    really believe that all preparation for life must, in the nature of things,
    take for its model the process of becoming a thirty-second degree Mason?"

48. Jerry Farber, *The Student as Nigger* (New York: Pocket Books, 1970).

49. Ellen Lurie, *How to Change the Schools: A Parents' Action Handbook on
    How to Fight the System* (New York: Vintage Books, 1970).

50. Article 26-3.

51. Naomi Feigelson, ed., *The Underground Revolution: Hippies, Yippies and
    Others* (New York: Funk and Wagnalls, 1970).

52. Since the time that I wrote this the amendment reducing the voting age
    to eighteen has been ratified. I am of the opinion that it will have important
    consequences bearing on the considerations in this essay.

JEROME KAGAN

A Conception of Early Adolescence

THE WESTERN mind is friendly toward the construction of discrete, abstract categories, each with its special set of defining characteristics, a prejudice best appreciated by comparing the perspective of the West with that of the classical Chinese. The latter preferred to view nature and experience as a contained and continuous whole. Day and night, to the Western eye, are two discrete entities separated by a transitional stage; to the Chinese they are part of one process, each being a diminution of the other. This conceptual posture had profound effects on the early development of physical science in each community. Western science, by celebrating atomism, made extraordinary advances in the physical theory of matter; early Chinese physics, by adhering to a philosophy of wholeness, focused on wave-like phenomena and made discoveries in fluid mechanics and sound that were in advance of the Europeans.

The particularism of the contemporary Western psychologist, perhaps an heir of atomism, leaps naturally to a view of human development as a sequence of discrete stages, each with its own unique attributes, catalyzed into manifest form by a delicate marriage of biological maturation and experience. "Now you see it, now you don't" is the metaphor for growth, and Western psychologists have provided us with a sequence of nodes called infancy, childhood, adolescence, and adulthood. Freud and Piaget invented four more exotic names to mark this journey, while Erikson expanded the list to seven by focusing on the changing profile of psychological conflicts, rather than the biological bases of sensuality or complexity of thought. Stage theorists have been enormously attractive to Western intellectuals and Freud, Erikson, and Piaget owe their justly earned popularity to the fact that they chose to describe development in a form that the larger community was prepared, indeed, wanted to believe.

90

These introductory comments are not intended to negate the simple observation that behavior changes with growth, or the less obvious fact that the rapidity of many of these changes is correlated with particular periods of time. A child's stature increases most rapidly during the first three years and again at puberty, and this knowledge is a sufficient reason to call these time epochs by some name that implies stages of physical development. It is reasonable, therefore, to ask if the period between ten and fifteen years of age should be regarded as a stage of psychological development. Are the changes that occur during this five-year epoch psychologically more coherent than those that occur during the five years that precede or succeed that time. We cannot answer this question easily for dramatically different environmental pressures operate during the successive five-year eras from kindergarten through college. We can tame the equivocation by noting that puberty, which occurs in the middle of this period for the vast majority of children all over the world, supplies a firm platform for further inquiry. This essay poses a simple question—Do the changes that occur around puberty justify the positing of a psychological stage called early adolescence?—and answers that question affirmatively.

The soundest basis for postulating a stage in psychological development occurs when biology has prepared the child for a change in cognitive structure, motive, affect, or behavior, with experience playing the role of inducer. Exquisite, time-locked mechanisms alter the individual's psychic competence so that he is able to react to events in a new way. An embryological analogy may be helpful. The concept of critical period, which was born in experimental embryology and nurtured in comparative psychology, is appropriately applied whenever there is a delimited period of time when certain events—internal or external—have formative effects on a developing physiological system, organ, or tissue. The biologists conceptualize this process in terms of an inherent biological competence potentiated by external forces. To illustrate, at a particular time in development certain ectodermal cells in the salamander acquire the potentiality to become the lens of the eye, if and only if certain inductive endodermal tissue is present in the vicinity to alter surface properties of cells and allow that competence to become manifest.[1] The lens will not develop if the inducing tissues and their appropriate chemical substances are introduced before the competence is acquired or after it has been lost. It is possible that biological developments of which we are unaware prepare the child for major psychological changes in early adolescence, if and only if the proper inducing experiences occur. If they occur too early or too late the psychological structures may be aberrant.

How shall this new psychological competence be characterized? Although man has been described as a sensory surface, a collection of responses, a reservoir of affect, or a structure of beliefs, we shall focus on the latter characterization because cognitive functions seem to be central to the changes that occur at puberty.

The essence of the argument is that the twelve-year-old has acquired a new cognitive competence—the disposition to examine the logic and consistency of his existing beliefs. The emergence of this competence, which may be dependent on biological changes in the central nervous system, is catalyzed by experiences that confront the adolescent with phenomena and attitudes that are not easily interpreted with his existing ideology. These intrusions nudge the preadolescent to begin an analytic reexamination of his knowledge.

Biological puberty is the only universal source of conflict inducing information, and it should be appreciated that cultures differ in how many additional inductive catalysts they provide. Since we have insufficient information about the detailed conflicts posed by other cultures, I shall restrict most of the discussion to the American community and consider those experiences that might induce cognitive conflict in American twelve-year-olds. It seems reasonable to suggest that these experiences are intimately yoked to family, school, religion, and sexuality.

The Nature of the New Cognitive Competence

During the few years prior to puberty the child is gradually acquiring several new and profound intellective capacities. First, he gains an ease in dealing with hypothetical premises that may violate reality. The twelve-year-old will accept and think about the following problem: "All three legged snakes are purple, I am hiding a three legged snake, guess its color?"

The seven-year-old is confused by the fact that the initial premises violate his notion of what is real and he will not cooperate. The younger child, unlike the adolescent, does not appreciate the discontinuity between the self-contained information in a hypothetical problem and the egocentric information he carries with him for more practical challenges. Hence if an adolescent is asked,

"There are three schools, Roosevelt, Kennedy, and Lincoln schools, and three girls, Mary, Sue, and Jane, who go to different schools: Mary goes to the Roosevelt school, Jane to the Kennedy school, where does Sue go?" he quickly answers "Lincoln." The seven-year-old may excitedly reply, "Sue goes to the Roosevelt school because my sister has a friend called Sue and that's the school she goes to."

To appreciate that problems can be self-contained entities solved by special rules is a magnificent accomplishment that is not usually attained until early adolescence.

The adolescent is more consistently able to induce rules from events with multiple attributes. Specifically, he is capable of inferring conjunctive and disjunctive concepts from appropriate data. An aunt is both a female and a blood relative; a mammal is an animal who nurses its young. A game is an activity that can be played either alone or with others; a strike is either swinging at a ball and missing it, or failing to swing at a ball thrown in the appropriate area. The adolescent can deal with multiple attributes simultaneously and is not limited to a one-at-a-time analysis. This ability allows the adolescent to think about events as arrangements of multiple dimensions, and to appreciate that an experience is often dependent on events not in the immediate field. He knows that his mother's anger can be provoked by any one of several violations, and realizes that her anger at dinner might be a product of yesterday's report card.

The adolescent can assume a relativistic view and is not troubled by the fact that the acceptability of a lie depends on both the situation and the intentions of the actor. He can excuse a hostile greeting from a friend if he believes the original incentive for the coolness occurred hours earlier in another context. The younger child is more absolute and mechanistic in his inferences. A lie is always bad; a hostile attack is seen as a direct and immediate result of the child's action or existence.

Of special relevance for this essay is the fact that the adolescent is disposed to examine his beliefs in sets, and to search for inconsistencies among them and between the beliefs and related actions. This inclination depends partly on the previous abilities, because critical examination of the logic of a set of related beliefs requires the capacity to consider multiple rules simultaneously. Thus, the fourteen-year-old broods about the inconsistency among the following three propositions:

(1) God loves man.
(2) The world contains many unhappy people.
(3) If God loved man, he would not make so many people un-
    happy.

The adolescent is troubled by the incompatibility that is immediately sensed when he examines these statements together. He
notes the contradiction, and has at least four choices. He can deny
the second premise that man is ever unhappy; this is unlikely for
its factual basis is too overwhelming. He can deny that God loves
man; this is avoided for love of man is one of the definitional qualities of God. He can assume that the unhappiness serves an ulterior
purpose God has for man; this possibility is sometimes chosen.
Finally, he can deny the hypothesis of God.

The last alternative, which has become the popular form of the
resolution in Western society, has profound consequences. This
conclusion is a denial of a belief that has been regarded as true for
many years, and invites the implication that if this statement is not
tenable then all other beliefs held at that moment are also in jeop-
ardy. Suddenly, what was regarded as permanently valid has become tentative.

A fourteen-year-old girl who was asked how her present beliefs
differed from those she held several years ago replied, "I had a
whole philosophy of how the world worked. I was very religious
and I believed that there was unity and harmony and everything
had its proper place. I used to imagine rocks in the right places on
the right beaches. It was all very neat and God ordained it all, and
I made up my own religion, but now it seems absolutely ridiculous."

Consider another inconsistency many adolescents discover and
try to resolve.

(1) Parents are omnipotent and omniscient.
(2) My parent has lost a job, or failed to understand me, or
    behaved irrationally—or any other liability the reader cares
    to select.
(3) If my parents were omniscient, they would not be tainted
    with failure and vulnerability.

The statements are examined together and the inconsistency
noted. As with the first example, the adolescent can deny the truth
of the second premise, but it demands too severe a straining of ob-
jectivity and is not usually implemented. The adolescent can invent a statement about parental motivation and excuse the show
of incompetence on the basis of willingness, rather than capacity.

This alternative is infrequently chosen because its acceptance elicits another troubling notion, for it implies that the parent does not care about the emotional consequences of his motivation for the affect life of the family. Hence, the child is tempted to deny the original hypothesis of parental omniscience. As with the denial of God, the fall of this belief weakens all the others.

A third set of propositions placed under analytic scrutiny involves sexuality:

(1) Sexual activity—self-administered or heterosexually experienced—is bad.

(2) Sexuality provides pleasure.

(3) If sex is pleasant, it should not be bad.

We shall forego the obvious analysis of these propositions and simply note that again the most likely conclusion is that the first assumption is not tenable. The increased masturbation at puberty forces the child to deal with the fact that he is violating, in private, a strong social prohibition. However, the consistent sensory pleasure cannot be denied and this silent violation has to be rationalized. As that rationalization is accomplished, the child is tempted to question a great many other standards and he begins to examine all prohibitions with the same skepticism.

Although the known physiological changes at puberty are not necessary antecedents to the increased sexuality, it is likely that they contribute to the ascendancy of sexual thoughts, feelings, and actions. The adolescent must deal with the temptations of masturbation, petting, intercourse, and homosexuality. The statistics unambiguously indicate that the frequent sexual behavior of the seventeen-year-old is not yet manifest in the eleven-year-old, who may be informed, but not yet active. One reason is that he is afraid; afraid of incompetence, parental discovery, and guilt. It is also likely that the sheer intensity of passion that is so urgent in the older adolescent is attenuated at this earlier age. The tension that is so overpowering in a seventeen-year-old is more like a tickle at eleven and, hence, more easily put aside. However, the eleven-year-old knows that his time is coming and he must prepare for it.

These major ideological conflicts pivot on the fact that old assumptions are challenged by new perceptions and the resulting incompatibility is resolved by delegitimizing the earlier assumption. The inducing perceptions include the acknowledgment of unhappy people, agnostic peers, and the pleasures of sexuality. The sequellae are a questioning of old beliefs and a search for a new set of premises. Each culture presents its children with a different set of beliefs to examine. In our society, standards surrounding family, religion, sexuality, drugs, and school are among the major ideological dragons to be tamed. Partial support for these ideas comes from interviews suggesting that American adolescents begin to wonder about the legitimacy of their belief systems, where, prior to this time, inconsistent propositions were not examined as a structure. Sometimes this analysis leaves the adolescent temporarily without a commitment to any belief. The author asked a fifteen-year-old about the beliefs she was most certain of: "None really. I just take in things and analyze them. Maybe it will change my opinion and maybe it won't. It depends, but I'm not really stuck to anything."

This open wondering produces a state of uncertainty and a need to resolve it. A fundamental principal of human psychological functioning states that child and adult are alerted by events and thoughts inconsistent with their prior understanding. These events provoke the mind to resolve the uncertainty and, through that work, premises are changed. A fourteen-year-old said, "I think religious attitudes change if you go to Sunday school. At that time you just accept it, but when you become older and start thinking about it and try to analyze it, that is, whether there really is a God, then it depends on what your religious beliefs are. I've asked myself this over and over again. I just started thinking about it at that time and I just can't get it off my mind; whether there really is a God. I ask myself questions. Is there a God and I have arguments inside myself. How there might not be, how there might be."

Many of the traditional solutions used to deal with uncertainty have lost their potency because a large portion of the population, including the child's friends, have stopped believing in the effectiveness of these slogans. Young people are confronted with the discrepant experience of knowing large numbers of adults and adolescents to whom they feel similar, but with whom they do not share beliefs about the rituals that heal. This inconsistency weakens the effectiveness of any ideology. As a result, many high school students are caught in a strangling web of apathy. They are confronted with all the major sources of uncertainty—a future that cannot be predicted, bizarre headlines, and persistent doubting of the simple truths their parents made them recite. But they have no effective set of ideas or behaviors to deal with these puzzles.

As hinted earlier, puberty qua puberty makes an important contribution to this process. The child's body changes visibly and there is an accompanying alteration in perceived feeling tone. The psychological accompaniments to this change include the rush of new thoughts, their evaluation, and their arrangement in a fresh structure. The adolescent dimly recognizes that he is capable of fertility and must decide how to handle this power, but many are unclear as to how conception occurs. One thirteen-year-old said, "Up until I was about ten years of age I was told that a seed produced the baby. So we go to this Chinese restaurant and they serve a little piece of candy with seeds all over it, so I said 'Hey, mom, I'm not going to eat this cause I don't want to have a baby.'"

Puberty is also interpreted as a signal that childhood is over, and a reminder that regressive actions and beliefs should be replaced, transformed, or eliminated. This character renovation requires the adolescent to generate a cognitive structure as sturdy as the one being replaced.

A fifteen-year-old girl was asked to recall her thoughts following her first menstrual period: "It was like growing up over night. I felt that I was not a little kid anymore. I couldn't ride my bicycle anymore; really I'm not kidding you."

Interviewer: "Were you happy?"
Girl: "No, but I just thought I was above riding a bicycle or playing with dolls. I thought I was cool."
Interviewer: "Did you feel that you had to act more grownup?"
Girl: "Yes, that's why I wouldn't ride a bicycle or play with dolls."

A second fifteen-year-old girl noted, "Friends became more important than toys. You had to have a lot of friends, that was more important than anything. And toys were a thing of the past. My mother would say, 'Are you going out to play now?' and I'd say, 'No, I don't play.' I went around to a lot of women and I asked them what it was like to have children. I didn't want to grow up."

Interviewer: "Was there something apprehensive about it, something you didn't like about this new role?"
Girl: "I didn't like it. I remember thinking I'd really hate to be an adult and I started staying in on Saturdays with my mother instead of going out. I didn't want to have to think for myself."

A third fifteen-year-old agreed. "I started thinking that I couldn't ride my bike and couldn't do things that made me look like a baby. I used to think, when are you going to start getting more attention from people. After a few years, I felt that people were treating me like I was older and in a different way from when I was younger. When I went to my grandmother's when I was little, I used to get a glass of milk or tonic, you know, but after I was a certain age I started getting a cup of tea or coffee."

The adolescent knows he must make his own decisions, but must feel free enough to ask adults for advice. He orients toward extrafamilial adults and tries on, with more seriousness than earlier, the beliefs and posturing of teachers and cultural heroes. Closer examination of adult characteristics leads to new insights that have to be assimilated. He notes defect and taint in adults, and he must find a rule that permits him to accept this disappointment, while not turning complete skeptic. He initiates heterosexual relationships, and must rationalize both his exploitative urges toward others, as well as potential or actual rejection by the beloved other. He must preserve the self's integrity in the face of massive, cognitive taunts.

There are also special institutional changes that occur during early adolescence, especially in Western culture, that are influential. In most communities in the United States the child between twelve and fifteen enters junior high or high school. There are two significant consequences of this structural change. First, unlike the elementary school, the junior high and high school contain many more individuals who hold different beliefs. The beliefs concern drugs, sex, authority, the value of study, and attitudes toward parents. Each ideological position has many advocates. The sources of these new views cannot easily be discredited and the adolescent must deal with the dissonance.

Second, many schools begin tracking at this age. This hard event forces each student to scrutinize his intellectual profile in some detail. Tracking often frightens those in the top track, many of whom do not believe they are talented enough to warrant the challenging assignment. It saddens and angers those in the lower track, who resent the invidious categorization and are forced to invent a rationalization against the importance of academic accomplishment. Once that rationalization crystallizes, it becomes incredibly resistant to change.

American adolescents must create a rationale for school attendance and, what is more difficult, continued effort. Earlier generations were given some incentives to promote involvement in the mission of the school. They were told that education prepared them for a vocation, status, and financial security. But as disbelief with this simple summary of life became public, the power of these incentives became eroded, and the adolescent found it increasingly difficult to accept the dissonance created by the school's arbitrary, monotonous, and often unworkable assignments. There is no reason for a student to work for A's in his courses if he has decided to ignore college and anticipates feeling no pain upon a rejected application. If prestige is empty and elitism wicked it is easy to forget about grades, for students of every age view the grade as a good conduct medal to be used in parades or to gain entry into hallowed halls, rather than as a confidential report on the state of their expertise. Youths are finding it increasingly difficult to rationalize working for grades. The adult community senses the danger and has reacted with an impulsive diagnosis that the school organization is defective and faculty incompetent. "Change the schools" is the cry and parents and teachers rush around in a frenzy, opening up classrooms, knocking down walls, organizing different kinds of outings, or creating nonschools under a variety of exotic names. The conflict is neatly set down:

(1) The child must be happy while he is learning the intellectual foundation of his culture.

(2) Children are not happy in school.

(3) Therefore, the school must be doing something wrong.

Rather than examine the first premise, we focus on the conclusion. The twelve-year-old is willing to believe that learning is valuable and that certain skills which seem irrelevant now are probably necessary for his role as adult. He needs a more persuasive adult community that believes what it professes, not a different place to learn.

The adolescent needs a firmer set of motivational supports that will allow him to work at school requirements while he is trying to fit the catechism of academic competence into the larger structure we call the self. Insufficient motivation has always been, and will always be, the primary problem in junior high and high school, and the reasons are not complicated. Man's major motives exist in a hierarchical structure, much like the dominance hierarchy of a group of baboons. One baboon, or a small group, is temporarily dominant until displaced. So too with motives. Although resolution of uncertainty, hostility, sexuality, and mastery are always potentially capable of seizing the motivational reins for a part of the day, the more specific goals that serve these general intentions change dramatically with development. The two-year-old is uncertain about the actions that will be punished or praised by his parents and he "tests the limits" to gain this information. The thirteen-year-old has solved that problem, but is unsure about his or her sexual attractiveness and, like the two-year-old, ferrets out those situations that will provide answers to the question of sexual adequacy.

The preoccupying motives for most American adolescents revolve around resolving uncertainty over sexual adequacy, interpersonal power, autonomy of belief and action, and acceptability to peers. The urgency of these questions dominates the weaker desire to acquire competence at mathematics, history, or English composition. Hence the school halls exude combinations of apathy and hostility. This mood is not a recent phenomenon. It has always been that way and will continue to be until we are able to help the thirteen-year-old find quick solutions to the four more pressing desires. There are some students, about 10 to 20 per cent of a typical classroom, who appear motivated, and the constancy of that proportion seduces many citizens into believing that "if some, why not all?" There is some basis for this optimistic mood of reform. A small group of children in every classroom have unusually strong affective relations with their parents, relations that combine the desire to please them with an intense identification with their values and roles. If these children happen to have parents whose lives and pattern of encouragement center on academic competence, motivation for mastery of school content is capable of competing with the motives listed earlier. But this contest among motives will not be actualized if the child has not established a belief in eventual success. It is this issue that weakens the power of the position that argues that all children can love school.

Man has two kinds of characteristics—a small set that are defined absolutely (hair and skin color, angle of teeth, and presence and thickness of bodily hair), and a much larger set of evaluative attributes that can only be defined in relation to a reference group. This set includes adjectives like intelligent, wise, athletic, brave, pretty, confident, independent, responsible, and sociable. Assignment to positions on these dimensions, by adult or child, requires the slippery judgment of comparison. Regardless of the absolute ability of the top six students in any classroom the child in rank six who perceives that there are five who are more talented than he will begin to doubt his ability either to perform with excellence or to challenge the expertise of the first five. As a result his motivation for geometry may descend in the hierarchy. It is likely that the adolescent only uses five categories to name levels of talent—the smartest, the very bright ones, those above average, those below average, and the dumb ones. Hence the top 25 to 30 per cent of any classroom have the easiest time maintaining motivation over the course of the school year, for they and their friends have come to an agreement about who has a better than average probability of success. The less fortunate two-thirds withdraw effort in proportion to their anticipation of less than average performance. As long as educators and children are forced to evaluate talent relativistically, most adolescents will require prompting to complete their assignments. The rank order structure of the school demands this psychodynamic result. There are mild antidotes to apply. The school can try to generate absolute standards of performance and ability. More realistically, it can promote more pluralism in the talents it rewards, and celebrate self-improvement as enthusiastically as it credits rises in the rank order. Teachers should defuse the salience of interstudent comparisons and acknowledge the significance of intrapersonal change. We should not be pollyannaish about the difficulty of averting the youth's gaze from his neighbor, but the school can do more to underplay the comparative philosophy of pupil evaluation which must, of necessity, leave two-thirds of the class with a barrier to serious involvement in the mission of the school.

There are a few special motivational conflicts, aside from expectancy of success, that affect some students. A few have decided that any semblance of power or status among their peers is corrupting of character. Since excellence in school often brings prestige, these adolescents avoid these tainted roles by restraining effort. Still others view passive acquiescence to adult authority as defiling, and view the teacher's assignments as commands rather than as suggestions for self-actualization. The third group views selected school subjects as inconsistent with sex role integrity. The twelve-year-old boy who is trying to quiet doubts over the solidity of his maleness may view French as feminizing. The plain girl who questions her attractiveness to boys may view the masculine halo of geometry as too much of a threat to the primary goal she is seeking.

In all three cases the obstacle to school motivation derives from a personal interpretation of the academic assignment that in turn is inconsistent with a motive that, at the time, dominates the hierarchy.

Although America's natural preference for idealistic solutions nudges us to assume that apathy is not a necessary ingredient in junior high school, history dictates a more skeptical conclusion. In 1970 most of the academically apathetic children in Boston were black; a century earlier they were Irish Catholic. The reasons are the same in both cases, although the actors have changed.

The schools have been given the impossible responsibility of proselytizing a faith that does not have intuitive validity for many adolescents. Since both parents and school faculty have been unsuccessful, they are throwing the responsibility of the persuasion back upon the child, hoping he will solve for himself the problem adults have never been able to resolve. We want the young adolescent to win the battle that we lost. The adult generation has lost faith in learning, but hopes that if the child can gain it, parents will have gained salvation for themselves. This dynamic is not unlike our vicarious identification with the youth's permissive attitude toward drugs, work, and sex. We are using the youth for our salvation, and that exploitation is selfish and dangerous.

If adolescents had another goal to replace school there would be less alarm, for there would be no apathy. But they do not; they are searching for a substitute. Several candidates are gaining popularity on high school campuses. The wish to test the depth and strength of one's emotional capacity has become one alternative. The availability of drugs has made this game exciting and easy to enter. Many adolescents ask themselves a question early generations never thought of: "How much pounding can my emotional self accept and assimilate?" The motive to master this challenge is likely to expend itself in a short while for the total intensity and variety of experience is soon exhausted and the answer to the original question clear. The adolescent will have learned how tough or fragile his inner self really is. A second goal is the search for honesty and intimacy in human encounter. Any ritual that carries the flimsiest decoration of artificiality is shunned, for it prevents contact and dehumanizes by forcing unnatural roles on unwilling actors who do not like the game of pretend. This code is more viable, for it is more profoundly human. Since it is, in the extreme, unattainable, it is forever laced with some uncertainty and, therefore, satisfies the main requirement for permanence. It is, fortunately, a more healing catechism than the individualistic competitiveness that captured the energy of earlier adolescent generations. If our community can nurture this freshly born objective, our several million adolescents may be able to find a more comfortable and involving morality that will be toxic to the boredom and hostility being carried into and throughout our institutional structures.

The early adolescent wants many friends, for he needs peers to help him sculpt his beliefs, verify his new conclusions, test his new attitudes against an alien set in order to evaluate their hardiness, and obtain support for his new set of fragile assumptions. However, he still needs his family, for it has several important psychological functions, even though the helplessness of childhood is past. The family provides the child with a set of arbitrary standards that give structure to his motives and actions. They provide models for identification which, if exploited, help establish a self-concept. The family provides the first set of adults who communicate their estimation of the child's worth. And many preadolescents still require this evaluation, because youth continue to award the family a special wisdom and legitimacy. The family's respect for his beliefs, taste in music, dress, or talk is reassuring for it persuades him that he is able to make reasonable decisions. One fifteen-year-old said succinctly, "I hardly ever see my mother because she has demanding jobs. She goes out at night. But I think that makes her even more important to me, for when she is there, it is a good thing; for she tells me I am right and that she's proud of me."

Adolescents of all societies must build a sense of self and the ingredients used in this construction vary with time and community. Each group announces the rules by which the adolescent infers the rate at which he is progressing toward maturity. In many cultures, acceptance of the simple, traditional roles of wife, mother, father, and husband are the only requirements. Our own community has placed a special obstacle in the path of the adolescent for it celebrates the primacy of an autonomous belief system—possession of a separate and distinct set of values—as a necessary prerequisite for a well-delineated identity. Since the ten-year-old realizes that his values are borrowed from his parents, he experiences a deep conflict between what he must attain and his current state. He strives to make alterations in his beliefs in order to persuade himself that the resulting arrangement is his creation, and not a "warmed over" catechism taken from his family.

One fourteen-year-old girl said, "Before I didn't know what I was doing, and now I feel that what I am doing is my own." She continued, "I think many adolescents are uncertain about their beliefs. They are preoccupied because they don't have their own individualism and they don't have their own beliefs yet. Their minds, their thoughts, are not concrete, they are just a lot of different thoughts." A thirteen-year-old boy added, "You begin to question what your parents have been influencing you to believe. Up to a certain time you are strictly going by your parent's ideals and until you are influenced by something else that's what you've got to go by. That's why junior high school is so important because it helps to determine what's going to influence you."

The ideational rebellion that has become definitional of adolescence does not primarily serve hostility, but, rather, the more pressing need to persuade the self that its mosaic of wishes, values, and behaviors derives from a personally constructed ideology. If "What one believes" were less central to the identity of the American adult than it is at the present time, the clash of values between child and parent might not occur with such ferocity.

Summary

We have argued that maturational developments, in a still not completely understood way, prepare the mind of a twelve-year-old to examine sets of propositions for logical consistency. This competence, when applied to his own premises, can produce new assumptions if it is catalyzed by encounter with experiences that jolt the mind into using this capacity. Puberty is one such inducing event in all cultures. Western society adds local phenomena surrounding school, drugs, sexuality, authority, and family, each of which generates uncertainty that the child must resolve. In so doing, he creates new beliefs. The specific form of the conflict and its resolution depend on the belief clash that initially generated the uncertainty, as well as the community in which the child lives. Contemporary middle-class American fifteen-year-olds are waging war against feelings of isolation, commitment to action and belief, loyalty to others, and capacity for love. Earlier generations grappled with the themes of social status, financial security, and petting. It is not clear what issues future generations will engage and subdue. It is usually the case that each era is marked by one or two social problems of enormous priority that give substantive direction to the brooding. Racial strife, density of population, and, more important, lack of a central transcendental ideology continue to loom as the potential catastrophes of the future. These themes will probably shape the form of the incompatible propositions that future adolescents will attempt to understand and comprise the heart of the essay on adolescence another psychologist will write in 1990.

Preparation of this paper was supported in part by grant HD4299, National Institute of Child Health and Human Development, U. S. Public Health Service, and a grant from the Carnegie Corporation of New York.

REFERENCE

1. A. G. Jacobson, "Inductive Processes in Embryonic Development," *Science*, 152 (1966), 25-34.

JOSEPH ADELSON

The Political Imagination of the Young Adolescent

THE YEARS of early adolescence, twelve to sixteen, are a watershed
era in the emergence of political thought. Ordinarily the youngster
begins adolescence incapable of complex political discourse—
that is, mute on many issues, and when not mute, then simplistic,
primitive, subject to fancies, unable to enter fully the realm of
political ideas. By the time this period is at an end, a dramatic
change is evident; the youngster's grasp of the political world is
now recognizably adult. His mind moves with some agility within
the terrain of political concepts; he has achieved abstractness, complexity, and even some delicacy in his sense of political textures;
he is on the threshold of ideology, struggling to formulate a morally
coherent view of how society is and might and should be arranged.

This essay will explore how this transition takes place. It will
lean heavily, though not entirely, on the work my colleagues and
I have done during the last several years.[1] We have conducted interviews with about 450 adolescents, a varied group, ranging in
age from eleven to eighteen, of both sexes, of normal to extremely
high intelligence, through the full spectrum of the social classes,
and in three nations, the United States, West Germany, and
Great Britain. About fifty of these youngsters form a longitudinal
sample, having been interviewed first at thirteen and then at
fifteen, or first at fifteen and then at eighteen.

Our aim was to discover how adolescents of different ages and
circumstances construe the world of political action, and how they
organize a political philosophy. Our early, informal interviewing
had suggested that it would be best to avoid talking to our youngsters about current political realities. To do so would obviously
make it difficult to compare children in different cultures, but beyond that we found that to do so risked being misled about the
child's grasp of the political. The younger adolescent may be in-

timidated by his lack of "knowledge," while the older adolescent may glory in the possession of it. In either case both child and interviewer become so mesmerized by the pursuit of facts and opinions that the quality of the child's thought may be obscured. At any rate we settled upon an interview format which offered the following premise: imagine that a thousand people venture to an island in the Pacific to form a new society; once there they must compose a political order, devise a legal system, and in general confront the myriad problems of government.

Having established this framework the interview schedule continued by offering questions on a large number of hypothetical issues. Our youngsters were, for example, asked to choose among several forms of government and to argue the merits and liabilities of each. They were asked didactic questions: what is the purpose of government, of law, of political parties? Proposed laws were suggested, and they were asked to offer opinions about them; for example, should the government require citizens over forty-five to have annual medical examinations? Problems of public policy were explored: should a dissenting religious sect be required to undergo vaccination, or what should be done when a law is commonly violated and hard to enforce? In general, we tried to touch upon the traditional issues of political philosophy—the scope and limits of political authority, the reciprocal obligations of citizen and state, the relations between majorities and minorities, the nature of crime and justice, the collision between personal freedom and the common good, the feasibility of utopia, and so on.

Let me offer here a brief synopsis of the findings. Surprisingly, it appears that neither sex nor intelligence nor social class counts for much in the growth of political concepts. There are simply no sex differences; and while there are some expectable differences associated with intelligence and social class (the bright are capable of abstract thought a bit earlier; the upper middle class are somewhat less authoritarian) these differences are on the whole minor. What does count, and count heavily, is age. There is a profound shift in the character of political thought, one which seems to begin at the onset of adolescence—twelve to thirteen—and which is essentially completed by the time the child is fifteen or sixteen. The shift is evident in three ways: first, in a change in cognitive mode; secondly, in a sharp decline of authoritarian views of the political system; and finally, in the achievement of a capacity for ideology. National differences in political thought, though present, are by no means as strong as age effects. A twelve-year-old German youngster's ideas of politics are closer to those of a twelve-year-old American than to those of his fifteen-year-old brother.

The Quality of Thought

The most important change that we find in the transition from early to middle adolescence is the achievement of abstractness. On the threshold of adolescence the child adheres to the tangible; he is most comfortable (and capable) with the concrete event, the actual person. As he matures he fights free of the concrete and its constraints and begins to reach for the abstract. As an example, consider these responses given by twelve- and thirteen-year-olds who have been asked "What is the purpose of laws?"

They do it, like in schools, so that people don't get hurt.

If we had no laws, people could go around killing people.

So people don't steal or kill.

Now compare these with the answers given by youngsters just two to three years older:

To ensure safety and enforce the government.

To limit what people can do.

They are basically guidelines for people. I mean, like this is wrong and this is right and to help them understand.

An essential difference between these two sets of responses—there are others, as we will see later—is that the younger adolescents are limited to concrete examples—stealing, killing, and the like. In some cases a more general principle seems to govern the concrete response, but ordinarily that principle cannot be articulated. The older adolescent, on the other hand, can move from the concrete to the abstract and then back again. Having stated a principle, he illuminates it by a concrete instance, or having mentioned specific examples, he seeks and finds the abstract category that binds them.

Several important consequences follow from the young adolescent's difficulty in managing the abstract. The processes and institutions of society are *personalized*. When we ask him about the law, he speaks of the policeman, the judge, the criminal. When we talk of education, he speaks of the teacher, the principal, the student. When we mention government, he speaks of the mayor, or the President, or the congressman, and much of the time none of these but rather a shadowy though ubiquitous set of personages known as "they" or "them." ("They do it, like in schools, so that people don't get hurt.") As one thirteen-year-old put it, when asked the purpose of government: "It's more or less a great leader and it makes our decisions and things of that sort."

The child's adherence to the personal and the tangible makes it difficult for him to adopt a *sociocentric* perspective. Since he cannot easily conceive of "society," or of other abstract collectivities, he does not take into account, when pondering a political action, its function for society as a whole. He thinks instead of its impact upon specific individuals. For example, when we asked adolescents the purpose of a law requiring the vaccination of children, the younger interviewers said that it is to prevent children from getting sick, while older adolescents replied that it is to protect the community at large.

To put it another way, at the threshold of adolescence the youngster gives few signs of a sense of community. Unable to imagine social reality in the abstract, he enters adolescence with only the weakest sense of social institutions, of their structure and functions, or of that invisible network of norms and principles which link these institutions to each other. Furthermore, the failure to achieve abstractness does not permit him to understand, except in a most rough and ready way, those concepts essential to political thought—such ideas as authority, rights, liberty, equity, interests, representation, and so on.

Once abstractness is achieved the adolescent enters into a distinctly new realm of thought and discourse. Let me illustrate this by describing the changing pattern of responses, through adolescence, to a question dealing with the problem of minority rights. The youngster was told that 20 per cent of the people on the island were farmers and that they were concerned that laws might be passed which would damage their interests. What might be done about this?

At the beginning of adolescence our subjects could do very little with the question. Much of the time they offered no response at all. Sometimes they denied, rather blithely, that there was a problem—people wouldn't hurt the farmers. Sometimes they expressed alarm, along with the wistful hope that something would be done for the poor farmers. And sometimes they resorted to *machtpolitik:* the farmers should fight, or should move to another part of the island, or should refuse to grow or sell food in order to get even. In the next phase, still in early adolescence, the idea of negotiation or communication takes hold: the farmers should talk to the rest of the people and make their problems understood. But there is as yet little grasp of institutionalized or collective means of carrying this out: an amorphous mass of farmers will somehow communicate with an equally amorphous mass of citizens. Toward the middle of adolescence youngsters acquire an understanding of the nature of collective institutions and of representation. Now they propose that the farmers form themselves into a union or some other organization, that they appoint representatives and have them petition or negotiate with the legislature. The final step takes place during the middle and later years of adolescence, when our subjects try to view the farmers' interests in the context of the entire community. They now observe that the farmers, having 20 per cent of the votes, can expect to have an equal proportion of legislators, and thus are automatically represented in the government and can exercise their will through the normal democratic processes. The more optimistic assume this is done by persuasion, the more cynical suggest bloc voting, logrolling, and the filibuster.

Time Perspective

Another important change in thought involves an extension of time perspective. In the early years of adolescence the child's mind is locked into the present. In pondering political and social issues he shows little sense of history or a precise and differentiated sense of the future. The past is not seen to weigh upon the present, via precedent and tradition, nor can the child perceive the manifold and varying potentialities within the present. The young adolescent will rarely look back to the antecedent sources of the present, and when he thinks of the future, or is forced to by the question we ask him, he can imagine only the immediate and direct outcome of a current event.

During the middle years of adolescence, we begin to see a distinct—though modest—extension of temporal range. A sense of the past begins to appear. In trying to decipher the causes of a human action—as in examining the roots of crime—the youngster may speculate about the miscreant's personal history: has he done this before? Is he known to be delinquent from his previous behavior? What was his upbringing like? When he offers his judgments on laws and institutions proposed for our hypothetical island, he will sometimes look to the past: where do the islanders come from? What was their earlier history? Are there successful precedents for this law?

Yet for most of our subjects, even the older ones, the sense of history is undeveloped. What is far more visible as the child passes through the early years of adolescence is a more powerful imagining of the future. Many of our questions asked youngsters to give their opinions on social and political proposals. At the entry into adolescence there seems to be little sense of the consequential; answers are brisk and brusque—that's a good idea or, that's a bad idea. Gradually he begins to look beyond the short-run impact of, say, a proposed law to wonder and worry about its long-term effect. As this capacity is consolidated we note that he can not only perceive the consequences of a single decision, but can also weigh and choose between alternative futures—that is, he can trace out the remote consequences of present possibilities: if A is chosen then X and later Y may follow, but if B is chosen, X' and later Y' will result. Thus, when offered possibility A, the adolescent may spontaneously add an alternative B, and choose between them on the relative merits of outcomes Y and Y'. What we have here, of course, is that leap from concrete to formal operations that Piaget and his associates have posited to be the key cognitive advances in the transition from childhood to adolescence.

Motivation

The youngster enters adolescence with a remarkably thin repertoire of motivational and psychological categories available to him. He is like a naïve behaviorist; he does not look beneath action to its internal springs. There is little sense of inner complication. Men act as they do because they are what they are. A man acts selfishly because he is selfish; the crime is committed because the man is a criminal. The vocabulary of motives is both impoverished and redundant. Character—character seen simplemindedly —is destiny.

All this changes very slowly. At the end of early adolescence few youngsters show much astuteness about motivation. Certainly we do not see those rapid and dramatic changes when more purely cognitive tasks are set. But changes there are—in a gradually thickening texture of psychological constructs, in the dropping out of black-white, good-evil judgments of personality, in a generally heightened sense of human complexity.

Consider the following: after a series of questions on crime and punishment, we introduced the problem of recidivism. Most people who go to jail seem to end up there again. Why? A hard question, certainly, and penetrating answers are hard to come by at any age. Yet there are clear differences in the quality of psychological inference between adolescents in the early and middle periods. The twelve- and thirteen-year-olds say such things as: "Well, they don't know anything, and you have to teach them a lesson," or "Well, it is in his mind that he has to do it and keep doing it over again," or "Well, their conscience might tell to do this or something." At fifteen a deeper sense of motive is apparent. One youngster says that "going to jail produces a grudge against others," another suggests that they "become bitter, or feel mocked," a third speculates that they brood and thus "establish themself as being a criminal."

The increased grasp of human complexity has an impact upon the child's apprehension of the political realm. On the topics of crime and punishment, for example, it produces the appreciation that men are subject to motivation, that if some motives may induce men to delinquency, other motives may persuade them to good behavior. Hence the child becomes responsive to education and rehabilitation, and sometimes even to psychotherapy, as methods of personal reform. Yet if he is more optimistic about human change in this domain, he is less so elsewhere, for his heightened understanding of human will leads him to a greater cautiousness, a greater skepticism about law and politics as ways of altering the human condition. He no longer, as the child does, sees men as infinitely tractable to the will of law. He now reckons with human resistance, with the human tendency to resist authority. While the very young adolescent, limited to an empty-organism model of the person, sees men as malleable, as yielding easily, even willingly, to authority, the older adolescent sees law as only one resort among many, and comes to recognize that indirection and inducement also serve as vehicles of social change.

Modes of Reasoning

One hesitates to say boldly that the young adolescent cannot reason about political problems, and yet one hesitates equally to say that he does. At the beginning of adolescence discourse is often so stark, so naked of embellishment, qualification, or nuance, that the listener cannot tune in, not confidently, to the modes of reasoning which may underlie and govern discourse. Given a problem to reason through, our younger interviewees, if they answered at all—and much of the time they could not—seemed to jump at the answer. Even when the answer was plausible—and much of the time it was not—it allowed little sense of the reasoning processes involved. A good deal of the time, then, the logical processes influencing response seemed entirely tacit, or solutions were, apparently, arrived at by an essentially intuitive logic, through some unspoken, unstatable framework of conviction.

Furthermore, one must reckon, in this age group, with an occasional descent into sheer confusion. What is one to make of the following statement? The young man, thirteen years old, has been asked why a certain law, forbidding the smoking of cigarettes on the island, has proved difficult to enforce. "Because people who are used to it now . . . well, if you say that you can't drive cars around, well that would be awful. Then people would go ahead and drive around, but you could see it. Well maybe you could have no newspapers, but then all the people in the newspaper business would go bapoof." What has happened here? Apparently, he begins by wanting to say that those who are habituated to smoking are unable to stop, but for some reason he does not complete the thought. He then introduces automobiles, and in all likelihood he means to say that cigarette smoking can be carried out surreptitiously, while automobile driving cannot. But the next statement, on newspapers, simply eludes understanding—newspapers have never been mentioned in the interview. Is he referring to newspaper advertising of cigarettes? Or to the prohibition of newspapers? Who can tell? Statements such as these, marked by a certain looseness of association, probably reflect the effects of anxiety upon the unready cognitive capacity of the young adolescent. This is an occasional, though not a common phenomenon in this age group; most young adolescents, unable to answer a question, remain mute, or answer monosyllabically or evasively. It is, however, quite uncommon among adolescents past the age of fifteen.

The significant transition in reasoning during the early years of adolescence involves the acquisition of a hypothetico-deductive capacity. We have already alluded to one example of this capacity in discussing the extension of temporal range: the ability to anticipate the remote consequence of a decision. A closely related variant is in the appearance of cost-benefit modes of reasoning, wherein the youngster, pondering the pros and cons of a political choice, can examine and compare explicitly the utilities involved. What are the costs to each party and what are the gains? The calculus of costs and gains will control the decision. Here, for example, are two bright fifteen-year-olds answering a question on eminent domain. The government on the island, they have been told, needs some land to construct a highway; the landowner is unwilling to sell. Who is right, and what is to be done?

"Well, maybe he owned only a little land if he was a farmer, and even if they did give him a fair price, maybe all the land was already bought on the island that was good for farming or something, and he couldn't get another start in life if they did buy it. Then maybe in a sense he was selfish because if they had to buy other land and change the direction of the road, why of course then maybe they'd raise the taxes on things cause it would cost more to change directions from what they already have planned."

"If it's a strategic point like the only way through a mountain maybe without tunneling, then I'm not too sure what I'd do. If it's a nice level stretch of plain that if you didn't have it you'd have to build a curve in the road, I think the government might go ahead and put a curve in the road."

Prior to the emergence of hypothetico-deductive reasoning, problems such as these are handled, when they are handled at all, by a brusque, simplistic decisiveness—affirmations and negations. Later on we see, as in these extracts, the appearance of the *conditional mode*—such locutions as "if" and "it depends upon" begin to dominate discourse on decisions. The youngster avoids either/or positions and thinks in terms of contingencies; the hard and fast absolutism of childhood and the first years of adolescence gives way to moral and conceptual relativism. Furthermore, the youngster begins to resist the either/or alternatives proposed by our questions. He *breaks set*—that is, he challenges the assumptions, tacit and otherwise, contained in the inquiry. Should the government do A or do B, we ask. Now he may say "neither," and suggest amendment, or compromise, or some entirely new solution which bypasses or transcends the terms of the question.

Let me conclude this section by a close analysis—an *explication du texte*, as it were—of a single response given by a fourteen-year-old boy, a child who has, cognitively speaking, put childish things away. The response is by no means representative—far from it—but it illustrates and highlights the conceptual achievements that separate early and later adolescent political thought. The question asked was "What would happen if there were no laws?" I will treat each sentence of the answer separately.

(1) *At first people would do as they pleased.* This is the conventional response to this question—a vision of self-indulgence and perhaps worse. But note the "at first," which suggests that he has already begun to look beyond the immediate.

(2) *But after a while someone or some party would come to power and impose laws, probably stricter ones than before.* He does indeed look past the immediate to remote, second-order consequences. What makes this statement unusual—in fact, unique in our experience of this age—is that it shows a grasp of social dynamics, in the suggestion that a period of anarchy would be followed by a period of stricter social control. He seems to be positing a kind of Newtonian social principle, that an action may generate an equal and opposing reaction, that reformation breeds counterreformation.

(3) *But a lot would depend upon the kind of society it was.* The conditional mode is brought into play. Also note the close connection he sees between law and society. Unlike younger adolescents he views law not as a given, unrelated to the social matrix, but as an integral expression of the social system.

(4) *Some societies have a strict social etiquette, like in ancient China, I think it was, where people were afraid to lose their place in society, because if they did something wrong everyone would look down on them.* An extraordinary statement, for several reasons. It breaks the set provided by the question; that is, it challenges the tacit assumption that laws are necessary for social control. It does so via an attempt at comparative sociology—*autre temps, autre moeurs.* The allusion to a distant and alien culture (and note the use of history) is employed to illuminate the relativism of social forms. The statement brings together the idea of informal social constraint with the idea of a legal code, and sees them as equivalent methods of control. It bespeaks the presence of a concept of social hierarchy, and beyond that the understanding that caste or class relations can compel conduct.

The Decline of Authoritarianism

Unless and until one has spoken at some length to young adolescents, one is not likely to appreciate just how bloodthirsty they can be. Herewith, some excerpts from interviews with three thirteen-year-old boys on crime, punishment, and rehabilitation.

On the best reason for sending people to jail: "Well, these people who are in jail for about five years and are still on the same grudge, then I would put them in for triple or double the time. I think they would learn their lesson then."

On how to teach people not to commit crimes in the future: "Jail is usually the best thing, but there are others . . . In the nineteenth century they used to torture people for doing things. Now I think the best place to teach people is in solitary confinement."

On methods of eliminating or reducing crime: "I think that I would . . . well like if you murder somebody you would punish them with death or something like this. But I don't think that would help because they wouldn't learn their lesson. I think I would give them some kind of scare or something."

Let me confess that I have chosen some unusually colorful examples; our youngsters were not typically quite so Grand Guignol, so Queen of Hearts in language. But the outlook expressed in these excerpts is entirely characteristic of younger adolescents when talking about law and order. Though they have a rough sense that the punishment should fit the crime, their view of that arithmetic leads them to propose Draconian measures even for innocuous misdeeds. If crime is to be stamped out, anything goes, and so they are ready to support elaborate and indeed Orwellian measures of control. To the question on what to do when a law prohibiting cigarette smoking is commonly violated, some of our younger subjects suggested, *inter alia,* such methods as hiring police informers, secreting spies in the closets of peoples' homes, and, yes, providing an elaborate network of closed-circuit television monitors in both public and private places. To achieve communal decorum, young adolescents are disposed simply to raise the ante: more police, stiffer fines, longer jail sentences, and, if need be, executions. To a large and various set of questions on crime and punishment, they consistently propose one form of solution: punish, and if that does not suffice, punish harder. At this age the child will not ordinarily conceive that wrongdoing may be a symptom of something deeper, or that it may be inhibited by indirect means. The idea of reform and rehabilitation through humane methods is mentioned by only a small minority at the outset of adolescence.

The young adolescent's views on crime and punishment reflect a more general, indeed a pervasive authoritarian bias. There is in fact no topic we explored which is free of that bias; wherever the child's mind turns—government, law, politics, social policy—we find it. Furthermore, at the onset of adolescence we find it in both sexes, in all social classes, and in the three nations we studied. It is, in short, a ubiquitous feature of early adolescent political thought.

Consider once again that set of interview excerpts, on the purpose of law, which initiated the discussion of cognition. In the sample of thirteen-year-olds we observe an exclusive emphasis upon constraint. The purpose of law is to keep people from bad behavior. At fifteen years the stress on restriction, though still present, is distinctly diminished. Now the youngster will far more often advert to the beneficial functions of law: it provides guidelines, he may say, or it ensures safety. An essentially similar pattern appears when we ask youngsters to describe the purpose of government. At the earlier ages they are more likely to answer in terms of constraint: government, they say, "prevents chaos," or it provides "better order in the city," or it keeps "the country from doing anything it pleases." In midadolescence there is a clear shift to the positive: government is now seen as "ensuring freedom," or fostering equality, or organizing efficient services.

What accounts for the authoritarian animus among the young? They are, to begin with, preoccupied by human wickedness. They see men as tending naturally toward the impulsive and the anarchic. They are Hobbesian—it is the war of all against all. They do not seem to have much faith in—or perhaps they do not cognize adequately—the human capacity for self-control, or the demands of conscience.

A second source, related to the first, is an ingenuous belief in the goodness and justice of authority. The young adolescent will not spontaneously imagine that authority might be capricious, arbitrary, or mistaken. He takes much the same position toward law. His first inclination—and his second and third—is to support any law, even when he is not altogether clear about its purposes. The underlying attitude seems to be: if a law is passed, or even proposed, there must be some good reason for it. And if the state makes a demand upon its citizens, it is their duty to obey, since solely benign (though perhaps inscrutable) motives actuate the state. In the early years of adolescence the child's orientation to government and law is trusting, uncritical, acquiescent. He transfers to these realms the habits of trust and obedience he has acquired in school and at home. (Interestingly enough, partisan politics does not share this exemption from critique. More often than not our youngsters tended to be cloudy about parties and the party system, but vaguely suspicious and uneasy. "Politics" in this sense is often associated with dispute—the prevailing images are of contention and acrimony. It is as though government and law partake of the sacred, while partisan politics are worldly, secular— and thus potentially corrupt.)

Another source of authoritarian attitude is the child's inability to grasp the idea of rights. It is too abstract, too evanescent a notion for the young adolescent fully to understand. It is only in the middle and, often, the later years of adolescence that the concepts of individual (and minority) rights are firmly entrenched. One example among several: we asked whether the government should require men over forty-five to undergo annual medical examination. Most younger subjects deem this a splendid idea; it is not until late in adolescence that youngsters (and even then only a minority) understand that a principle might be involved, that the citizen's rights of privacy and self-determination might outweigh the tangible benefits of the medical check-up. The young adolescent responds affirmatively to *evident* good. If what the state proposes, or demands, is visibly, concretely beneficent, he cannot look beyond or beneath to more remote and abstract violations of principle. Should the government require all houses to be painted every five years? Only older adolescents suggest that this law might represent an excessive degree of interference by the state. Should the government insist upon the vaccination of religious groups opposed to it? Only the older adolescents are troubled by the idea of state intrusion upon religious principles.

Finally, the child's authoritarianism can be seen to stem from a certain conservatism of mind, which leads him to view values and institutions as fixed and immutable. He does not readily imagine those processes of change, planned and unplanned, which characterize social and political phenomena. What is, has been; what is, will be. Perhaps the clearest expression of this disposition is to be seen in the moral absolutism we mentioned earlier. Moral judgments at this age are marked by a blessed simplicity. Good and evil do not vary over time or between situations, and we see little of the moral relativism which will later complicate clear conviction.

So much may be obvious, but what may be less apparent is that a similar habit of mind dominates the child's perception of social and political institutions. One of our most interesting findings is that the young adolescent does not spontaneously entertain the concept of amendment. If you suggest to him that a law is not working out as expected, he will likely propose that it be enforced more rigorously. He may also suggest, though far less often, that it be abolished. But he will almost never conceive that it can be altered to make it more effective. What it amounts to is that at the onset of adolescence the child cannot think of human actions as provisional, tentative, empirical. He has little sense that social and political decisions are responsive to trial and error. He does not see the realm of government as subject to invention, and thus to experiment, to tinkering, to trying out. It is as though law (and other human artifacts), like the Decalogue, descended from the mountaintop. Once given, once announced, the citizen's duty is to submit and obey.

At fourteen, fifteen, and beyond, the youngster's mood begins to be critical and pragmatic. Confronting a proposal for law or for a change in social policy, he scrutinizes it to determine whether there is more to it than meets the eye. Whose interests are served, whose are damaged? He asks these questions not out of a reflexive suspiciousness, but because he weighs heavily, as the younger adolescent does not, the obstacles between the will and the act. He senses that law and social policy must take account of the dead hand of the past, entrenched privilege, human stubbornness, the force of habit. He now understands that law and policy must accommodate competing interests and values, that ends must be balanced against means, that the short-term good must be appraised against latent or long-term or indirect outcomes.

To sum up, the young adolescent's authoritarianism is omnipresent. He has only a dim appreciation of democratic forms (for example, he is more likely to favor one-man rule as against representative or direct democracy); he shows little sensitivity to individual or minority rights; he is indifferent to the claims of personal freedom; he is harsh and punitive toward miscreants; his morality is externalized and absolutistic. The decline and fall of the authoritarian spirit is, along with the rapid growth in abstractness (to which it is related), the most dramatic developmental event in adolescent political thought. Lynnette Beall developed an index of authoritarianism based on our interview items. At the threshold of adolescence a remarkable 85 per cent of our subjects are high on the index; by the senior year in high school only 17 per cent score in the high range.

Ideology and Utopia

It is commonly assumed that adolescence is a period marked by political idealism, a preoccupation with utopian reconstructions of society, and a disposition toward the formulation of ideologies. We hear it said that the youngster, once he discovers politics as a vehicle for the free exercise of mind, leaps exuberantly into its possibilities, into ideation, speculation, fantasy, into the building of brave new doctrines and worlds. A utopian impulse, fed by idealism and by newly won cognitive capacities, captures the adolescent imagination. The youngster then gives himself over, both in the privacy of thought and in excited exchange with like-minded friends, to the criticism of current institutions and the search for a more just society.

In plain fact, and for better or worse, nothing very much like this takes place among the great majority of adolescents. Why we think it does is a puzzle: perhaps we remember (and perhaps falsely) our own exceptional lives in adolescence; or perhaps we are attracted by those rare and spectacular instances of precocity in that fraction of articulate, politically engaged adolescents, and then generalize to the total body of the young. Be that as it may, the evidence we have speaks to the contrary. Utopian ideals are not only uncommon in adolescence, the mood of most youngsters is in truth firmly antiutopian. As to idealism, though it is present, it is by no means modal, let alone universal, and is less common than skepticism, sobriety, and caution as a characteristic political affect. As to ideology, with which I will begin, that is a most complicated matter.

The root of the complication is that we may adopt either a weak or a strong definition of ideology. By the latter we mean a highly structured, hierarchically ordered, internally consistent body of general principles from which specific attitudes follow. Used in this strong sense, the ideological capacity in adolescence is extremely rare, almost never found before the later years of high school, and even then only among the most intelligent, intellectually committed, and politically intense. In a weak definition, we construe ideology to involve the presence of attitudes *roughly* consistent with each other, and *more or less* organized in reference to a more encompassing, though perhaps tacit, set of political principles. Used in this sense, we can say that ideology is dim or absent at the beginning of adolescence, and that the criteria for achieving ideology are apparent only during the middle period. It is in the latter sense that I will use the term.

It should be clear that the child cannot achieve a personal ideology, even in the most modest sense, until he has acquired and to some degree mastered the cognitive skills of the stage of formal operations. He must be able to manage abstractness; he must be able to synthesize and generalize his observations beyond the specific instance; he must be able to transcend the present and imagine the future. So much we have already seen, and now we must add another vital quality: the mastery of principles.

At the onset of adolescence, the youngster's grasp of principle is dim, erratic, shifting. Much of the time, of course, he is simply unaware of the principles which might govern a political decision, but even when he is, his command is too uncertain, too unsteady to allow him to bring it to bear on the specific instance. We see examples of this in the early adolescent's penchant for political catch-phrases and slogans, which generally serve as a substitute for and approximation of the general principles he senses are relevant but does not truly grasp. To a question on voting the child will say, brightly and confidently, "The majority rules," and a moment later we learn that by majority he means unanimity. Or he may allude solemnly to "freedom of speech," and shortly thereafter call for the total abridgment of dissent. In these and like instances the child senses that a given class of political decisions is controlled by or subsumed under some governing principle, but his mind cannot fully contain the principle or cannot articulate the connection between the specific case and the controlling generality. The cognitive failure or slippage leads him to flail about until he finds an apparently relevant phrase which relates to and stands in place of the more vaguely felt principle.

The steady advance of the sense of principle is one of the most impressive phenomena of adolescent political thought. Once acquired, it spells an end to the sentimentality which so often governs the young adolescent's approach to political issues; it allows the child to resist the appeal of the obvious and the attractive, particularly where individual or communal *rights* are concerned. Our youngest subjects are so often capricious about individual rights not merely because they idealize authority, but also because they have so little sense of those principles which should limit the sway of government. Confronted with an appealing proposition, the younger adolescent proclaims brightly that it "sounds like a real good idea"—a recurring phrase, by the way—and cannot look beyond immediate advantages to discern violations of principle. The same tendency can be found in the opposite direction, in that the child will favor the individual against the government when the former's case is immediate and attractive and the latter's is based on principle. To our question on eminent domain, for example, younger subjects favored the landowner because his case was concrete and attractive, and showed little recognition of the parallel rights of the community.

Knowledge

The growth of ideology in adolescence also feeds upon the child's rapid acquisition of political knowledge. By knowledge I mean more than the dreary "facts"—for example, on the composition of county government—that the child learns, or better, is exposed to in the conventional civics course taught to most American ninth graders. Nor do I mean by knowledge only information on current political realities. Aside from these facets of knowledge the adolescent also absorbs, often unwittingly, a feeling for those many unspoken assumptions about the political system that make up the common ground of understanding—such matters as what is "appropriate" for the state to demand of its citizens, and vice versa, or the "proper" relationship of government to subsidiary social institutions, such as the schools and churches. Much of the naïveté that characterizes the younger adolescent's grasp of politics stems not from an ignorance of "facts" but from an incomplete apprehension of the common conventions of the system, of what is and is not customarily done, and of how and why it is or is not done.

And yet, while I would not want to scant the significance of increased knowledge in the forming of adolescent ideology, let me also say that over the years I have become progressively disenchanted about its centrality, and have come to believe that much current work in political socialization, by relying too heavily on the *apparent* acquisition of knowledge, has been misled about the tempo of political understanding in adolescence. Just as the young child can count many numbers in series and yet not grasp the principle of ordination, so may the young adolescent have in his head many random bits of political information without a secure understanding of those concepts which would give order and meaning to the information.

Like a magpie, the child's mind picks up bits and pieces of data. If you encourage him, he will drop these at your feet—Republicans and Democrats and the tripartite division of the federal system and Nixon and Agnew and Kennedy and, if he is prodigal enough, the current secretary of labor and the capital of North Dakota. But without the integumental function that concepts and principles provide, the data remain fragmented, random, disordered.

Cathexis

To this point I have emphasized—to put it mildly—the cognitive component of the adolescent's political imagination. That side of things is, after all, the most visible, the most easily discerned and measured, and no one conversant with adolescent thought can escape the compelling force of the child's rapid growth in sheer understanding. But clearly there is another aspect to the growth of ideology—the youngsters increasing *investment* in matters political. For the typical young adolescent politics is personally remote. Though he answers your questions politely, even earnestly, it is quite clearly, one senses, alien territory. He wants to please you, he wants to get the answers "right," but aside from that he is essentially indifferent to the political world. By the middle period of adolescence this indifference—perhaps neutrality is a better word—has given way, at least in some cases, to a more keenly felt sense of connection to the political. There is less distance between the cognizing, valuing self and the realm of politics. What accounts for this change?

Clearly, no single thing. The various events of the adolescent experience accumulate and interact to move the child toward a cathexis of the political. His growing intellectual facility stimulates interest, and the political, now cognitively accessible, becomes comfortable and, beyond that, engaging. In turn, interest can be the engine of intellectual growth; the cathecting of the political stimulates and challenges the child's mind, activating heretofore latent capacities for formal thought in the political vein. Add to this an obvious but most important fact—the youngster's increased sense of autonomy, his anticipation of adulthood, his rehearsal of mature modes of self-definition, among which is the readiness for citizenship, and with it the need to have opinions, make judgments, discourse on the world of affairs.

These are the normative pressures and opportunities which move all adolescents toward a greater investment in political ideas; all children experience and respond to them. Yet there are profound individual differences in political cathexis. Some youngsters, even of fifteen, seem deeply involved in political talk and thinking; most do not. To some degree this difference reflects general intellectual capacity and interest, but there are many exceptions. Some of our most astute interviewees at this age seem largely disengaged affectively. One of the most advanced interviews I have ever done was with a fourteen-year-old who showed a remarkable grasp of political concepts and information. He told me, for example, that he had been reading Trotsky's *History of the Russian Revolution* and could discuss it intelligently. Yet he did not read any newspaper, nor did he watch television news, nor did he discuss politics with family or friends. He said he found politics "boring." On the other hand, a fifteen-year-old much given to long-winded and dogmatic assertions of political opinion, many of them eccentric (among other things, he has given serious thought to being dictator of the world), showed only modest attainments in political cognition. Such anomalies abound in the middle period. Not only do youngsters show surprising gaps in knowledge, and between levels of understanding from one topic to another, one also can find astonishing discrepancies between cathexis and cognition.

And yet we can venture some generalizations about those youngsters intense about politics and striving toward ideology. The most apparent common denominator is their origin in families which are politically active and for whom politics are morally passionate. The youngster takes not only the direction of political thought from his parents, but also their moral intensity. It is an unusual phenomenon in the adolescent population, but a memorable one when it appears, and we find it on both left and right. On the right the religious component in politics is often not far from the surface; politics is only moderately displaced from piety. One of our adolescents, the daughter of a John Birch Society leader, in fact made little distinction between political goals and the fundamentalist values she held; both were oriented toward the assurance of order and the reduction of wickedness. On the left, political earnestness seems more a substitution for than a mere extension of the religious impulse. We find here a politics dominated by guilt, where the themes of restitution and atonement command the political perceptions. In a sense, however, both right and left politics are dominated by guilt. In the former case, the moral impulse is largely externalized and others must be coerced into goodness; in the latter, an internalized sense of guilt, an aching sense of one's own unmerited privilege, is dominant, at least initially, although in many cases (as these last years remind us) the moral passion is ultimately directed toward external enemies. We note in these cases a decided absence of playfulness, irony, or detachment, at least when politics are discussed. Politics have come under the sway of the superego. Whatever losses and gains may follow from this state of affairs, there can be no question that among the consequences are a heightened attention to the political, some considerable precocity of attitude, an early crystallization of belief, and a strong sense of family unity.

We have now approached the important but difficult topic of ideology's connection with psychodynamics. It is difficult first because we made no systematic effort to explore personality, and beyond that because both ideology and personality at this age seem too fluid, too shifting to allow us more than the most hesitant of impressions. But let me venture one impression: that a certain consistency of motif, based in part upon psychodynamics, dominates the political thought of certain adolescents in the middle period. There is, for example, a politics of dependency (found with unusual frequency in the German sample, as we will see later), in which the imagined and described political world is organized around the idea of government as a succoring parent and the citizen as a receptive child. There is a politics of envy, of resentment, dominated by the conviction that the high and mighty unjustly retain the world's resources for themselves. And there is a politics of power, in which we can discern a preoccupation with domination and control. These themes—guilt, dependency, envy, power, and no doubt others—seem to emerge from an interaction between salient values in the child's milieu and certain dispositions in personality. When felt strongly enough they order the political perceptions and provide a framework for the organization of ideology.

Let me offer a brief example. The young man in question was one of the longitudinal sample, interviewed first in the ninth grade, then three years later as a high school senior. He is one of the two or three most intelligent adolescents in the entire sample; at fifteen his views are unusually well developed. Unlike most of our highly intelligent youngsters, there is nothing in the least liberal about his opinions. He expects to become a scientist, like his father, who is a manager of scientists working in the defense industry and a Goldwater-style Republican; he has, he tells us, taken over his father's political ideas. Government is too powerful, too intrusive; it has stifled autonomy and initiative. So he believes, or believes he believes. Once the interview is under way, however, it becomes evident, in the way he talks about the specific problems that the interview proposes, that he cherishes not the government's weakness but the government's strength. He wants the government to be efficient, tough, powerful. He is the consummate technocrat: hard-headed, "rational," scornful of human muddle, disdainful of the incompetent. Though he will not say so, not at this time, one senses that he yearns for an engineered society.

At eighteen he tells us that he has thought out a scheme for governing society. He has, in fact, developed a fully elaborated utopia. (He is the only adolescent we have ever interviewed to do so.) It is based upon a science-fiction novel he once read, and he has since made his own improvements on the germinal idea. In his ideal society, political power would be completely in the hands of an elite whose nature seems partly militaristic, partly technocratic. The governing class would be self-selected. Young men would volunteer for a five- to ten-year period of service and training, during which they would undergo tests of courage, submission, and discipline. They would also be trained for political and technical leadership, and would enter the ruling class upon successful completion of the regime. The common people, being well served by their leaders, would devote themselves only to leisure and self-realization, and would not need to bother with politics, policy, or planning.

We have here an example—an unusually choice one, as it happens—of the growth of ideology, of some of its determinants, and of its consistency over time. We note a well-developed identification with the father, one which draws our young man toward a technocratic political ideal; social problems will vanish when in the hands of a tough-minded, scientifically trained, quasi-monastic elite, a kind of twenty-first century Knights Templar. We see an emphasis on submission and sacrifice, upon the testing of the self by trials of devotion, upon the ritual initiation into maturity —all the archetypical concerns of some forms of adolescent idealism. Above all, we observe the persistence of the theme of power. At the age of fifteen it is relatively muted, a tendency, a bias, not yet clearly an ideology; at eighteen the ideal of power has flowered into a carefully elaborated fantasy of totalitarian control, one in fact not far removed in some of its details (as in the two-tiered caste system) from *Brave New World*.

I want to stress again how nearly singular the case is. It was, as I have mentioned, the only fully articulated utopia we came across. The belief in naked power is extremely unusual. But it is unusual too in less obvious ways. Rarely do we find so consistent a view, realistic or utopian, of the political world. If we think of ideology not merely as the presence of attitudes and principles, but also as involving the successful attempt to *bind* them, to give them internal coherence, in that sense ideology is an unusual event in adolescence, even at eighteen. Most of our subjects' ideologies seemed very much ad hoc. They answered each question as it came, seeming to make little effort to construct a model which would relate principles to each other. In the great majority of instances, the child merely soaks up the tacit assumptions of the milieu. Those few youngsters who cathect politics are those who will try to delineate, clarify, and justify the tacit, or those who resist it. It is in this sense that, for the most part, political grasp and political energy fuel each other; without a high cathexis of the political world there is, at least in adolescence, little effort given to the construction of a consistent political ethic.

Idealism, Utopianism, and Other Political Affects

The revival of political activism on college campuses has given new life to an older vision of the young as intensely political creatures, motivated by messianic or, at the least, idealistic sentiments. From the first, a central goal of this research was the exploration of this putative state of affairs. In earlier work with adolescents I had seen few signs of deep political involvement, much less so political idealism. Nor had other data I had consulted suggested it; to the contrary. But the political beliefs of adolescents had not, at that time, been much studied; nor had the problem of political idealism been studied head on. Hence, several of the items on the interview schedule directly (and many more, indirectly) were addressed to searching out ideals and idealism. Specifically: would it be possible in an ideal society to eliminate crime; would it be possible to diminish or do away with disputes and disagreements among people; what kind of ideal society would you set up? Let me quickly grant the limitations of the questions for providing a full answer to the assessment of adolescent idealism. In particular, I now believe that we should also have included items dealing with more feasible social goals, such as the elimination of poverty or racial strife (as we are now in fact doing in research currently in progress). But we were more interested in determining whether the child could imagine social possibilities beyond those offered by conventional liberalism.

We had expected to discover more idealism among the young than we did, but we were not overly surprised to find it generally absent. What we were totally unprepared for was the prevalence of antiutopian views and the fierce strength with which they were held. Otherwise sleepy interviewees could bestir themselves to lecture us on the limits of human nature and social change. One became accustomed, when the "utopianism" questions were asked, to a shake of the head, a gentle smile, and a polite but determined dismissal of such naïve notions. Antiutopian sentiment is found to about the same degree at all ages and in all three nations.

I think we get some insight into its sources when we examine some characteristic interview responses:

Because you can go back into history and human nature has always been the same—people want things and if they see no other way to get it they'll steal it or kill. Because basically everybody is selfish. So I don't think—no matter what kind of government or system has been devised—there will always be crime. Because you can go back as far as you want and people have always been the same basically.

People are always out to gain things for their own ends, and if they can gain great wealth quite easily without working for it, and the temptation is there, then it is human nature and they are going to take the chance and the crime is committed.

"You can't change human nature . . . people are basically selfish . . . people will always disagree"—these are the constant refrains heard in the interview when it touches upon the possibilities for substantial changes in human conduct. Our youngsters believe, as many of the Founding Fathers did, in "the assertive selfishness of human nature." They would most likely agree with Madison on "the propensity of mankind to fall into mutual animosities." They might even believe, with Hamilton, "that men are ambitious, vindictive, and rapacious." They are saying that man is a creature of interest, that interest will overcome goodness, if not all of the time, then some of the time, and if not in all men, yet certainly in some. Hence, the political order, though it may strive to attain perfection in men, should not expect to achieve it. To the contrary, society must be arranged to take account of and counter the human tendencies toward self-interest and faction.

There are, I suppose, varying attitudes we can take about the anti-idealism of the young. A colleague of mine, a devotee of Herbert Marcuse and the counterculture, sees in this finding a reflection of how the competitive conditions of capitalism stifle the natural openness and generosity of the young. Another colleague is delighted to learn of it; he believes that utopianism is essentially romantic and that political romanticism is sooner or later antidemocratic. Another feels that this mood among the young suggests no more than the triumph of the Lockean over the Rousseauian tradition in Western political thought. However we understand the counteridealism of our adolescents, we should be clear about what it is not. It is not the thoughtless authoritarianism of the very young, for older subjects are rather more skeptical of human goodness than younger ones. Furthermore, it is our most reflective and sensitive youngsters who offer some of the most telling arguments against what they take to be naïve idealism. Nor is it gutter cynicism, or anything like it; it appears in those who are otherwise fairly sanguine about the prospects for man and society.

The anti-idealistic attitude is, I suspect, among other things, a reflection of that striving toward realism which is as important as, and far more prevalent than, the reach toward idealism. The child moves during this period toward what he conceives to be an "adult" understanding of the world, which sometimes seems to mean relinquishing what he deems to be "childish"—naïveté, or simple-mindedness, or sentimentality. The strain toward "maturity"—that is, toward coolness, prudence, sober judgment, and the like—is as strongly felt as the more idealistic impulses. The striving toward realism, and the consequent tension between "idealistic" and "realistic" modes within the person, has been much neglected by students of adolescence, so enthralled have they been by the myth of adolescent idealism.

In view of this it should come as no surprise that few adolescents show signs of having given serious thought to the radical revision of society. That there is little interest in the construction of utopia among the youngest adolescents is hardly unexpected. As we have seen, they have such a rudimentary sense of the concept of society that it would be implausible to find them indulging in social critique, let alone proposing schemes of social betterment whether modest or exalted. But in the middle period, with the capacity for political reasoning established—though not altogether consolidated—we would expect to see, and we do in fact see, the emergence of both critical and melioristic outlooks. These largely span a rather narrow range of attitude. To the question on devising an ideal society, most responses range from fatuous complacency to sharp and succinct wishes for change, the latter very much within the system.

A great many youngsters say, "I like it just the way it is," or some variant thereof, and will not be budged even when pressed by further questioning. Some of the American youngsters, in particular, think their country ideal, or close to it. Many responses are rather diffuse: for example, "Well probably one where the people could do what they wanted . . . not what they want. What I mean is not go out and have riots and things like that, but do things that they would enjoy and have fun in that and not get into trouble or anything." Others offer only modest goals: "A society that would have laws and that would be run by the people, and a country that everyone under eighteen should go to school and everyone over eighteen should go to college, and make something out of themselves." Some propose a utopia by exclusion: "Let's see, I would try to make it better. All the people causing trouble should be sent away by themselves. They could make all the trouble out there. So they wouldn't bother anybody."

Among the more focused responses, three themes seem dominant. There is a *law-and-order* and/or serenity motif, in which the stress is upon the absence of crime, riots, narcotics, and the like, and the consequent achievement of a tranquil, peaceful, kindly community. There is an *abundance* motif, which emphasizes the elimination of want. One child proposes that everything be free, another a credit-card utopia, with cards to be in bountiful supply. There is an *equality* motif, which aims at the leveling of differences, both economic and racial. These themes—serenity, bounty, equality—are the elements of most millenarian visions, but it should be emphasized that they seem not to be felt strongly, that these are attenuated millennial dreams, both in their scope and in their affective intensity. On the whole, the mood of our youngsters is conservative. Grievances against the system, when present, do not seem deeply held; the apocalyptic or chiliastic mentality so often imputed to adolescents is scarcely to be found.

We should not find any of this in the least surprising. Our samples in all three nations were drawn largely from youngsters of the more or less contented classes of the community, from that vast range of the population extending from the stable working class to the nonintellectual upper middle class. In regard to politics they will ultimately become either passive spectators or intelligent consumers; signs of this are already evident. They are consumed neither by grievances nor by moral passion, and in this respect they are almost certainly very much like their families. And it is no surprise either that the impulse to utopian thought, in the few instances we find it, appears among inner-city adolescents, largely black but some white, who feel themselves despised and rejected, and by young suburban intellectuals, morally troubled, and feeling in themselves the destiny to innovate and lead. These, too, are no doubt much like their families. The inclination to utopia, in short, is a matter of class and social position, not fundamentally a youth phenomenon.

National Variations

What follows should be read with the utmost caution. They are sketches of national styles in adolescent political thought, attempts to capture the distinctive qualities—the dominant tonalities, as it were—of the three political cultures. To do so, I have stressed what is unique to each, at the cost of ignoring the many more ways in which American, German, and British adolescents are alike. Thus the typical German adolescent is not as preoccupied with order and obedience as the sketch given below would suggest; yet taken as a whole the set of German interviews do show such a preoccupation when we compare them with the other two national samples.

The Germans

I begin with the German interviews because they are the easiest to grasp. The distinguishing themes can be stated boldly and simply. They are also familiar—eerily so. Reading some of these interviews—not all, but a substantial minority, perhaps 30 per cent of them—we feel ourselves drawn or thrown back thirty or forty years, to those sentiments about citizen, state, and society which we then took to be "uniquely" German. Despite at least two decades of successful democratic practice, despite the earnest attempt of most educated Germans to wash their hands of the past, much of that political spirit persists—as many observers have noted, and as our interviews made painfully plain. Consider the following statement by an eighteen-year-old German girl, responding to a question on the purpose of government. Nothing like it, nothing remotely like it, appears in the American or British interviews. "We have to have someone who takes responsibility for us, so that they don't become confused, the whole community, so that there's one person who governs us, and shares an interest in what we do and everything."

In this brief extract we catch a glimpse of several of the motifs that distinguish the German interviews: the fear of confusion; the identification of government with a single person; and, above all, the view of authority as parental and of the citizen as a child. The governing power is seen as wise and benevolent, the citizen as weak and dependent, the two joining symbiotically. Given this nuclear view of the political enterprise, most of the singular features of German political thought fall into place.

The ordinary citizen is seen as weak, or stupid, or incompetent. He does not know enough to come in out of the rain. A disdain for "the people" runs through the interviews: "people must all be guided somehow . . . they can't otherwise make sense out of what happens to them," "the laws are created because otherwise when one lives without laws . . . then one cannot tell if what one is doing is right."

Indeed, it is sometimes implied that stupidity, or a sheeplike docility, *should* be the proper state of mind for the citizen:

[Laws are needed] so that all the people can live in such a way that they don't have to think about what's going to happen to them very much.

There should be [a law forbidding smoking] because . . . otherwise people would have to decide for themselves if it's good or bad for their health or not.

They wanted to have a guiding principle that one could defer to without further ado, without reflecting on his deeds and considering whether something is correct or false.

These last quotations point to a recurrent theme in many of the German interviews: the anguish of ambiguity, the pain of deciding among alternatives. Ambiguity begets confusion, and confusion is an internal state most deeply feared. Out of the fear of ambiguity, and the deeper fear of confusion, of being adrift in a sea of possibilities, comes the need to reduce diversity, to seek order, clarity, and direction. Hence the German youngster turns to the strong leader. Without firm leadership, there will be chaos, anarchy. By anarchy he has in mind not that state of nature where it is the war of all against all (an Anglo-Saxon notion, to judge by our interviews), but a state of anomie, of being lost, rootless, perplexed, without beacons or guideposts, besieged by a Babel of separate voices. The clear, loud, coherent voice of authority can overcome Babel. It is this consideration which seems to attract a disproportionate number of German adolescents to one-man rule. (Over-all, the German sample preferred one-man rule twice as often as the American and British subjects. At the age of thirteen, an astonishing 50 per cent prefer it over representative or direct democracy.)

Well, when one man rules it is always better than when many rule. There are no others who have a different opinion and such, and there should be only one ruling. With [a representative system] the people could not determine anything at all, because there are always different voices.

[One-man rule] I like—that only one person decides; otherwise they might argue. And with [representative democracy] they won't get to agree, and with [direct democracy] there is probably more confusion, when they all at once say this and that.

Even when the choice is made for a representative system, the reasoning is the same:

If each person decided individually, there would almost certainly be a tremendous chaos, and when only a certain number of people rule, then they guide the people much better. They realize what's important for individual people.

The leadership—whether a single man or a ruling group—is assumed to be, as one youngster put it, "smarter and wiser" than the people they rule, and thus entitled to rule. There is little of the cynicism and distrust of authority we find so commonly in the American and British interviews. The omnicompetence of the leader allows the citizen to turn over responsibility to him without qualms, secure in the sense that a strong and wise leadership will provide order, ensure unity, and thus protect the country from chaos and weakness. What haunts the imagination of a few youngsters is the idea of a disunited country weak in the face of its enemies.

If a state didn't provide any order, in my opinion, if there weren't any internal order, in Germany, then other states would begin to overrun the country because no one would provide unity then.

[The purpose of government] is first to keep order in the country and then—most of all to unite, perhaps, during a war.

The state must not only be strong, it must *appear* to be strong. If the government gives even the appearance of weakness, then all may be lost. When asked what the government should do about a law being violated by the citizenry, one seemingly unworkable, we have these responses:

Keep [the law] but alter it. To abolish it they would more or less admit that they had been wrong . . . and, of course, if the government is wrong, the people would have no confidence in it.

Repealing the law completely would be admitting defeat and so I would disagree.

Well, they should stiffen the law maybe now, because if they let the people get away with [smuggling], then it would be a very weak government.

The fear of disorder, and of the confusion and weakness that would follow, influences political judgments in many areas. Some German youngsters view the party system, for example, not as a means of expressing political conflict, but almost as a way of inhibiting it. They stress the orderliness that the party system provides:

[Purpose of political parties] So that there is order. Well, because otherwise everyone could almost do as he pleases.

[Why did parties emerge?] So that there are no disturbances in the country and that everything is in order in the country.

Thus, the Germans: they are not "authoritarian" in the sense that they wish to bully the weak, or even to wield authority over others. To the contrary, they seem to see themselves as weak, childlike, and inept, and they yearn for the strong, comforting hand of a benign and vigilant leader. Offered it, they will follow.

The British

The British were the most difficult of our samples to understand. They are rugged individualists, laissez-fairists of the H. L. Hunt stamp; and yet they are the most welfare-oriented of the national groups, determined that the government provide goods and services. They resent any attempt to do away with their pleasures; and yet they take a low view of their fellow-men on the grounds that they are too obsessed by pleasure. They are edgy and irritated about authorities, whom they suspect to be bossy and hypocritical; and yet they want and expect the authorities to govern, and no nonsense about it. Their politics is a marvelous, bewildering mixture, derived partly from Hobbes, from whom they draw a mordant view of man and his doings; from John Stuart Mill, with whom they share a fierce devotion to liberty; and from the Fabians and their successors, who have taught them to look to the state for welfare and security.

To find our way into the British political temper, let me begin, once again, with a representative quotation from an interview with a thirteen-year-old responding to a question on laws: "There must be certain laws, otherwise people would just go round and eat other people's apples off the next door neighbor's trees or something."

This rather innocuous excerpt contains within it two elements which reflect British preoccupations: the oral emphasis, on food and stealing, and the implicit concern with boundaries—the sense of territory, and the fear of trespass.

Reading through the British interviews, one is struck most forcefully by their ubiquitous orality. There is a more than usual frequency of oral metaphors and phrasings, as in the example given, but even more evident is what amounts to an obsessive emphasis on greed, envy, theft, and self-indulgence, all of these oral motifs. The concern with stealing is especially prominent. When Americans think about a world without law, they mention murder and other forms of personal violence; the British mention theft and its variants, and only later, as a second thought, think to mention killing. To an open-ended, general question on crime, 49 per cent of the British subjects spontaneously cited stealing as an example; to the same question, only 18 per cent of Americans did so.

When we look more closely into what they imagine to motivate theft, we find once again a stress upon oral motifs. People steal because they are *greedy*—that is, they are voracious, insatiable, unsatisfied by what they have. Or they are consumed by *envy*—that is, they cannot abide the prosperity of the other in the light of their own deprivation. Or they are truly *deprived*—that is, poor and in want. Or they are merely *self-indulgent*—unwilling to work as the rest of us must, they take the easier path of theft.

I mention this pervasive orality, this obsessive stress on getting and taking, not as a psychoanalytic curiosity, but because it has a vital connection to the political thought of our British adolescents. What matters to the British—far more than to the American or German youngsters—are such issues as the equitable distribution of supplies, the government's stance toward the pursuit of pleasure and self-interest, the enhancement of economic well-being, and other matters bearing upon the materialistic interests of the citizen.

As Judith Gallatin has pointed out, the British, in contrast with both the Germans and Americans, are disposed to think in terms of distributive rather than aggregative utility when considering a political proposal. That is to say, they measure the value of a law or political decision by its benefit to the individual citizen rather than its advantages to the community as a whole. Germans, as we have seen, tend to think first in terms of strengthening the state; Americans, as we will see, think in terms of enhancing the common good. For the British, what comes first is the well-being of the individual citizen. Whereas the German or American might say that what's good for the community is good for the citizen, the British clearly believe that what's good for the citizen is good for the country.

The maintenance of material well-being is seen as being very much a governmental responsibility. While both the American and German adolescents more or less ignore the government's economic role, the British put it at the forefront of concern. It is only in the British interviews that we find such statements on the purpose of government as the following: that it should "control the economy," "sustain existence," "look after the economic side," "help old people," "look after the welfare of the country," and "increase export and trade."

The government's role vis-à-vis supplies is expected to go beyond the enhancement of the nation's well-being. It must also make sure that what there is (and it is taken for granted that what there is is in short supply) must be distributed equitably—fair shares for all. As one British youngster puts it, one of the functions of government is "to see that everybody gets their own share of everything."

What makes this a difficult task is the tendency toward greed and self-interest commonly imputed to at least some of one's neighbors. It is not, I hope, overly cynical to point out that while the British child sees himself as wanting no more than his due (and no less), he is ready to imagine that others are not nearly so modest in their wants; the mechanism, projection, is familiar enough. This preoccupation with the avarice of others is a steady drumbeat in the British interviews, and it does not diminish much with age.

Everyone would take advantage of everyone else. Nobody would mind taking something from the person next door.

The majority of people steal because they want to live above what they have been used to.

I think people would turn greedy, dishonest, and selfish.

So the British youngster is fretful lest he be deprived of his share of the pie, yet vigilant that others may cheat and steal to get more than they merit. It is this mixed mood that seems to generate a peculiarly ambivalent view of authority. If authority is too weak, then men will plunder. One's territory, one's goods, one's privacy, one's autonomy—and the British hold all of these dear—will be despoiled. Hence authority must be firm enough, alert enough, and, above all, disinterested enough to keep human predation in check and to ensure equality of supply. Yet his need of authority does not lead the British adolescent to exalt it. His leaders too are made of human clay; they too may be actuated by self-interest or the vanity of office. At their best his leaders may indeed be disinterested, but in this vale of tears, who will count on that? It would be going too far to say that the British are suspicious of authority. It does not quite amount to that. Let us say that they are unillusioned, skeptical. Authority is a necessary evil, necessary because of man's self-love. The British are anarchists *manqués;* were it not for the beastly nature of man, they would as soon do without authority.

Though the British youngster's skepticism about authority is usually polite, or *sotto voce,* it emerges nevertheless, almost despite itself. He half suspects that his leaders are hypocrites, that they will deprive *him* of things that they permit *themselves.* (On the question of controlling cigarette smoking, it was the British alone who felt that dissuasion of the young by authority would not work because teachers and other elders would continue to smoke, even while inveighing against it for the young.) And if they are not hypocritical, then they are bossy, intrusive, officious— eager to interfere with simple pleasures, ready to invade one's privacy. (As one youngster put it, commenting scornfully on an intrusive law: "Some bureaucrat in an office thought of that!") It should be clear that the British do not see in authority a potential tyrant, a man on horseback. The thought does not even cross their minds. They see authority as, potentially, a Scrooge, or a Mrs. Grundy, or—above all—a Pecksniff.

And so we return to that "fierce devotion to liberty" we talked about at the outset of this argument. The British are not much given to airy sentiments about freedom, much less so than our Germans and Americans, both of whom, each in their way, tend toward philosophy, by which I mean the high-flown and the full-blown. The British love of liberty is earthy, concrete, material, and in many ways selfish; it is, at bottom, based on such self-regarding sentiments as "keep your hands off my sweets" and "get off my turf." It is the British, not the Americans, who emerge in our interviews as "rugged individualists." They have a tough, gritty independence, a stubborn determination to be left alone—to have each man be a tight little island of his own—and at their best, a live and let live attitude toward others.

But I have no wish to sentimentalize. Their independence, their refreshing individualism, is but one side of the coin. The other side is a potential callousness to others, a tendency toward selfishness which the British themselves have named and lamented: "I'm all right, Jack." In that balance between the individual and the collective good that all political cultures must somehow compose, the British clearly emphasize the citizen's self-interest, and at some cost, actual or potential, to the total community. Nor are the British always quite so indulgent of others, so live-and-let-live in outlook as they are at their best. Their tolerance for eccentricity, their acceptance of diversity are often under some strain and they readily lapse into peevishness, malice, and even vindictiveness as they reflect on the greed and self-indulgence they impute—projectively, I believe—to others. The Pecksniffism and Grundyism they so quickly suspect in their leaders is in fact to be found in themselves. More so than the Germans and Americans, the British seem to struggle with their impulses. The struggle takes its toll in an ambivalent shuttling back and forth between their wish to be generous and fair toward others and their tendencies toward envy and resentment. Let me conclude by showing that struggle directly, in an excerpt from a fifteen-year-old girl's interview. She is composing her ideal society, and what she tells us speaks more vividly than para-phrase of British ambivalence:

I'd like darkies to be accepted because they're not as bad—I don't think they're as bad as they're made out to be. Some are very nice and then again there are some who are horrible. I think they're more nice than horrible. Try to get on with them, you know. They're nice to talk to sometimes. I think they should be accepted because after all they're no different really, except for the color of their skins. The only thing I don't like about them is the way they come over here and in a few days—well, before they've been over here very long, they seem to have got a good job, and they've got a great big car and they've got loads of clothes and it just seems a wonder how they get them—those jobs—just like that as they come over.

The Americans

I begin with four statements, two taken from the press, two others drawn from the interviews:

What people have to do is build that collectivist spirit. To overcome that notion of bourgeois individuality which separates one person from the next and which defines the individual as someone who can assert himself at the expense of his neighbor, at the expense of his brother by destroy-ing his brother.

What we are really into is living together . . . Living in community, learn-ing to love one another . . . Learning to live together! This and not land-ing a space ship on the moon is the great adventure of our time.

[The purpose of law] Just to set a certain basis for society so that people can get along together.

[The purpose of government] to enable . . . a great many people to live together in harmony.

The first quotation is by Angela Davis; the second is from an effusion celebrating life in hippie communes; the third is from a young lady mentioned earlier, the daughter of a John Birch Society leader and a Bircher herself; the fourth is also from a youngster discussed earlier, the boy who wants to be dictator of the world. If we ignore the rhetorical flourishes in the first two excerpts, we can observe that all four speakers are say-ing much the same thing. They are emphasizing community, to-

getherness, social amity. And in doing so, and despite their no
doubt bitter differences each from the other, and all from the
center of American thought, the four do share a togetherness,
a community of a sort—they are all Americans, and they share
the deep American belief in community, and the American ambivalence about unbridled individualism.

To simplify: if what mattered to the German adolescent was
the leader's wisdom and strength, and to the English youngster
the needs of the individual, what mattered to the American was
the citizen's connection to the community. In the American interviews the preoccupying themes are those of group and community: how to produce harmony between factions within the community; how to reduce differences in status among members of
the community; how to find a balance between the citizen's rights
and the group's needs. With remarkable consistency the American
sample was the most likely of the three to adduce community welfare and community needs as the essential goals of political action.

What we have, in a sense, is an other-directed politics, a politics of togetherness. But in saying this I do not mean to offer the
common and to my mind vulgar idea that Americans are slavishly
conformist to the opinions of others. Our data in fact showed that
the Americans were the *most* likely of the three national samples
to fear the tyranny of the majority, to uphold minority rights, and
to emphasize the right of dissent. (For that matter, the Americans
were—by a considerable margin—the least authoritarian of the
three samples, a good thing to keep in mind in these hysterically
self-flagellating times.) What I do mean to say is that the Americans seemed to be ever mindful of the total community—of its
needs, its just demands, its potential for tyranny. The ideal of
government is social harmony, the reduction of frictions so that
people can live together amicably.

In the pursuit of social amity, a number of specific political
goals are stressed. First, there must be harmony among factions,
or potential factions within the community. In the good polity, no
single group profits at the expense of others. Conflicts should be
mediated, differences compromised; a balance among competing
interests must be achieved. The concept of *balance* seemed to be of
particular importance to the American youngsters:

To keep people free—worship, free speech, way of thinking . . . so the
people have rights . . . and the civilization will balance.

The purpose of government is to balance individual and group interests so that no one group has advantage over others.

The idea of equity among competing factions is extended to minority groups. As I remarked earlier, there is a distinct emphasis upon the protection of minority rights. All voices should be heard, all interests accommodated whenever possible. The wish to reduce differences within the community is seen in its strongest form in the emphasis upon equality. Richard Hofstadter, among others, has pointed out that Americans tend to equate democracy with equalitarianism. Our interviews do much to confirm this. We find a vigorous egalitarian bias, so much so that for some of our subjects a prime function of government is the fostering of equality.

The American interviews, then, emphasized social harmony, democratic practices, the maintenance of individual rights, and equality among citizens. An optimistic view of government: the state not as the antagonist of the citizen but as his collective extension. Does all this seem too good to be true? To some minor degree. In some part the "democratic" quality of these interviews stemmed from a penchant for democratic rhetoric. In some degree it reflected a complacency about "the American way of life"—the Americans were, as I may have mentioned, the most self-consciously patriotic of the national samples. Yet neither of these tendencies—neither the occasional reciting of democratic set-pieces, nor the occasional indulgence in national self-congratulation—is the essential source of the American ambience. The optimistic, expansive liberalism of the American interviews could be seen in the most unconscious, most unselfconscious moments of discourse, in the tacit assumptions made while groping toward solutions of the problems posed by the interview.

But there is a fly in the ointment. Beneath the generally optimistic view of government we find some real tensions, involving the potential collision between equally prized values—individualism and the public good. Some of the time the American handles this conflict by a kind of denial. He imagines a social contract between the individual and society wherein the social order protects personal freedom and initiative in the understanding that the individual will voluntarily limit his pursuit of self-interest when this conflicts with the greater good sought by the community. When the spirit of Pollyanna is upon him, the American adolescent wills himself to the belief that the terms of the contract are easily met, that this concert of aims is achieved automatically. In the best of all possible political worlds, individual freedom enhances the common good, the lion of self-interest lies down with the lamb of public good.

In his darker moments we find a fear of unchecked individualism, an apprehension that the citizen will exploit and abuse the opportunities for freedom offered by the community. Let me offer a hypothesis here: that the American handles this political anxiety —at least in part—by displacing it from the realm of politics to the world of crime. There is a striking discrepancy in the American findings between the liberal, humanistic emphasis in the areas of government and political philosophy and the hard, harsh, cold line taken toward crime. (I should mention here that much of our interviewing was done before the consciousness of crime was as acute as it has since become; our American youngsters were as obsessed about the control of crime in 1963 as they are in our latest studies.)

The Americans tend to see crime as a social act. It is a betrayal of the community, a violation of the contract that binds men together in amity. When the American youngster speaks of crime, he speaks not so much of impulses (as the British do) as of its effect upon other people. The criminal is one who, willfully or otherwise, has broken his connection with the community, with other people.

Well we send people to jail to protect other people in the community. And well if he's a thief or murderer I think that it's his place to be somewhere else where he won't hurt someone else.

Crime is another way of expressing discontent for existing institutions.

[Lawbreakers] might not have very good relationships with their families or the community and I think that would have an awful lot to do with it.

The outlaw haunts the American imagination—unfettered, free, free of community and thus of constraint, free and thus alone. Crime, in the deepest American consciousness, is individualism writ large, individualism corrupted, individualism out of control.

REFERENCE

1. I cannot emphasize too strongly how much this report owes to the gifted group of students I have worked with during the last several years: Drs. Robert O'Neil, Bernard Green, Lynnette Beall, Judith Gallatin, Marjorie Bush, Bernard Banet, Maury Lachor, and Mrs. Ruthellen Josselson. Detailed findings from our research are available in the following publications

and dissertations: J. Adelson and R. O'Neil, "The Development of Political Thought in Adolescence: The Sense of Community," *Journal of Personality and Social Psychology*, 4 (1966), 295-306; J. Adelson, B. Green, and R. O'Neil, "The Growth of the Idea of Law in Adolescence," *Developmental Psychology*, 1 (1969), 327-332; J. Adelson and L. Beall, "Adolescent Perspectives on Law and Government," *Law and Society Review* (May 1970), pp. 495-504; J. Gallatin and J. Adelson, "Individual Rights and the Public Good," *Comparative Political Studies* (July 1970), pp. 226-242; unpublished doctoral dissertations (all University of Michigan) by Robert O'Neil (1964), Lynnette Beall (1966), Judith Gallatin (1967), and Marjorie Bush (1970).

LAWRENCE KOHLBERG AND CAROL GILLIGAN

The Adolescent as a Philosopher: The Discovery of the Self in a Postconventional World

Those whose exterior semblance doth belie
Thy Soul's immensity;
Thou best Philosopher . . .

Thou little child, yet glorious in the might
Of heaven-born freedom on thy Being's height,
Why with such earnest pains dost thou provoke,
The years to bring the inevitable yoke?
Thus blindly with thy blessedness at strife?
Full soon thy Soul shall have her earthly freight,
And customs lie upon thee with a weight
Heavy as frost, and deep almost as life!

The thought of our past years in me doth breed
Perpetual benediction; not indeed
For that which is most worthy to be blest;
Delight and liberty, the simple creed of childhood . . .
But for those obstinate questionings
Of sense and outward things,
Fallings from us, vanishings;
Blank misgivings of a creature
Moving about in worlds not realized,
High instincts before which our mortal Nature
Did tremble like a guilty thing surprised:

—Wordsworth, *Intimations of Immortality*

THE CENTRAL themes of this essay are first, the definition of adolescence as a universal stage of development; second, the way in which the universal features of adolescence seem to be acquiring unique colorings in the present era in America; and third, the implications of these changes for education.

144

Adolescence as a Role Transition and as a Stage of Development

In turn-of-the-century America, G. Stanley Hall launched developmental psychology with his discussion of adolescence as a stage of development. For the next fifty years, however, most American educators and psychologists tended to think about adolescence not as a stage but as a period in life, "the teens." The teenager was viewed as half-child, half-grown up, with a half-serious peer "culture" or "youth culture" of his own. Textbook after textbook on adolescence was written telling in statistical detail the sort of information which could be gathered from reading *Seventeen* or Harold Teen.

Even with the textbook description of the teenager, one could surmise that the central phenomenon of adolescence is the discovery of the self as something unique, uncertain, and questioning in its position in life. The discovery of the body and its sexual drive, and self-conscious uncertainty about that body, is one stock theme of adolescent psychology. The romantic concerns and hopes for the self's future has always been another element of the stock description of the adolescent. The third stock theme implied by the discovery of the self is the need for independence, for self-determination and choice, as opposed to acceptance of adult direction and control. The fourth stock theme implied by the adolescent discovery of self is adolescent egocentrism and hedonism, the adolescent focus upon events as they bear upon his self-image and as they lead to immediate experiences. (While the child is egocentric and hedonistic, he is not subjective; he focuses upon events, not upon his subjective experience of the events, as what is important.)

While the discovery of the self in the senses just listed has been a stock theme in American discussion of adolescence, it has been subordinated to another theme, the theme of adolescence as a marginal role between being a child and being grown-up. The adolescent sense of self, with its multiple possibilities, its uncertainties, and its self-consciousness has been viewed as the result of a social position in which one is seen and sees oneself, sometimes as adult, sometimes as child. In the marginal role view, the adolescent's need for independence and fantasies of the future are seen as the desire to "be grown-up," his conflicts and instabilities are seen as the conflict between the desire to be grown-up and a role and personality not yet consistent with being grown-up.

This social role view of adolescence, the adolescent as teenager, places the instability of the adolescent self against the background of a stable society. Against the background of the moods and tantrums and dreams of the American teenager lay an unquestioned acknowledgment of the stability and reality of the social order the adolescent was to enter. Underneath the hedonism and rebellion of the teenager lay the conformist. Harold Teen and Andy Hardy's first law was conformity to the norms of the peer group. Beneath this conformity to the peer group, however, was the teenager's recognition that when the chips were down about your future you listened to dear old Dad. An extreme example in reality of the American image of the teenager as cutting up while basically conforming is a group of California suburban high school seniors of the late 1950's. This group celebrated graduation by a summer of well-planned robberies. Their one concern while they engaged in their delinquent activities was that if they were detected, they would not get into the college of their choice.

Conformity to the peer culture, then, was the first theme of the American treatment of the adolescent in the fifties, of August Hollingshead's *Elmtown's Youth,* James Coleman's *Adolescent Society,* Albert K. Cohen's *Delinquent Boys.* The second theme was that this peer culture was itself determined by the realities of adult social class and mobility in which the peer culture was embedded. Whether grind, jock or hood, glamour girl, sex kitten or Plain Jane, the teenager's discovery of self led to the enactment of the stock roles of the adolescent culture. At a different level than the sociology of the teenager, American literature also presented adolescence as accepting unquestioningly the reality of adult society. Adolescence was presented as an imaginative expansion of the innocence of childhood facing the sordid but unquestionable reality of adult life. From *Huckleberry Finn* to *Catcher in the Rye,* the true American adolescent brought the child's innocence to a new awareness of adult reality, leading to a vision of the phoniness and corruption of the adult world, which was, however, unquestioned in its reality. Sherwood Anderson's story of the fourteen-year-old finding his father figure with a prostitute is titled "I Want to Know Why." While the American adolescent might be shocked by the sordid elements of adult life and might "want to know why" there was no question that he would eventually enter and accept "adult reality." Even when he wanted to know why, the American adolescent seldom questioned the American assumptions of progress and upward mobility, the assumption that society was moving ahead. Rather, he questioned the wisdom of his parents because they were old-fashioned. This questioning was itself an expression of faith in the adult society of the future. The adolescent's sense of the superiority of his values to those of his parents was an expression of the adolescent's belief in a greater closeness to the adult society of the future than his parents had; it was a faith in progress.

Today, we are aware of the possibility of a deeper questioning by the adolescent than was true at earlier times. Our image of the adolescent must accommodate to the phenomena of the counterculture, of the hippie and the revolutionary who does not believe in progress and upward mobility. Both the hippie and the New Left reject not only the *content* of adult society but its *forms*. The new radical refuses to organize as his revolutionary predecessors of the thirties did. Unlike the revolutionary of the thirties, he does not want to be a grownup, to really transform and govern the adult society of the future. And beneath a questioning of social *forms* is a questioning of social *functions*. The current radical rejection of adult society seems to be the rejection of any adult society whatever, if an adult society means one including institutions of work, family, law, and government. Radicals have always questioned the social *forms* of authority, of competitive achievement, and of the nuclear privatistic family and have dreamed of a more egalitarian and communal society. The essential realities of the social *functions* of work, child rearing, and of an organized social order were never questioned, however. Since Paul Goodman's *Growing Up Absurd*, we have been aware that the reality of work and making a living has come into question. Now the new ethics of population control and the Women's Liberation Movement leads to the questioning of the supreme reality of adulthood, being a parent and having children. Finally, the reality of social order is in question. When current adolescents talk of revolution, they do not seem to mean merely that adult society is evil and is resistant to rational change. More deeply, they seem to be saying that there is no real social order to destroy anyway. Social order is a myth or illusion in the adult's mind and revolution is not the destruction of an order, whether good or bad. On the optimistic side this is the message of Charles Reich's "revolution in consciousness," the idea that the young can transform society without entering or dealing with it. On the pessimistic side, the popular versions of the counterculture reiterate the theme of *Easy Rider*, the theme that the adult culture is hostile and absurd, that it does not want you to join it but that it envies you and will destroy you in the end no matter what you do.

To summarize, all accounts of adolescence stress both the sense of questioning and the parallel discovery or search for a new self of the adolescent. Usually this questioning and search for self has been seen as the product of the adolescent's marginal role between childhood and adulthood. Usually, too, it has been assumed that there are underlying givens beneath the questioning, that whatever uncertainties the adolescent has, he wants to be a grownup. Recent experience makes real for Americans the much deeper forms of questioning which may characterize adolescence, one which is not merely a matter of roles. The potential for a deeper questioning by the adolescent is implied by the identity conflict central to Erik Erikson's psychohistorical stage theory of adolescence. It is the philosophic doubting about truth, goodness, and reality implied by J. Piaget's epistemological stage theory of adolescence. It is the doubting represented by Dostoevsky's adolescents, not Mark Twain's. Deeper doubting is still a rare phenomenon, for adolescents. Beneath most hippie exteriors is an interior more like Harold Teen than Hamlet or Raskolnikov. But theoretical understanding of adolescence as a stage must stress its ideal type potential, not its "average" manifestations.

The importance of taking adolescent questioning seriously is not only important for psychological theory, it is also central to a successful resolution of the current problems of the American high school. For education, the problem of meaning just raised is the problem of whether the high school has meaning to the adolescent. We said that American psychology placed the adolescent discovery of the self against a stable but progressive social order. It saw the discovery of self within a desire to be "grown up," however confused or vague this image of the grownup was. The high school had a double meaning to the adolescent from this point of view. First, it was the locus of the peer culture in which he found his immediate identity, whether as grind, jock, or hood. Second, on the academic side, it was a point of connection to a place in the adult world. In most high schools these meanings still remain and the questioning of the reality of adulthood is not that deep. In others, however, it is a serious problem and high school is essentially a meaningless place. Before we can solve the problem of the felt meaninglessness of the high school, a clearer view of adolescent questioning is required. For this, we must turn to stage theory of the Erikson and Piaget variety.

The Meaning of the Stage Concept—Illustrated from the Preschool Years

To understand the universal meanings of adolescence as a stage and its implications for education, it will help to examine briefly an earlier stage and its implications for education, one more thoroughly understood than the stage of adolescence. Almost all cultures implicitly recognize two great stages or transformations in development. Adolescence, the second transformation, traditionally terminated compulsory schooling. The first transformation occurring from five to seven years of age initiated compulsory schooling.[1] This five-to-seven shift is termed the "onset of the latency period" by Freudian theory, the onset of concrete logical thought by Piaget. As embodied in educational thought, the Freudian interpretation of the five-to-seven shift implied letting the child grow, letting him work through his fantasies until he had repressed his sexual instincts and was ready to turn his energies into formal learning. This Freudian interpretation of the preschool stage suffered both from lack of confirmation by empirical research and from irrelevance to the intellectual development and everyday behavior with which the schools were concerned. When the Great Society decided to do something for the disadvantaged child, the Freudian "let him work through his oedipus complex" implications of the five-to-seven shift were dismissed as a luxury for the wealthy. Programs of preschool intellectual stimulation and academic schooling were initiated, with the expectation of long-range effects on intelligence and achievement. These programs failed to fulfill their initial hope of changing general intellectual maturity or long-range achievement.[2]

One reason they failed was because they confused specific teaching and learning with the development of new levels of thinking truly indicative of cognitive maturity. The evidence of limitations of these early education programs, together with growing positive research evidence of the existence of cognitive stages, convinced early educators of the reality of the stage transformation at the age five to seven. The stage transformation of the period five to seven is now conceived in quite a different way than in the vogue of Freudian education. In the Freudian view, the preschooler was in a stage of domination of thought by sexual and aggressive fantasies.

The new stage which succeeded this was defined negatively as latency, rather than positively. Under the influence of Piaget, more recent thinking sees the preschool child's fantasy as only one aspect of the preschooler's pattern of prelogical thought. In the prelogical stage, subjective appearance is not fully distinguished from "reality"; the permanent identities of things are not differentiated from their momentary transformations. In the prelogical stage view, the preschool child's special fantasy is not the expression of an instinct later repressed but of a cognitive level of thought. The decline of fantasy in the years five to seven, longitudinally documented by R. Scheffler,[3] is not a repression; it is closely related to the positive development of concrete logical patterns of thought.

The child's changed orientation to reality in the five-to-seven period is part of the development of concrete logical operations then. During this period the child develops the operations of categorical classifications, of serial ordering, addition, subtraction, and inversion of classes and relations. This development occurs in the absence of schooling in African and Taiwanese villagers in much the same way that it occurs in the American suburban child.[4]

As a concrete example, Piaget and the writers have asked children if they had had a bad dream and if they were frightened when they woke up from their bad dream.[5] Susie, aged four, said she dreamt about a giant and answered, "Yes, I was scared, my tummy was shaking and I cried and told my mommy about the giant." Asked, "Was it a real giant or was it just pretend? Did the giant just seem to be there, or was it really there?" she answered, "It was really there but it left when I woke up. I saw its footprint on the floor."

According to Piaget, Susie's response is not to be dismissed as the product of a wild imagination, but represents the young child's general failure to differentiate subjective from objective components of his experience. Children go through a regular series of steps in their understanding of dreams as subjective phenomena. The first step, achieved before five by most American middle-class children, is the recognition that dreams are not real events. The next step, achieved soon thereafter, is the realization that dreams cannot be seen by others. The third step is the notion that dreams are internal (but still material) events.

By the ages six to eight children are clearly aware that dreams are thoughts caused by themselves. To say such cognitive changes define stages implies the following things:

(1) That young children's responses represent not mere ignorance or error, but rather a spontaneous manner of thinking about the world that is qualitatively different from the way we adults think and yet has a structure of its own.

(2) The notion of different developmental structures of thought implies consistency of level of response from task to task. If a child's response represents a general structure rather than a specific learning, then the child should demonstrate the same relative structural levels in a variety of tasks.

(3) The concept of stage implies an invariance of sequence in development, a regularity of stepwise progression regardless of cultural teaching or circumstance. Cultural teaching and experience can speed up or slow down development, but it cannot change its order or sequence.

The concept of stage, then, implies that both the youngest children's conceptions of the dream as real and the school age children's view of the dream as subjective are their own; they are products of the general state of the child's cognitive development, rather than the learning of adult teachings.

Cross-cultural studies indicate the universality of the basic sequence of development of thinking about the dream, even where adult beliefs about the meaning and significance of dreams is somewhat different from our own.[6] While the stage of concrete operations is culturally universal and in a sense natural, this does not mean it is either innate or that it is inevitable and will develop regardless of environmental stimulation. In the United States, the doctrine of stages was assumed for sometime to mean that children's behavior unfolded through a series of age-specific patterns, and that these patterns and their order were wired into the organism. This indeed was the view of Gesell and Freud, and Americans misunderstood Piaget as maintaining the same thing. The implications of the Gesellian and Freudian theory for early education were clear; early teaching and stimulation would do no good since we must wait for the unfolding of the behavior, or at least the unfolding of the readiness to learn it.

In contrast, Piaget used the existence of stages to argue that basic cognitive structures are not wired in, but are general forms of equilibrium resulting from the interaction between organism and environment. If children have their own logic, adult logic or mental structure cannot be derived from innate neurological patterning because such patterning should hold also in childhood. (It is hardly plausible to view a succession of logics as an evolutionary and functional program of innate wiring.) At the same time, however, Piaget argued that stages indicate that mental structure is not merely a reflection of external physical realities or of cultural concepts of different complexities. The structure of the child's concepts in Piaget's view is not only less complex than the adult's, it is also different. The child's thought is not just a simplified version of the adult's.

Stages, or mental structures, then, are not wired into the organism though they depend upon inborn organizing tendencies. Stages are not direct reflections of the child's culture and external world, though they depend upon experience for their formation. Stages are rather the products of interactional experience between the child and the world, experience which leads to a restructuring of the child's own organization rather than to the direct imposition of the culture's pattern upon the child. While hereditary components of I.Q., of the child's rate of information processing, have some influence on the rate at which the child moves through invariant cognitive sequences, experiential factors heavily influence the rate of cognitive-structural development.[7] The kind of experience which stimulates cognitive stage development is, however, very different from the direct academic teaching of information and skills which is the focus of ordinary schooling. Programs of early education which take account of cognitive stages, then, look neither like the permissive "let them grow" nursery school pattern nor like the early teaching programs popular in the sixties. They are a new form now coming into being.[8]

Cognitive Stages in Adolescence

The older children get, the more difficult it is to distinguish universal stage changes from sociocultural transitions in development. We said that the core phenomenon of adolescence as a stage was the discovery of the subjective self and subjective experience and a parallel questioning of adult cultural reality. The manifestations of this discovery, however, are heavily colored not only by historical and cultural variations, but also by previous patterns of life history of the child.

In our first section, we discussed one manifestation of the discovery of the self, the discovery of the body and its sexual drives. In part this is, of course, a biological universal, the physical growth spurt marking adolescent puberty and an accompanying qualitatively new sex drive. If there is anything which can be safely said about what is new in the minds of adolescents, it is that they, like their elders, have sex on their minds. These changes, of course, have been the focus of Freudian thinking about adolescence as a stage. If anything, however, Freudian thinking has underestimated the novel elements of sexual experience in adolescence. For the Freudian, early adolescent sexuality is the reawakening of early childhood sexuality previously latent, with a consequent resurrection of oedipal feeling. Although it is true that adolescent sexuality bears the stamp of earlier experience, it is not the resurrection of earlier sexual feelings. Adolescent sexual drive is a qualitatively new phenomenon.[9]

While sexual drives are awakened at puberty, there are vast individual and cultural variations in the extent to which they determine the adolescent's behavior and experience. Sexuality is a central concern for the self of some fourteen-year-olds; it is something deferred to the future for others. What is common for all, however, is an intensified emotionality whether experienced as sexual or not. This emotionality, too, is now experienced as a part of the self, rather than as a correlate of objective events in the world. C. Ellinwood studied the age development of the verbal experiencing and expression of emotion in projective tests and in free self-descriptions. She found that prior to adolescence (aged twelve or so), emotions were experienced as objective concomitants of activities and objects. The child experienced anger because events or persons were bad; he experienced affection because persons were good or giving; he felt excitement because activities were exciting or fun. At adolescence, however, emotions are experienced as the result of states of the self rather than as the direct correlate of external events.[10]

The difference may perhaps be clarified by reference to middle-class drug experiences. Occasionally, a psychological preadolescent may take drugs, as he may drink beer or sneak cigarettes. When he does this, he does this as an activity of an exciting forbidden and grown-up variety. For the adolescent drug-taker, drugs represent rather a vehicle to certain subjective moods, feelings, and sensations. In many cases, the drug experience is a vehicle for overcoming depression, felt as an inner subjective mood. In any case, drug-taking is not an activity with an objective quality; it is a mode of activating subjective inner feelings and states. The same is true of such activities as intensive listening to music, an activity characteristically first engaged in at early adolescence (ages eleven to fourteen). The rock, folk-rock, and blues music so popular with adolescents is explicitly a presentation of subjective mood and is listened to in that spirit.

Associated with the discovery of subjective feelings and moods is the discovery of ambivalence and conflicts of feeling. If feelings are objective correlates of external good and bad events, there can be little tolerance and acceptance of feeling hate and love for the same person, of enjoying sadness and feeling sad about pleasure. Ellinwood's study documents that adolescents are consciously expressing such ambivalence, which is of course the stock in trade of the blues and folk-rock music beamed to them.

We have spoken of the adolescent discovery of subjective moods and feelings as linked to puberty. More basically, it is linked to the universal cognitive stages of Piaget. We have said that the five-to-seven transition is defined by Piaget as the transition to *abstract, reflective* thought. More exactly, it is the transition from logical inference as a set of *concrete operations* to logical inference as a set of *formal operations* or "operations upon operations." "Operations upon operations" imply that the adolescent can classify classification, that he can combine combinations, that he can relate relationships. It implies that he can think about thought, and create thought systems or "hypothetico-deductive" theories. This involves the logical construction of all possibilities—that is, the awareness of the observed as only a subset of what may be logically possible. In related fashion, it implies the hypothetico-deductive attitude, the notion that a belief or proposition is not an immediate truth but a hypothesis whose truth value consists in the truth of the concrete propositions derivable from it.

An example of the shift from concrete to formal operations may be taken from the work of E. A. Peel.[11] Peel asked children what they thought about the following event: "Only brave pilots are allowed to fly over high mountains. A fighter pilot flying over the Alps collided with an aeriel cable-way, and cut a main cable causing some cars to fall to the glacier below. Several people were killed." A child at the concrete-operational level answered: "I think that the pilot was not very good at flying. He would have been better off if he went on fighting." A formal-operational child responded: "He was either not informed of the mountain railway on his route or he was flying too low also his flying compass may have been affected by something before or after take-off this setting him off course causing collision with the cable."

The concrete-operational child assumes that if there was a collision the pilot was a bad pilot; the formal-operational child considers all the possibilities that might have caused the collision. The concrete-operational child adopts the hypothesis that seems most probable or likely to him. The formal-operational child constructs all possibilities and checks them out one by one.

As a second example, we may cite one of Piaget's tasks, systematically replicated by D. Kuhn, J. Langer, and L. Kohlberg.[12] The child is shown a pendulum whose length may vary as well as the number of weights attached. The child is asked to discover or explain what determines the speed of movement (or "period") of the pendulum. Only the formal-operational child will "isolate variables," that is, vary length holding weight constant, and so forth, and arrive at the correct solution (for example, that period is determined by length). Success at the task is unrelated to relevant verbal knowledge about science or physics, but is a function of logical level.

In fact the passage from concrete to formal operations is not an all or none phenomenon. There are one or two substages of formal operations prior to the full awareness of all possibilities just described. These substages are described in table 1, which presents an overview of the Piaget cognitive stages. For simplifying purposes, we may say that for middle-class Americans, one stage of formal operations is reached at age ten to thirteen, while the consideration of all possibilities is reached around fifteen to sixteen. At the first formal-operational stage, children became capable of reversing relationships and ordering relationships one at a time or in chains, but not of abstract consideration of all possibilities. (They are capable of "forming the inverse of the reciprocal," in Piaget's terminology; but not of combining all relationships.) A social thinking example of failure to reverse relationships is shown in concrete-operational children's responses to the question: "What does the Golden Rule tell you to do if someone comes up on the street and hits you?" The typical answer is "hit him back, do unto others as they do unto you." The painful process of the transitional formal-operational child in response to the question is given by the following response: "Well for the Golden Rule you have to like dream that your mind leaves your body and goes into the other person, then it comes back into you and you see it like he does and you act like the way you saw it from there."[13]

We have described Piaget's stage of formal operations as a logical stage. What is of special importance for understanding adolescents, however, is not the logic of formal operations, but its episte-

Table 1.   Piaget's eras and stages of logical and cognitive development.

Era I (age 0-2) The era of sensorimotor intelligence
Stage 1.   Reflex action.
Stage 2.   Coordination of reflexes and sensorimotor repetition (primary circular reaction).
Stage 3.   Activities to make interesting events in the environment reappear (secondary circular reaction).
Stage 4.   Means/ends behavior and search for absent objects.
Stage 5.   Experimental search for new means (tertiary circular reaction).
Stage 6.   Use of imagery in insightful invention of new means and in recall of absent objects and events.

Era II (age 2-5) Symbolic, intuitive, or prelogical thought
Inference is carried on through images and symbols which do not maintain logical relations or invariances with one another. "Magical thinking" in the sense of (a) confusion of apparent or imagined events with real events and objects and (b) confusion of perceptual appearances of qualitative and quantitative change with actual change.

Era III (age 6-10) Concrete operational thought
Inferences carried on through system of classes, relations, and quantities maintaining logically invariant properties and which *refer to concrete objects.* These include such logical processes as (a) inclusion of lower-order classes in higher order classes; (b) transitive seriation (recognition that if a > b and b > c, then a > c); (c) logical addition and multiplication of classes and quantities; (d) conservation of number, class membership, length, and mass under apparent change.
Substage 1.   Formation of stable categorical classes.
Substage 2.   Formation of quantitative and numerical relations of invariance.

Era IV (age 11 to adulthood) Formal-operational thought
Inferences through logical operations upon propositions or "operations upon operations." Reasoning about reasoning. Construction of systems of all possible relations or implications. Hypothetico-deductive isolation of variables and testing of hypotheses.
Substage 1.   Formation of the inverse of the reciprocal. Capacity to form negative classes (for example, the class of all not-crows) and to see relations as simultaneously reciprocal (for example, to understand that liquid in a U-shaped tube holds an equal level because of counterbalanced pressures).
Substage 2.   Capacity to order triads of propositions or relations (for example, to understand that if Bob is taller than Joe and Joe is shorter than Dick, then Joe is the shortest of the three).
Substage 3.   True formal thought. Construction of all possible combinations of relations, systematic isolation of variables, and deductive hypothesis-testing.

---

mology, its conception of truth and reality. In the previous section we said that the child's attainment of concrete operations at age six to seven led to the differentiation of subjective and objective, appearance and reality. The differentiation at this level was one in which reality was equated with the physical and the external. We cited the child's concept of the dream, in which the unreality of the dream was equivalent to its definition as an inner mental event with no physical external correlate. The subjective and the mental are to the concrete-operational child equated with fantasies, with unrealistic replicas of external physical events. The development of formal operations leads, however, to a new view of the external and the physical. The external and the physical are only one set of many possibilities of a subjective experience. The external is no longer the real, "the objective," and the internal the "unreal." The internal may be real and the external unreal. At its extreme, adolescent thought entertains solipsism or at least the Cartesian cogito, the notion that the only thing real is the self. I asked a fifteen-year-old girl: "What is the most real thing to you?" Her unhesitating reply was "myself."

The lines from Wordsworth introducing this essay represent his own adolescent experience described by him as follows: "I was often unable to think of external things as having external existence, and I communed with all that I saw as something not apart from, but inherent in, my own material nature. Many times while going to school have I grasped at a wall or tree to recall myself from this abyss of idealism to the reality. At this time I was afraid of such processes."[14]

Wordsworth's adolescent solipsism was linked to his awakened poetic sense, to his experience of nature, and to his transcendental religiosity. It seems that for all adolescents the discovery of the subjective is a condition for aesthetic feeling in the adult sense, for the experience of nature as a contemplative experience, and for religiosity of a mystical variety. It is probably the condition for adolescent romantic love as well. This whole constellation of experiences is called romantic because it is centered on a celebration of the self's experience as the self enters into union with the self's counterpart outside. The common view of romanticism as adolescent, then, is correct in defining the origins of romanticism in the birth of the subjective self in adolescence.

If the discovery of subjective experience and the transcendental self is one side of the new differentiation of subjective and objective made by the adolescent, the clouding and questioning of the validity of society's truths and its rightness is the other. To consider this side of adolescence we must turn from cognitive to moral stages.

Before we turn to adolescent moral thought we need to note a real difference between the development of concrete operations and the development of formal operations. There are two facts which distinguish the adolescent revolution in logical and epistemological thinking from the five-to-seven revolution in thinking. The first is that the adolescent revolution is extremely variable as to time. The second is that for many people it never occurs at all. With regard to concrete operations, some children attain clear capacity for logical reasoning at five, some at eight or nine. But all children ultimately display some clear capacity for concrete-logical reasoning.[15] This is not true for formal-operational reasoning. As an example, the percentage of 265 persons at various ages showing clear formal-operational reasoning at the pendulum task is as follows:

Age ten to fifteen: 45 per cent
Age sixteen to twenty: 53 per cent
Age twenty-one to thirty: 65 per cent
Age forty-five to fifty: 57 per cent[16]

The subjects studied were lower-middle and upper-middle-class California parents (age forty-five to fifty) and their children (age ten to thirty). The figures indicate that it is not until age twenty-one to thirty that a clear majority (65 per cent) attain formal reasoning by this criteria. They suggest that there is no further development of formal reasoning after age thirty. This means that almost 50 per cent of American adults never reach adolescence in the cognitive sense. The figures should not be taken with too great seriousness, since various tasks requiring formal operations are of somewhat varying difficulty. In the study cited another problem, a "correlation problem," was used which was passed by even fewer members of the adult population. It is possible that easier tasks could be devised which would lead to more people displaying formal reasoning. The point, however, is that a large proportion of Americans never develop the capacity for abstract thought. Most who do, develop it in earlier adolescence (age eleven to fifteen), but some do not reach full formal reasoning until the twenties. We should note, too, that rate of attainment of formal operations is not simply a function of I.Q.: the correlations between Piaget and I.Q. measures are in the 50's. Finally, in simpler cultures—for example, villages in Turkey—full formal operations never seem to be reached at all (though it is reached by urbanized educated Turks).

The high variability in age of attainment of formal operations, then, indicates that we cannot equate a cognitive stage with a definite age period. Puberty, the attainment of formal operations, and the transition from childhood to adult status are all components of adolescence variable in time and in their relations to one another.

Moral Stages in Adolescence and Their Relation to Cognitive Stages

Joseph Adelson, in this volume, documents the way in which the adolescent's thinking about political society is transformed by the advent of formal-operational thought. To understand the adolescent's social thinking, however, we need to be aware not only of logical stages but also of stages of moral judgment. In our research, we have found six definite and universal stages of development in moral thought. In our longitudinal study of seventy-six American boys from preadolescence, youths were presented with hypothetical moral dilemmas, all deliberately philosophical, some of them found in medieval works of causistry.

On the basis of their reasoning about these dilemmas at a given age, each boy's stage of moral thought could be determined for each of twelve basic moral concepts, values, or issues. The six stages of moral thought are divided into three major levels, the *preconventional*, the *conventional*, and the *postconventional* or autonomous.

While the preconventional child is often "well-behaved" and is responsive to cultural labels of good and bad, he interprets these labels in terms of their physical consequences (punishment, reward, exchange of favors) or in terms of the physical power of those who enunciate the rules and labels of good and bad. This level is usually occupied in the middle class by children aged four to ten.

The second or conventional level usually becomes dominant in preadolescence. Maintaining the expectation and rules of the individual's family, group, or nation is perceived as valuable in its own right. There is concern not only with conforming to the individual's social order, but also in maintaining, supporting, and justifying this order.

The postconventional level is first evident in adolescence and is characterized by a major thrust toward autonomous moral principles which have validity and application apart from authority of the groups or persons who hold them and apart from the individual's identification with those persons or groups.

Within each of these three levels there are two discernable stages. At the preconventional level we have: Stage 1: Orientation toward punishment and unquestioning deference to superior power. The physical consequences of action regardless of their human meaning or value determine its goodness or badness. Stage 2: Right action consists of that which instrumentally satisfies one's own needs and occasionally the needs of others. Human relations are viewed in terms like those of the market place. Elements of fairness, reciprocity, and equal sharing are present, but they are always interpreted in a physical, pragmatic way. Reciprocity is a matter of "you scratch my back and I'll scratch yours," not of loyalty, gratitude, or justice.

At the conventional level we have: Stage 3: Good-boy-good-girl orientation. Good behavior is that which pleases or helps others and is approved by them. There is much conformity to stereotypical images of what is majority or "natural" behavior. Behavior is often judged by intention—"he means well" becomes important for the first time and is overused. One seeks approval by being "nice." Stage 4: Orientation toward authority, fixed rules, and the maintenance of the social order. Right behavior consists of doing one's duty, showing respect for authority, and maintaining the given social order for its own sake. One earns respect by performing dutifully.

At the postconventional level we have: Stage 5A: A social-contract orientation, generally with legalistic and utilitarian overtones. Right action tends to be defined in terms of general rights and in terms of standards which have been critically examined and agreed upon by the whole society. There is a clear awareness of the relativism of personal values and opinions and a corresponding emphasis upon procedural rules for reaching consensus. Aside from what is constitutionally agreed upon, right or wrong is a matter of personal values and opinion. The result is an emphasis upon the legal point of view, but with an emphasis upon the possibility of changing law in terms of rational considerations of social utility, rather than freezing it in the terms of Stage 4, law and order. Outside the legal realm, free agreement and contract are the binding elements of obligation. This is the official morality of American government, and finds its ground in the thought of the writers of the Constitution. Stage 5B: Orientation to internal decisions of conscience but without clear rational or universal principles. Stage 6:

Orientation toward ethical principles appealing to logical comprehensiveness, universality, and consistency. These principles are abstract and ethical (the Golden Rule, the categorical imperative); they are not concrete moral rules like the Ten Commandments. Instead, they are universal principles of justice, of the reciprocity and equality of human rights, and of respect for the dignity of human beings as individual persons.

These stages are defined by twelve basic issues of moral judgment. On one such issue, Conscience, Motive Given for Rule Obedience or Moral Action, the six stages look like this:

1. Obey rules to avoid punishment.

2. Conform to obtain rewards, have favors returned, and so on.

3. Conform to avoid disapproval, dislike by others.

4. Conform to avoid censure by legitimate authorities and resultant guilt.

5A. Conform to maintain the respect of the impartial spectator judging in terms of community welfare.

5B. Conform to avoid self-condemnation.

In another of these moral issues, the value of human life, the six stages can be defined thus:

1. The value of a human life is confused with the value of physical objects and is based on the social status or physical attributes of its possessor.

2. The value of a human life is seen as instrumental to the satisfaction of the needs of its possessor or of other persons.

3. The value of a human life is based on the empathy and affection of family members and others toward its possessor.

4. Life is conceived as sacred in terms of its place in a categorical moral or religious order of rights and duties.

5. Life is valued both in terms of its relation to community welfare and in terms of being a universal human right.

6. Belief in the sacredness of human life as representing a universal human value of respect for the individual.

We call our types "stages" because they seem to represent an invariant developmental sequence. True stages come one at a time and always in the same order.

All movement is forward in sequence and does not skip steps. Children may move through these stages at varying speeds, of course, and may be found half in and half out of a particular stage. An individual may stop at any given stage and at any age, but if he continues to move, he must move in accord with these steps. Moral reasoning of the conventional or Stage 3-4 kind never occurs before the preconventional Stage 1 and Stage 2 thought has taken place. No adult in Stage 4 has gone through Stage 6, but all Stage 6 adults have gone at least through 4.

While the evidence is not complete, our study strongly suggests that moral change fits the stage pattern just described. Figures 1 and 2 indicate the cultural universality of the sequence of stages which we found. Figure 1 presents the age trends for middle-class urban boys in the United States, Taiwan, and Mexico. At age ten in each country, the order of use of each stage is the same as the order of its difficulty or maturity. In the United States, by age sixteen the order is the reverse, from the highest to the lowest, except that Stage 6 is still little used. The results in Mexico and Taiwan are the same, except that development is a little slower. The most conspicuous feature is that at the age of sixteen, Stage 5 thinking is much more salient in the United States than in Mexico or Taiwan. Nevertheless, it is present in the other countries, so we know that this is not purely an American democratic construct.

Why should there be such a universal invariant sequence of development? In answering this question, we need first to analyze these developing social concepts in terms of their internal logical structure. At each stage, the same basic moral concept or aspect is defined, but at each higher stage this definition is more differentiated, more integrated, and more general or universal. When one's concept of human life moves from Stage 1 to Stage 2 the value of life becomes more differentiated from the value of property, more integrated (the value of life enters an organizational hierarchy where it is "higher" than property so that one steals property in order to save life) and more universalized (the life of any sentient being is valuable regardless of status or property). The same advance is true at each stage in the hierarchy. Each step of development, then, is a better cognitive organization than the one before it, one which takes account of everything present in the previous stage, but making new distinctions and organizing them into a more comprehensive or more equilibrated structure.

What is the relation of moral stage development in adolescence to cognitive stage development? In Piaget's and our view, both types of thought and types of valuing (or of feeling) are schemata which develop a set of general structural characteristics representing successive forms of psychological equilibrium. The equilibrium of affective and interpersonal schemata, justice or fairness, involves many

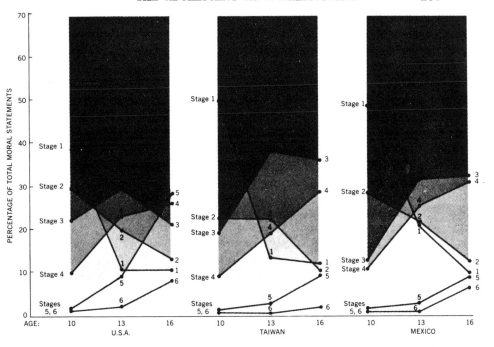

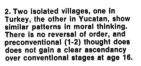

1. Middle-class urban boys in the U.S., Taiwan and Mexico (*above*). At age 10 the stages are used according to difficulty. At age 13, Stage 3 is most used by all three groups. At age 16 U.S. boys have reversed the order of age 10 stages (with the exception of 6). In Taiwan and Mexico, conventional (3-4) stages prevail at age 16, with Stage 5 also little used.

2. Two isolated villages, one in Turkey, the other in Yucatan, show similar patterns in moral thinking. There is no reversal of order, and preconventional (1-2) thought does does not gain a clear ascendancy over conventional stages at age 16.

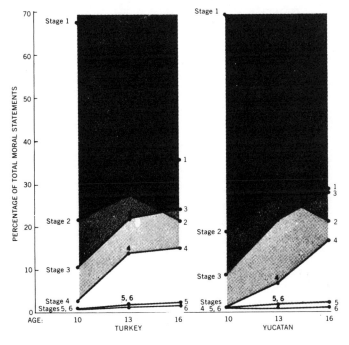

of the same basic structural features as the equilibrium of cognitive schemata logicality. Justice (portrayed as balancing the scales) is a form of equilibrium between conflicting interpersonal claims, so that "in contrast to a given rule imposed upon the child from outside, the rule of justice is an imminent condition of social relationships or a law governing their equilibrium."[17]

What is being asserted, then, is not that moral judgment stages are cognitive—they are not the mere application of logic to moral problems—but that the existence of moral stages implies that normal development has a basic cognitive-structural component.

The Piagetian rationale just advanced suggests that cognitive maturity is a necessary, but not a sufficient condition for moral judgment maturity. While formal operations may be necessary for principled morality, one may be a theoretical physicist and yet not make moral judgments at the principled level.

As noted in the previous section, Kuhn, Langer, and Kohlberg found that 60 per cent of persons over sixteen had attained formal operational thinking (by their particular measures). Only 10 per cent of subjects over sixteen showed clear principled (Stages 5 and 6) thinking, but all these 10 per cent were capable of formal-operational logical thought. More generally, there is a point-to-point correspondence between Piaget logical and moral judgment stages, as indicated in table 2. The relation is that attainment of the logical stage is a necessary but not sufficient condition for attainment of the moral stage. As we shall note in the next section, the fact that many adolescents have formal logical capacities without yet having developed the corresponding degree of moral judgment maturity is a particularly important background factor in some of the current dilemmas of adolescents.

Adolescent Questioning and the Problem of Relativity of Truth and Value

The cornerstone of a Piagetian interpretation of adolescence is the dramatic shift in cognition from concrete to formal operations by which old conceptions of the world are restructured in terms of a new philosophy. Piaget defined the preschool child as a philosopher, revolutionizing child psychology by demonstrating that the child at each stage of development actively organizes his experience and makes sense of the physical and social world with which he interacts in terms of the classical categories and questions of philos-

Table 2.   Relations between Piaget logical stages and
Kohlberg moral stages.
(all relations are that attainment of the logical stages is necessary,
but not sufficient, for attainment of the moral stage)

Logical stage	Moral stage
Symbolic, intuitive thought	*Stage 0:* The good is what I want and like.
Concrete operations, Substage 1 Categorical classification	*Stage 1:* Punishment-obedience orientation.
Concrete operations, Substage 2 Reversible concrete thought	*Stage 2:* Instrumental hedonism and concrete reciprocity.
Formal operations, Substage 1 Relations involving the inverse of the reciprocal	*Stage 3:* Orientation to interpersonal relations of mutuality.
Formal operations, Substage 2	*Stage 4:* Maintenance of social order, fixed rules, and authority.
Formal operations, Substage 3	*Stage 5A:* Social contract, utilitarian law-making perspective.
	Stage 5B: Higher law and conscience orientation.
	Stage 6: Universal ethical principle orientation.

ophers concerning space, time, causality, reality, and so on. It is, however, only in adolescence that the child becomes a philosopher in the formal or traditional sense. This emergence of philosophic questioning has been studied most carefully in the moral realm.

The transition from preconventional to conventional morality generally occurs during the late elementary school years. The shift in adolescence from concrete to formal operations, the ability now to see the given as only a subset of the possible and to spin out the alternatives, constitutes the necessary precondition for the transition from conventional to principled moral reasoning. It is in adolescence, then, that the child has the cognitive capability for moving from a conventional to a postconventional, reflective, or philosophic view of values and society.

The rejection of conventional moral reasoning begins with the perception of relativism, the awareness that any given society's definition of right and wrong, however legitimate, is only one among many, both in fact and theory. To clarify the issue of moral relativism as perceived by an adolescent, we will consider some adolescent responses to the following dilemma:

In Europe, a woman was near death from a very bad disease, a special kind of cancer. There was one drug that the doctors thought might save her. It was a form of radium that a druggist in the same town had recently discovered. The drug was expensive to make, but the druggist was charging ten times what the drug cost him to make. He paid $200 for the radium and charged $2,000 for a small dose of the drug. The sick woman's husband, Heinz, went to everyone he knew to borrow the money, but he could only get together about $1,000 which was half of what it cost. He told the druggist that his wife was dying, and asked him to sell it cheaper or let him pay later. But the druggist said, "No, I discovered the drug and I'm going to make money from it." Heinz got desperate and broke into the man's store to steal the drug for his wife.

Should the husband have done that? Was it right or wrong? Bob, a junior in a liberal private high school, says:

There's a million ways to look at it. Heinz had a moral decision to make. Was it worse to steal or let his wife die? In my mind I can either condemn him or condone him. In this case I think it was fine. But possibly the druggist was working on a capitalist morality of supply and demand.

I went on to ask Bob, "Would it be wrong if he did not steal it?"

It depends on how he is oriented morally. If he thinks it's worse to steal than to let his wife die, then it would be wrong what he did. It's all relative, what I would do is steal the drug. I can't say that's right or wrong or that it's what everyone should do.

Bob started the interview by wondering if he could answer because he "questioned the whole terminology, the whole moral bag." He goes on:

But then I'm also an incredible moralist, a real puritan in some sense and moods. My moral judgment and the way I perceive things morally changes very much when my mood changes. When I'm in a cynical mood, I take a cynical view of morals, but still whether I like it or not, I'm terribly moral in the way I look at things. But I'm not too comfortable with it.

Here are some other juniors from an upper-middle-class public high school:

Dan: Immoral is strictly a relative term which can be applied to almost any thought on a particular subject . . . if you have a man and a woman in bed, that is immoral as opposed to if you were a Roman a few thousand years ago and you were used to orgies all the time, that would not be immoral. Things vary so when you call something immoral, it's relative to that society at that time and it varies frequently. [Are there any circumstances in which wrong in some abstract moral sense would be applicable?] Well, in that sense, the only thing I could find wrong would be when you were hurting somebody against their will.

Elliot: I think one individual's set of moral values is as good as the next individual's . . . I think you have a right to believe in what you believe in, but I don't think you have a right to enforce it on other people.

John: I don't think anybody should be swayed by the dictates of society. It's probably very much up to the individual all the time and there's no general principle except when the views of society seem to conflict with your views and your opportunities at the moment and it seems that the views of society don't really have any basis as being right and in that case, most people, I think, would tend to say forget it and I'll do what I want.

The high school students just quoted are, from the point of view of moral stage theory, in a transitional zone. They understand and can use conventional moral thinking, but view it as arbitrary and relative. They do not yet have any clear understanding of, or commitment to, moral principles which are universal, which have a claim to some nonrelative validity. Insofar as they see any "principles" as nonrelative, it is the principle of "do your own thing, and let others do theirs." This "principle" has a close resemblance to the "principles" characteristic of younger children's Stage 2 instrumental egoistic thinking. The following examples of a ten-year-old naïve egoist and a college student transition relativistic response are more clearly of this instrumental egoistic form.

Jimmy (American city, age 10): It depends on how much he loved his wife. He should if he does. [If he doesn't love her much?] If he wanted her to die, I don't think he should. [Would it be right to steal?] In a way it's right because he knew his wife would die if he didn't and it would be right to save her. [Does the druggist have the right to charge that much if no law?] Yes, it's his drug, look at all he's got invested in it. [Should the judge punish?] He should put him in jail for stealing and he should put the druggist in because he charged so much and the drug didn't work.

Roger (Berkeley Free Speech Movement student, age 20): He was a victim of circumstances and can only be judged by other men whose varying value and interest frameworks produce subjective decisions which are neither permanent nor absolute. The same is true of the druggist. I'd do it. As far as duty, a husband's duty is up to the husband to decide, and anybody can judge him, and he can judge anybody's judgment. If he values her life over the consequences of theft, he should do it. [Did the druggist have a right?] One can talk about rights until doomsday and never say anything. Does the lion have a right to the zebra's life when he starves? When he wants sport? Or when he will take it at will? Does he consider rights? Is man so different? [Should he be punished by the judge?] All this could be avoided if the people would organize a planned economy. I think the judge should let him go, but if he does, it will provide less incentive for the poorer people to organize.

Relativity, Moral Stages, and Ego Identity

We first came across extreme relativist responses in some of our longitudinal subjects shortly after college entrance in the early sixties.[18] At that time, we interpreted their responses as a regression to Stage 2 thinking. Fifteen per cent of our college bound male students who were a mixture of conventional (Stage 4) and social-compact-legalist (Stage 5) thought at the end of high school, "retrogressed" to an apparent Stage 2 instrumentalist pattern in college.

In terms of behavior, everyone of our retrogressed subjects had high moral character ratings in high school, as defined by both teachers and peers. In college at least half had engaged in anticonventional acts of a more or less delinquent sort. As an example a Stage 2 Nietzschean had been the most respected high school student council president in years. In his college sophomore interview, however, he told how two days before he had stolen a gold watch from a friend at work. He had done so, he said, because his friend was just too good, too Christ-like, too trusting, and he wanted to teach him what the world was like. He felt no guilt about the stealing, he said, but he did feel frustrated. His act had failed, he said, because his trusting friend insisted he lost or mislaid the watch and simply refused to believe it had been stolen.

The forces of development which led our 20 per cent from upstanding conventional morality to Raskolnikov moral defiance eventually set them all to right. Every single one of our "retrogressors" had returned to a Stage 5 morality by age twenty-five, with more Stage 5 social-contract principle, less Stage 4 or convention, than in high school. All, too, were conventionally moral in behavior, at least as far as we can observe them. In sum, this 20 per cent was among the highest group at high school, was the lowest in college, and again among the highest at twenty-five.

In other words, moral relativism and nihilism, no matter how extensive, seemed to be a transitional attitude in the movement from conventional to principled morality.

Cognitive Moral Stages and Ego-Identity

In considering further the meaning of relativism in adolescence, it is helpful to relate logical and moral stages to Erikson's stages of ego-identity. Logical and moral stages are structures of thought through which the child moves sequentially. Erikson's stages are rather segments of the life histories of individuals; they define the central concerns of persons in a developmental period. An adolescent does not know or care that he is moving from concrete to formal thought; he knows and cares that he is having an Erikson "identity crisis."

Cognitive-developmental stages are stages of structure, not of content. The stages tell us *how* the child thinks concerning good and bad, truth, love, sex, and so forth. They do not tell us *what* he thinks about, whether he is preoccupied with morality or sex or achievement. They do not tell us what is on the adolescent's mind, but only how he thinks about what is on his mind. The dramatic changes in adolescence are not changes in structure, but changes in content. The adolescent need not know or care he is going from conventional to principled moral thinking, but he does know and care that sex is on his mind. In this sense cognitive structural stages may be contrasted with both psychosexual and Eriksonian stages.[19]

When we turn to Erikson's ego stages, we are partly dealing with a logical sequence as in logical and moral stages. Within Erikson's stages is the logical necessity that every later disposition presupposes each prior disposition, that each is a differentiation of prior dispositions. Erikson's ego stage centers around a series of forms of self-esteem (or their inverse, negative self-esteem). The first polarity trust-mistrust is one in which self and other are not differentiated. Trust is a positive feeling about self-and-other; mistrust is a negative feeling. The next polarity, autonomy versus shame, involves the self-other differentiation. Autonomy is a trust in the self (as opposed to the other); shame is a depreciation of self in the eyes of another whose status remains intact. Shame, however, is itself a failure to differentiate what one is from what one is in the eyes of the other, a differentiation implied in the sense of guilt. Similarly, initiative (I can be like him, it's all right to be or do it) is a differentiation from autonomy (I can do it). Such sequential progressive differentiations in self-esteem are involved throughout the Erikson stages. While there is an inherent logical (as opposed to biological) sequence to the Erikson ego stages, they are not hierarchical in the way cognitive stages are. Resolutions of identity problems are not also resolutions of trust or initiative problems, that is, each of the earlier problems and dispositions persists rather than being integrated into or being hierarchically dominated by the next. As a result, when we turn to Erikson's stages as defining focal concerns, we have a stage scheme which is so multidimensional as to resist empirical proof in the sense in which Piagetian stages may be proved. Ultimately the Erikson stages are "ideal-typical" in Weber's sense. They are not universal abstractions from data, but purifications and exaggerations of typical life histories. They do not predict regularities in the data, they aid in establishing historical connections in case histories. As Erikson uses his stage schema, it helps to suggest historical connections in a particular life, like Luther's. The truth of the stage schema is not in question; the truth of particular historical connections is. The stage schema helps select and illuminate these historical connections. In this sense, the stage of identity formation is not a step in an abstract but observable universal sequence, but is an ideal-typical characterization for a concrete historical period of adolescence.

As such, it need not have any exact logical relation to logical and moral stages, as they must to one another. While Erikson's stages cannot be defined, measured, or logically handled in the same sense as cognitive-developmental stages, suggestive empirical relations between ego-identity terms and moral stages are found.

M. H. Podd[20] gave an ego-identity interview to 134 male college juniors and seniors as well as the moral judgment interview. Following J. E. Marcia,[21] the identity interview covered occupational choice, religious beliefs, and political ideology. "Crisis" and "commitment" are assessed in each of these areas and serve to define each identity status. When an individual undergoes active consideration of alternative goals and values he is said to have experienced a "crisis." "Commitment" is the extent to which an individual has invested himself in his choices. The identity statuses operationally defined are: (1) identity achievement—has gone through a crisis and is committed; (2) moratorium—is in crisis with vague commitments; (3) foreclosure—has experienced no crisis but is committed to goals and values of parents or significant others; (4) identity diffusion—has no commitment regardless of crisis.

Subjects in the Podd study could be grouped into three major groups, the conventional (Stages 3 and 4), the principled (Stages 5 and 6), and the transitional. The transitional subjects could in turn be divided into two groups, those who were a combination of conventional and principled thinking and the extreme relativists who rejected conventional thought and used more instrumental egoistic ("Stage 2") modes. Two-thirds of the principled subjects had an "identity achievement" status. So too did about 40 per cent of the conventional subjects, the remainder being mainly in "identity foreclosure" (a status missing among the principled). None of the morally transitional subjects had an identity achievement status, and very few had foreclosed identity questioning.

Essentially, then, morally transitional subjects were in transition with regard to identity issues as well as moral issues. Stated slightly differently, to have questioned conventional morality you must have questioned your identity as well, though you may continue to hold a conventional moral position after having done so.

The impact of the Podd study is that the relativistic questioning of conventional morality and conventional reality associated with logical and moral stage development is also central to the adolescent's identity concerns. As a corollary, morally conventional subjects have a considerable likelihood of never having an identity crisis or an identity questioning at all. Erikson's picture of an adolescent stage of identity crisis and its resolutions, then, is a picture dependent upon attainment of formal logical thought and of questioning of conventional morality. It fits best, then, the picture of adolescence in the developmentally elite and needs further elaboration for other adolescents.

Historical Change in Adolescent Relativism

We have linked adolescent relativism to a transition from conventional to principled morality, associated with identity crisis. This picture emerged most clearly from our longitudinal data from the late fifties and early sixties reported in the Kohlberg and Kramer article (see note 18). In this data only a small minority of college students entered a phase of moral nihilism and relativism in the transition from conventional to principled morality. Typically they attempted to construct or select an ideology of their own in this transitional phase, ideologies which ranged from Nietzschean racism to Ayn Rand objectivism to early S.D.S. New Left formulations. In these college subjects of the early sixties it was possible to see an intense identity crisis, in Erikson's terms. These college relativist-egoists were rare, and they all seemed to have been moralistic and guilt prone in high school. As part of their identity crisis, they seem to have had strong problems in freeing themselves from childhood moral expectations and guilt.

There were two universal developmental challenges to conventional morality to which these "regressors" were also responding: first, the relativity of moral expectations and opinion; second, the gap between conventional moral expectations and actual moral behavior. It is clear that these developmental challenges are universal challenges; the integration of one's moral ideology with the facts of moral diversity and inconsistency is a general "developmental task" of youth in an open society; its solution is the formation of a universal principled morality.

For our extreme relativists or amoralists, there seemed to be an additional task in the need to free themselves from their own early "rigid" morality. In Erikson's terms our retrogressors were living in a late adolescent psychosocial moratorium, in which new and nonconforming patterns of thought and behavior are tried out. Their return to morality or moral thought is the eventual confirmation of an earlier identification as one's own identity. To find a sociomoral identity requires a rebellious moratorium, because it requires liberation of initiative from the guilt from which our retrogressors suffer. At the "stage" of identity the adult conforms to his standards because he wants to, not because he anticipates crippling guilt if he does not.

By the 1970's the extreme doubt and relativism which earlier characterized only a minority of college students appears both earlier and much more pervasively. It is now sometimes found toward the end of high school.[22] In our own Harvard undergraduate course for freshmen and sophomores, about two-thirds of the students assert that there are no such things as valid moral rules or principles, no objective sense in which one thing is morally better than another. It appears that a majority rather than a minority of adolescents now are aware of relativism and of postconventional questioning, though it is still a minority who really attempt postconventional or principled solutions to these questions.

Parallel historical changes seem to have occurred in the relationship of extreme moral relativism to identity issues. Podd's findings from the *late* sixties differed from those of Kohlberg and Kramer in the *early* sixties in one important way. Kohlberg and Kramer found their extreme relativists, the Stage 2 or regressed subjects, in a condition of moratorium, in a state of "crisis" with vague and uncertain commitments. In contrast, Podd found them in a condition of identity diffusion with no sense of commitment and not necessarily a sense of crisis. In other words, extreme relativism no longer appeared to be a temporary ego-developmental maneuver of a small group of subjects in crisis, but rather to represent a more stable, less crisis-like pattern of low commitment. It seems likely to us that the psychological meaning of extreme relativism had changed in the five to ten years between the data reported by Kohlberg and Kramer (1969). Extreme relativism is no longer the struggle for independence from a strongly internal conventional morality in a period of moratorium and crisis in one's identity.

The relativistic rejection of convention, once individuality and spontaneously developed by adolescents in the course of reflecting on their own experience, is now manufactured as a cultural industry called the "counterculture." Further, the adult culture itself offers a very unsteady counter to the counterculture, particularly from the viewpoint of the adolescent to whom it offers a dwindling number of jobs and a world already overcrowded and crying out for less rather than more. It is clearly seen that one result of affluence, technology, and increased longevity has been to decrease the need of the adult community for its adolescents. Instead, it has some stake in keeping them in the youth culture since in one sense they only further threaten an already defensive adult world with fewer jobs and still more people. Thus the adults at once produce and market a counterculture and present themselves as a less than appealing alternative to it.

From the point of view of the adolescent, the counterculture has other meanings. The rejection of the conventional culture can be seen as a rebellion which can either turn into submission spelled backwards, or into the formation of principles. In our terms, the former remains conventional in form with only the content changed by being stood on its head. Although the impetus for the counterculture may have been once either principled or the expression of young people in identity crisis, the manufacture of the counterculture transforms it into yet another conventional system, although one lacking the solidity of the traditional conventional society.

While only a minority of adolescents actually have a postconventional view of morality and society, many more live in a postconventional culture or society. As a specific example, the majority of a sample of Haight-Ashbury hippies[23] emerge as mixtures of preconventional Stage 2 and conventional Stage 3 thinking. While hippie culture appears to be postconventional, it is almost entirely a mixture of Stage 2 "do your own thing" and Stage 3 "be nice, be loving" themes. The hippie culture continually questions conventional morality but on Stage 3 grounds of its being harsh and mean, or Stage 2 grounds of "Why shouldn't I have fun?" rather than in terms of its irrationality. Many hippies, then, belong to a counterculture which is largely conventional in its appeal but which lacks the solidarity of traditional conventional society and is not embedded in it. As moral counterculture, the hippie culture differs primarily from the conventional culture in its extreme relativism and consequent fluidity, not in any positive forms of moral thought different from the conventional.

In most eras of the past, the adolescent went through questioning of value, meaning, and truth in a world of adults apparently oblivious to these doubts. Reflective adolescents have always considered adults as benighted for accepting conventional norms and imposing them on youth, for never doubting the truth and goodness of their world. The questioning adolescent has always seen the adult acceptance of the conventional social world as reflecting the hypocrisy, insensitivity, and dreariness of the adult. Equally, the questioning adolescent has always expected to remake the adult world nearer to his heart's desire, and at given moments in history has succeeded. What is new is the creation of a questioning culture providing half-answers to which adolescents are exposed prior to their own spontaneous questioning.

The adolescent is faced then with not one but two cultures offering alternative ideologies and ways to live. Both present resolutions to the postconventional doubt which now appears to be so pervasive. Both may be embraced in our sense conventionally for the set of answers they provide, or may be seen in principled terms, their validity as social systems resting on the principles of justice they more or less successfully embody.

Implications for Education

The extreme relativism of a considerable portion of high school adolescents provides both a threat to current educational practice and a potentiality for a new focus of education.

We said earlier that the five-to-seven shift has been traditionally represented in education by the beginning of formal schooling. The traditional educational embodiment of the adolescent shift has been a different one, that of a two-track educational system dividing adolescents into two groups, an elite capable of abstract thought and hence of profiting from a liberal education and the masses who are not. At first, this division was made between the wealthy and those who went to work. As public high schools developed, the tracking system instead became that of an academic school or lycee leading to the university and a vocational school. The clearest formulation of this two-track system as based on the dawn of abstract thought was found in the British 11+ system. Based on his score on an intelligence test given at the dawn of adolescence, a child was assigned to either a grammar (academic) or a modern (vocational-commercial) high school.

The aristocratic tracking system just described rested on the assumption that the capacity for abstract thought is all or none, that it appears at a fixed age, and that it is hereditarily limited to an elite group in the population. The evidence on formal operational thought does not support these assumptions. However, when democratic secondary education ignored the existence of the adolescent cognitive shift and individual differences in their attainment, real difficulties emerged. Most recently this ignoral occurred in the wave of high school curriculum reform of the late fifties and early sixties in America, the "new math," the "new science," and the "new social studies." These curricula reforms were guided by the notion that more intellectual content could be put into high school and that this content should not be factual content and rote skills, but the basic pattern of thinking of the academic disciplines of mathematics, physics, or social science. The focus was to be upon understanding the basic logical assumptions and structure of the discipline and the use of these assumptions in reflective or critical thinking and problem-solving. Clearly the new curricula assumed formal-operational thought, rather than attempting to develop it. Partly as a result of this ignoral, some of the most enlightened proponents of the new curricula became discouraged as they saw only a subgroup of the high school population engaging with it. The solution we have proposed is that the new curricula be reformulated as tools for developing principled logical and moral thought rather than presupposing it.[24]

Experimental work by our colleagues and ourselves[25] has shown that even crude efforts based on such objectives are challenging and are successful in inducing considerable upward stage movement in thought. Hopefully, our efforts are the beginning of reformulating the "new" high school science, mathematics, social studies, and literature as approaches using "disciplines" as vehicles for the stimulation of the development of thought, rather than making young Ph.D.'s.

The difficulties and failures of the new curricula and of the general movement to democratize higher learning or liberal education, then, is not due to hereditary differences in capacity used to justify the two-track system. They represent, instead, the failure of secondary education to take developmental psychology seriously. When stage development is taken seriously by educators as an aim, real developmental change can occur through education.

In saying this, we return to the thought of John Dewey which is at the heart of a democratic educational philosophy. According to Dewey, education was the stimulation of development through stages by providing opportunities for active thought and active organization of experience.

The only solid ground of assurance that the educator is not setting up impossible artificial aims, that he is not using ineffective and perverting methods, is a clear and definite knowledge of the normal end and focus of mental action. Only knowledge of the order and connection of the stages in the development of the psychical functions can, negatively, guard against those evils, or positively, insure the full maturation and free, yet, orderly, exercises of the physical powers. Education is precisely the work of supplying the conditions which will enable the psychical functions, as they successively arise, to mature and pass into higher functions in the freest and fullest manner. This result can be secured only by a knowledge of the process of development, that is only by a knowledge of "psychology."[26]

Besides a clear focus on development, an aspect of Dewey's educational thought which needs revival is that school experience must be and represent real life experience in stimulating development. American education in the twentieth century was shaped by the victory of Thorndike over Dewey. Achievement rather than development has been its aim. But now the achieving society, the achieving individual, and even the achievement tests are seriously questioned, by adults and adolescents alike. If development rather than achievement is to be the aim of education, such development must be meaningful or real to the adolescent himself. In this sense education must be sensed by the adolescent as aiding him in his search for identity, and it must deal with life. Neither a concern with self or with life are concerns opposed to intellectuality or intellectual development. The opposition of "intellect" and "life" is itself a reflection of the two-track system in which a long period of academic education provided a moratorium for leisurely self-crystallization of an adult role identity by the elite while the masses were to acquire an early adult vocational identity, either through going to work or through commitment to a vocation in a vocational high school.

Our discussion of adolescent relativism and identity diffusion suggests that the two tracks are both breaking down and fusing. Vocational goals are evaded by relativism and counterculture questioning as are deferred goals of intellectual development. An identity crisis and questioning are no longer the prerogative of the elite, and they now occur earlier and without the background of logical and moral development they previously entailed. If the high school is to have meaning it must take account of this, which means it must take account of the adolescent's current notion of himself and his identity. Like most psychologists, most adolescents think the self has little to do with intellectual or moral development. The relativistic adolescent is content to answer "myself" to questions as to the source and basis of value and meaning. Like most psychologists he tends to equate the content of self-development with the ego, with self-awareness, with identity. The other pole of ego or self-development, however, is that of new awareness of the world and values; it is the awareness of new meanings in life.

We discussed the moral strand of ego development, which is clearly philosophical. We have also noted aesthetic, religious, metaphysical, and epistemological concepts and values born in adolescence. One side of ego development is the structure of the self-concept and the other side is the individual's concept of the true, the good, the beautiful, and the real. If education is to promote self-development, ego development must be seen as one side of an education whose other side consists of the arts and sciences as philosophically conceived. We have pointed to the need for defining the aims of teaching the arts and sciences in developmental terms. In this sense one basic aim of teaching high school science and mathematics is to stimulate the stage of principled or formal-operational logical thought, of high school social studies, the stimulation of principled moral judgment. A basic aim of teaching literature is the development of a stage or level of aesthetic comprehension, expression, judgment. Behind all of these developmental goals lie moral and philosophic dimensions of the meaning of life, which the adolescent currently questions and the school needs to confront. The adolescent is a philosopher by nature, and if not by nature, by countercultural pressure. The high school must have, and represent, a philosophy if it is to be meaningful to the adolescent. If the high school is to offer some purposes and meanings which can stand up to relativistic questioning, it must learn philosophy.

178   LAWRENCE KOHLBERG / CAROL GILLIGAN

S. H. White, "Some General Outlines of the Matrix of Developmental Changes Between Five to Seven Years," *Bulletin of the Orton Society,* 20 (1970), 41-57.

L. Kohlberg, "Early Education: A Cognitive-Developmental Approach," *Child Development,* 39 (December 1968), 1013-1062; A. R. Jensen, "How Much Can We Boost I.Q. and Scholastic Achievement?" *Harvard Educational Review,* 39 (1969), 1-123.

R. Scheffler, "The Development of Children's Orientations to Fantasy in the Years 5 to 7," unpublished Ph.D. dissertation, Harvard University, 1971.

L. Kohlberg, "Moral Education in the School," *School Review,* 74 (1966), 1-30; Kohlberg, "Early Education."

Kohlberg, "Moral Education in the School."

Ibid.

Cognitive stage maturity is different from I.Q., a separate factor, though the two are correlated. (See L. Kohlberg and R. DeVries, "Relations between Piaget and Psychometric Assessments of Intelligence," in C. Lavatelli, ed., *The Natural Curriculum* [Urbana: University of Illinois Press, 1971].) General impoverishment of organized physical and social stimulation leads to retardation in stage development. Culturally disadvantaged children tend to be somewhat retarded compared to middle-class children with the same I.Q.'s in concrete-operational logic. Experimental intervention can to some extent accelerate cognitive development if it is based on providing experiences of cognitive conflict which stimulate the child to reorganize or rethink his patterns of cognitive ordering.

Kohlberg, "Early Education."

Kohlberg, "Moral Education in the School."

10. C. Ellinwood, "Structural Development in the Expression of Emotion by Children," unpublished Ph.D. dissertation, University of Chicago, 1969.

11. E. A. Peel, *The Psychological Basis of Education,* 2d ed. (Edinburgh and London: Oliver and Boyd, 1967).

12. D. Kuhn, J. Langer, and L. Kohlberg, "The Development of Formal-Operational Thought: Its Relation to Moral Judgment," unpublished paper, 1971.

13. Another example of transitional stage response is success on the question: "Joe is shorter than Bob, Joe is taller than Alex, who is the tallest?" The transitional child can solve this by the required reversing of relations and serial ordering of them but will fail the pendulum task.

14. Wordsworth's note to ode on *Intimations of Immortality* quoted in Lionel Trilling *The Liberal Imagination* (New York: Viking, 1941).

15. Kohlberg, "Moral Education in the School."

16. Taken from Kuhn, Langer, and Kohlberg, "The Development of Formal-Operational Thought."

17. J. Piaget, *The Moral Judgment of the Child* (Glencoe, Ill.: Free Press, 1948; originally published in 1932).

18. L. Kohlberg and R. Kramer, "Continuities and Discontinuities in Childhood and Adult Moral Development," *Human Development,* 12 (1969), 93-120.

19. J. Loevinger, "The Meaning and Measurement of Ego Development," *American Psychology* (1966), 195-206.

20. M. H. Podd, "Ego Identity Status and Morality: An Empirical Investigation of Two Developmental Concepts," unpublished Ph.D. dissertation, 1969.

21. J. E. Marcia, "Development and Validation of Ego Identity Status," *Journal of Personality and Social Psychology,* 3 (1966), 551-558.

22. C. Gilligan, L. Kohlberg, and J. Lerner, "Moral Reasoning About Sexual Dilemmas: A Developmental Approach," in L. Kohlberg and E. Turiel, eds., *Recent Research in Moral Development* (New York: Holt, Rinehart and Winston, 1972).

23. N. Haan and C. Holstein, unpublished data, 1971.

24. L. Kohlberg and A. Lockwood, "Cognitive-Developmental Psychology and Political Education: Progress in the Sixties," speech for Social Science Consortium Convention, Boulder, Colorado, 1970; L. Kohlberg and E. Turiel, "Moral Development and Moral Education," in G. Lesser, ed., *Psychology and Educational Practice* (Chicago: Scott, Foresman, 1971).

25. L. Kohlberg and M. Blatt, "The Effects of Classroom Discussion on Level of Moral Judgment," in Kohlberg and Turiel, eds., *Recent Research in Moral Development.*

26. J. Dewey, *On Education: Selected Writing,* ed. R. D. Archambault (New York: The Modern Library, republished 1964).

EDWARD C. MARTIN

Reflections on the Early Adolescent in School

EARLY ADOLESCENTS in America spend, for better or worse, considerable time in school. The problems and tensions, as well as the pleasures and growth, of these youngsters manifest themselves there. Those of us who teach in these schools witness much, some of which we understand, some of which we do not. In those chatty moments in the teachers' lounge we talk glibly about the terrible eight's (eighth graders) in much the same way parents will talk about the terrible two's. We also talk about the naïveté and enthusiasm of seventh graders and the growing responsibility and pseudoworldliness of ninth graders. These are gross impressions but nonetheless express the view of most adults, that early adolescence is a hard age to understand, one characterized by rapid change and confusion.

The perspective of the youngsters themselves must also be part of the general picture. They feel keenly the stresses and strains that confront them. They seem to think that there is something better ahead to look forward to; and also something better behind that they may have lost.

While on the subject of perspective the reader should know more about my own. I taught high school for seven years prior to four years of junior high teaching. My perceptions of the early adolescent come fundamentally from the contrast between the students I taught in these two age groups. Obviously I can speak only about these students. The reader must judge how accurately my descriptions fit other situations. I hasten to add that the community in which I taught was a ring city of Boston, classified by most as a comfortable suburb, but with many more poor people than it liked to admit, and considerable religious and ethnic diversity.

I

When I moved from high school to junior high school teaching

180

I was an experienced teacher with a recognized reputation for good performance. I went to my class of eighth graders with confidence and the nervousness I always feel at the beginning of a school year. After forty-five minutes I knew I had entered a different world and would have to begin learning about teaching again. This time I had other reasons to be nervous. These were people who were different from the fifteen- to eighteen-year-olds I had been teaching.

On Being a Twitch

The most obvious differences are physical, not just the tremendous disparity of sizes (with most girls towering over many of the boys) nor that early pubescent body, but a general twitchiness. Movement was the standard—tapping of hands or fingers, wiggling bodies, turning heads, bouncing, jiggling, squirming. These were not the exuberant and free movements of small children, nor the coordinated and powerful movements of youth, but rather an uncontrolled display and use of body.

This physical confusion was often matched by a general sense of intellectual and emotional confusion. One of my boys sat and read through class after class. His parents told me that was all he ever did at home. This was not the reading that comes from boredom with class, but seemed to be a way for him to detach himself from external reality. His parents and guidance counselor were worried about this behavior and wanted him to be more outgoing. I saw their point but let him read in my class because he seemed to want or need some time alone to resolve a confusion he did not understand or wish to divulge. Other confusions were more overt, such as the girl who would alternately love and hate me, displaying both sentiments as actively as possible in class. She was not the sixteen-year-old who had some sense of her emotions and knew about crushes; this was a thirteen-year-old without subtlety and with much bravado. Then there was the boy who wanted to sit in the rear of the class. His confusion in school was quite typical but extreme. He never did his homework and rarely paid attention. I knew he was having trouble with his school work, but I did not find out, until two weeks after I should have, that he was reading on a fourth grade level while in the eighth grade, that his brother was in jail, and that his parents were in serious personal difficulty. Less dramatic but as serious to the individual was the girl who just could not understand. She worked so hard but could not put together her thoughts. Finally, there were always youngsters who had been sheltered from experience and found their more worldly peers frightening. These problems are only suggestive of the myriad of small and large confusions that are part of the lives of these youngsters.

On Being Full of Enthusiasm

Enthusiasm is much a part of the world of the early adolescents I have seen—the instant complete commitment to some person, idea, activity, or event, which may vanish just as quickly as it appears or consume what seems an inordinate amount of time and energy. Four months after I had stopped teaching a particular group of seventh grade students, I appeared in the school lunchroom where many from the class were eating. A cry went up "there's Mr. Martin" and suddenly I was surrounded by eight bubbling girls and boys all talking at once, all asking a string of questions about where I was and what I was doing. By the time I had recovered from the charge and my ego had hopelessly swelled, I realized I was alone again. The eight had returned to their other activities just as fast as they had come. That scenario was repeated on several different occasions during the rest of the year. It would not happen in the high school in which I taught. Even with the same intentions the scenario would read more like *Romeo and Juliet* than *A Midsummer Night's Dream*.

Having enthusiasm for people is very much a quality of this age, just as is the transient quality of those enthusiasms. In school work this applies more dramatically. Since I think this age often works best in small groups of four to six, I organize most of my classes in this way. One of the greatest difficulties is that the initial enthusiasm that gets a student committed to working in one group ("I like so-and-so," or "that's an exciting subject") often disappears and you are besieged with requests to switch projects or groups. (As one of my colleagues explained to her classes, "I assign you to groups because the person you hate today you will probably love tomorrow.")

Almost as typical is the process of being consumed by some activity ranging from reading to sports to daydreaming. The oft-joked about boy who takes his bat and glove to bed with him is not unreal for this age. This kind of passion means putting everything else aside—a total commitment. Often this means not wanting

to find out about anything else. One of my more humorous encounters with this kind of enthusiasm came with a boy who liked
to draw airplanes (all over everything). I thought I could use his
interest in drawing to get him involved in the material we were
working on in class. I approached him with this proposal only to
be told he did not like to draw anything but airplanes.

Another aspect of this enthusiasm is a healthy lack of sophistication. Once involved, these students get really excited about
finding out something they did not know before. Learning is not taken
for granted, nor do they have the facility of high school students
for sorting experiences in a way that sifts out what is discontinuous
with established categories. The twelve-year-old often approaches
the world without set categories and can be both insufferable and
delightful in his refusal to screen out data. For example, one class
period I posted a half dozen 2 feet by 3 feet reproductions of
Breughel's *Flemish Fair,* a painting rich in detail. In groups of five
the class was to make a list of activities they observed in the picture
and sort these into categories such as children's games, religious
practices, eating and drinking, and so on. By my reckoning it would
take the groups about twenty minutes to list all the activities and
about ten minutes to sort them. One hour later group leaders
were running up to me excitedly stating they had just located
activity number 159 which was a boy eating an apple in the window
of one of the background houses of the picture. In the end, they
had so many items to sort that it became virtually impossible to
get reasonably meaningful groups. This kind of unbridled enthusiasm
makes teaching this age an exciting and sometimes overwhelming
experience.

"Dump"—an Example in Depth

Before the reader is left with the impression of youngsters who
are physically disconnected and mentally scattered, I must balance
this with a description of one series of classes which indicates
otherwise. There is a quite simple simulation which I call "Dump."
Students are given a map of a mythical town. Each student is
assigned one lot on the map and the town is then given the problem
of deciding where to put a new town incinerator. This simulation
provided a week's worth of activity and discussion in my class,
indicating that the enthusiasm of these twelve- and thirteen-year-
olds could result in an exciting and depthful educational experience
for the whole class. After explanation of the game and assignment

Town of Middleboro

Problem: Where do we build the incinerator?

The town of Middleboro has a rubbish disposal problem. Until now, everyone has taken care of his own trash, with the result that the town lands, the marsh, the quarry, pond, stream, beach, and forest have become quite littered, polluted, and unattractive. The store areas are dirty and infested with rodents. Individual burning of trash is becoming a health hazard.

Money has been assigned for the construction of a town incinerator. A town meeting is to be held to decide where it is to be built, and its location must have the approval of a majority of four-fifths of the members of the community.

Each child is to pretend to be the owner of one of the properties lettered A-Z, the dairy, golf course, garage, lumber yard, or gas station or to represent the school or the church. He is to shade in lightly with pencil his land on the map.

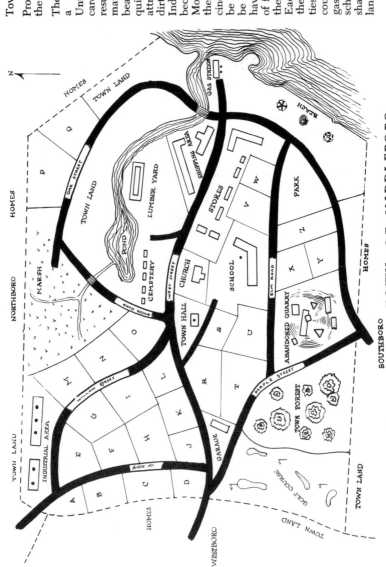

TOWN OF MIDDLEBORO

of lots, the decision process was thrown into a town meeting. After a chairman was selected to preside, the proposals began and with them the inevitable arguments pro and con for each position. Some of the issues raised were zoning, ecology, recreation needs, individual versus community rights, eminent domain, and even whether or not they had any obligation to the neighboring town. Conclusions were reached on some of these issues, not on others, and most frustrating, no decision could be made about the location of the incinerator. Before and after school and between classes the students carried on the debate with friends. Early in one class period at about the time I decided they had settled on the marsh as the site (against the protests of a few), the chairman called for a vote. The marsh site was resoundingly defeated. As is often the case, the teacher is the last to know why. As it turned out, just by chance the science teacher had shown a film on marsh life which had convinced the students to vote down the site as ecologically unsound. (As a side note, I am always impressed by how powerful such correlations can be and how rarely they are made in schools. Students see their activities in different subjects as disconnected pieces that do not fit into any puzzle.) With the marsh site ruled out, full-scale argument resumed with final resolution coming when the two central protagonists got together around an obscure and unmarked section of the map and agreed to put it up as a compromise spot. After the decision we spent one day discussing how the decision was reached and what and who influenced it. Although we moved on to other things, the "dump game" proved throughout the rest of the year a seminal referent for many discussions.

What the "dump" experience points out is how the enthusiasm of these youngsters can focus. They were involved in considering some important political, moral, and ethical issues. They handled them in a way that was intelligent, analytic, and purposeful. They responded to the moral issues and ideas with an openness and reflectiveness that is often rare with adults and later adolescents. The "dump" example also is important because of the quality of honesty displayed by students in the follow-up discussion. They talked with ease about sometimes voting as they did to be popular or to support a friend and with equal candor about how they felt if they were defeated.

The Beginnings of Discontent

Another cluster of characteristics of early adolescents is the beginning of discontent with self and others which expresses itself in anger, rebellion, and fear. The anger and rebellion is liable to be physical rather than verbal as in older students. Schools with this age student experience considerable physical fighting between students, often girls being as violent as boys. Anger against the adults in the school expresses itself in bursts which frequently end in tears. This anger is not focused as it is in high school students who can express what they do not like about schools, teachers, or classmates in logical and reasoned statements. The anger of the thirteen-year-old is highly emotional and usually short-lived. Because it is often unpredictable and highly charged it is difficult to deal with in a classroom. One cannot reason with an angry tearful girl or boy. Once I removed a boy from class for bothering another student. I asked him to wait in the hall until we could talk. Later we calmly discussed his actions and what to do about them. When I left for the day I noticed some writing on the wall just outside the classroom door. I had to look closely since it was so small. The half-inch letters were carefully traced over and over in a way that made them thicker each time. The message was simple: MARTIN SUCKS.

There is of course considerable discontent expressed about courses. Some complaints are relatively minor and part of the sparring between the young and the old: "How come we have to clean up the shop?" "Why can't we see more movies?" "Why do we have so much homework?" "How come we have to cover our books?" Other complaints, involving boredom and confusion, are more serious and often go unspoken: "Why are we studying this?" "Why is it important?" Often we do not treat these questions seriously enough or we fail to explain sufficiently our answers. This adds to the confusion. The main complaint of twelve- and thirteen-year-olds is not the *irrelevance* of their studies: it is rather that they are not let into the secret of the importance of what we ask them to study.

The discontent is often turned toward oneself at this age. The result is fear—a kind of fear that must be very hard to handle. A typical manifestation in school is the boy who refuses to go to gym because he will not take a shower in front of other boys or the girl who worries about beginning menstruation. These are personal fears which are part of the life in schools. Since they are hidden, we teachers often miss the less obvious ones. They involve not only fears of inadequacy but fears of other students—of being laughed at, or pushed around, or being isolated with no friends.

The Power of a Touch

Perhaps one final discovery I made about teaching thirteen-year-olds that first year will further clarify these rambling impressions. A teacher in high school rarely touches a student, although in these days of affective education and improvisational drama it is more common. The reasons are many, but centrally for a male teacher to touch a female student is liable to be seen as a sexual act. Everyone understands it as improper. Likewise, for a male teacher to touch a male student is also improper either for sexual or territorial reasons. These are cultural understandings in a school of fifteen- to eighteen-year-olds. When I started teaching twelve- and thirteen-year-olds I found it was quite the opposite. Touching these youngsters was a way of showing affection, of reasoning with a student, of showing trust and respect. It came to symbolize for me something about the need for both reliance and autonomy in these youngsters. I also learned to sense when a touch would be seen as demeaning and treating someone like a child, but I was not always able to hit this right because they are an unpredictable lot.

In the space of three years the change is drastic. At twelve (usually seventh grade) they are clearly on one side of limbo, at fourteen on the other. I always saw my high school students as people becoming adults. They had the size and shape of adults, the physical and mental abilities of adults; they were clearly becoming someone. Early adolescents are a different story. They are also in the process of becoming, but they move erratically back and forth between the world of childhood and the world of adolescence.

II

What is it like to be in school if you are twelve to fourteen years of age? What does and doesn't it mean to you? Before I attempt to deal with these questions one should know something about how I approach the school as an institution. The school, as we are all aware, is that institution created to house the young of America for at least ten years of their lives, 180 days each of those years, and six hours each of those days. School is also presently an institution that is under attack from a broad range of critics. The criticisms come from varied sources—professors, teachers, students, and parents; businessmen, laborers, and government officials; blacks, browns, and whites. They confront the schools with a wide range of complaints: "You must stop the drug problem," "sex education is a conspiracy," "poor children are not reading," "social studies is making children radical," "there isn't enough discipline in the schools," "school is irrelevant." In schools themselves there is a substantial sense of failure, the feeling that somehow schools are not meeting the ideals of helping every individual fulfill his or her potential. In this general context sits the American junior high school, essentially the great wasteland of the American public school system.

It is a wasteland for many reasons, not the least of which is that the structure of the junior high school, although theoretically designed specifically for this age group, in practice does very little other than put them physically together. Whatever real theoretical base existed has lost its power to shape the institution and no new set of ideals has taken its place to set a direction. In essence the junior high is seen as a transition point to the high school and as such the structure and program are often watered down high school schedules and courses. The schedule divides subjects into blocks of time with different teachers. In junior high schools with grades seven, eight, and nine, the ninth grade is considered the first year for high school graduation credits. The academic courses in the junior high are often seen as the *basic knowledge* needed if one will be successful in high school courses. For example, it is assumed that in eighth grade United States history students will learn the basic chronology which can be relied upon in the eleventh grade United States history course. At times this attitude is conveyed by the staffs of high schools to their colleagues in the junior high as "You teach the basic rote material so that we can get to some real thinking in our respective subject fields." Because of the hiring policies of many junior high schools, this condescending message is often accepted by junior high school teachers. Junior high schools are often composed of teachers who are considered by themselves or those who hire them as not quite qualified for the high school. Many try to prove themselves and wait around for a chance to "move up."

To complicate matters, the physical removal of twelve- to fourteen-year-olds into separate institutions has many serious negative aspects. They are already removed physiologically, emotionally, and intellectually from younger and older children and from adults. An eight-year-old is still clearly dependent on adults. A sixteen-year-old has the physical and emotional maturity to participate in the adult community. The twelve-year-old, caught in between, finds that his school further isolates him. This isolation seems to add to his confusion and disorientation.

What I am suggesting is that on top of a school system which is not functioning well we have one section of it that receives very little serious attention and energy on the part of the educational community. It is within this context that I will consider the central issues that concern twelve- to fourteen-year-olds in school. The reality is that no matter what our criticisms, the schools are significant (relevant if you will) and important to these children, sometimes in negative and destructive ways, sometimes in positive and constructive ways.

III

How do these students see school? The popular answer to this question has been provided by Edgar Friedenberg, John Holt, and now Charles Silberman: schools are perceived as irrelevant to the real needs of students and repressive of individuality and humanity. As an adult who has been involved in education all his life, I cannot basically disagree with this as an evaluation, but I do disagree that this is what junior high school students perceive. The wave of great discontent with American schools focuses on the high school. By the age of fourteen students entering high school have picked up the rhetoric and the real feelings and thoughts about how and why school is so bad. Before that age their perceptions are different, possibly because they are less focused, but mainly because their view of school is vastly different from either elementary or high school age students. Obviously I cannot speak for all children; I cannot speak for even those children I have taught. We are all impressionable and changeable; twelve-year-olds even more so. What I can do is give my perceptions of what the twelve- to fourteen-year-olds I know see in school—what they love about it and what they hate about it. *Love* and *hate* are their terms.

Fundamentally, for most American twelve-year-olds, school is *where it's at*. School occupies the time and concerns of all the people you know—your friends, your parents, people you meet.

People are always asking what you do in school and how you like school. School is often a source of contention between you and adults. Why did you get low grades? Why did you play hooky? Why don't you play school sports or join clubs or work harder or work less, and so forth? You are always telling people you don't like school, but often you don't mean it because school is comfortable and they at least want you around. Also you think school is important and even fun. But these things can't be said too openly.

On Being with One's Peers

Friends and enemies are a large part of school, perhaps the largest. One comes to school to see friends, one fears school because enemies are there also. Some of the most important parts of the school day are the walk or ride there, changing between classes, the few minutes before the class gets started, the study hall, and the end of school. These times are the intense periods of "seeing the other kids," or realizing you have no one to see. One of those unwritten rules of teaching is "begin the class on time." It makes the teacher appear efficient and purposeful and gives the task to be done a sense of importance. When I started teaching in junior high I still believed this rule, until I began to realize how much there is to learn about students by observing or participating in the three minutes before class started. (I can hear my radical educational friend now saying, "Ah-ha, the beginnings of a conversion experience.") Perhaps, but my interest in the friendship group has been not to join it but to figure out ways to tap it when it made sense to do so. The usual separation of the interests of these groups and the classroom is not necessarily a bad separation. Doing the peer group's thing all the time would be as deadly as doing the teacher's thing all the time.

The case of a student staying home, being ill, or skipping a class because he fears some group of students is more common than most adults imagine. Threats are used frequently by students although fortunately not often carried through. For two weeks a group of girls were harassing another girl in and out of classes. The girl under attack was literally terrified, although she sought to hold her ground by appearing casual and unafraid. When this failed she would seek the help of adults or just burst into tears. For the group of antagonists, this aggressiveness was a source of unity and camaraderie. They relished the times of confrontation and the times of subtle teasing. Individuals took pride and received group praise devising more exciting methods of taunting their foe. There was always the daring aspect of avoiding that line where the full force of adult intervention would be imposed. The several adults involved did not know what to do. One teacher tried to give some perspective on the situation by showing the long-run absurdity of such behavior, another by attempting disciplinary tactics—essentially tongue-lashing and keeping the aggressive group after school. The guidance counselor tried to talk it through with all the students involved. The situation improved on the surface, but we all knew the individual girl's fear remained and the group's resentment toward her and power over her continued. We also realized that there was very little we could do about it but make sure it did not become violent. I am always surprised at how brutal students this age can be toward each other. It reminds me again of how important a book Golding's novel *Lord of the Flies* is for teachers.

The intense friendship groupings in junior high obviously have another side—the youngster who has no friends, no group to which he has allegiance or which sees him as a part. Several kinds of students in my experience fall into this category and it means different things to each. John was an outgoing intellectual student who spoke in an affected way and assumed he had the right answers. Other students saw him as a "freak" and made it clear to him that was how they regarded him. Sharon was a quiet withdrawn girl who talked with no one and to whom no one talked. She seemed not to be bothered by this isolation. Bob was a class leader. He demanded everyone's attention and when he did not get it was bound to provoke it. Although the students saw him as an important person to be reckoned with, he was really not a part of any group. Adults at one time or another are isolated from others by choice or happenstance, but the isolation of a twelve-, thirteen-, or fourteen-year-old is particularly difficult. There is a pain brought on by not being like everyone else when it is important that you be like others. This comes at a time in physical, emotional, and intellectual development when change is so rapid that many individual youngsters are either behind or ahead of the mass of their peers. Aggravating these gaps is the intolerance of this age group toward diversity and their delight in making an issue over those who are different. The boy who does not start to spurt in physical stature is called a "shrimp" and sees himself as a shrimp. The girl who gets seriously interested in a boy does not quite fit with her giggly friends. The peer group of the twelve- to fourteen-year-old has most of the mechanisms of keeping members in line but often lacks the moral, ethical, and intellectual substance of the so-called "youth culture" of older students.

Before leaving the discussion of peer group, I should say a few things about sex. Twelve-year-olds hang around in groups by sex. It is a rare exception when a member of one sex risks associating with members of the opposite sex. The students make this issue an important one, for example, when they work in groups and strongly prefer one-sex grouping. The attitude displayed toward the opposite sex is often humorous—"Ugh, she's a girl"—when you realize what he will be saying in three years. In another vein, girls like school and do better in it than boys. Statistics on grades in the schools where I have taught indicate this though not as dramatically as it really exists, given the fact that far more boys than girls are turned off by school. Women's liberation has taught us to see the male orientation of most institutions. In this respect the junior high is closer to the female orientation of the elementary school measured by how students respond. Sex is obviously important in other ways to early adolescents. It comes out in forms of flirting, teasing, nondating, dating, all of which are reflected in school, but not nearly as visibly as the equivalent forms in the senior high school.

On Classrooms and Teachers

In schools, the classroom is seen as the center of the educational experience. Whether or not it is in effect is beside the point. Students see it as such. For the student, in class is where you are or should be *learning*. Learning is often associated with how hard one has to work, how much one has to produce, and, of course, what grade one gets. As part of the recent reaction against the educational reforms of the post-sputnik age, there is less enthusiasm about these conceptions. Hard work, after all, often has little to do with real learning. Quantity of production does not necessarily correlate with quality. And grades cannot really indicate what a student has learned and they tend to make the process of learning punitive if you get low grades and deceptive if you get high ones. Although I agree with these criticisms, nonetheless students still see these things as important and sense how deeply rooted they are in our whole culture. I have heard myself described by students as both an easy teacher—"a soft touch who doesn't make you work and learn"—and as a hard teacher—"He's real tough and you learn a lot." My most comic example of this (there are many I consider tragic) was the boy who discussed with another teacher why I was no longer teaching his class: "Oh, I bet they got rid of him because he was too easy. We didn't have much homework and he gave us all good grades. He was too nice."

Students seem to like subjects where they are physically active —art, gym, laboratory science, and industrial arts—although there are plenty of exceptions. Many students, particularly the verbal ones, like subjects where they are involved in general discussions such as English and social studies. Most students have a pet dislike of a specific subject. "I hate math and I always have." By and large, however, students in junior high find their courses boring. This has to do with going through the same pattern every day in every subject with very little variety. It has to do with a good deal of ignorance on our part about how to tap their interest. It has to do with the fact that many of the students are in limbo or as some describe themselves, *spastic*. It has also to do with inferior materials, bad pedagogy, and rigid school structures.

In the center of the classroom experience is the teacher. Students most often describe and define their courses in terms of the teacher. He or she is the one who makes a class great or terrible. Curriculum reform projects of the past ten years in the academic disciplines have tried to improve schools by producing better materials, some of which could be taught by *any* teacher. Most of them now realize that with a bad teacher students will feel the new course is as bad as the old. Parents, principals, and guidance counselors keep telling youngsters it should not matter who the teacher is. They say you should be able to learn from someone you do not like. This is true only when personal dislike is mild and is overpowered by respect for the teacher's fairness and competence. Most teachers accept the necessity of being liked by their students; some turn this into an end in itself. Students want a positive personal relationship with their teachers, but they want more.

The teacher, whether or not he considers himself a benevolent despot or a partner in learning, is a model. He is usually the only adult in a room of thirty people. He is the one most different and the one who is expected to do something to make that class good. If he does not, he is not a good teacher. He is the one turned to when the going gets rough. One day I brought six candy bars into class for a lesson on the distribution of goods. I put the candy bars on the desk and told the class they were welcome to have them and should agree on how to divide them. For the rest of the period and part of the next, alternatives were presented and discussed. Several boys from the track team suggested, only half in jest, that the candy be placed at one end of the room and the class race for it. Generally, this solution was opposed. Other proposals were made including equal division, grades, fighting, working, bidding, and drawing lots. None, by the way, suggested that I as teacher decide. Finally, drawing lots was agreed upon as the best method. As I moved the candy bars to another spot in the room, the elected class chairman grabbed at one. I asked him why, since all had agreed to do the division by lots. He said he wanted one. I held out the bars and he took one, opened it, and proceeded to eat it. The universal reaction of the class was silent confusion. I thought they would be outraged and I suppose they were, but in this case they expected me to take action, to stop the violation of their hard-reached decision. I finally did ask the boy why he disregarded the class's decision, rather mildly chewed him out, and ruled him out of the drawing of lots.

This incident illustrates many things and raises many questions. Clearly I had violated the expectations of the students, either by letting their classmate take the candy or by not acting when he did. They expected me to handle this situation even though all but the assignment of the task was in their control and they had made the decisions. Perhaps I had asked them to step too far out of their notions of authority and the security that a teacher is expected to provide in the classroom. Another reason I was surprised at the class's lack of reaction was their usual strong reactions to injustice. Students measure teachers, generally with a high degree of accuracy, on a continuum from just to unjust in treatment of people. Twelve-year-olds often use a double standard—canons of fairness are strictly applied to others, much less strictly applied to themselves. Connected to both the security and justice issues is the whole question of authority. Although much less sensitive about authority than sixteen-year-olds, the twelve-year-old in school is keenly aware of who makes decisions and what role he has in the process. In the case of the candy bars, I was expected to act as the authority. No doubt I was naïve about how students viewed the authority relationships in class to think they would exercise some control on their classmate. This age student is more committed to the distinction between himself and adults. He is more willing to go along with the authorities, but is beginning to question. By the time he leaves junior high school, the question of legitimate authority is a central part of things about which he is "bugged."

A final point about the candy bar incident. The actions of the boy represent, in the extreme, a serious problem for most youngsters in junior high school: *How do I establish and develop individuality in an institution that treats me as. one of a group with similar characteristics?* Most of the students I teach want to be seen as individuals, just as we all do. A school is a difficult if not impossible place to get a great deal of individual treatment. The students want to be members of the group, but they also want to be someone unique. Since all the children have this problem and since there is considerable pressure toward group conformity, they are not much able to give each other this sense of individuality. The teacher is often the only one able to legitimatize pluralism, but he is hampered because he deals with so many children and almost always as a group.

The structure of the classrooms, the logistics of schedules, and the courses taught all seem to encourage the teacher to deal with groups of thirty. Most good teachers seek ways to deal with students individually. They advise clubs, coach teams, use free periods to help youngsters with work, or any number of other methods. I have even found that keeping students after school for discipline has served as a way to get to know a student as an individual and to give him the attention he wants and often needs. I cannot say honestly that this miraculously improves behavior in class, but at least I know more about the individual and usually have more sensible options with which to respond.

IV

Most of what I have written is descriptive rather than prescriptive. The schools for early adolescents that I have taught in and seen need changing. The changes we undertake need careful thought, not only in terms of restructuring the school, but, more important, in terms of what we want for the young, and what they want for themselves.

Two final thoughts seem worth conveying as a postscript to this essay. The first is from Urie Bronfenbrenner in *Two Worlds of Childhood.* He writes: "What is called for is a greater involvement of parents, and other adults in the lives of children, and—conversely—greater involvement of children in responsibility on behalf of their own family, community, and society at large. Given the fragmented character of modern American life—its growing separatism and violence—such an injunction may appear to some as a pipe dream, but it need not be. For just as autonomy and aggression have their roots in the American tradition, so have neighborliness, civic concern, and devotion to the young. It is to these that we must look if we are to rediscover our moral identity as a society and as a nation."

The second is from many of the students I have taught. When asked the qualities of a good teacher they respond with some version of three ideas: "cares about me as a person," "is fair," "is excited about and knows something about what he teaches." In broader terms this says, we want classrooms and schools in which an individual can exist and be nourished, in which there is social justice, and in which the adults have some commitment to what they do and what they believe.

JOHN JANEWAY CONGER

A World They Never Knew:
The Family and Social Change

In our society, adolescence has traditionally been viewed as a more difficult period in the lives of children and their parents than either the middle-childhood years which precede it or the years of emerging adulthood which follow it. While a number of recent investigations suggest that the extent of adolescent and parental turmoil during this period has frequently been exaggerated,[1] there is, nevertheless, general agreement that adolescence, and particularly early adolescence, is likely to be a challenging and sometimes trying time for both the young themselves and their parents.[2]

Furthermore, the difficulties of this period appear to be increasing—partly as a consequence of continuing changes in the family itself and in its relations to society, and partly as a consequence of the accelerated *rate* of these changes. The purposes of this essay are, first, to examine briefly the nature of some of these changes, and then to consider some of their effects, presumed and actual, upon contemporary adolescents and their parents. Finally, an effort will be made to suggest some of the steps that will have to be taken if we are to fulfill our responsibilities to society's most valuable resource—its adolescent young.

The Family and Social Change

There can be little doubt that the present century has been one of fundamental, in some respects even radical change for our society. Increasing urbanization and geographic mobility have been altering the face of the country and the nature of its social institutions, including the family, at a rather astonishing rate. In 1900, nearly two out of every three persons in America lived in a

197

rural area, either on farms or in small towns. Today that figure has declined by half, to only about one person in three.³ Significantly, the greatest population shift has been away from the traditional "heartland of America"—the central Midwest and South—and toward the burgeoning metropolitan areas along the east and west coasts and the southern shores of the Great Lakes.⁴ Even for those already living in such urban areas, however, mobility has not ceased.

Incredible as it may sound, in the last decade more than half of all families in the United States have moved every five years.⁵ All population groups have been affected, from the nomadic corporate executive at one end of the socioeconomic spectrum, for whom "the price of position and social mobility includes a willingness to be geographically mobile,"⁶ to the hundreds of thousands of agricultural workers—black, brown, and white—who have been forced off the land by increasing agricultural automation and re- stricted land use into urban slums with which they are ill- prepared to cope.

These changes have tended to weaken the stability and inter- dependence of communities, impair communication between the family and other social and political institutions, and shrink the size of the family (and its sources of both material and psychological support) from the extended family of an earlier day to today's relatively isolated nuclear family. All of these changes have made the family's burdens greater and increased still further the dif- ficulties of child rearing.

Furthermore, because of the rapidity of the rate of change, to- day's adolescents and their parents have grown up in markedly different worlds. As the sociologist Kingsley Davis observed more than thirty years ago, and as Kenneth Keniston has emphasized again recently,⁷ when the developmental experiences that shape our personalities and the social changes that must be confronted vary markedly from adults to young people, from parents to their children, generational differences in cultural values and outlook— even in knowledge—tend to be magnified. In short, as current jargon has it, the greater the rate of social change, the larger the generation gap may be expected to be. Thus, to the extent that today's parents look only to their own experience as adolescents for expectations about their children's probable adolescent behavior, or for guidance in understanding their needs, outlooks, and goals, they are almost bound to encounter frustration, bewilderment, or disappointment.

A World They Never Knew

The parent of today's young adolescent is most likely to have been born in the early 1930's and to have entered adolescence in the middle 1940's. Thus most of his preadolescent development took place in the, at least relatively, simpler era that preceded World War II. True, the lingering shadow of the Great Depression may have hung over his family, but by and large it was still a smaller, more intimate, and in many ways a more predictable world— at least for the broad middle class.

Although the nation's flight to the metropolitan centers and their suburban satellites, like that of lemmings to the sea, was already under way, nearly half of all Americans still lived on farms and in the traditional small towns that are enshrined in American mythology and the paintings of Norman Rockwell.[8] Even in our larger cities, we still had neighborhoods. Consequently, many of today's parents grew up in informal, often daily association, not only with members of their immediate family, but also with other relatives of all ages, who, if they did not live in the same household, could often be found down the street or around the corner. As Urie Bronfenbrenner has observed:

> Everybody in the neighborhood minded your business . . . If you walked on the railroad trestle, the phone would ring at your house, and your parents would know what you had done before you got back home. People on the street would tell you to button your jacket, and ask why you were not in church last Sunday. Sometimes you liked it and sometimes you didn't—but at least people *cared*.
>
> Your also had the run of the neighborhood. You were allowed to play in the park. You could go into any store, whether you bought anything or not. They would let you go out back where you could watch them unpack the cartons, and hope that one would break. At the lumberyard, they let you pick up the good scraps of wood.[9]

It is this older, less rapidly changing world that many of today's parents seem to be recalling when they talk of the world their own adolescent children face. In a recent study by Daniel Offer of normal, largely middle-class, midwestern adolescent boys, parents were asked to describe their own early years:

> Most of the parents, particularly fathers, said their families had been affected by the Depression, were less affluent, harder working. Nearly all said their sons had more things, more knowledge, more opportunities —and they were glad of that. But there was a strong hint, as these parents talked, that their sons were not better off, despite the things and opportunities. The suggestion was that one *should* have to work hard for rewards, that it all should not come as easily as to today's young.

There was some nostalgia, too, as expressed by one father: "I grew up in the Depression and everybody worked to keep the family going. We were a large and closely knit family. I had a good time." Or this from another father: "In my day the world was small and there was more mystery to things—there were still kids—you know."[10]

The great social issues that today bombard our senses and confuse and divide us as a people—war, racial and socioeconomic injustice, simultaneous growth and destruction of our cities, pollution of the environment—had not yet exploded on the national consciousness, although obviously below the surface the seeds were being sown. But the exhaustibility of our resources was not yet so evident, and ever-increasing technology could still be equated with progress.

Even though the late middle-childhood or early adolescent years of these parents were overshadowed by World War II, at least it was a war, probably the last one, that the country as a whole believed in and identified with. Soldiers and sailors were everybody's heroes, and not merely, as now, the unfortunate victims of a new kind of Russian roulette in an otherwise "business as usual" society. When the nation's adults began to pick up the pieces again in the aftermath of that war, it was primarily with a passion to restore their own childhood and adolescent conceptions of "normality." This was the familiar era of the "split-level" and the "silent generation," with its single-minded devotion to home, family, and security. This was the atmosphere in which many of today's parents completed their own adolescence and crystallized their values and expectations. In many ways, it may be said that today's adolescents have grown up with the consequences.

Born in the 1950's, today's adolescents have been nursed on the uneasy peace that followed the Korean war and weaned on a diet of increasing social malaise, discord, and divisiveness. By the time they entered school, we had plunged into the hectic decade of the 1960's—initially with the dream that accelerated technology would bring unprecedented progress in the "war against poverty," in education, in civil rights, in the salvation of our cities, in peace, and in an ever increasing prosperity for all. What was to have been a new era, however, turned instead into what Andrew Hacker has called the Age of Rubbish, characterized by violence, separatism, and a rudderless morality. In short, to a virtually unprecedented degree, today's adolescents have been exposed to an adult society deeply divided within itself.

Decline of adult authority. One of the inevitable and most important consequences in the minds of today's young has been a decline in adult authority. In an earlier generation in this country, and in other less fragmented and less rapidly changing cultures, adolescents have been able to view adult society as at least relatively homogeneous. While adolescents may have felt that "they" —the adults—were misguided, compromising, apathetic, or just plain wrong, nevertheless, there was an identifiable, reasonably self-confident, confrontable "they." Parents, particularly the father, could be viewed with considerable justification as the adult society's resident ambassadors in the family court. As such, parents derived authority and wisdom—implied or real—from their position as representatives of the adult power structure and could serve as sympathetic guides to its mysteries and as effective models for success in gaining entry into it.

A majority of today's adolescents in this country are denied such coherent perceptions. At least from middle-childhood on, they have been exposed to increasingly bitter divisions among prestigeful adults on almost every front, from the broadest social issues to the most intimate questions of personal standards and morality. Even to the limited extent that adolescents have been able to view adult society as speaking with one voice and planning a unified attack on society's mounting problems, the evidence of its capacity to achieve success has not been overly reassuring. Consequently, the "authority" of the adult culture is compromised in the eyes of many adolescents, and with it the authority derived by parents from their position as family representatives of this culture.

As will become evident, all of this is not to say that parents can no longer serve as effective role models for their children. But it does suggest that their authority may no longer be derived simply from their status as representatives of a unified adult society, as would be the case in more static, more homogeneous cultures. It must come more from their own individual strengths and resources, or at most from their position as representatives of only a limited segment of adult society. This, of course, does not make the task of the parent any easier, for he too is confronted with "a world I never made," despite some adolescents' rather naïve and occasionally arrogant assertions to the contrary.

At any rate, the older assertion that "father (that is, adult society) knows best" is likely to be met—not merely for psychodynamic, but for increasingly reality-based reasons as well—with the adolescent response of "who's kidding whom?"

The rise of "youth culture." A related difference between the worlds in which parents and their adolescent sons and daughters have developed lies in the increasingly prominent role of "youth culture" and its potential effects on younger adolescents. In a day when at least a majority of young people went to work at seventeen or eighteen after graduation from high school, we were faced with two fairly discernible groups, adolescents in the traditional sense, and adults (including young adults). Currently, increasing visibility has been assumed by a third group, variously identifiable as "post-adolescents" or, more simply, "youth." With greater numbers of these young people in our society than ever before,[11] and with more and more of them denied access to full adult status for longer and longer periods of time (whether as college or graduate students in the case of the advantaged, or as rootless unemployed or under-employed in the case of the disadvantaged), the size of this group has grown, along with its visibility, definability, seeming cohesiveness, and social impact upon both adults and young adolescents.

As a consequence, young adolescents are currently exposed, not only to age-mate peers and to an older adult society, but also to a widely publicized older youth culture, a culture which is frequently viewed as in conflict with these other groups for the loyalty and emulation of young adolescents. The situation is further complicated by the fact that this youth culture as perceived by young adolescents (and to a large extent also by adults) often bears little resemblance to the actual behavior, attitudes, and value systems of the average post-adolescent or youth.[12] What the young adolescent perceives is, of course, influenced in part by personal observation of the post-adolescent generation. But it is also influenced to a significant degree by the popular stereotypes of this group which have been created and sustained by the mass media, and by commercial interests eager to tap what is by all odds the most affluent generation of young people in history. (Some of the recent rock festivals provide particularly distasteful examples of highly commercialized and cynical exploitation of young people under the guise of encouraging "love," "freedom," and independence of "materialistic" values.)

Because of such illusory but powerful stereotypes, some young adolescents may be led to view their youthful elders as more influential, more homogeneous, and more active in a wide variety of behaviors (for example, sexual activities, preoccupation with drugs, revolt against "the system") than is actually the case for many of them. Thus, the possibility arises that a young adolescent may think he is merely emulating older youth when, in fact, he is actually going beyond them, and leaping into life styles and behaviors that older youth themselves may not be prepared to follow. While the available evidence[13] indicates that the average young adolescent has not risen to such lures, more vulnerable minorities clearly have done so.

Age segregation. Accompanying the growth of an older adolescent youth culture has been a reduction in the extent of interaction among age groups, both within the family and in the community. In the words of a task force of the recent White House Conference on Children, children and adolescents are currently

deprived not only of parents but of people in general. A host of factors conspire to isolate the young from the rest of society. The fragmentation of the extended family, the separation of residential and business areas, the disappearance of neighborhoods, zoning ordinances, occupational mobility, child labor laws, the abolishment of the apprentice system, consolidated schools, television, separate patterns of social life for different age groups, the working mother, the delegation of child care to specialists—all these manifestations of progress operate to decrease opportunity and incentive for meaningful contact between children and persons older, or younger, than themselves.[14]

Herbert Wright and his associates at the University of Kansas have recently compared the daily life of children still growing up in a small town environment with that of the far greater number living in metropolitan areas. Among the principal differences that they found was that "unlike their urban and suburban age-mates, children in a small town become well acquainted with a substantially greater number of adults in different walks of life, and are more likely to be participants in the adult settings which they enter."[15] This may be one reason why relatively few of today's adolescents follow in the occupational footsteps of their fathers. A survey by James Coleman has revealed that 23 per cent of high school boys in small towns, as contrasted with only 9.8 per cent of boys in city and suburban schools, planned to enter their fathers' occupations.[16] Indeed, under conditions of life in many of today's cities and suburbs, the adolescent may never have seen anybody actually performing the type of work he is considering upon completion of his education. In social activities, too, this same trend toward age segregation may be observed: "Whereas invitations used to be extended to entire families, with *all* the Smiths visiting *all* the Joneses, nowadays every social event has its segregated equivalent for every age group down to the toddlers. The children's hour has become the cocktail hour. While the adults take their drinks upstairs, the children have their 'juice time' in the rumpus room downstairs."[17]

Members of the White House Conference task force found this situation increasingly disturbing:

> The young cannot pull themselves up by their own bootstraps. It is primarily through observing, playing, and working with others older and younger than himself that a child discovers both what he can do and who he can become—that he develops both his ability and his identity. It is primarily through exposure and interaction with adults and children of different ages that a child [or adolescent] acquires new interests and skills and learns the meaning of tolerance, cooperation, and compassion. Hence to relegate children to a world of their own is to deprive them of their humanity . . . Yet, this is what is happening in America today.[18]

Consequences of Social Change

There can be little doubt that recent and continuing changes in the nature of the family and in its relations to society, and the rate of these changes, have increased the stresses confronting today's nuclear family. But have they also, as is so widely asserted, produced a virtually unbridgeable generation gap between today's average parents and their adolescent sons and daughters? Has the contemporary nuclear family become obsolete? Have parents become irrelevant as models for their children's psychological and social development? And have contemporary adolescents forsaken their parents and become the captives of an all-powerful peer culture? Each of these questions will be addressed briefly, in the hope of restoring some perspective to a topic that has become unduly burdened by rhetorical extremes.

Dimensions of the Generation Gap

The avid follower of the mass media's instant sociology might easily conclude that there is not merely a universal generation gap between today's parents and their adolescent sons and daughters, but an abyss. What are the facts, insofar as we can ascertain them at the present time?

The best answer appears to be that there *is* a generation gap between the average parent of today and his adolescent young, but that this gap is neither as wide nor as totally new as we have been led to expect, nor is it qualitatively very similar to popular stereotypes. In recent representative national surveys[19] of both younger and older adolescents and of their parents, approximately two out of three young people and seven out of ten parents expressed the view that a gap exists but that it has been exaggerated. Only about one young person in four, and a like percentage of their parents, felt that there was a large gap, while only a small minority of both groups (about one in twenty) felt that there was no gap. Intensive investigations of more limited samples have yielded similar findings.[20]

Popular notions that a state of cold or hot war exists between today's average parents and their own adolescent young, that the average adolescent disapproves of the way he has been reared, that he views his parents as unhappy, frustrated people who have "sold out" their basic values to the establishment, and that he is uncomfortable in their presence and unable to communicate with them also received little support. When asked to describe their present relationships with their parents, a majority of both younger and older adolescents (57 per cent) stated that they got along fine with their parents and enjoyed their company. Approximately one in three said that they were fond of their parents but had trouble communicating with them. Only a small minority (4 per cent) stated that they did not enjoy spending time with their parents. Interestingly, among the one-third who felt they had trouble communicating, only 18 per cent expressed the view that it was their parents' fault; 6 per cent said it was their own fault; and an overwhelming majority (74 per cent) said it was "both our faults." Furthermore, when asked if they felt their upbringing had been "too strict, too permissive, or about right," over 80 per cent felt that it had been about right.

Nor does the average adolescent view his parents as unhappy, frustrated souls who have "sold out." Three out of four adolescents fifteen and older expressed the belief that their father "has been happy in his work." Four out of five stated that their parents had "lived up to their own ideals." In addition, approximately three out of four adolescents, both younger and older ones, stated that they were in general agreement with their parents' ideals. Indeed, a variety of studies indicate that in many areas the values of a majority of today's adolescents are surprisingly unsurprising.

Current trends in adolescent values. While significant and probably growing minorities of contemporary adolescents have become profoundly disillusioned and "turned off" by a society that they view variously as unjust, cruel, violent, hypocritical, superficial, impersonal, overly competitive, or immoral, the average adolescent still shares many traditional values with his parents. Thus, a substantial majority of today's adolescents and their parents subscribe to such beliefs as the following: competition encourages excellence; the right to private property is sacred; depending on how much character a person has, he can pretty well control what happens to him; society needs some legally based authority in order to avoid chaos; and compromise is essential to progress. Approximately two out of three contemporary adolescents express the view that hard work leads to success, and that success is worth striving for.[21]

While many adolescents speak of their opposition to "materialistic values," paradoxically they seem to accept readily this generation's relative affluence. Seventy-six per cent of a national sample of adolescents regarded shopping as "one of the experiences I most enjoy."[22] It would appear more accurate to say that many contemporary adolescents are finding that materialistic goals are insufficient to produce a sense of personal fulfillment, rather than to say that adolescents generally are opposed to material values.

Although the average adolescent has retained many traditional values, he is not overly impressed with the current state of society and its principal institutions.[23] For example, only 22 per cent of adolescents have a "great deal" of confidence in the government's ability to solve the problems of the 1970's, 54 per cent have "some confidence, but not a lot," and 22 per cent have "hardly any" confidence. A substantial majority believe that most of our social institutions, including big business, the military, political parties, and the mass media, including television, are in need of at least moderate reform. It should be noted, however, that only a portion of this skepticism reflects a generation gap. Although the young are more critical of these institutions than their parents, adults have also shown an attitude shift recently in the direction of greater skepticism.

Nevertheless, generational differences do exist, even for the average adolescent and his parents, both in their current views and also in comparisons of the views of today's adolescents and those of their parents when they were the same age. Although only a small minority, especially of younger adolescents, are militant activists on social or political issues, most do appear to have a greater concern than their parents did at the same ages, or do now, with such issues as socioeconomic discrimination and racial prejudice. Thus, for example, adolescents are far more willing than their parents to have increased school integration and to have blacks or other minority group members as neighbors.[24] Interestingly, in their attitudes they seem to be reflecting flexibility, tolerance, and lack of prejudice, as much as or more than crusading zeal.

This attitude of relative tolerance, of a greater willingness to let others (except possibly parents) "do their own thing," pervades much of adolescent thinking—younger and older alike. It is accompanied by a relatively high value placed on open, honest, and "meaningful" interpersonal relationships with others. Thus, while they are more tolerant than their parents of premarital sexual relationships in which love and commitment are present, they appear generally opposed to promiscuity, not only in principle, but for the most part in behavior. They are far more convinced than their parents of the importance of sex education in their high schools, and believe that it should be taught in coeducational classes. Three out of four believe that though a double standard of sexual behavior still exists, it is wrong.[25]

Most are interested in job success as conventionally defined, but they are, at least relatively, less concerned with achieving status and recognition by society in their future jobs than earlier generations were, and more concerned with finding work that is "meaningful" and enjoyable and in which they can have pride.[26] Three out of four say they would not work for a company that causes substantial pollution, and four out of five say they could not accept easily a job in which they were treated impersonally. A majority believe that "business is overly concerned with profits and not with public responsibility."[27] In our junior and senior high schools, today's abler, better informed students are far more concerned than their parents with student participation in policy-making and with innovation and "relevance" in curricula; in contrast, their parents are more concerned with maintenance of discipline and the development of orderly routines of study.[28]

Two other characteristics of current adolescents deserve brief mention, although they are difficult to document. Despite their often impressive intellectual capability, many adolescents today appear less knowledgeable about the past and less convinced that there are lessons to be learned from it. They are more inclined to view the future as either unpredictable, or at best full of options that need not be explored yet. Relatively, though only relatively, they do appear to be more of a "now" generation.

In a related vein, it is essential to realize that while both parents and adolescents are confronted with the irrational and chaotic forces increasingly abroad, and our apparent inability to control them effectively, many parents are still able—with their own childhood experiences as a frame of reference—to view this unhappy state of affairs as a deviation from a subjective conception of "normality." In contrast, their children for the most part have no such frame of reference. While they may have found elements of stability within their homes, the uncertainties of the world outside its walls are not new for them—not a deviation from prior expectancies. They are in fact normal, for to these young people these uncertainties have, in greater or less measure, always existed. In a survey by Louis Harris for *Newsweek,* a nationwide sample of adolescents age thirteen to seventeen described the world they live in as "warlike," "impersonal," "competitive," and "fast moving" and fraught with constant change.[29]

This important difference between the perspectives of parents and their adolescent sons and daughters may help to explain some current adolescent preoccupations that puzzle or alarm many parents. While parents frequently cling nostalgically to the symbols of a simpler, more rational past, the "now" generation looks for ways of living in the present, for finding meaning in uncertainty and irrationality. They look for meaning in seeming meaninglessness— "happenings," elaborate "put-ons" in dress and manner, distortions of "reality" in light shows and movies, the current preoccupation with astrology and, in some older adolescents, with Eastern religions.[30]

Finally, and perhaps most significantly, today's adolescents reveal a pervasive need for a world in which there is more true friendship and love. Indeed, no other values are as strongly and consistently held. Nine out of ten contemporary adolescents—whether younger or older, affluent or disadvantaged, conservative, middle-of-the-road, liberal, or revolutionary—are in agreement about the importance of these values (although they may differ widely in many of their other beliefs). They consistently find these values in short supply. Less than one in five adolescents agrees strongly that "most people will go out of their way to help someone else," or that they "can be depended on to come through in a pinch."[31]

In brief, the average contemporary adolescent appears to be relatively more ready than his more self-conscious predecessors of earlier generations to put into practice a philosophy of "live and let live" and of pragmatic idealism. More than earlier generations, he appears to be a sophisticated and critical exponent of the art of the possible—not illusioned, but not disillusioned either. With considerable justification, James A. Wechsler, editor of the *New York Post,* has termed today's adolescents a generation of "flaming moderates."[32] Whether this will continue to be the case, or whether the size of the profoundly disenchanted minority will continue to grow, is still an open question.

How can we reconcile these rather wide discrepancies, not only between the apparent facts and popular stereotypes about the size and nature of the so-called generation gap, but also between what we might expect theoretically, on the basis of the nature and rate of social change? I think we can look to at least five factors that should be considered, but which tend frequently to be overlooked:

1. Many current pronouncements about the generation gap are based on faulty analysis and inappropriate conclusions. They derive largely from comparing nonrepresentative samples of adults with equally nonrepresentative samples of young people. Both the popular media and a number of social scientists as well have tended to picture adolescents, whether favorably or unfavorably, in terms of the manifest characteristics of visible, controversial, sometimes highly articulate minorities: high school and junior high school activists, minority group militants, hippies and "teeny boppers," even, at times, hard drug users and delinquents. Particular attention has focused on a counterculture of elite, affluent, urban, upper-middle-class adolescents of all ages, especially on the east and west coasts.[33] In contrast, although the statistical and semantic justification is doubtful, to say the least, adults have been most commonly characterized recently as members of a "silent majority" of "middle Americans."

In fact, however, as David Riesman has recently noted, a number of current so-called generational conflicts could better be described as class conflicts—between a minority of relatively affluent middle-to-upper-middle-class adolescents whose families have long been secure in their social and economic status and a minority of working-class adults who have only recently, and sometimes rather tenuously, gotten hold of the lower rungs of the middle-class ladder.[34] Similar observations could be made regarding some other so-called generational conflicts that actually more closely reflect ethnic and other divisions.

Such simplistic adolescent-adult comparisons ignore the fact that ours has long been a heterogeneous society, rather than simply a "melting pot," both for adults and adolescents, and it appears to be becoming ever more so. Any number of recent investigations[35] make clear that the variations among important subgroups of adolescents are at least as great, and frequently greater than those between the average adult and the average adolescent, whether in the areas of political and social values, sexual attitudes and behavior, patterns of drug use, or educational and vocational goals.

2. Popular stereotypes also tend to confuse and confound comparisons between adults and adolescents generally with those between individual parents and their own adolescent sons and daughters, despite the fact that these may differ significantly. Thus in one recent study,[36] while two-thirds of adolescents fifteen years of age and older replied "yes" to the question, "Do your parents approve of your values and ideals?" a majority of these same adolescents responded negatively to the question, "Do they approve of the way *your generation* expresses their ideals?" Adolescents also tended to be more critical, generally in rather stereotyped terms, of the "older generation" taken as a whole than of their own parents.

When adults were asked what they disliked about today's adolescents as a group, the most frequently mentioned complaints involved: a lack of respect for authority, undisciplined behavior, lack of ambition or motivation, overindulgence and overpermissiveness by parents and others, lack of responsibility, lack of manners, "too smug and self-assured," and, interestingly, "lack of dialogue with elders." Similarly, when young people were asked about their parents' generation, the most commonly cited complaints were that they were "too set in their ways" and that there was a lack of communication ("they won't listen to us").[37] Furthermore, as Keniston and others have shown,[38] in a number of instances adolescents may come into conflict with the values of some adult authority figures in their society precisely because those values conflict with values the young person has acquired from, and shares with, his parents.

3. There is also a widespread tendency to confuse generational differences that may be truly new, either in kind or in magnitude, with those that have traditionally separated parents and children—if for no other reason than that successive generations occupy differing positions in the life cycle. The adolescent who is just becoming aware of the insistent stirring of sexual impulses will inevitably differ from the middle-aged adult who perceives their urgency waning. Adolescents need ways to consume their energy; adults

look for ways to conserve it. Young people are concerned about where they are going; adults are concerned about where they have been. Adults, having personally experienced the many partial victories and defeats and the inevitable compromises of living, tend to be tempered in their enthusiasms and cautious in their moral judgments. Young people, in contrast, tend to be impatient, impulsive, and given at times to imperious moral judgments that allow little room for shades of grey. They are more likely to move rapidly from the heights of profound joy to the valley of despair. Adults must worry more about their children; adolescents must worry more about themselves. The psychological defense mechanisms of adolescents are in flux and only partially effective; those of adults tend, like arteries, to harden with age.

Consider the following brief quotation:

> The young are prone to desire and ready to carry any desire they may have formed into action. Of bodily desires it is the sexual to which they are the most disposed to give way, and in regard to sexual desire they exercise no self-restraint. They are changeful too, and fickle in their desires, which are as transitory as they are vehement . . . They are passionate, irascible, and apt to be carried away by their impulses . . . They have high aspirations; for they have never yet been humiliated by the experience of life, but are unacquainted with the limiting force of circumstances . . . Again, in their actions they prefer honor to expediency . . . If the young commit a fault, it is always on the side of excess and exaggeration . . . They regard themselves as omniscient and are positive in their assertions; this is, in fact, the reason of their carrying everything too far.[39]

While this description might easily have been taken from John Aldridge's recent popular book, *In the Country of the Young*, the fact is that it was written by Aristotle over 2,300 years ago. Obviously, *all* aspects of the so-called generation gap are simply not that new.

4. Even some of the more sophisticated formulations of generational conflict have tended, I believe, to underemphasize the potential of parents, as well as adolescents, to change with changing times. It has recently been observed, although systematic data are lacking, that adults who are currently the parents of adolescents are more likely to be sympathetic and "understanding," not only toward their own children, but toward adolescents generally. At any rate, it is clear that many of today's parents have undertaken an "agonizing reappraisal" of a number of their own attitudes and beliefs in the face of social change—not infrequently as a

consequence of exposure to the concerns of their own adolescent sons and daughters.

5. Finally, there is a widespread tendency to overlook the possibility that parents and adolescents may be able to differ in some of their values and modes of behavior and still remain capable of mutual understanding and respect.

As should already be evident, none of this is to say that there are not a significant and probably growing number of adolescents, younger and older alike, for whom the gap between themselves and their parents is not only wide, but in some cases virtually unbridgeable. It is simply to say that they do not *presently* represent a majority of contemporary adolescents. Whether the ranks of the disenchanted minority will continue to grow will depend in large measure on the steps taken by parents and by the leaders of our society to stem the decline of a sense of community among young people and adults alike, and to restore a sense of genuine moral and social concern.

Continued Relevance of Parental Models—Fact or Fiction?

It has also become increasingly fashionable lately in some circles to assert that because of the nature and rate of recent social change, parents have become largely irrelevant as models or guides to their adolescent young's current and future development. Indeed, some social critics, such as David Cooper, the British psychiatrist and author of *Death of the Family*,[40] have gone so far as to proclaim that the family has become, not simply irrelevant to the needs of children and adolescents, but a malignant force that acts only to frustrate the fulfillment of these needs.

A more moderate position has been assumed recently by Margaret Mead and others.[41] Mead's essential argument is that in earlier and more stable cultural eras—which she terms "postfigurative" and which are most dramatically exemplified by some relatively static preliterate societies—children and adolescents could realistically look to their parents and other adults for guidance because these adults were, in fact, the best, most experienced guides to the social and vocational roles that the younger generation would eventually assume.

In the more recent past, characterized by a moderate rate of social change and a culture termed by Mead as "cofigurative," the young had to look more to their peers and less to parents and other adults for clues to successful adaptation.

In . . . cofigurative cultures the elders are still dominant in the sense
that they set the style and define the limits within which cofiguration is
expressed in the behavior of the young . . . But at the same time, where
there is a shared expectation that members of a generation will model
their behavior on that of their contemporaries, especially their adolescent
age mates, and that their behavior will differ from that of parents and
grandparents, each individual, as he successfully embodies a new style,
becomes to some extent a model for others of his generation.[42]

But in view of the extremely rapid rate of change that our
young currently face, and that they will continue to face in the
world of tomorrow, Mead finds both the postfigurative and the
cofigurative models inadequate. Instead, she sees a "prefigura-
tive" culture developing—one in which "it will be the child and
not the parent or grandparent that represents what is to come . . .
As I see it, children today face a future that is so deeply un-
known that it cannot be handled, as we are currently attempting to
do, as a generation change with cofiguration within a stable, elder-
controlled and parentally modeled culture in which many postfigurative elements are incorporated."[43]

For Mead, all of those, including today's parents, who grew up
before World War II are pioneers, immigrants in an unexplored
land—the "country of the young." In this new terrain, the young
person will have to chart his own paths, without significant as-
sistance from either parents *or* peers. Under such circumstances,
about all that parents can provide—and contrary to some popular
misconceptions of Mead's message, she considers them of vital importance—are love and trust.

While I would agree that contemporary parents can learn, and
indeed need to learn, much from their adolescent young about
adaptation to inevitable change, there is little or no evidence to
support the notion that the converse is not equally the case. A
background of love and trust are, as Erik Erikson asserts, fundamental.[44] Without them, the child's chances of becoming a reasonably happy, effective, contributing adult, of developing a positive
self-image and a sense of his own identity, are seriously impaired,
as clinical experience and any number of more systematic investigations make abundantly clear.

But, as will also become evident, the role that parental models
play in fostering or hindering the child's and adolescent's psychological development, and preparing him to meet the challenges
of emerging adulthood, extends far beyond these essential ingredients.

Parent-child relationships and the developmental tasks of ado-lescence. What often tends to be lost sight of amid the polemics of the generation gap and our—often legitimate—concerns about the nature and rate of current social change is that while the rapidity of change increases the difficulties of adolescent adaptation for both parent and child, the basic developmental tasks which the adolescent must master if he is to become a competent, autono-mous, responsive, and responsible adult still remain.[45] The period between puberty and nominal adulthood may be relatively short (as in the case of the blue-collar youth who may be employed, married, and a parent at nineteen) or relatively long (as in the case of the upper-middle-class youth who may still be involved in his education, unmarried, and largely dependent on his parents at twenty-five). It may also, depending on cultural and familial cir-cumstances, be relatively simple or complex.

Nevertheless, adolescence still involves the accomplishment of a number of critically important developmental tasks: adjustment to the physical changes of puberty and later adolescent growth and to the flood of new subjective impulses brought on by genital maturity; the development of independence from parents or other caretakers; the establishment of effective social and working relationships with same- and opposite-sex peers; preparation for a vocation; and, withal, the development of a system of values and a sense of identity—some kind of personal answer to the age-old question, "Who am I?"

The fact that in today's rapidly changing world these tasks may be more complex, and that both parent and child have fewer consistent blueprints to guide them in their accomplishment, does not fundamentally alter the situation. Sexual and social roles of men and women may change, as indeed they are changing today; the responsibilities and privileges associated with independence may change; the difficulties of projecting the vocational needs of the future may increase; and the kind of personal and social iden-tity that will be viable in both today's and tomorrow's world may alter. But regardless of the particular forms assumed, each remains a critical and indispensable task of adolescent development.

Despite romantic or hostile assertions to the contrary, the single most important external influence in aiding or hindering the average adolescent (particularly the young adolescent) in the accomplish-ment of these tasks—at least in today's relatively isolated nuclear family—is his parents. The real question, then, is not whether parental models are any longer important; rather, it is what kinds of parental models are necessary and appropriate in preparing contemporary adolescents to cope with the largely unpredictable world of tomorrow.

Models of parent-child interaction. In the case of adolescents, this question obviously involves the effects, not simply of current parental models and patterns of parent-child interaction, but a long history of prior ones, extending back to early childhood. Whether parents are loving or rejecting; calm or anxious; involved or uninvolved; rigid or flexible; controlling, guiding, but encouraging of autonomy or laissez-faire—all have been found, singly and in combination, to influence the child's subsequent behavior and adjustment.[46] For example, the child who is subjected to covertly hostile, restrictive parental child-rearing practices is likely to internalize his angry feelings (as in the case of many neurotic children and adolescents); in contrast, the child who is reared under hostile but lax conditions is more likely to act out his resentment (as in the case of many delinquents).

The behavior of the child whose parents are high on the dimension of love (warmth) may also vary, depending on coexisting conditions. Thus, children reared in warm but restrictive (as opposed to autonomy-encouraging) homes are likely to be more dependent and conforming; less aggressive, dominant, and competitive with peers; less friendly; less creative; and more hostile in their fantasies. In contrast, those reared in homes where parental love is evident though not cloying, and where the child is given considerable age-appropriate autonomy, are likely to emerge as more active, outgoing, socially assertive, and independent, as well as friendly, creative, and lacking in hostility toward others or self. While such children may also tend to be somewhat disobedient, disrespectful, and rebellious on occasion, these behaviors appear to manifest themselves largely because of feelings of security and lack of severe punitive response from parents, and to be "more easily turned on and off in response to reinforcing conditions,"[47] rather than reflecting chronic anger and frustration, or uncontrollable expressions of deep-seated but dammed-up feelings of hostility.

In short, it appears clear that the heritage of parent-child relationships that the young person carries into adolescence will affect the relative ease with which he adjusts to the changed roles and new demands of this period. The overprotected child, who may have achieved a workable modus vivendi within the circumscribed confines of the family during middle-childhood, may find coping with the demands of others for independence and self-reliance during adolescence extremely difficult to handle. Similarly, the over-indulged child as he approaches adolescence may find the society's unwillingness to provide a like degree of indulgence frustrating. The child of hostile parents may until adolescence have controlled his counterhostility reasonably well, only to lose this control under conditions of increased stress, conflict, and opportunities for acting-out behavior that accompany adolescence.

Furthermore, the appropriateness of particular patterns of prior and current parental behavior may vary markedly with cultural conditions and with the speed of social change. Thus, the child reared in Mead's postfigurative culture, where change is slow and the requisite skills and patterns of living demanded by the culture are handed down from one generation to another essentially intact, is in a very different position from, for example, an upper-middle-class child in American society in 1971. Whereas authoritarian and even autocratic parental models may serve reasonably adequately in the former instance, where conformity and diligence are more important to the adolescent than creativity, curiosity, and independence, they do not serve very well in a rapidly changing culture, where the parent can often neither predict nor control the types of challenges his adolescent young will face.

Much nonsense has been written recently by anxious or angry adults, asserting that all dissent among today's young can be blamed on their "permissive" upbringing, with Dr. Benjamin Spock usually perceived as the omnipotent, all-pervasive villain of the piece.[48] Aside from the inherent absurdity of attributing all dissent either to permissiveness or to Dr. Spock as its alleged agent, a case can certainly be made independently about the unwisdom of unrestricted permissiveness.

One needs, however, to be careful about what is meant by permissiveness. Does it mean indulgence, intimidation of parents by children, a laissez-faire parental attitude, or simple neglect? In this connection, Urie Bronfenbrenner makes the interesting point that many studies originally interpreted as indicating a universal trend toward permissiveness in child rearing in this country since World War II could as well be interpreted as indicating a progressive decrease in "recent decades in the amount of contact between American parents and their children."[49]

Or does the term "permissiveness," at least as employed by

some authoritarian adults, really refer to the encouragement of autonomy and of adolescent participation in decision-making, albeit under parental guidance and ultimate authority? The presumed alternative to so-called permissiveness in the minds of many vociferous critics seems to be a return to an authoritarian or autocratic model, which might (or might not) have prepared an adolescent for some simpler, postfigurative era, but certainly not for today's unpredictable world, where change and readiness for change are the name of the game. In effect, what these latter-day Minniver Cheevys seem to be crying out against is not so much the changing behavior of the players as the changing rules of the game itself. Adolescents in tomorrow's world will require discipline (ultimately self-discipline), but they will also require independence, self-reliance, adaptability, creativity, and the ability to distinguish between assertiveness and hostility, not to mention a sense of humor. And these characteristics are fostered, as we shall see, neither by permissiveness or parental neglect, nor by autocratic or authoritarian child-rearing methods.

The development of adolescent independence. The development of independence is central to any discussion of the tasks of adolescence, not only in its own right, but also because of its intimate relationship to the accomplishment of other tasks. Thus, the adolescent who does not ultimately resolve the conflict between a continuing, regressive dependence and the newer demands (and privileges) of independence in the direction of independence will encounter difficulties in most other areas as well. Without the achievement of separation and autonomy, the adolescent can hardly be expected to achieve mature heterosexual or peer relationships, confident pursuit of a vocation, or a sense of identity, which requires a positive image of the self as separate, unified, and consistent over time.[50]

The relative ease or difficulty of establishing independence depends in great part upon prior and continuing parent-child relationships. The parent who provides a successful model of independence himself, one which is rewarding and with which the child can identify, and who balances controls and realistically age-graded opportunities for independence behavior, will make the task a great deal easier.

Extensive studies by Glen Elder and Charles Bowerman found that adolescents subjected to "democratic" child-rearing practices (in which the adolescent freely participates in discussion of issues relevant to his behavior, and may even make decisions, but where parents retain ultimate control) were far more likely to consider their parents fair and reasonable in their "ideas, rules, or principles about how you should behave" than either "autocratic" parents (who "just tell" their children what to do) or "permissive, laissez-faire, and ignoring" parents. These democratically reared children were also far less likely to report feelings of having been unwanted as children (about 10 per cent) than were the children of auto-cratic mothers or fathers (about 40 per cent).[51]

Most relevant to our purposes here, parents with such varying techniques of parental control (or lack of it) were also further subdivided into those who attempted to make their exercise of power "legitimate"[52] by frequently explaining their rules of conduct and expectations versus those who did not. The relationships of the ensuing subcategories to the development of adolescent self-confidence and independence were then examined. Interestingly, it was found that both confidence and independence occurred most frequently among the children of democratic (and permissive) parents who also frequently provided parental explanations. Lack of confidence and dependence occurred most frequently among children of autocratic parents who infrequently provided parental rules of conduct and expectations. Other studies have yielded similar results. For example, Morris Rosenberg has recently found that confidence and self-esteem were highest among adolescents whose parents expressed strong interest in, and knowledge about, their opinions and activities and who encouraged autonomous behavior and active participation in family affairs.[53]

In brief, it appears that democratic practices, with frequent explanations by parents of the reasons for their rules of conduct and expectations, foster responsible independence learning in several ways: (1) by providing opportunities for increasing autonomy, guided by interested parents who communicate with the child and exercise appropriate degrees of control; (2) by promoting positive identification with the parent, based on love and respect for the child, rather than rejection or indifference; and (3) by themselves providing models of reasonable independence, that is, autonomy within the framework of a democratic order. In contrast, the child of autocratic or indifferent parents is not presented with models of responsible, cooperative independence; he is not so likely to be encouraged by parental acceptance to identify with adults; and he is not given age-graded experiences in the orderly assumption of responsible autonomy.[54]

While a number of these studies were conducted several years ago, they appear, if anything, more rather than less relevant today. The democratic child-rearing structure (as defined here), providing as it does for perceptions of parental fairness, for feelings of personal security and being wanted, and for the development of both responsibility and increasing autonomy, seems especially important in a turbulent period of rapid social change such as the present, where the need for adult autonomy is at a premium, where there are few clear-cut social guidelines and responsibility must come largely from within, and where the opportunities for generational conflict, hostility, and alienation are legion.

Autocratic, or at least authoritarian patterns of parental behavior may have been more workable in other times and other cultures where the adolescent could expect to be reasonably successful simply by following in a father's or mother's footsteps, assuming similar tasks and responsibilities in the same manner and at the same ages. Under such cultural conditions, carefully defined, even rigid channels were also more likely to be provided by the society for coping with the greater intergenerational hostility that more classically oedipal confrontations associated with an autocratic structure appear likely to provoke. Furthermore, in such situations the autocratic posture of the parent, while it may have been frustrating to the adolescent, was more "legitimate"—in the sense that the parent really did "hold all the cards," and was the repository of most of the relevant power and skills that the adolescent was seeking. Today, however, parents can, under favorable circumstances, provide for their children models of successful, autonomous, flexible, problem-solving behavior, and they can provide love and a fundamental underlying security; but they cannot provide detailed blueprints for mastering the changing demands of a society in headlong transition.

Conversely, the laissez-faire or ignoring parent—permissive but uncommunicative, and frequently not emotionally involved—also makes the task of achieving responsible independence especially difficult in the current world. Despite contrary claims, other influences on adolescent behavior—age-mate peers, the older adolescent youth culture, the adult world in general—frequently cannot provide adequate or consistent guidelines for assuming the kind of responsible independent behavior required by our changing times.

As Bronfenbrenner notes in his thoughtful study of American and Soviet child-rearing practices,[55] where there is a systematic, consistent, supervised effort by adults to employ the peer group as models in adult standard setting, peers may play such a role (as is the case with Soviet children and adolescents). Such, however, is not the prevailing situation in countries like the United States and England. Bronfenbrenner argues that one of the reasons for the relatively higher rates of antisocial behavior in these latter two countries is that, to an increasing extent, parents have been isolated from their children—and from child-rearing—without providing planned substitutes adequate to the task (for example, schools, the church, peers or older adolescents, and extended family and neighbors).

Parental and Peer Influences—a False Dichotomy?

Finally, there is a well-worn cliché that at adolescence the young person turns away from his parents and becomes the captive of his peers. There can be little doubt that the peer group assumes increasing importance during adolescence, as dependency on the family decreases,[56] and also that a number of recent social changes—including the decline of the extended family and neighborhood and increasing age segregation—have tended to heighten peer-group dependence. However, a number of recent studies indicate that this cliché also contains a considerable element of mythology, at least as applied to most adolescents.

In the first place, there is usually considerable overlap between parental and peer values because of commonalities in their backgrounds—social, economic, religious, educational, even geographic. Thus, for example, a white, Catholic, lower-middle-class, ethnic blue-collar adolescent's peers in one of our larger cities are likely to share more common values (for example, educational, vocational, sexual, social, political) with his parents than with his own upper- or upper-middle-class WASP contemporaries.[57] In this sense, then, peers may actually serve to reinforce parental values.

Second, as Clay Brittain, Lyle Larson, and others have demonstrated,[58] neither parental nor peer influence is monolithic. The weight given to either will depend to a significant degree on the adolescent's appraisal of its relative value in a specific situation. For example, peer influence is more likely to be predominant in such matters as tastes in music and entertainment, fashions in clothing and language, patterns of same- and opposite-sex peer interaction, and the like; while parental influence is more likely to be predominant in such areas as underlying moral and social values and understanding of the adult world.[59]

✓ It is also important to recognize that in many instances where the peer group assumes an unusually dominant role in the lives of adolescents, it is likely to be due as much or more to the lack of attention and concern at home, as to the inherent attractiveness of the peer group. Thus in a recently completed study by John Condry, Michael Siman, and Urie Bronfenbrenner of younger adolescents, it was found that those who were strongly peer-oriented were more likely than those who were adult-oriented to hold negative views of themselves and the peer group.[60] "They also expressed a dim view of their own future. Their parents were rated as lower than those of the adult-oriented children both in the expression of affection and support, and in the exercise of discipline and control. Finally, in contrast to the adult-oriented group, the peer-oriented children report engaging in more anti-social behavior such as 'doing something illegal,' 'playing hooky,' lying, teasing other children, etc."[61]

These investigators conclude that "the peer-oriented child is more a product of parental disregard than of the attractiveness of the peer group—that he turns to his age-mates less by choice than by default. The vacuum left by the withdrawal of parents and adults from the lives of children is filled with an undesired —and possibly *undesirable*—substitute of an age-segregated peer group."

✓ Somewhat similar findings have emerged from a very recent investigation by Lyle Larson of seventh, ninth, and twelfth grade boys and girls.[62] He found, among other results, that parental influence was greatest where "parent-adolescent affect" (that is, the quality of the parent-child relationship, as measured by parental interest and understanding, willingness to be helpful, amount of shared family activity, and so forth) was highest. Furthermore, adolescents with high parent-adolescent affect were significantly less likely than those with low affect to see a need to differentiate between the influence of their parents and their best friends.

Not surprisingly, parental influence was found to be greatest at the sixth grade level and least at the twelfth grade level. Interestingly, it was also found that at the seventh grade level the extent of parental influence was only minimally a function of the quality of the parental relationship. At later grade levels, however, where the potential impact of peer-group influence had increased significantly, parent-adolescent affect assumed markedly increased importance as a determinant of parental influence. In short, a parent may be making a serious mistake if he thinks that because he can influence his children at the beginning of adolescence without concerning himself with the quality of the relationship with his children and his contributions to it, he will continue to be able to do so in middle and later adolescence.

Finally, we tend to overlook the important fact that the need for rigid conformity to either parents or peers varies enormously from one adolescent to another. Thus, more self-confident, more autonomous (democratically reared) adolescents may be able to profit from the views and learning experiences provided by both parents and peers, without being strongly dependent on either or unduly troubled by parent-peer differences. Ironically, the adolescent who has gained most confidence in his own self-image as a result of such child-rearing techniques and who is least concerned with popularity "and goes his own way may find that his peers flock around him as a tower of strength."[63]

Sources of difficulty. It appears that where serious difficulties are most likely to arise and where the parent is most likely to find himself feeling helpless is where: (1) there is a very strong, homogeneous peer group with patterns of behavior and attitudes that differ markedly from those of parents; (2) a rewarding parent-child relationship is lacking at the outset, due to a lack of parental interest and understanding, manifest willingness to be helpful, and shared family activities; (3) the parents' own values and behaviors are inconsistent, uninformed, unrealistic, maladaptive, or obviously hypocritical; (4) the adolescent lacks either the self-confidence (based on a positive self-image) and the independence training to act autonomously without undue concern; or (5) as it is phrased on multiple-choice examinations, "all of the above." In most cases where young people have forsaken or renounced family values for those of deviant peer groups, one or more of these conditions is likely to obtain.

Obviously, the task of the parent may be simpler in the kind of traditional, geographically remote small town described earlier— one characterized by extended kinship and neighborly ties and by continual interaction between parents and other adults, peers, the schools, and other social institutions. Under such circumstances, fundamental values and customs are often more firmly held and widely shared among both adults and adolescents. In contrast, the parents' task (as well as that of the adolescent) may be much more difficult in other settings, such as that of a large city, where both the nuclear family and the peer group may be relatively isolated from community-wide interaction or even communication. Where, for example, such an isolated peer group is heavily involved in experimentation with the more serious drugs, with varied forms of early sexual activities, or with delinquent behavior, and where the group is homogeneous and exerts strong social pressures for conformity, parents may be confronted with seemingly insurmountable problems.

Among the typical mistakes in discussing contemporary adolescence is, of course, the tendency to assume that such situations either do not exist or are exaggerated; or, conversely, that they are universal, which they are not. But where they do exist, it is most often where the older sense of community has been dissipated, whether in the urban ghetto or, ironically, in a number of our "swinging," affluent, suburban "bedroom communities."

The more discrepant or deviant the peer group setting, however, the more important does it appear for parents to attempt to provide the kind of confidence-inspiring, autonomy-inducing democratic child-rearing discussed earlier. And the more crucial do efforts at communication and understanding—and active interaction—between parent and child become. The parent who is laissez-faire—providing neither guidance nor a strong model of basic standards and values with which the adolescent can identify —and the parent who is authoritarian—certain of his own views and neither understanding nor feeling any need to understand the views and problems of his adolescent son or daughter—are both likely to vitiate whatever influence they might have had and to leave the adolescent vulnerable to deviant and destructive peer-group influences.

A Final Word

While the stresses that today's parents face cannot be minimized, it is increasingly essential that they preserve some perspective on what values and behaviors are fundamental and "nonnegotiable," and what are either peripheral or in need of an "agonizing reappraisal." This requires both patience and the courage of self-analysis, but it is vital. Recently, I have encountered increasing instances of parents who become so explosive (threatened?) that they refuse to allow a basically sound, well-intentioned adolescent to come home on vacation because of the length of his hair, or because he or she has once tried marijuana, or confessed to a sexual experience, or been engaged in orderly protest against some aspect of the establishment which the parent views himself as representing.

Such parents, whether they are aware of it or not, are pretty well insuring that any future parent-child communication, influence, or understanding will be further vitiated, leaving the adolescent more rather than less vulnerable to more serious and perhaps irreversible experiences, as recent studies of runaways and alienated young adolescents, for example, make clear. These parents would do well to ask themselves how sound and consistent are their own values; how much they really love their children; and how threatened they are themselves by the reefs and shoals of a changing world.

These are indeed difficult and complex times, but if there is one single word that would appear most important to stress to both parents and adolescents, it is *communication*. It is significant that among the intergenerational criticisms cited earlier, adults mentioned a "lack of dialogue with elders," while adolescents complained that "they won't listen to us." Despite the admittedly difficult problems posed by an increasingly complex, fragmented, rapidly changing world, the channels of communication must be kept open, or in some cases reopened, between parents and their adolescent sons and daughters. For the fact is that they need each other, now as much as ever. The view of some social observers that parents and other adults have become irrelevant or even barriers to the psychological and social development of adolescents, particularly young adolescents, may, as I have implied, have a certain romantic appeal, but it is not substantiated by the facts. *Peter Pan* has its indisputable charm, but *Lord of the Flies* is probably more relevant.

In the world of tomorrow, adolescents will have to grow beyond the models their parents can provide, but they still need appropriate parental models to build on, and they need their parents' love and active concern.[64] By the same token, parents need their children, not only for the greater meaning these young people can lend to existence, but also for the very real contribution they can make to the parents' own continuing development and their flexibility in understanding and coping with the inevitabilities of change. While adolescents clearly do not have as many answers to the problems of a troubled society as many of the more articulate among them think they do, they are often far more sensitive than adults to the relevant questions. By acknowledging the legitimacy of these questions, by struggling, through the alchemy of love, to understand the unique needs, problems, and concerns of today's adolescents, parents and other adults may gain a better understanding of their own world and, hopefully, even of themselves.

But if they are to succeed in this task, parents and young people will need a great deal more help from a society that loudly proclaims its devotion to children and adolescents, but that, in fact, does little to demonstrate this concern in practice. The problem is most urgent for the family of poverty, "where the capacity for human response is crippled by hunger, cold, filth, sickness, and despair." But, as the task force of the White House Conference on Children succinctly states, "Even for families who can get along, the rats are gone, but the rat race remains."[65]

Ways need to be found to guarantee to all children and adolescents, as a basic minimum, adequate housing, health care, nutrition, and meaningful educational and vocational opportunities. In addition, we need consciously to plan and carry out ways of reversing current trends toward ever greater age segregation, not only within the family, but in the social life of the community— and in the work setting. While too many children and adolescents still work long hours at physically, mentally, and emotionally debilitating jobs, despite child labor laws, a far larger and more challenging problem to remedy is the absence of meaningful and appropriate work experiences for today's adolescents, who in many ways have become the unwanted stepchildren of our complex, technologically oriented society.

As attempts by an increasing number of young people, and some adults as well, to devise new forms of communal living bear witness,[66] we also need ways to restore a sense of community. Ultimately, this may be done only by breaking down our currently metastasizing urban and suburban sprawls into manageable-sized political, social, and economic units, in which meaningful communication and interaction between all elements of the community —from families to schools, to businesses, to local government, and to the cop on the corner—become possible. At the same time, we need to work at translating possibility into action—through innovative school curricula that involve the wider community; through apprenticeship opportunities for young people in government, business, and community agencies; through work schedules for adults that permit adequate participation in family life; through eliminating the exploitation of young people and their families in misleading or demeaning advertising; through community-wide projects in recreation, ecology, social service, and the like. The list, though not endless, is extensive. But as the White House Conference task force points out, these are things that *can* be done if government, business and industry, and individual citizens really mean what up to now they have only been saying. And they are things that must be done. As we have seen, a substantial majority of adolescents have not as yet given up in their hopes for society or for themselves, and there is still time. But time may be running out. In the words of the task force:

> The failure to reorder our priorities, the insistence on business as usual, and the continued reliance on rhetoric as a substitute for fundamental reforms can have only one result: far more rapid and pervasive growth of alienation, apathy, drugs, delinquency, and violence among the young and not so young in all segments of our national life. We face the prospect of a society which resents its own children and fears its youth. Surely this is the road to national destruction.[67]

I am reminded of the currently popular slogan, "I need all the help I can get." Today's parents and their adolescent sons and daughters are embarked on a perilous voyage, with stormy seas ahead and no port in sight. We can only wish them well.

REFERENCES

1. For a current review of the concept of adolescent turmoil, see Irving B. Weiner, *Psychological Disturbance in Adolescence* (New York: Wiley-Interscience, 1970). See also Elizabeth Douvan and Joseph Adelson, *The Adolescent Experience* (New York: John Wiley, 1966) and Daniel Offer, *The Psychological World of the Teen-Ager: A Study of Normal Adolescent Boys* (New York: Basic Books, 1969).

2. See Erik H. Erikson, "The Problem of Ego Identity," *Journal of the American Psychoanalytic Association,* 4 (1956), 56-121; Anna Freud, "Adolescence," *Psychoanalytic Study of the Child,* 13 (1958), 255-278; and Catherine S. Chilman, "Families in Development at Mid-Stage of the Family Life Cycle," *The Family Coordinator* (October 1968), pp. 297-313.

3. *The American Almanac for 1971* (*The Statistical Abstract of the United States*, 91st ed.) (New York: Grosset and Dunlap, 1971).

4. Lawrence A. Mayer, "New Questions about the U. S. Population," *Fortune* (February 1971), pp. 82-85. Source: U. S. Census, 1970.

5. Hans Sebald, *Adolescence: A Sociological Analysis* (New York: Appleton-Century Crofts, 1968). See also Charles W. Hobart, "Commitment, Value Conflict and the Future of the American Family," *Marriage and Family Living*, 25 (1963), 406.

6. Sebald, *Adolescence*.

7. Kingsley Davis, "The Sociology of Parent-Youth Conflict," *American Sociological Review*, 5 (1940), 523-536; Kenneth Kenniston, *The Uncommitted: Alienated Youth in American Society* (New York: Dell, 1960). See also Vern L. Bengston, "The Generation Gap: A Review and Typology of Social-Psychological Perspectives," *Youth and Society*, 2 (1970), 7-32.

8. *American Almanac*.

9. Urie Bronfenbrenner, *Two Worlds of Childhood: U. S. and U.S.S.R.* (New York: Russell Sage Foundation, 1970), p. 96.

10. Offer, *The Psychological World of the Teenager*, p. 64.

11. Mayer, "New Questions about the U. S. Population."

12. For example, see Daniel Yankelovich, *Generations Apart* (New York: Columbia Broadcasting System, 1969); Louis Harris, "Change, Yes—Upheaval, No," *Life*, 70 (January 8, 1971), 22-27; and Douvan and Adelson, *The Adolescent Experience*.

13. Harris, "Change." See also Paul Henry Mussen, John Janeway Conger, and Jerome Kagan, *Child Development and Personality*, 3d ed. (New York: Harper and Row, 1969).

14. *Children and Parents: Together in the World*, Report of Forum 15, 1970 White House Conference on Children (Washington, D. C.: Superintendent of Documents, 1971).

15. Herbert Wright and others, "Children's Behavior in Communities Differing in Size" (unpublished manuscript, Department of Psychology, University of Kansas, 1969), cited in Bronfenbrenner, *Two Worlds of Childhood*.

16. James S. Coleman, *The Adolescent Society* (New York: Free Press, 1963), p. 7.

17. Bronfenbrenner, *Two Worlds of Childhood*, p. 100.

18. *Children and Parents*.

19. For example, see Harris, "Change," and Yankelovich, *Generations Apart*.

20. Offer, *The Psychological World of the Teenager*; Douvan and Adelson, *The Adolescent Experience*; Mussen, Conger, and Kagan, *Child Development*.

21. Harris, "Change."

22. Louis Harris, "The Teen-Agers," *Newsweek* (March 21, 1966), pp. 57-72.

23. Harris, "Change." See also Mussen, Conger, and Kagan, *Child Development,* and Yankelovich, *Generations Apart.*

24. L. Harris and others, "What People Think About Their High Schools," *Life* (May 16, 1969), p. 32. See also Mussen, Conger, and Kagan, *Child Development.*

25. Ira L. Reiss, "The Scaling of Sexual Permissiveness," *Journal of Marriage and the Family* (1964), pp. 188-199; Morton Hunt, "Special Sex Education Survey," *Seventeen* (July 1970), pp. 95ff; Harris, "Change"; Vance Packard, *The Sexual Wilderness: The Contemporary Upheaval in Male-Female Relationships* (New York: David McKay, 1968); Bernard Rosenberg and Joseph Bensman, "Sexual Patterns in Three Ethnic Subcultures of an American Underclass," *Annals of the American Academy of Political and Social Sciences,* 376 (1968), 61-75.

26. Harris, "Change."

27. Yankelovich, *Generations Apart.*

28. Harris, "What People Think." See also Charles E. Silberman, *Crisis in the Classroom: The Remaking of American Education* (New York: Random House, 1970).

29. Harris, "The Teenagers."

30. Mark Gerzon, *The Whole World Is Watching* (New York: Paperback Library, 1970); Naomi Feigelson, *The Underground Revolution* (New York: Funk and Wagnalls, 1970); Lewis Yablonsky, *The Hippie Trip* (New York: Pegasus, 1968).

31. Yankelovich, *Generations Apart.*

32. Mussen, Conger, and Kagan, *Child Development.*

33. For example, see Theodore Roszak, *The Making of a Counter Culture* (New York: Doubleday Anchor Books, 1969); Joel Fort, *The Pleasure Seekers: The Drug Crisis, Youth, and Society* (New York: Grove Press, 1969); Gerzon, *The Whole World Is Watching;* Yablonsky, *The Hippie Trip;* Feigelson, *The Underground Revolution.*

34. T. George Harris, "The Young are Captives of Each Other: A Conversation with David Riesman," *Psychology Today* (October 1969), 28ff.

35. See, for example, Richard Scammon and Ben J. Wattenberg, *The Real Majority* (New York: Coward-McCann, 1970); Richard S. Blum and others, *Society and Drugs* (San Francisco: Jossey-Bass, 1969); Mussen, Conger, and Kagan, *Child Development;* Adelson, "What Generation Gap?" Packard, *The Sexual Wilderness;* Rosenberg and Bensman, "Sexual Patterns."

36. Harris, "Changes."

37. George H. Gallup, Jr., and John O. Davis, III, "Gallup Poll," *Denver Post*, May 26, 1969, and Harris, "What People Think." An apparent failure to distinguish clearly between parent-child and youth-adult conflicts is seen in Lewis S. Feuer, *The Conflict of Generations* (New York: Basic Books, 1969).

38. Kenneth Keniston, *Young Radicals: Notes on Committed Youth* (New York: Harcourt, Brace, and World, 1968); Edward E. Sampson, Harold A. Korn, and others, *Student Activism and Protest* (San Francisco: Jossey-Bass, 1970).

39. *Rhetoric of Aristotle*, cited in Norman Kiell, *The Universal Experience of Adolescence* (Boston: Beacon Press, 1964), pp. 18-19. For comparisons, see Otto Fenichel, *The Psychoanalytic Theory of Neurosis* (New York: Norton, 1945) and John W. Aldridge, *In the Country of the Young* (New York: Harper and Row, Perennial Library, 1971).

40. David Cooper, *Death of the Family* (New York: Pantheon, 1970).

41. Margaret Mead, *Culture and Commitment: A Study of the Generation Gap* (New York: Doubleday, 1970).

42. *Ibid.*, pp. 32-33.

43. *Ibid.*, pp. 62, 88.

44. Erik H. Erikson, *Childhood and Society*, 2d ed. (New York: W. W. Norton, 1963). See also E. James Anthony and Therese Benedek, *Parenthood: Its Psychology and Psychopathology* (Boston: Little, Brown, 1971).

45. Joan Aldous, *The Family Development Approach to Family Analysis* (prepublication manuscript, Family Study Center, University of Minnesota, 1967), chap. 4.

46. For comprehensive reviews, see Wesley C. Becker, "Consequences of Different Kinds of Parental Discipline," in Martin L. Hoffman and Lois Wladis Hoffman, eds., *Review of Child Development Research* (New York: Russell Sage Foundation, 1964). See also Mussen, Conger, and Kagan, *Child Development*, esp. chaps. 12, 14, and 15; Lois Meek Stoltz, *Influences on Parent Behavior* (Stanford, Calif.: Stanford University Press, 1967); and Earl S. Schaefer, "A Configurational Analysis of Children's Reports of Parent Behavior," *Journal of Consulting Psychology*, 29 (1965), 552-557.

47. Becker, "Consequences of Different Kinds of Parental Discipline," p. 197.

48. Matt Clark and Jean Seligmann, "Bringing up Baby: Is Dr. Spock to Blame?" *Newsweek* (September 23, 1968), pp. 68-72; and Benjamin Spock, "Don't Blame Me!" *Look* (January 26, 1971), pp. 37-38.

49. Bronfenbrenner, *Two Worlds of Childhood*, p. 98.

50. Erik H. Erikson, *Identity: Youth and Crisis* (New York: W. W. Norton, 1968); Douvan and Adelson, *The Adolescent Experience;* Mussen, Conger, and Kagan, *Child Development*, esp. pp. 622-635.

51. Glen H. Elder, Jr., "Structural Variations in the Child Rearing Relation-

ship," *Sociometry*, 25 (1962), 241-262; and Charles E. Bowerman and Glen H. Elder, Jr., "Variations in Adolescent Perception of Family Power Structure," *American Sociological Review*, 29 (1964), 551-567.

52. Glen H. Elder, Jr., "Parental Power Legitimation and Its Effect on the Adolescent," *Sociometry*, 26 (1963), 50-65.

53. Morris Rosenberg, *Society and the Adolescent Self-Image* (Princeton, N. J.: Princeton University Press, 1965). See also Diana Baumrind, "Authoritarian vs. Authoritative Control," *Adolescence*, 3 (1968), 255-272.

54. Mussen, Conger, and Kagan, *Child Development*, pp. 630-631.

55. Bronfenbrenner, *Two Worlds of Childhood*.

56. Philip R. Costanzo and Marvin E. Shaw, "Conformity as a Function of Age Level," *Child Development*, 37 (1966), 967-975; Elias Tuma and Norman Livson, "Family Socioeconomic Status and Adolescent Attitudes to Authority," *Child Development*, 31 (1960), 387-399.

57. For representative findings, see Mussen, Conger, and Kagan, *Child Development*.

58. Clay V. Brittain, "Adolescent Choices and Parent-Peer Cross-Pressures," *American Sociological Review*, 28 (1963), 385-391; Clay V. Brittain, "A Comparison of Rural and Urban Adolescents with Respect to Parent vs. Peer Compliance," *Adolescence*, 13 (1969), 59-68; and Lyle E. Larson, "The Relative Influence of Parent-Adolescent Affect in Predicting the Salience Hierarchy Among Youth" (paper presented at the annual meetings of the National Council on Family Relations, Chicago, October 1970).

59. Douvan and Adelson, *The Adolescent Experience*.

60. John C. Condry, Jr., Michael L. Siman, and Urie Bronfenbrenner, "Characteristics of Peer- and Adult-Oriented Children" (unpublished manuscript, Department of Child Development, Cornell University, 1968).

61. Bronfenbrenner, *Two Worlds of Childhood*, pp. 101-102.

62. Larson, "The Relative Influence of Parent-Adolescent Affect." See also Charles E. Bowerman and John W. Kinch, "Changes in Family and Peer Orientation of Children Between the Fourth and Tenth Grades," *Social Forces*, 37 (February 1959), 206-211.

63. L. Joseph Stone and Joseph Church, *Childhood and Adolescence: A Psychology of the Growing Person* (New York: Random House, 1957), p. 291.

64. Konrad Lorenz, "The Enmity Between Generations and Its Probable Ethological Causes," *The Psychoanalytic Review*, 57 (1970), 333-377.

65. *Children and Parents*.

66. Sara Davidson, "Open Land: Getting Back to the Communal Garden," *Harper's* (June 1970), pp. 91-102; "The American Family: Future Uncertain," *Time* (December 28, 1970), pp. 34-39; and "The American Family," *Look* (January 26, 1971), pp. 21-86.

67. *Children and Parents*.

JOHN H. GAGNON

The Creation of the Sexual in Early Adolescence

ANY DISCUSSION of the sexual in human development must recognize
and come to terms with the degree to which modern thinking has
been dominated first by the work of Freud and second by the work
of Kinsey and his coworkers. Of the two, Freud has surely been of
greater influence in shaping theoretical models of development and
in the penetration of his ideas into the cultural ambience; however,
it is in the work of Kinsey that we find the largest body of empirical
data about sexual behavior, regardless of the strictures that one
might wish to put on its generalizability. Despite the predominance
of these two men in the discussion of the sexual, there is, from the
point of view of the history of science, a curiously nonconsequential
quality about their work. That is, while the status of their ideas as
cultural events has been substantial, there has been a painful lack
of scientific followup of either their concepts or their data. This is
not to say that there is not a substantial literature that has developed
out of the psychoanalytic tradition, but in the largest part it has
been narrowly concerned with the Talmudic imposition of Freud's
original models on clinical case histories or the reading of collective
and sociocultural events and processes using a narrowly individual
explanatory style (for example, swaddling of individuals in childhood produces national imperialism in adulthood). The immediate
commitment of the psychoanalytic movement to a specific clinical
program (regardless of its sophistication) insulated it from academic science, and the intellectual and moral dominance of Freud
over his colleagues made the internal debates over psychoanalytic
doctrine occasions for divisiveness or affirmation of the central dogma
rather than scientific discussions.[1] Kinsey's scientific fate has been
perhaps ruder than Freud's, since very little research of any sort
has followed upon the publication of his two major works, perhaps
two to three papers of merit each year. The two large volumes continue to be undigested lumps in the craw of the research community.

231

While Kinsey had serious consequences in changing and creating cultural attitude, in bringing the language of sex into general public discussion (as Freud had among intellectuals a generation before), at the level of science, there has been only a minimal increase in activity.[2]

To some degree this failure to develop a research concern for sexual matters in the conventional disciplines can be laid at the door of scientific and cultural prudery, but equally it is a function of two other forces: the historical (and perhaps reactive) self-insulation of "sexological" researches and researchers from the mainstream disciplines and the continued commitment—shared by both Freud and Kinsey—to a belief in "biological knowingness" or to the wisdom of nature in the explanation of sexual behavior and development. The very idea of a sexology tends to insulate those interested in sexual behavior from both theoretical and methodological developments that occur on a broad front within the human sciences. Because sex is culturally isolated in general, researchers often claim exemption from normal methodological strictures and become deeply and defensively invested in the substantive content of sexuality while remaining indifferent to the rest of social life. The very specialness of sex makes its students special, both to themselves and others, and their possession of secret cultural knowledge is in itself sometimes intellectually disabling since it often is used as a device to disarm criticism.

Intersecting this adisciplinary tradition in sex research, there is a continued commitment on the part not only of researchers but also of the larger society to see sex behavior as the working out of some immanent biological plan. This tradition is surely present in Freud with his emphasis on a drive model of development, a libidinal thrust that sequentially organizes intra- and extrapsychic life as well as the very meaning of the part of the body. In Kinsey, while some of the broader connections that Freud would have argued existed between tactality and sexuality in early life are disputed, it is asserted that "orgasm is distinct from any other phenomenon that occurs in the life of an animal, and its appearance can ordinarily if not invariably be taken as evidence of the sexual nature of an individual's response."[3] This direct relation between the external signs of physiological events and necessary motivational and cognitive states (the analog to the Freudian interpretation of the infant's genital gesture as equivalent to masturbating) is a given for nearly all students of sexual behavior whose frequent error is to confuse the outcomes of sexual learning with their apparent origins.

In large measure our sense of the role of sex in human development departs considerably from the Freudian or Kinseyian traditions, especially to the degree that they promote the prevailing image of the sexual drive as a basic biological mandate which presses against and must be controlled by the cultural and social matrix. This drive reduction model of sexual behavior which is then mediated by cultural and social controls is preeminent in sexological literature. Explanations of sexual behavior that flow from this control-repression model are relatively simple. The sex drive is thought to exist at some constant level in any cohort of the population and in some rising and falling level in the individual life cycle. It presses for expression, and in the absence of controls, which exist either in the external laws or mores or in appropriate internalized repressions learned in early socialization, there will be outbreaks of abnormal sexual activity. In the more primitive versions of drive theory, there is a remarkable congruence between the potentiating mechanisms for either specifically sexual or generally sinful behavior. The organism is inherently sexual (sinful) and its behavior is controlled by the presence of inhibitory training and channeling, internalized injunctions, and the absence of temptations. If these mechanisms fail there will certainly be sexual misconduct (sin). More sophisticated models than this can be found in functional theories in sociology or in revisionist psychoanalytic models, but fundamental to each is a drive reduction model that sees sex as having necessary collective and individual consequences because of its biological origins.[4]

In contrast to these traditions that have grown up in research on human sexuality, it is our sense that sexual behavior can be understood only through determinining its complex relations with the rest of social and psychological life and that in no sense is there evidence that sexuality as a drive or experience assumes any particular priority in human development. An understanding of sexual behavior (or more accurately, sexual conduct, which is, in the words of Ernest Burgess, sexual behavior that is evaluated, judged, and has meaning in cultural situations) derives not from some special understanding of the content of sexual activity, but from the consideration of that activity through the intellectual frameworks provided by the conventional disciplines of behavioral science.[5] Central to this commitment of the behavioral sciences is a commitment to sexual conduct (and even activity) as learned behavior, not learned in the simplicity of behaviorist psychology, but learned in the sense of the coordination of individual and collective cultural elements which will vary over the individual life cycle, differing within sub-cultures of any one society and cross-culturally in both its historical and geographical dimensions. There is no necessary meaning attrib-uted to any specific joinings of organs, for these couplings exist only as one more element that derives its meaning from the surrounding domain of cultural life. In large measure the biological domain will tell of limitations, parameters, and will provide constants around which the interesting variations of cultural life will play themselves out. At no point will the biological framework directly determine the content of cultural life.

In contrast to views that argue in a complete or mixed fashion for a biological mandate for sexual expression that begins at birth and has predictable early signs (for example, orgasm or mastur-bation in infancy), it is the view of this essay that in the particular cultural conditions of the West, that period of early adolescence is largely a break with the past and that the outcome of changes as-sociated with this period in development in no respect assures a priority or special importance to those elements that external ob-servers have determined to be sexual. During the period of early adolescence the young person begins to respond in intrinsically sex-ual ways, that is, in ways that are discontinuous with prior experi-ence that is labled sexual, either in psychoanalytic or the Kinsey tradition. Neither the homologous physical experiences which are observed by adults in infant masturbation and childhood sex play, nor the orgasms observed by the Kinsey group among infants, carry with them meanings and motivations that are congruent with what an adult actor would apply to his own or others' behavior.

As William Simon and I have argued elsewhere, in an earlier at-tempt to point out the dynamic interaction between overt activities and symbolic meanings in sociosexual and psychosexual develop-ment, sexual behavior is not

the masked or rationalized expression of some primordial drive. The in-dividual learns to be sexual as he or she learns sexual scripts, scripts that invest actors and situations with erotic content. One can easily conceive of numerous social situations in which all or almost all of the ingredients of sexuality are present, but which remain nonsexual in that no sexual arousal occurs. Thus, combining such elements as desire, privacy, and physically desirable alter of the opposite sex, the probability of something sexual occurring will, under normal circumstances, remain exceedingly small until one or both actors organize these elements into an appropriate script. The very concern with foreplay in sexual behavior suggests something of this order. From one point of view foreplay might be described as progressive physical excitement, or what the authors have elsewhere referred to as the "rubbing of two sticks together to get a fire going" model. From another point of view, this activity may be described as a method of eroticizing the body and as a method for transforming mute, inarticulate gestures and motions into a sociosexual drama.[6]

By positing this discontinuity in sexual development between childhood and adolescence it is not meant that man becomes sexual all at once; however, the elements of prior socialization that have most effective continuity are those which have the least directly "sexual" content from an adult observer's point of view. The past influences this period, but most profoundly through the forms of gender role training. From this point of view the early years around puberty, say from eleven to fourteen, are of major significance in integrating new definitions of a potentially sexual self with prior gender role training which together are the ground work for the sexual component in adult character structure.

Self-Definition and Physical Change

In the early years of adolescence there is the beginning of a major series of changes in the conformation of the bodies of males and females as a result of the hormonal changes. Menstruation in the female, ejaculation in the male, pubic and other axillary hair, breast development, voice change in the male, and a general shift in body shape make apparent to both the developing child and adults around him that significant and (more important) collectively visible changes are going on. As far as can currently be told, the hormonal changes that are occurring at this time are not directional in terms of a necessary outcome in developing masculine or feminine personality structure, but are rather activational in character. There is no evidence that differing androgen levels in the two sexes will account for differing rates of overt sexual behavior either within or between genders and no evidence that these same biological events produce variations in meanings attributed to these behaviors.

These years represent a difficult and inchoate period, from physical, psychological, and social points of view. These varying developments or status changes are often triggered by a remarkably uneven appearance of or completion of the physical signs of development. From the recall data in the Kinsey volumes (which in the aggregate

conform to those observational data collected at the same ages)
women reported the median appearance of pubic hair at 12.3 years
(varying from 8 to 18 years), the median appearance of breasts at
12.4 (varying from 8 to 24 years), menses at 13.0 years, and completion of growth in height at a median age of about 16. The cumulative incidence of menses is that 21 per cent menstruate at age 11.9 or
before, 29 per cent in their twelfth year, 29 per cent in their thirteenth year, and 21 per cent in their fourteenth year and after.[7] In
contrast, males recall pubic hair at a median age of 13.4, growth
completion at a median of 17.5, and, probably most significantly,
first ejaculation at a median age of 13.9. The cumulative percentage
of first ejaculation was 8 per cent at age 11.9 and before, 19 per cent
at age 12.0, 29 per cent at age 13.0, 25 per cent at age 14.0, and 18
per cent thereafter.[8]

While the aggregate figures seem orderly, young people of the
same age and same year in school often appear extremely different in terms of their physical development. Some twelve-year-old
girls will have moderately complete breast development and will
be taller than boys their own age, while other girls will not menstruate until fourteen and may, in consequence, feel that they are
somehow deficient in a womanly characteristic. Early completion
of general bodily growth in a boy can lead to adults believing that he
is more psychologically advanced than he might be, or to patterns
of masturbatory behavior that are far in advance of his peer group.
A grammar or middle school teacher, who is facing a classroom of
children in the fifth, sixth, seventh, and eighth grades is often teaching children with vastly different levels of physical development
and with extremely varied levels of private experience.[9] The sex
education course in the sixth grade will be speaking to girls who
have been menstruating for a year and a half and others who will not
menstruate for two years, and to some boys who have been masturbating to orgasm a number of times a week while others are still
involved in games and other boyish pursuits.

This wide variety of available experiences within a limited age
grading, an age grading whose members are often kept in close social-psychological interaction by the schools, is quite problematic
for the child. The external physical signs of adolescence are differentially available to different sets of judges within the local environment. Inevitably, problems of comparison emerge between children
which relate to physical strength and size and masturbatory prowess
among boys or the appearance of breasts and menses among girls.

The more public changes require judgment by the self, peers of the same sex, peers of the opposite sex, parents, and teachers. Some changes are (or seem) apparent only to the self, others to narrower or wider publics.

However variable the physical changes that mark the beginning and middle of early adolescence, it has meaning as a period of development because it is the time when society at large (and more approximately, parents, peers, schools, and media) recognize and, in part, impose on and invent the conventional sexual capacity of the individual. Even though the capacity for orgasm (as distinguished from ejaculation in the male) is available far earlier in life and even experienced by some infants and children, there is no sense in which the society promotes the utilization of or organization of this capacity into preadolescent experience.[10] Even though some few young people enter into adolescent sexual behavior before they are publicly defined as adolescents, for the majority this passage into overt sexual behavior is linked with the social transition as defined either by peers or by parents. Other than prepubertal sex play (and *play* is the appropriate word for the behavior), it is the entry into the new social status that triggers an increase in the rates of overt sexual behavior and the attribution and integration of new meanings for the behavior. In these earliest stages of the transition, extensively mixed modes of behavior occur; hence it is possible for young boys to be both playing games of tag and using *Playboy* to masturbate. At this same moment physically precocious young girls will be covertly admired by older males and a generous amount of seductive behavior may be engaged in by such females without any conception of the mental constructs that it produces in the sexually experienced of either gender.

The sexually nonspecific character of the biological change in its minimal identification as being sexual by the experiencing child is evidenced by the numbers of children who report erection or orgasm from physical activities that were only generally arousal producing, for example, tree climbing or fright, without it being defined as sexual. Only in a few cases prior to adolescence is there evidence that there was any attempt to repeat this behavior, even though it might have been experienced as pleasurable. While one problem clearly for the child is the mechanics of making orgasm occur again (erections from the fear, anxiety, and excitement of climbing trees do not automatically translate into manual masturbatory repertoires), more significantly the event occurs without being bound into an organized set of behaviors which insure its reproducibility (except by climbing more trees, perhaps). This suggests the limitations of pure stimulus response interpretations of sexual activity in that the single pleasurable act requires an integration into a large and more complex structure of organized activities. As Kinsey states:

> The record suggests that the physiologic mechanism of any emotional response (anger, fright, pain, etc.) may be the basic mechanism of sexual response. Originally, the preadolescent boy erects indiscriminately to the whole array of emotional situations, whether they be sexual or nonsexual in nature. By his late teens the male has been so conditioned that he rarely responds to anything except a direct physical stimulation of genitalia or to psychic situations that are specifically sexual. In the still older male even physical stimulation is rarely effective unless accompanied by such a psychologic atmosphere. The picture is that of the psychosexual emerging from a much more generalized and basic physiologic capacity *which becomes sexual as an adult knows it,* through experience and conditioning.[11]

As is common in the Kinsey volumes there is a limited understanding of the psychological or social explanations of the processes of development; however, the observations themselves are most accurate.

The Emergence of Sexual Conduct

The phrase "which becomes sexual as an adult knows it" is the critical element in the transition between the general disorder of the beginnings of adolescence and participating in sexual activity with all of social and psychological elements that adults attribute to it. The tentative sexual-like behaviors and the physical signs of adolescence are enriched by differential adult and peer imputations of motives, desires, and needs, which through their very imputation become the occasion for the child's learning them. Sexual behavior and the desire for sexual activity become the occasion for attributing both old and new meanings to a novel and unexplored domain. Previously learned moral categories and oppositions (good and evil, purity and degradation, modesty) and gender role activities (aggression and submission, control and freedom, needs for achievement and affiliation) are integrated into new scripts, at first private and then collective, which contain new meanings to be applied to organs, orifices, activities, and people which make up the conventional sociosexual drama.

Masturbation, Gender, and Fantasy

Both in its onset and in the culmination of this period it is required that the developmental process as it takes place in the male and female be distinguished. The two genders share the experience of transition from childhood, but the early outcomes of these transitions serve to further estrange each gender from the existential character of the other's sexual experience. For males early adolescence is commonly characterized by the onset of overt sexual activity which is conducted in the context of secrecy experienced in tension with the public masculine striving associated with homosociality. In contrast, among females overt sexual activity is infrequent; they, like males, live in a world dominated by their own gender, but it is a more public world designed to promote future heterosociality. Within two years after puberty most males have had their commitment to sexuality reinforced by orgasm, commonly through masturbation, though there is some social class variation in the early onset of heterosexual contacts to orgasm. These sexual experiences occur nearly universally in situations of secrecy, with their most public affirmation in the context of male peers, the secret society of the male alliance.[12] As part of this secrecy and the inability to share except in indirect and anxious ways what is a powerful and novel experience, an experience for which there is no social provision either in terms of adult instruction or localized places for performance, there is engendered feelings of guilt and anxiety. The available social world is composed of peers with the same feelings of separation and fearfulness, but this peer group world does provide a set of meanings that can be applied to both masturbation and heterosexuality.

Unlike the male experience, either during this period or later in life, few females masturbate to orgasm (only about two thirds ever do so), and they do so at far lower frequencies. Not only are the rates of behavior different, it appears that as a result of a differing surrounding context, the experience of masturbation is far more idiosyncratic for women. The existence of male-male discussions, aspersions, and comparisons serves to regularize and order and further motivate the behavior; among women the experience of early masturbation seems often unconnected with any other domain of behavior. The crucial difference seems to be the lack of collective or social sources to provide a larger set of social meanings.

The differences in rates can only in part indicate these psychological processes; however, the major differences between men and women is expressed in the Kinsey data collected between 1938 and 1948: [13]

ACCUMULATIVE INCIDENCE OF
MASTURBATION TO ORGASM

By age	12	15	20
	%	%	%
Male	21	82	92
Female	12	20	33

A more recent set of figures taken from a 1967 national sample of college students (average age around 18.5 when interviewed) indicates a remarkable continuity and stability for these figures on gender differences in masturbation.[14]

FREQUENCY OF MASTURBATION
IN HIGH SCHOOL

	Twice a week or more %	Ever to once a month %	Never %	Number of cases
Male	77	12	11	586
Female	17	23	60	581

The key difference between males and females is that for the latter the organizing experience of puberty is the encouraging and furthering of the reality of marriage rather than the reality of sexual activity. Females live in a homosocial world as do males, but it is a homosocial world composed of both adult women and peers who primarily value the girl for her ultimate status as wife and mother. In this sense the girl is prepared for heterosociality, if not for heterosexuality. It is a world of women and girls training a girl for behavior with reference to men without a concomitant understanding of the diverging pattern of sexual development being experienced by men. This linkage of the young girl with the woman's role and the publicly valued institution of marriage means that the female lives most of her life as preadult in a public status where the coercive forces of normal socialization are present.

The key role of the presence or absence of early sexual activity, either in terms of masturbation or early heterosexual involvement, cannot be underestimated in the reinforcing of a divergence in gender development. Nearly universally for males, even though the majority find masturbation pleasing, there is guilt and anxiety attached to the masturbatory experience.[15] While we no longer believe that there is a connection between insanity and the expenditure of these vital bodily essences, there is little evidence that there has been any reduction in the anxiety associated with masturbatory practices by the young who are beginning their sexual lives. Indeed, it is possible to hypothesize that it is the existence of this anxiety about masturbation that supports our experiential belief that the sexual drive is one of extreme potency. We presume that we are experiencing a biologically powerful experience when in fact it is the guilt and the anxiety associated with arousal identified as sexual which is provoking our sense of intensity. We mislocate the source of the intensity, attaching it to a bodily state rather than to the psychological processes that accompany the experience.

This guilt and anxiety is not a simple consequence of the fact that society disapproves of the behavior. It rather derives from a number of sources. Masturbation is performed in secret, not because of specific sexual prohibition, but because most things connected with the genitals are performed in private. Here earlier training in modesty comes into play, a training that children do not experience as sexual, though their parents may, in which the genitals become part of the excluded and private zone. Most early acts involving the genitals are involved with excretion, and privacy is part of this exclusion. The beginning manipulation of the genitals for purposes of pleasure retains this exclusion, and is further intensified by the beginnings of fantasies of doing sexual things with oneself and with others. These fantasies are the preliminary rehearsals and the vicarious organization of sociosexual dramas using the primitive symbolic resources that are available. This activity in the private zone increases the breach between male child and parents (and other members of the immediate family) where the sentimental and the erotic are complexly intertwined. Often the utilization of available effectively bonded figures (sisters, relatives) in sexual fantasy creates an attachment between sexual performance and normative violation. Further anxiety is generated by the ambivalent attitudes of peers toward masturbation and sexual activity in general. While the peer group is supportive of predatory achievement-oriented and aggressive styles of sexual performance (once again deriving from general gender role training and not a hunting instinct), masturbation is treated with great suspicion unless performed in the context of heroic sexual contest.

Viewed from this perspective, which shares many of the concerns for the symbolic meaning of behavior generated by the psychoanalytic perspective without sharing its concept of drive or unilinear biological causality, masturbation becomes a complex and ambiguous event in socialization. The age at onset, its frequency, its absence if it does not occur, its embeddedness in peer and parent relations, its relation to past socialization, are all interactively tied to other dimensions of social and psychological life.

The general absence of masturbation among women is, when contrasted with the male experience, commonly explained in one of three ways. It is assumed that masturbation is universal and that females repress their memories of it, or it is assumed that women's sexual drive is more inhibited or repressed than that of men, or it is assumed that the sexual drive itself is biologically weaker among women. These kinds of interpretations seem to be ill-founded and lead to endless confusions and misunderstandings about female sexuality. As has been argued, the assumption of a universal biological mandate for any sexual activity or for a gender variation in the strength of biological impulse is not supported by any body of data on human beings. Further, the psychoanalytic model which imposes on women a male history of development makes the development of female sexuality far more mysterious than it need be, though as an existential experience men can still see it only through a glass darkly.

The lack of an upsurge in sexual activity at adolescence among females indicates that there is less of a break between the nonsexual training experiences of childhood and the experiences of early adolescence for females than for males. The future valued status of womanhood, with its comparatively narrow commitments to wifehood and childrearing, seems more or less continuous with earlier experiences in gender training. Gender-linked training in submissiveness and lack of aggression toward parents link to similar roles that are expected of female adults with reference to husbands. Girls are trained to occupy essentially reactive roles, roles in which they are to be scheduled by the behavior of others, including their future children.

Similarly to boys, girls are trained in notions of modesty; they are not trained in sexual performances nor is their quasisexual behavior defined in any directly sexual manner for them. It is not women's sexual drive that is inhibited, for the language of "drive" and "inhibition" are both faulty; it is that women receive no training in sexual activity while being positively trained in docility. It would be easier to explain the low rates of overt female sexuality by the existence of a positive event (like repression), but what is apparent for women is that what we must posit is an *absence* of sexual training, rather than the inhibition of a native talent.

During this period of sexual nontraining females are offered a wide range of other nonsexual experiences which link to conventional gender role performance and which are coordinated with it. Menstruation (properly so, in most senses) is fundamentally linked to the capacity for pregnancy rather than sex. The desire for the social occasions of romance, love, and marriage are universally reinforced by the conventional social order composed of both peers and parents. Parents are more protective in terms of controlling a girl's time and likelihood of sexual involvement, though this is not specifically inhibitory, but rather limits the occasions in which she might fall into sexual encounters. Since masturbation among females is linked to so few other important social experiences, it rarely becomes organized into other patterns of behavior. For boys there is achievement, fear, aggression, and normative violation to attach to bodily manipulation; for the girls only a modest sense of anxiety unlinked to more powerful motivations. It remains until a period later than the one with which we are concerned for women to experience overt sexual behavior in concordance with the powerful collective dimensions of romance, violation of taboos, and consequent emotional feelings that enhance sexual acts. It is important to note that in the Kinsey data nearly half of the females in the sample who did masturbate did so after the first orgasm in sociosexual experience.

One of the key socialization effects of the differences in masturbatory behavior between men and women is the differential specification of the central loci of sexual response on the body. It is clear from cross-cultural evidence that the sequence of sexual foreplay that is seen as necessary to the production of orgasm in the West is a cultural invention rather than a biological necessity. The erogenous zones of the body are in large measure learned locations rather than special congeries of nerve endings that have built-in sexual meaning. Masturbation tends to focus the male sense of feeling of sexual desire in the penis, giving the genitals centrality in the physical and symbolic domains. This shift to genital priority occurs for women at a far later date if it occurs at all. Genital localization of erotic response is a function of reactive sexual contacts with males rather than through masturbatory sexual experience. It is this diffuse character of responsiveness that results from a differential staging of sexual socialization that has created the false dichotomy between the clitoral and vaginal orgasm. It is only through believing that the vagina is the "natural" place to feel response (since coitus involves intromission and this is the "natural" form of sexual behavior) that has made us misunderstand the sociopsychological sources of bodily eroticism. In some measure, females may well be more flexible sexually than males in this matter and be able to respond with a wider definition of the parts of the body as participating in sexual performances. This contention that these matters are learned is also applicable to the breasts, where external definition of them as primary erotic signs is learned by women through their contact with men and the later autonomous erotic pleasure they take in them is created by this prior reading of the body.

Another distinction which must be made in terms of significance of masturbation as an early form of overt sexual behavior is its provision of an arena for the acting out of specifically sexual fantasies which are tied to other social motives. Here there are differences not only between the genders, but between males of various social classes. Once the tension release aspects or the physiological dimensions of the masturbation are deemphasized, what is observable is that there is a complex feedback loop between what is defined as a physically pleasurable act and the reinforcement of newly organized sexual scripts. The masturbatory act in the most conventional learning theory terms reinforces a good deal of symbol manipulation, and this symbolic commitment tends to take on an independence significance later in life.

The differences between the symbolic commitments of males and females in sexuality, and especially as they accompany masturbation, are only partially known. As we have noted, not many females masturbate and those who do, do so at rates that are much below those of males. Further, the fantasies that we know about (and the information is both retrospective in most cases and sparse) among females tend to support the belief that their fantasies on the level of specific sexual acts are commonly limited to the sexual things that they have done, and further, that the context of social arrangements that surround the thoughts of sexual acts are those which emphasize love, marriage, social attachment, and in some cases, mild forms of masochism. The participants in the act are either known or actors with the kind of social status that would be appropriate for marriage. In contrast, the male sexual fantasy, which can appear to the naïve observer to be denuded of social factors (though as with pornography, there are explicit sexual elements) is rich in specifically sexual behavior. The targets of sexual activity are the notorious (hence the erotic) and local females who have high status in peer structures that surround the male. There are commonly themes of sexual aggression, the use of transgressive sexual techniques (mouth genital contact and the like), and fantasies of sexual cornucopias (the harem). The more complex sexual fantasies develop later in this period, say from fourteen to sixteen. The sexual acts are often suggestive of needs for achievement (the making of the unattainable), the acting out of moral transgression, and reduction of anxiety through fantasies of omnipotence. What is central here is that the sexual act is being tied to nonsexual motives that preexist in gender role training. The masturbatory fantasy prefigures ultimate male attitudes and in the case where it occurs among females suggests the degree to which gender role training is coercive in ultimate development.

While the incidence of masturbation across social class among males is quite similar, there is substantial variation across social class in its use and meaning.[16] From the Kinsey data and other studies, it appears that middle-class boys tend to masturbate more frequently and accompany it with relatively complex fantasies. Indeed, there is no reason why this pattern of symbolic elaboration should not develop, given the already existing commitment on the part of middle-class males to symbolic manipulations in other spheres of life. Already directed into lines of development that emphasize socioemotional skills and an attachment to cognitive achievement, there is no reason why these skills should not be put to use in the originating portions of sexual development. In contrast, working- and lower-class males masturbate less often and, while fantasy occurs, it does so with less complexity and further, as a result of other factors in working-class life, masturbation is reduced in significance. Masturbation is thought to be unmanly in working-class situations, an unmanliness that is reinforced by the presentation of alternative patterns of early heterosexual commitment. The middle-class male who tends to have earlier affective contact with females, finds them considerably less accessible physically than does the working-class boy, though these differences have often been exaggerated.

Heterosexuality and Homosociality

It is this phasing of the movement into heterosexual experience, either directly or as a fundamentally valued experience that can replace masturbation, that distinguishes between males of various social classes. It is apparent that there are pre- and early pubertal entries into coitus in all social groups, but these are quite exceptional in the middle classes and only slightly more frequent in working lower-class communities. At age thirteen there are very few boys who are capable of handling the relatively complex social skills required to perform the social manipulations necessary to have coitus with a female of the same age. That it does happen is not doubted, but it does not represent the main drift of sexual socialization during this period. The proportion of white males in the Kinsey college educated group who had intercourse in the sequence of years during this period were by age twelve, 1 per cent, by age fourteen, 6 per cent and by age sixteen, 16 per cent.[17] In contrast, the percentages for the same ages for white working-class males were 9 per cent, 20 per cent, and 40 per cent.[18]

What is significant about these acts of coitus is not the specific acts themselves, which are sporadic and infrequent even for the most successful male, but rather the milieu in which they are performed. This period is dominated by *homosociality*, that is, a period in life when valuation of the self is more keyed to those of like gender than it is to those of opposite gender. This male world, full of rather primitive predatory sexual values focusing on the moral differences between good girls and bad girls, and acting out achievement motives involved in seeing "how far one can get," uses sexual contacts with females as a device for confirming social status among males. What is critical is not the act, but to whom the act is referential. The higher incidence of coitus among working-class males and the value system of sexual predation often means that such early sexual experience essentially limits (though it does not have to in other social milieus) the capacity for heterosocial commitments later in life. By heterosocial, I mean the development of the capacity to perform sexual acts which value the woman and which bind together males and females in contrast to those sexual performances with females that bind together males.

Homosocial values exist among middle-class males at this time, but there is far more interpenetration of male social life by females (mothers and peers) in middle-class than in working-class environments. The efflorescence of early dating patterns in middle-class contexts, which are so worrisome to many parents because they seemingly increase the risk of early sexual experience, may well serve to increase male commitments to heterosociality. Much of the sexual contact during this period is petting above the waist with some genital contact, but such contacts do not commonly easily proceed to coitus. These steady dating experiences may well serve to increase the young male's investment in the rhetoric of love and emotional commitment which seem so necessary a part of the marriage pattern of this society. Even when the young male's protestations of affection are cynical affectations to achieve greater sexual access, what must be kept in mind is that we often become what we thought we were only pretending.

Since coitus requires that males have a partner, there clearly must be, at least, some females in this age period who have these extensive sexual contacts. The Kinsey percentages for sexual intercourse among white nondelinquent females for this period are as follows: [19]

ACCUMULATIVE INCIDENCE OF COITUS
FOR FEMALES, AGES 13 AND 15

Educational level	13	15
	%	%
0–8	9	18
9–12	1	5
13–16	–	2
17+	1	1

What is most apparent is that there is little difference between educational levels (except for educational level 0–8), and from data gathered by William Simon and the author in 1967, there is little difference in the incidence of coitus for these ages between the Kinsey data gathered on college women from 1938 to 1950 and for females presently in college. What seems to occur during this period is that a limited number of females become the targets for the sexual interests of a larger number of males. The "easy lay," the "bad girl," the "peg board" reinforce the male imagery of purity and corruption that is one of the central symbolic dimensions of sexuality.

These females, for whatever reasons, become that small pool who are involved in sexual experience early in life. While they are the targets of male sexual interest, they are also the targets of female rejection.

The general absence of overt sexual activity by females during this period does not preclude the fact that they are receiving training experience which will link to sexual activity later. In the homosocial world in which females live, during this period there are sets of informing goals that link to competition, not in the sexual marketplace, but in the marriage marketplace. Competition in this marketplace requires learning to present the self to males as a marketable commodity, in some sense as a potential sexual object. On the cosmetic level, nearly all young females, especially in the more recent past, have begun to learn these skills early. In another place this process has been described as learning all of the postures of sex, except pleasure, but there is the possibility that this pattern has aided in the development of females' attitudes toward attractiveness that has some sexual overtones. The content of the sexual role for the female retains its essential commitment to service for the male, a service that is to be provided far in the future, and in the context of love and marriage.

While this period of life is filled with moral injunctions toward young girls, it does not appear to us that much of this instruction is directed toward specifically sexual prohibitions. Few parents tell their daughters not to copulate in so many words (given the limited existential link between the verbal sign and the behavior, one wonders what such an injunction could mean), they rather hedge in girls' lives with notions of good companions, early hours, and restricted dating. As a consequence, certain forms of sexual behavior in this period are linked to testing these injunctions of control rather than for the ambiguous pleasure that exists in the sexual act itself.

In this period, the male and the female are being trained in essentially opposed modalities, though there is more interconnection between boys and girls in middle-class than in other social locations. The central themes for females are commitment to affect-laden relationships and to the rhetoric of romantic love. It is not so much that their sexual development is inhibited, though it is policed, but that it exists as a vacuity and can only be experienced as an absence. The male themes are more complex. There is a growing and developing commitment to sexual acts, in part for themselves, and in part as acts as they relate to other main patterns in male gender role training: autonomy, aggression, control, achievement, normative transgression. What most males, except for the middle class, are not learning are socioemotional skills that are directed toward females. Both through masturbation and heterosexual contact males can be committed to directly sexual activities and, in some part, to gratification from them; females, even when they report sexual arousal, do so in the haze of romantic as opposed to erotic illusions.

Homosexuality

The other major form of sexual activity during this period is homosexuality. By major I do not mean that it is especially frequent, or even that it has a very great incidence. It does appear that for many adult males who become homosexual, first experiences can and do occur during this period; however, of the vast majority of males who have a single homosexual encounter at this time, few carry it on into adulthood. In a previously published reanalysis of the incidence figures from the Kinsey research, it was noted that among the college educated about 30 per cent of the males reported a single homosexual experience. Fifteen per cent of the total number of males (50 per cent of those experienced) had experiences only during the period twelve to sixteen with no later experience, and some 10 per cent of the total number of males (33 per cent of those experienced) had experiences during this period with some experiences at seventeen and eighteen, but nothing after that.[20]

The meaning of these experiences is difficult to determine, as is that of all phenomena that are transient and seemingly without consequence. Most of the homosexual contacts that occur between males early in the period (say ages eleven, twelve, thirteen) are more like prepubertal sex play in their motives, even though they may be accompanied by ejaculation. Curiosity, mutual instruction, the influence of slightly older males, result in physical exploration. What is risky for the youth is that the uninstructed adult will impose on this behavior the complex meanings which adult homosexuality has for him and behave accordingly toward the young people. This can only be demoralizing and disrupting. Homosexuality in the latter part of this period has a number of meanings depending on the social location and the prior social and sexual experiences of the actors. It can be the transient response to opportunity where there is arousal in private situations, or it can have more emotional depth between an admired older boy and a follower. In a sense adolescent homosexuality is not integrated into the mainstream of sexual development (though there is no reason it could not be), though some homosexual activity does result from the normal conditions of the male alliance (a homo-*social* commitment) in early puberty where strong dyadic affective ties can produce incidental as well as ultimately exclusive homosexual interests. In working- and lower-class environments, some homosexual contacts can result from the exploitation of weaker males (this can happen in boarding schools as well) or through contacts as male prostitutes. While these latter events are somewhat rare, they are instructive in that they provide another instance of the way in which a sexual act can be symbolically transformed. The exterior view is that such contacts are homosexual, while the young male defines himself and his act, because of his role, as continuously heterosexual.[21]

Evidence on early homosexual relations among females is extremely sparse, perhaps more sparse than the behavior. There is a good deal of body contact among females during this period—hand-holding, sleeping together, or being partially nude. Except for the rare girl, none of this is found to be erotic or sexual. It has been argued elsewhere that the development of female homosexuality is directly linked to the development of normal femininity and gender role in the society. During this period (and for most women, throughout the life cycle) the feminine gender role training integrates and constrains the sexual component in behavior as powerfully and similarly in homosexuality as it does in heterosexuality.[22]

Continuity and Change

At the present time in American society a confirmed sense of sexual identity as distinguished from gender identity begins to emerge around puberty as the surrounding environment begins to treat differently the newly pubescent child. It seems that for the most part this period of integration of a newly sexual self for both males and females will continue to be built on conventional models. Indeed, at the level of overt sexual activity there seems a remarkable continuity with patterns that have been normative in American society since the 1930's.

While it is not of major scientific interest to develop a general stage model of human development (following, say, Erik Erikson) since such models tend to become reified and, rather than serving to

draw our attention to culturally limited and flexible modal processes, become objects of interest in themselves, it is useful to delineate some of the activities that are central to this society's version
of "normal" early adolescence, in order to indicate potential sources
of stability and change. *It should be noted that neither the period
of development nor its contents are seen as necessary, either within
or across cultures, nor necessary in some task-solving human development scheme.* This period and its content is roughly what happens
in the middle 1960's in a complex Western society, largely to its white
working- and middle-class populations, and in large measure to those
persons of most ethnic and racial minorities who are attached to
these modal schemes of development, or who have not been entirely
alienated from them. There can be vast reversals and changes in
the design of human sexuality from the feelings it evokes to the
kinds of behavior that are appropriate to or included in its performance elements. The age and moment when specific behaviors
can be introduced, performed, and lived will vary enormously, so
that any fixity in the sequence and content behavior is most likely
to occur in infancy and little after that.

The following elements (which have been described in more
detail above) are central to the creation of a sexual identity in early
adolescence (ages eleven to fifteen or twelve to sixteen), in which
the central agencies of sexual socialization are the family, same-sex
peers, opposite-sex peers, and the media:

—first societal identification as a conventional sexual performer
—first overt physical sexual activity with self or others
—development of sexual fantasy materials
—beginning of a male/female divergence in the content of overt
sexual activity
—application of gender package to meaning of sexual acts
—application of prior moral values and categories to emergent sexual behavior
—privatization of sexual activity
—same-sex peers reinforce homosocial values
—family begins to lose moral control
—media reinforce conventional public adult content of gender/sex
roles
—media attaches consumer values to gender role behavior
—basic attachment to youth culture formed

If there are to be changes in this period of life they will be
dependent on change that will result from shifts in later rather than

earlier periods of life. At this moment the softening of the gender training package which is assembled prior to age eleven is occurring in a limited segment of the population (limited by race, class, and life style) so that it does not appear that the input population to early adolescence will change significantly, at least for a generation. The societal changes that seem most significant for this period are linked to the increased and changed interpenetration of the mass media with the youth culture, and changes in the family produced by increasing role flexibility on the part of adults rather than children.

At the present time, it is apparent that adults personally and in media constructions are reacting to young people during early (and especially late) adolescence as being sexual, indeed, as being more sexual than they really are. Thus, in the fantasy life of adults, there is a kind of constant eroticism among the young, and the overreaction of adults to the cosmetic sexuality on the part of youth begins to confirm its acting out. Thus, females in early puberty dress in what are sexually provocative styles, appearing not as girls, but as women. While this shift in social identity has always been the pattern in adolescence, and the reactions of others have always been the process through which the young of both genders have assembled the sexual role with prior gender commitments, the feedback loop now seems to occur somewhat earlier in development, with adults reacting to young people's dress and styles closer to puberty.[23] This is explicitly true for young girls whose dolls (though still without genitals) now have breasts, beauty contests, boy friends, and rock concerts. While the gender role definitions of the children's toy world are conventional, the sexual implications seem more intense and significant. The young are more exposed to a wider range of explicit sexual stimulii in the media than they have ever been in this society, and they are presented with images of their own sexuality, that is characteristic of, at this point, a minority of the young.

While the young are becoming cosmetically more eroticized, they nearly all share in or reject vicariously other social movements (women's liberation, students' rights, sexual liberation, antiwar activities) which enhance the content of youth culture and deepen the rhetoric of generational differences and the moral inferiority of their elders. Such specific issues, whatever their transience, operate to strengthen the image of rebellion and foster other forms of guerilla warfare against parents and authority figures. Sexual activity and participation in drug subcultures begin, in part, for most young people as personal vendettas with parents and then become, for a minority, political in character (that is, a testing of the ultimate basis of the parent-child relationships which rest in part on the physical and economic power of the former). As this political rhetoric of the family emerges it can become, for a few young people, a serious alternative allegiance to familial authority. However, for the majority, each separate cause usually becomes a mixture of justification and rationalization that falls far short of ideology.

At the same time that the eroticism of the social backdrop is increasing, which should at least enhance the increased probability of sexual activity on the part of the young, there is not a great deal of evidence that such increases are being acted out at this moment by this generation of high school students. While the temperature of the adolescent hothouse seems to be higher now than ever before, there has not been a concomitant increase in early sexual activity on the part of the young. The earlier and more intense definition of the young as sexual does not seem to be acted out by the young themselves, that is, there is no direct conversion of a new level of erotic identification into specific forms of behavior. It is likely that this is in part a function of the continued existence of prior conventional gender role commitments on the part of the majority of the young, as well as the continued commitment of both young men and women to the rhetoric of love, interpersonal attachment, and, ultimately, marriage. At the present time there is little social or interpersonal payoff for sociosexual activity of any sort during early adolescence, and minimal payoff for coitus during later adolescence. Outside of the conventional routes to marriage, the payoff for young women in both periods is close to zero, though for males there do exist some rewards of homosocial adulation for heterosexual success (though these pleasures are not unalloyed). Sexual activity during this period can become symbolic of antiadult attitudes and can be performed by either gender, or young women can drift into sexual activity at the behest of young men who are still acting out of an older male sex exploitation ethic, but there is no other specific societal linkage or payoff system that makes the behavior appropriate. Until the ideology of "sex is fun" or that "sex is good in itself" is more widespread, the acting out of sexual commitments does not seem to be likely in early adolescence.[24] However, when these young people enter later adolescence, and especially during the early period of serious mate selection, it is likely that these earlier (in the life cycle sense) definitions may well tend to increase the amount of premarital sexual activity on the part of the young. During the mating period the definition of sex as a pleasure to which the young have a right can be combined with a payoff system (dating-mating-marriage) that is currently in existence.

A new element that will affect the period of early adolescence is the increasing flexibility of parental figures in their role performances. While the youth movement among parents is greeted by the young with derision, it is an amusement often mixed with more than a little anxiety. During the early 1960's parents who did the twist were figures of fun, but now the serious sexuality of older persons is becoming more apparent to young people. Using the conventional language of psychoanalysis, the central problem of adolescence can be seen as an attempt to solve again the oedipal dilemmas of early childhood, and to come to terms with an independent sexual identity. In the past, parental figures were assumed, during this time period, to be stable objects, if not inside themselves, at least in their representation to children. Indeed, from the Freudian point of view, as the objective correlative of the super ego, parents were to remain parents to their children throughout their lives, evincing a continuity of moral character that could serve as a firm basis for either acceptance or rejection of parental values.[25] The emerging role flexibility supplied to adults by affluence has eroded both the fact and illusion of this phenomenon, and parents have become increasingly ambiguous figures for their adolescent children. In this struggle children often revolt, not to be different, but in order to coerce their parents to remain conventional parents, and there is in consequence a mutual identity struggle between parent and child, with the latter often having a more rigid definition of the parent's behavior than the parent has of his child's.

It may well be that the significant sexual changes that are occurring presently are more apparent in an older generation whose response to the increasing sexual openness of the society can be acted out with fully formed sexual commitments. The existence of these commitments is more apparent to the young in this generation than it was previously, and the young are rarely prepared for the dynamic changes that can occur in adults. This does not mean that young people will not adapt to the experience of parents who change, even during this period which is critical to the development of sexual identity. It means only that this period will increase in complexity for this generation of young people. In the long run (one to two generations away) it is likely that there will be a great deal more heterosexual activity in early adolescence and perhaps an increase in sexual activity between persons of a wider range of ages, which will serve to introduce sexual activity more widely among the young.

Conclusion

The period from twelve to sixteen is the period of priority in developing and integrating the sexual into general patterns of gender development in Western societies. The beginning signs of physical changes are cues to parents and to youths themselves to begin to conceive of the young person as potentially eligible to occupy what are conventional sexual roles in the society. The specific sexual acts themselves are then linked to prior gender role categories (not prior sexual experiences) and it is through this integration that meanings can be attributed to newly developed physical capacities and conformations. Even the very experience of the body must be translated through meanings that are drawn from nonsexual domains. The experience of sexual activity as achievement on the part of young men, or as a form of social service on the part of females, does not result from immanent meanings derived from biology, but from the invented and created role categories that are available to members of a society.

The increased salience of sex as a moral category is also significant during this period. Sexual behavior in the West has been inextricably linked to dramas of good and evil as part of the phenomenon of excess and restraint. The imagery of the moral value of restraint (virginity) and the moral failure of excess (the orgy) take their symbolic roots from scarcity societies that have transmuted their values through a secularized protestantism. These exist as values today best codified in modern fiction. Children during this period are learning some of the primitive elements of what is an ultimately sophisticated and complex dramatistic conception of the sexual.

The development of the sexual comes relatively late in character development, and rather than being the engine of change, it takes its meaning primarily from other sources of personal development. It rarely becomes an autonomous area of behavior and retains its dependent status for nearly all persons. If there is a strain toward moral autonomy during this period, it occurs relatively late and

256   JOHN H. GAGNON

rather more frequently with males than with females. Because sex
is at the service of so many other motives, the rules that constrain
it seem more external and less flexible than in other domains.

The boundaries of the period in question are diffuse and variable, especially across cultures (and even within subsectors of a
society), but in the West it seems to be a critical moment for people
in terms of psychosexual development. One's identity as sexual
gains much of its shape during this period as society and, quite
secondarily, biology combine to mark the end of childhood.

Support for this research was provided by United States Public Health Service
grants HD 04156 and HD 04157.

REFERENCES

1. While the deeply beleaguered condition of psychoanalysis as a movement
accounts for at least some of the sectarian politics of its earlier days, the
adherence to doctrinal purity on the part of younger analysts may be equally
attributed to the ambiguous conditions under which therapy is practiced;
see John H. Gagnon, "Beyond Freud," *Partisan Review*, 34 (Summer 1967),
400-414.

2. The publication of the two volumes by Masters and Johnson appear at some
level to be as noncumulative as Kinsey and to be similar kinds of cultural
rather than scientific events.

3. A. C. Kinsey and others, *Sexual Behavior in the Human Female* (Philadelphia: Saunders, 1953), p. 101.

4. Kingsley Davis, "Sexual Behavior," in R. K. Merton and R. Nisbet, eds.,
Contemporary Social Problems (New York: Harcourt, Brace, Jovanovich,
1970), pp. 313-360.

5. For the distinction between sex as behavior and sex as conduct see E. W.
Burgess, "The Sociologic Theory of Psychosexual Behavior," in Paul H.
Hoch and Joseph Zubin, eds., *Psychosexual Development in Health and
Disease* (New York: Grune and Stratton, 1949), pp. 227-243. A more recent but parallel distinction is made between sex as behavior and sex as
experience in Paul Bohannan's review of D. S. Marshall and R. C. Suggs,
eds., *Human Sexual Behavior* (New York: Basic Books, 1971) in *Science*,
175 (September 17, 1971), 1116-1117.

6. William Simon and John H. Gagnon, "On Psychosexual Development," in
David Goslin, ed., *Handbook of Socialization Theory and Research* (New
York: Rand McNally, 1969), p. 736.

7. Kinsey, *Sexual Behavior in the Human Female*, pp. 122-125.

8. A. C. Kinsey and others, *Sexual Behavior in the Human Male* (Philadelphia: Saunders, 1949), pp. 182-187, esp. table 35.

9. An exemplary description of this period from a teacher's point of view is James Herndon, *How to Survive in Your Native Land* (New York: Simon and Schuster, 1971).

10. Kinsey, *Sexual Behavior in the Human Female*, pp. 104-105.

11. Kinsey, *Sexual Behavior in the Human Male*, p. 165 (emphasis added).

12. Evelyn Hooker has suggested that the beginning of sexual activity for males in the social context where only other males are socially valued could have potentials for producing at least some homosexual experience, if not homosexual careers.

13. Table constructed from percentages on p. 173, Kinsey, *Sexual Behavior in the Human Female*.

14. Table taken from J. H. Gagnon, W. Simon, and A. J. Berger, "Some Aspects of Sexual Adjustment in Early and Late Adolescence," in Joseph Zubin and Alfred N. Freedman, eds., *Psychopathology of Adolescence* (New York: Grune and Stratton, 1970), p. 278.

15. Gagnon, Simon, and Berger, "Some Aspects of Sexual Adjustments," pp. 275-295, reported that among college-going males who masturbated during high school 22 per cent felt guilt often, while 39 per cent felt guilt some of the time when they masturbated.

16. Kinsey, *Sexual Behavior in the Human Male*, pp. 374-377, 506-516.

17. *Ibid.*, table 136, p. 550.

18. P. H. Gebhard, J. H. Gagnon, W. B. Pomeroy, and C. V. Christensen, *Sex Offenders* (New York: Harper and Row, 1965), table 55, p. 564.

19. Kinsey, *Sexual Behavior in the Human Female*, table 75, p. 337.

20. William Simon and John H. Gagnon, "Homosexuality: The Formulation of a Sociological Perspective," *Journal of Health and Social Behavior*, 8 (1967), 177-185.

21. Albert J. Reiss, "The Social Integration of Queers and Peers," *Social Problems*, 9 (Fall 1961), 102-120.

22. William Simon and John H. Gagnon, "Femininity in the Lesbian Community," *Social Problems*, 15 (Fall 1967), 212-221.

23. This is not the same as the past with early marriage or early definition as sexual in preindustrial and early industrial societies. In those situations reproductive maturity and sexual maturity were coterminous with marriageability, and such culturally approved transitions are vastly different from emergent sexual identity without legitimate sexual behavior, marriage, or reproduction.

24. Nelson Foote, "Sex as Play," *Social Problems*, 1 (April 1954), 159-163.

25. The injunction by psychiatric advice-givers not to be permissive is based on the notion that constructive rebellion or rejection requires solid parental figures.

The Weather of the Years

LATE NOVEMBER in New Orleans the rain comes down hard and with it a chill can challenge the city's sense of itself as deeply southern and a gateway to Latin America. For the poor those damp, cold days are particularly difficult; they have to be fought off, and to do so requires money that is scarce indeed. So, children go to school shivering or even wet, because they haven't good sweaters, and often enough lack a raincoat; and families hover around old and dangerous gas burners, the only source of heat for many who live in the port city's black slums.

In the autumn of 1960, when four black children, each of them six years old, prepared themselves for the ordeal of initiating school desegregation in New Orleans, the weather (of all things) was very much on their minds—just as the weather was on their minds ten autumns later in 1970. Here is what one little girl said to me in November of 1960: "It's bad. It's real bad—the weather. I'm afraid that when I get to the school those white kids will have sweaters and they'll have raincoats and they'll have umbrellas— and I'll be wet through and through. My daddy said I should pray for rain, the more the better, because then people won't leave their homes to cause trouble for us outside the school, but I told him that I'd rather have the people shouting at me with the sun out and no clouds than no one around except the rain. When you go inside the building, you close the door on the bad people and all their words. But if you're soaking wet and your bones are shaking from the cold, you might as well not go to school, because all day you're trying to warm up and dry out, and the teacher won't look on you as very nice."

For a while the girl had no worries, at least none supplied by "those white kids." The school she attended was almost totally boycotted, and every day her main problem was to get by mobs—angry, noisy, threatening mobs. With the help of federal marshalls the mobs did not achieve their often stated purpose: "to keep that little nigger girl out of our schools." The girl appeared every morning; men and women were waiting to shout obscenities every morning; the girl emerged every afternoon and left for home—and they were back, shouting and screaming. In the words of one of the federal marshalls: "It's a regular game we have here between the little child and these so-called grown-ups. They just have to see her and swear their hearts out at her. And I tell you, I don't believe she lets them bother her much. She worries about her teacher and how sad the other teachers must be, because the white kids aren't coming to school. But when it's raining and there's no one there to heckle her and taunt her and scream at her, she looks as if she almost misses them. I guess you get used to almost anything, isn't that right?"

The little girl did indeed get used to anything. She got used to rudeness and meanness and loneliness. She got used to uncertainty and a kind of lingering sadness she could sometimes shake off—only to find it return unexpectedly. And yes, she got used to being inward. Under constant stress, she stood fast and went to school and learned and moved along from grade to grade, but all along she wondered about things to herself, asked herself questions, became her own rather severe taskmaster. I have already described how she (and others like her) managed the immediate months of school desegregation in the South—at a time when the region was jittery and sullen and all too openly violent.[1] Now I would like to describe how those same young children have grown up, have lived through the 1960's; and in doing so become sixteen and seventeen, become what one young lady I have known these last ten years calls "worldly."

Here she is at age fourteen using that word, and contrasting herself "no longer a child" and herself years before, when she and her struggle prompted from a federal marshall the remarks I have just quoted: "I'm coming to be a grown woman, I guess. It's hard to know when you're all grown and when you've still got some growing to do. My grandmother tells me there's no one alive who doesn't have growing to do. She says I've been wise for a long time—because of what I went through. She says I should go on up to Washington, D.C., and talk to those people who run our government. But I don't know what I'd say. I don't feel any wiser than anyone else. I feel I know a lot about white people that some of my friends don't know; but I'm a girl of fourteen, and we're all just beginning to find out about the world, that's what I think—so I'm as worldly as the others, but no more. Every once in a while one of them will be just like my grandmother; she'll tell me I know everything, because I had my picture on television and in the newspaper and I got all those letters and I've been with the whites for so long, and she'll keep on talking—until I tell her to stop, please, and let me speak. Then I remind her that I was a little girl like her, and there was just so much I could learn. In the last few years, I'd say since I was ten or eleven, I've been learning things I never knew before. I'm no longer a child now. I know what's going on in the world, and sometimes I think this to myself: if I ever knew what I know now about people back when I was a little girl and going past those mobs outside the school—well, I would have told those people a few things, yes I would have given them something to go home and think about, just like they gave me a lot to get upset about."

What has she been learning these recent years? How is one to describe the particular way she has slowly been growing up, and at the same time indicate the things she shares with others in New Orleans, in Louisiana, in the South, and in the United States? And is there any point in getting schematic about her life; I mean, is there something all that different about the character of her mind now, in 1971, when she is going on seventeen, something that contrasts with her manner of thinking five years ago or ten years ago? I again turn to her. I turn to her at fifteen, in late 1969: "In some ways I don't feel much different now than I did when you first started visiting us. I'm the same me is what I'm trying to say. Of course, I'm older. I'd be a fool if I didn't say that! But I'll get to talking with my grandmother, and we both agree that if you stop and look around, you will see that a lot of time the world doesn't change as much as you think. Because you've added ten years on to your life and you've seen a lot happen doesn't mean you've come into a different world. I will say this, though: I'm always wondering what will happen next. I mean, I'm not bored. Well, I'm not *often* bored. Sometimes I just sit and listen to my records and they don't do anything to me, they don't register. That's when I know I'm bored. Another time is when I watch the news on TV, or look at a newspaper. It looks to me as if there are good things happening in the world—but the bad side is always waiting, ready to get even and set us back. We've lost Dr. King and we've lost Robert Kennedy. My grandmother keeps on saying they were so young, and it was terrible—but the minister told us Jesus Christ was even younger when they killed Him, so I guess you have to expect the worst all the time, even when it does look good, the world you're a part of.

"I'm sure I'd be thinking a lot different now if I wasn't living in the city here, but was over in Mississippi, living with my cousins. As bad as it is for us, it's worse for them. I don't think they minded when they were smaller, but they're getting big, growing up, like I am—and they tell me there's nothing for them to do, there's nothing ahead of them. I'll ask them why they don't pack up and come on down to New Orleans. They'll glare and glare—as if to tell me they know I'm trying to be smart, but instead I'm just fresh and sassy. Then I'll know I've said the wrong thing. Then I'll know I haven't stopped and thought about *them*. My grandmother says a person can't just up and leave, not unless she wants to or she has to. My cousins want to and they have to, but even so they're scared and they think it's bad all over, so they stay put. They tell me I'm headed for trouble, they're sure of it, because I have 'big notions,' that's what they say. I tell them that all I want is to finish high school and meet a man who is good and God-fearing, and then marry him and have a girl and a boy—no more than those two children. I tell them I'd like to live free—yes, that's how I say it. And I don't have to explain myself; a black woman who talks about 'living free' has only one subject on her mind: the white people. You can't grow up and be black and not have the whites on your mind. I know I'm special. I know I've been with them all these years—and you know my friends tell me I've been whitewashed. But I do believe, I honestly do, that those friends of mine are more under the spell of them, under a white spell, than I am. I'll tell you why. I've learned all about the white people. I've seen them. I've heard them. I've talked with them. I've listened to them talking about me. By now I've become tired of them—tired of thinking about them and tired of talking about them. All I want is to be myself and think of my own life. Do you know, the black person has a hard time growing up and finding herself, because she can't shake them off—all those white girls and those white boys, and all the grown-up whites who won't stop running everyone's life, even if she's a black girl like me.

"I'm no girl any more. I have to say that. To a white man, we're all girls. I have two white friends, white girls, who have admitted to me it's true: we're never looked on as grown-ups by a lot of white people, and not only those who live in the South, I'm sure of that. Some kids can be sure they're grown up; I'm speaking of white kids. If you're black and live in the state of Louisiana you can't be sure everyone is going to look upon you as grown if you're seventy, never mind seventeen or fifteen. Sure, the country is changing. Even Louisiana is changing. I've been with whites in every grade. They don't shout at me any more. They don't boycott me. They leave me alone. I think they're glad to leave me alone. I heard one say the other day (she was walking ahead of me and she didn't see me behind her) that we never grow up, not really, because we don't have the intelligence to grow up. I almost ran up to her. I almost made some trouble. But I have enough intelligence to know there's no point in trying to talk with a little child like that in the corridor of a high school. She's worrying about us; she thinks we'll never be men and women. Maybe we won't. Maybe you're not really a man or a woman until you can look at yourself in the mirror and feel there's no one owning your life. But I believe a white girl who can't do any better than call black people *children* is a baby herself. She's not a child, mind you. She's not up to my little sister in intelligence. She's a baby; she's one or two, and she gets nervous when she sees a new face.

"Once my grandmother saw my sister start crying; she was about a year old, I believe, maybe less, and a stranger came and tried to be nice to her. Well, she got scared. She cried. She stared for a second, and tried to smile, but she couldn't, so she burst out into a long, long cry for herself. I tried to do everything to stop her. I talked to her and I sang to her; but all she wanted was to go away. She didn't want to see any strange faces in front of her. She wanted to be with us, and with no one else. She was a baby, that's what. My grandmother came over and told me that; she said a baby is afraid of everyone except the few people she knows, so the only thing you can do is indulge her, that's right. 'Someday she'll grow up,' that's what I can remember my grandmother saying. And you know, for a second in school I wanted to go up to that white girl, that white child, that white baby she is, and tell her that I'm praying for her, yes I am; I'm praying that she won't forever be a little baby—all dressed up as a big girl, a woman I guess we're becoming these days, but still a baby in her head.

"Don't ask me what it takes to become all grown up. I'm halfway there; that's what my grandmother says, and I think she's right. I asked her when she got all the way there—and she said no one ever does. I guess I didn't follow her, because my face looked puzzled, and she said I shouldn't be a child, and I asked her what I was thinking that was wrong, and she said that a child is someone who thinks she's going to stop being a child one of these days. I scratched my head and said I couldn't see what that meant. My grandmother didn't explain herself. She just told me I was twelve, going on thirteen, and when I was seventy I'd be six going on seven and twelve going on thirteen and twenty going on twenty-one, because she's found out it happens that way in life.

"I'm old enough now to understand more and more of the advice I heard when I was small from my grandmother. I think you're no longer a child when you catch yourself thinking back. I used to think I'd be all grown up when I have a million things to anticipate as around the corner. I used to think the day would come when I couldn't hardly keep up with all the plans I'd be making. But now I'll catch myself wondering how I ever got by those people in front of the school, and I'll pinch myself and say I never *did* get by them, it was only a dream. But it wasn't a dream, I know. If you were to ask me whether I'd go through the same thing over again, now that I've had almost ten years to think about it, I'd say yes; I'd say I can't imagine what I'd be like if I hadn't gone past that crowd (that mob, the marshalls always called them) every day. And I can't imagine who I'd be if I hadn't stayed and stayed and stayed, until I saw one white girl and then another one come back to school, and after a while even sit near me in the classroom. 'Don't try to think of some other life you might have had'; that was my daddy's advice before he died. My grandmother told me she'd whispered that in his ears when he was a little boy, and he was always asking her why he couldn't be rich and white and up in some city like Chicago. I learned what the white people are like when I was six years old, so I never wanted to be white. I wouldn't mind being rich, but I'd never want to go to Chicago. I'm from the South, and I hope to stay right here all my life. Now that I'm in high school I've been doing some thinking about where I'd like to live. I've thought of other cities, like in Florida or up in Atlanta. But I think I'll stay here. It depends on the man I meet and marry, of course. But maybe he'll listen to me as much as I listen to him. Like my grandmother says, women aren't the niggers they used to be!

"I'd like to be able to understand the world like my grand-mother does—that's my chief ambition. Then I could talk to my children and my grandchildren the way she does. I used to think that when I got to high school I'd be like my grandmother—I'd be smart and I'd know what to think and what to say, no matter how tough the trouble I was in. But you can't race ahead of yourself. You can only keep up with yourself, if you keep at it. And it's hard, not falling behind. If you don't watch out you're losing ground in your school work and you're slow about what to wear and what to say and what records to buy and what to watch on television. There was a time when I'd only look forward to lunch or supper after I had breakfast; now I'm worrying about what I'll wear when I grad-uate from high school, and that's two or three years from now. And by then they may have new styles, so there's no percentage in figuring out what you'll be wearing that far ahead.

"My boyfriend says I should be wise about all that—the newest clothes, the best food to eat if you don't want to get fat. He thinks the white folks know everything, and they taught what they know to me. I tell him he's a child. Fred, I say, when you were five or six you probably thought your own parents knew everything; now you think it's the white man who is so clever. You're twice wrong, I tell him. He should grow up and know there's more to this world than anyone can figure out, no matter how old he is, or how white. But I do believe you learn new things each and every year, and that's what growing up is all about."

As I go over all I have heard her say and try to summarize something called her "psychological development" I keep on won-dering whether the rather unusual experiences she went through as a young child may have caused her to be especially thoughtful and almost uncannily ironic and detached. All the insults and near-disasters, all the fear and doubt she knew, all the special at-tention she received from her own community, may have fostered in her mind a kind of precocious resignation such as philosophers struggle to obtain and demonstrate to others—or so I sometimes think. Yet she has never let me get away with that line of reason-ing. She sees herself as a rather "ordinary teenager." She sees her-self as thirteen or fourteen or fifteen. She sees herself as black, as a resident of New Orleans, as a southerner who lives in Louisiana. She reminds herself from time to time that she is more and more a woman, and is becoming a woman at a moment in history when women all over the United States are breaking down barriers, even as she began doing likewise in late 1960. And there is more: she calls herself "fortunate," and at other times, "lucky"; and she has in mind a whole range of circumstances when she uses those words. She does not go hungry. She is going to graduate from high school. She has some attractive clothes. She owns a record machine and some good music to play when the mood suits her. She has (and has had) the attention of boys she likes.

Not that the young lady comes from a well-to-do family. Because she was a pioneer, neighbors and friends have saluted her over the years—and perhaps more than made up for the suffering a bewildered little girl went through day after day for two years, really; by which time a degree of "quiet" (as the girl once put it) if not full-fledged normalcy had settled upon her daily school life. So, no doubt about it, she has been given much, singled out again and again—by grateful neighbors who know well how white men and women singled out the first black children to enter the South's white schools. On the other hand she reminds me again and again that her grandmother has lived a long and hard life, has known extreme poverty and trembled in her own time before whites, perhaps not assembled in front of a school building, but no less desperate and vindictive. And in the face of that life the old lady has more than survived; she has sustained her children and her grandchildren: "she has taught us how to grow up."

By no means does the grandmother constantly figure in her granddaughter's conversation; nor is the young lady I am writing about constantly talking self-consciously about "growing up." We who think and write about "adolescence" can turn the youths we presumably hope to understand into cannon fodder for the theoretical wars we so often wage. And for me it is especially dangerous to quote from a girl at such-and-such an age, then from the same person later—now become a "youth" or a "young lady," as her grandmother refers to her. By selecting this or that remark for presentation in an essay, I make a case of sorts—and run the risk of failing somehow to indicate the breadth and depth of a particular life. Perhaps others should be allowed to speak about the black woman I have been seeing all these years, even as she should be given a chance to reply in kind. For example, a white girl who returned eventually (in 1961) to the boycotted school once had this to say about her black classmate: "I've been at school with her for most of the year now. She's nervous, I believe. She doesn't look at me unless she can't help it. She's not nearly as dirty as my mother

told me they are. She's just another girl, only she's colored—and
they're different. I don't mind her. There isn't anything we can
do: they're here because the federal government in Washington,
D.C., has forced them on us. But I play with her sometimes; I do.
It's only for a few minutes, and she's alright. She smiles a lot."

Later, years later, the same "girl," now fourteen and in high
school, looks both back and ahead: "I remember all that trouble
every once in a while; there will be something in the news about
Negroes and I listen and think of all we lived through. Then I'll
see her in the corridor, and we'll say hello. I don't harbor any bad
feelings against her. She's a nice person—quiet and neat. She has
good manners. If only all the colored people had the poise she has.
I think they mature faster than we do. I read someplace that
they do. That's why they're good athletes, and the girls look so
grown up. They have a rhythm to them; it's hard to describe—and
I don't only mean that they're musical. They seem to move along
faster than us down the corridor, and they laugh more easily—some
of them. Of course it's like with us, you find all kinds, provided
you get to meet enough people. Maybe the day will come, like our
minister says, when we all trust one another in this country. But
like I've said before, it's only natural that the races stay apart from
each other in a lot of ways. I still believe that."

She believes many things. She is also growing up, parting company with her childhood, feeling herself more aware of a future,
less tied to the immediate, concrete present of the school and the
neighborhood. As a result, she makes comments and observations
about an increasing number of people and customs and events, not
because she is becoming a social analyst of sorts, but because,
again, she is getting some distance on herself and her life, and yes,
on life in general, on time's flow as each of us comes to know it. At
nine and ten she would make particular remarks about one or another black child she sat near in class or watched playing in the
schoolyard. At thirteen and fourteen she would talk more generally, more philosophically, it can be said, more conceptually—
though I hesitate to describe what comes across as natural and unselfconscious with words that strait-jacket a rather subtle development, much of it not a matter of phrases used or ideas mobilized,
but rather "thoughts that get really felt." I use that last expression
because I once heard the white girl just mentioned speak so, and
I can't at all improve on her way of putting what she has been going
through these recent years: "When you start going to high school

you realize that you're really on the way—yes, sir. I never thought much about life until now. I never asked myself any important questions. I guess I never really looked around and stopped and considered what was ahead of me. But now I catch myself hearing a song or listening to what a man says on a television program— and all of a sudden it's *me* who's there, and I have a picture of myself getting married, or I recall something I did five years ago, maybe, and I wonder if my own child will go through the same experience I had.

"With the colored kids I know, I'll bet their children won't look upon us whites with the same amount of fear. For us white people it will be different, too: when we're parents, we won't talk about the colored the same way our parents did, so naturally our children will grow up with different ideas on the subject of race. Who you are depends on where you grow up as much as what your parents believe, don't you think? Our minister said that, and I couldn't help turning his words over and over again in my mind. There are some thoughts that get really felt—you just can't put them out of your head. That's why I think I'll always be a southerner, even if I meet someone who comes from another part of the country, and he takes me away to live there and not here."

Yes, there is nothing all that surprising or original in her remarks. Like many millions of young adolescents she daydreams about her future and becomes moody, introspective, sentimental, hesitant, then thoroughly sure of herself. Most of all, though, she feels herself emerging from the day-to-day life of childhood; and as she does so she summons her mind to the task of finding for herself a certain coherence. As I have gone back South to talk with her I have watched that coherence develop, heard it revealed now in an aside, now in a full-fledged declaration. That is to say, I have heard her take note of the music she likes, the politics she finds appealing, the reading she does, the hopes she nourishes, the fears she sometimes can't quite (but mostly does manage to) put aside, the hobbies and "interests" she pursues, the food she is "partial to," the clothes she has or wants to have, the television programs she won't under any circumstances miss, the sermon she has heard in church and not by any means forgotten the next day, the nation she is proud to call her own, the region she loves, the state she refers to as "our Louisiana," the city she wishes never to leave, the streets she walks down, the buildings she passes every day, the stores she goes to, the house that is unmistakably hers (however much it strikes an observer as like all the others nearby), the bus she boards, the soldiers she sees walking, the policeman she sees driving by, the firemen who stand outside and smile at her and talk to her—because her uncle is one of them, but also because she is "getting pretty," they tell her, "looking real nice," they declare, "becoming quite a young lady," they comment, "growing up real fast," they observe, "turning into a real, lovely woman," they remind both me and themselves.

What those men take note of does not escape the young lady. She recognizes her growing attractiveness. She dresses in such a way, walks and sits in such a way, touches her hair and moves her bracelet in such a way as to make clear her developing sense of herself as a woman, "a real lovely woman" whom men stare at and no doubt think about in their thoughts and daydreams (their "fantasies" some call them) just as she can "catch sight of" a young man and find herself much later on wondering whether he looks like the man she one day will marry, and, again, quite possibly move with to another city or state. In her few but important words: "A woman takes a man's name and becomes fulfilled by making a home and family for him, wherever the place may be." Nor can the pieties she learns from her parents and at school or at church be dismissed as mere chatter. All sorts of high-sounding notions (her "femininity," her "unconscious attitudes," her "sexual identification," her "role" as a woman) can in a flash come across as not necessarily a great confusing mystery to her—but rather as something settled and lived with, or as people like me would have it, "resolved."

Meanwhile there are her boyfriends, and she is careful to watch them, even as she is anxious to have them keep an eye on her. One of her "nice boys," a young man she calls "a great person," came back to school the same day (in 1961) she did. At the age of six he described that return like this: "I didn't ever want to go to school, because my daddy told me you can't learn with the colored all over the school. But they only brought in three, and now that I'm back there's only one in the room with the rest of us—the white kids. She's always looking around at us; I guess she's worried we may not like her. I don't think she's bad. I'd rather play with my own friends, though. Sometimes I play with her, and she's good at running after a ball, as good as the boys are. My daddy says the colored can run fast.

"They won't stay long with us, I was told that. My uncle told me it won't be long before we'll be all-white again, because colored kids don't stay in school. I said I don't want to stay in school, either; we have a better time at the playground, all of the kids do. But when you get bigger there's a lot of homework to do; I know, because my cousin is in high school and my aunt and uncle said I won't have to worry: no colored boys will be on our baseball team or basketball, either, when I'm fourteen, like my cousin, and in the ninth grade, like he is. The colored wanted to try and get some of their people into the high schools, too; but they didn't get their way, like they did when the judge ordered our school to let in those girls. One of them told me yesterday that she'd probably leave school in a year or two, and maybe go back to Mississippi, if her parents decide to leave New Orleans. She said her parents are thinking of leaving because they're scared. She says even now, with no more people shouting at her, she can't make her brother believe she's doing okay in school. He thinks she'll get killed. He's afraid she won't live to grow up. But she says she will grow up, and I hope she does."

She did grow up, as did he. When he was twelve he was far more comfortable with black children than he once dreamed possible. More of those children had been admitted to the school he attended, and though he never in the elementary grades became very friendly with his black classmates, he did take note of them— indeed, watched them more closely than his parents ever imagined. Just before his thirteenth birthday he took note of the coming milestone in his life, and made some interesting forecasts about his future: "I'll be a teenager next week. My dad reminded me my birthday wasn't just another birthday. He said I have a lot of common sense, and I'll study hard in high school next year. I told him yes, I will. My father wants me to go to college. He never finished high school, because when he was a boy growing up there wasn't any money around, and his father was sick in bed all the time and my dad had to go and get a job. He did everything. He swept floors. He unloaded the ships. He worked for a grocery market. He worked in a hotel, carrying suitcases up to rooms. He was glad to have a job, any kind of job. He says a lot of the jobs he once had, the Negroes now have them. The white people are moving up, and the colored are glad to have jobs. Before they picked cotton over in Mississippi and here in Louisiana. Now they've been coming into New Orleans. One of the colored boys sits in front of me, and he told me he expects to go right through high school, the same as I do. He said he might even be able to go to college. My dad says they are always pushing on us, trying to get everything the white man has—but a lot of them aren't willing to work too hard. Some of them are pretty dumb, but we have some real smart ones in my school. You can't figure them out; they talk different than we do, and they dress different and they bring different food to school. But I think they're people, like us, and the ones I know in school are mostly just trying to better themselves, and there's nothing wrong with that, our minister says. I hope I can better myself, and I hope the Negro kids do. They seem a lot older than us, even if they're actually the same age. I can't explain why, but they do.

Three years later, at fifteen years and ten months, he could indeed explain why the black youths he knew "seem a lot older." He could explain to me that blacks are poorer, and are more on their guard, feel rather awkward in the presence of whites, hence become more "quiet" and more "grown up." He could insist that by and large "the races should still be separate," but go on to remind me that "times are changing," and because they are "you can't stand still, you have to go along." What held for his father does not hold for him: "The Negro people are entitled to be left alone. I wish they'd leave us alone, but they won't. So, the way I see it, the only thing to do is what we've gone ahead and done: let them go to school with us and try to be as fair and square with them as you can, but not do them any special favors. A black boy growing up should have every chance I do, but he should live with his own people and try to better them. It's all right for them to be at school with us, but that's as far as it should go. Even my dad says school integration is one thing, but when it comes to socializing, that's another.

"Anyway, the Negro kids of my age have a good time socializing among themselves. Those people, the colored, they are natural-born athletes and natural-born musicians. I believe they're made different from us. I'm on the track team and I play basketball, and I can't keep up with them. We're glad to have a few of them at school with us: they help us out in sports. They can be sharp dressers but they're kooky, you know: they put on wild, wild clothes, and they're always touching one another, bumping into one another, laughing with one another—when they figure we're not watching, when they're in the cafeteria by themselves. Sometimes I wish the white guys could be as loose as they are; my mother says it's because they're like children a lot, so they fool around.

But I think they're more relaxed. They can laugh quicker than we can. I think it's easier for them to grow up and become men. For one thing, their bodies don't take the time ours do to get up to our full height, and besides that, a Negro kid who is fifteen or sixteen is probably going to be up against it: whether he studies and stays in school, or he's headed for the unemployed, which is where so many of them are. I'd be scared if I was a Negro.

"Of course, I get to worrying now myself. I hope I'll be able to get a good job one day. I'd like to go to college, but I doubt I will. I'd like to learn a trade. I'd like to be an electrician, I think; maybe a carpenter. It's hard to decide right now. Sometimes I forget about all that stuff—the future, the kind of job I'll have ten years from now, my grades, the summer work I'll be needing. All I want to do is run, or shoot the ball. All I want to do is turn on our hi-fi or watch the tube. Who cares what you'll be doing for work a long time from now! I mean, you've got to care, but there's going to be plenty of time later to be worried sick over the size of your pay check and the bills. I can go through the week and keep pretty relaxed. I can take each day by itself. That's what you ought to do—the best you can, and it's hard to expect more of yourself. My girl agrees.

His girl: she is his age, in his school; and she lives three blocks away. He has known her "off and on" for a long time, but now he is "really getting to know her"—though there are times when he concludes that "women are a strange bunch, and I don't think they even understand themselves, so how can a man hope to figure them out?" A Methodist, a believing Methodist from a devout Methodist home, he wants to "get close" to his girlfriend, "but only so close." He would not respect a girl who "wants to give in too much." He reads in the newspapers and hears on television that "there's a lot of drugs being used" and that "kids of my age are just going off and having sex, or something pretty close to it." And he needs no sociologist to explain *who* and *why*: "It's a lot of spoiled rich kids. Our minister says we're all lucky around this neighborhood to be sober and without too much money. (Not that my dad would mind having more cash!) If you've got nothing to worry about, if you've got thousands and thousands of dollars, then you take drugs and you lose your good judgment about what's right and what's wrong. I hear the poor are the same way, especially the Negro people. They've just given up. They don't have any ambition for themselves. That's a bad state to let yourself get in—not thinking of your future. I can't see how a fellow can let it happen. I don't think a day passes that I don't catch myself daydreaming: I picture the car I'll be driving a few years from now; or I'll picture myself in the army, or maybe the air force. I wouldn't mind flying a plane, I'll tell you—that would be a job for life. But they don't need too many pilots now, and I think you have to have a college degree. Besides, I like to work with my hands. I like to build things. I've built myself a small workshop, a chair and bench, so I can build other things. I never buy my kid brothers presents. I make them a toy boat or a small car, you know, with wooden wheels. I built them a small ladder, so they can climb up to the window and crawl into the house. I built a dog house for us. I love our dog as much as anyone in this world. She's only a mongrel, but she won't let go of me. She's the most reliable, dependable one in the world—I was going to say the most dependable *person!* I'll get into a tiff with my girl—over nothing, nothing at all—and I'll think to myself I'd like to go get my mutt and take a walk and not hear all that dreamy talk, and big ideas, lots of big ideas. Women are full of big ideas—but it's the men who work and work and bring in the hard cash. You know, there can be a day when I agree with what my dad says: men are the niggers of this world; it's up to them to be slaves, so the woman can go and buy her earrings and her fancy shoes, and always be worrying about how her hair is, her coiffure, you know. But I guess you want them looking pretty for you."

He goes on to observe what he says applies to blacks as well as whites; his black classmates are in that respect no different—the young men look for work after school or for summer jobs, and their girlfriends talk about "dream houses" and dresses and "how they look, all dolled up." And he is right, some of his black classmates talk very much like he does; and let it be known how serious they are or will be, how tough it will be for them to keep ahead of bill collectors, and not least, the appetites of their girlfriends, some of whom may be their wives in a not too distant span of time. Yet, the black youths feel by and large more hard-pressed, less confident about getting and keeping jobs; and at the same time more or less aware that the girls, the young women they think of as frivolous and self-centered, may well have better luck at finding work than their "men-folks." Consequently there are differences between the way black and white boys come to think of themselves as they "turn the corner and get going on the big-time stretch," as one black boy of eleven described for me the beginning of his manhood.

In fact, he had demonstrated himself to be a rather impressive young man two years before, at the age of nine, when he entered an all-white elementary school in New Orleans against substantial resistance—though not of the hysterical and violent kind the city had experienced several years earlier. "I'm one of thirteen in the school," he told me in 1964. "I'm doing okay. Yes, I am. We stick together. So long as we can spot each other one or two times a day, we're all in good shape. But if I had to be the only one in this school, with all the whites there—well, I'd still be willing to go. We've got to fight for our rights. I don't want to grow up and be like my uncle. He says he's afraid to look at white people. He says they're the devil, and they can snap their fingers and that's the end of you. It's not just because he drinks—that's not why he's so scared and talks like he does about the white man. He's never even dared look at himself in the mirror, never mind look at the white man; that's what I think. I hope that when I'm a man I'm really a man. I hope I don't sit around waiting for some bossman to smile down on me and pat me on the head—or kick me in the pants. Some other kids, my own cousins—they're too good: they say white people don't mean us harm, and we should be nice to them, and they'll be nice to us. I laugh out loud when I hear them talking like that. They ask me why I go to the white school if I'm so against the white man, and I tell them that I want to learn all I can, and I want to see what they're like, kids who will be wanting to boss us around in a few years when they're bigger. Then maybe I'll be wise enough about them to fool them; they've been tricking us ever since they brought us over here, and it's about time we learned to get even with them. My big brother says he wishes he had the chance; he wishes he could have gone to school with whites. If he'd gone, he thinks he'd be better off today. He'd be up to the whites. He'd know their number. I hope in a few years I won't be sitting around feeling regrets, like he does now. I hope I'll be in the ring, fighting it out with the man. Our minister always says life is a boxing match, and he's right."

In 1970 he was fifteen and as tough as ever, though somewhat more philosophical. He still had no great love for white people, but he had had ample time to become acquainted with them and see their failings, their limitations, their blind spots. They appeared less threatening, more approachable—maybe because American society itself had changed along that direction in the intervening six years, maybe because he had come to know certain white children as individuals, and maybe because (in addition) he himself was growing up to be a particularly strong-minded and able man who could increasingly appreciate his own worth, and who will not easily be intimidated by anyone, regardless of race. I asked him that year what he saw ahead for himself and he replied by first looking back: "I have to stop and think every once in a while, and when I do I catch myself remembering the first few days—when I came to that school and suddenly found myself surrounded by white kids. I was scared, I guess. I didn't feel scared then, but as I think back to those days, I was. The weather is changing you know; I realize that now. There's a different climate now between the races. The white people have to watch their step, just like we've always had to watch our step. It used to be the sun always shined on them, and it was raining on us. Now we've got some of the sun and they have some rain. That's what I believe. So far as I'm concerned, I'm pretty hopeful. When I was a kid I used to fear growing up. I'd look at my big brother and my uncle, and I'd think of how my daddy died—in jail, because a white man hit him and then called the police and got them to arrest my daddy, and not the white man—and I'd get low, real low. I'd think to myself: there's no good life ahead for a colored boy like you.

"But I'm not a colored boy. I'm a black man. Not all my people really grow up to be black men and black women. A lot of us are still colored; we're still niggers, or if we have a little money but no respect for ourselves, we're Negroes. To be black you have to feel you're going to get somewhere, and no one's going to stop you, no sir. A while back I used to have a dream, a nightmare, that there was a tornado coming up, like the kind that killed my granddaddy. I would be standing there, a little colored boy, I guess, and soon I'd be gone. I'd wake up thinking I was dead and gone, and expecting to see my granddaddy who is in his grave, near where the tornado killed him. I don't have the dream any more. After studying in school and playing basketball and studying some more and working and trying to hold on to my girl—well, no wonder I fall into bed and the next thing I know it's morning, and I've never had a thing to dream about. If I did dream I think there'd be no tornadoes. Since I've gotten older I believe I've become more optimistic: I think I'll be able to do all right. I think the weather ahead will be pretty good. Actually, the weather has been getting better and better the last few years, and I guess I picked the right time to be born and to grow up."

He elaborates. He talks about his prospects—the work he'd like to do (law or engineering), the kind of life he'd like to live—"comfortable but not spoiled-comfortable." He also talks about his fellow-man. Like others of his age from Louisiana I have talked with these past years (of both races) he can be at once cool, calculating, self-centered—and open, idealistic, compassionate, and impressively dedicated. I have learned to respect the imagery he uses. When he talks about weather he talks about himself; he lets me know that he once felt afraid and vulnerable, but now feels more confident, less dependent, less at the mercy of life's arbitrary side, more intact and self-sufficient. The outside world does not threaten him as much as it once did; he is growing up, feeling his developing competence as a student, an athlete, a man. He has borne up against certain difficult challenges, survived his own anger and bitterness as well as his doubts and misgivings, and all in all weathered a time in this nation's history as well as a "period" in his own life.

Sometimes when I listen to the young men and women I have quoted in this essay I find myself taking note of the troubles they have, the contradictions within themselves (not to mention within our society) they struggle with, the inconsistencies and ambiguities they try to cover over one way or another. Yet, the more time I have spent with these youths, the less troubled they have struck me as being. Perhaps one can only know about a life by staying with the particular person in question long enough to get a sense of his or her history. What seems like a pathological moment out of a *case*-history can often enough be revealed (only in time, though) as part of someone's *life*-history—and maybe a necessary and valuable part, too. So, in a way, I have in the past decade been growing up myself—becoming a little less apprehensive about the various "things" I see and hear. I do not mean to whistle in the dark, or blindly dismiss the South's still very serious racial situation as "solved"; but I think the decade and more I spent with black and white children like those from Louisiana described here has been an important period of time for them as individuals as well as for the region, not to mention all the United States. The South has changed enormously and for the better, even as these youths who have just spoken have also changed. And who can separate (except those theory-minded ones who are determined to do so) the growth of a country from the growth of individuals like these young men and young women?

Again and again I hear the Louisiana children and youths I visit talk about their particular experiences as members of particular families; but I also hear them talk as southerners, black or white southerners, and southerners who were six in 1960 (not 1940 or 1950) and sixteen in 1970 (not 1950 or 1960). Put differently, I hear them express the fears and hates and aspirations which their parents, as southerners, are heir to—the latent populism of the region, the racism in the region, the passivity and obsequiousness characteristic of blacks some call Uncle Toms, the meanness and narrowness characteristic of whites some call rednecks. True, such youths have been "special," have been pioneers of sorts. They have led their race into white schools or been the first generation of whites to study with black children. Yet, they have also been thoroughly "ordinary" or "normal"; they have carried on over the years, fought with their mothers and fathers, brothers and sisters, friends and acquaintances—and also felt drawn to, close to those same people. They have "held the torch" of their people (the way one black youth of fifteen put it) or they have "helped move the South along to a better day" (the way a white youth the same age put it). I suppose, if I had to tidy it all up, collect my thoughts and put them into a sentence or two, I would say that I have found myself in 1971 looking back at the way certain young Americans have (in the last third of the twentieth century) managed to weather some important years in their lives and in the life of their region and their country. Especially in recent years, especially since 1965 or 1966 (after school desegregation began in New Orleans and Atlanta, after the Mississippi Summer Project took place, after Dr. King's efforts in Birmingham and Selma had their effect), the youths I have been privileged to know in states like Louisiana and Georgia have found it possible to have new ideas, new assumptions, new expectations. And how lucky for them and all of us that such was the case just as they were growing up, becoming men, becoming women, feeling suddenly stronger, more themselves and less children of their parents, more weathered as individuals as well as participants in the South's, in America's coming of age.

REFERENCE

1. *Children of Crisis: A Study of Courage and Fear* (Boston: Atlantic-Little, Brown, 1967).

PHYLLIS LA FARGE

An Uptight Adolescence

EARLY ADOLESCENCE, perhaps more than other periods in life, feels in memory as if it were uniquely one's own. No one else could have been so tentative, so lyrical, and so despairing by turns. At the time one felt unique, too, perhaps especially in my generation. When I was an adolescent there was far less of a youth culture supporting and generalizing as well as blunting the experience of the individual. I was doubtful that anyone else felt as I did and uncertain in my attempts to interpret the self emerging in me. Enough of this still lingers so that I feel most comfortable if I do not generalize but speak of my own adolescence in specifics.

I was twelve in 1945. For me the end of World War II in Europe came during recess in a girls' private school in New York City. It was announced by the sallow hysteric whose title was Head of the Middle School. That very winter she had disbanded our French class after we had reduced the white Russian emigré teacher to tears once too often. The hysteric thought she could make us guilty enough so that we would sign up for a new French class in a more docile frame of mind. Her strategy failed. No one signed up, not even the class goody-goody, me. We knew that there was no real question of the school's discontinuing French. We waited out a week of extra study halls and sure enough we were back with Mme. T., with her black suit buttoned too tightly over her large breasts, her braids coiled over her ears, and, just in front of her braids, a neatly trimmed fringe of black sideburns.

The end of the war in the Pacific came on an island off the coast of Maine where I was visiting with my mother and my sister. The day was brilliant. My mother and I walked on a path that was a foot-worn trough in the pine mulch, looking at the headlined *Times* we had picked up at the dock. "But it is not the same for us as it is for other people," she said. She meant that the fathers and husbands of others would return, whereas my father, who had died in the war, would not. This is the only time in those years that I can remember her mentioning what she thought grief had done to us— that it had set us apart.

Set apart from my peers and from an important part of my younger life: these sensations of isolation and discontinuity were the strongest experiences of my early adolescence. While the war went on I felt a continuity, even if of an abstract sort, with my father. The newsreels at the 85th Street Translux on Madison Avenue proved that we were still living in the same piece of time in which he had died; in my consciousness the jiggly black and white images (Dresden, Salerno) were of a piece with the event of his death. But when the war was over we were in a new time he had not known.

There were other, more specific discontinuities. A year or so before the end of the war my mother had sold the house in the country where we had lived and taken an apartment in New York where she herself had been raised. We spent most of the summer in my maternal grandmother's Westchester house where my mother had lived as a child. There was continuity but it was with my mother's earlier years (we had spent no more than a few weeks there each year as small children). Continuity with my own and my sister's earlier experience was broken.

My mother's decisions gave me a latter-day Jamesian adolescence. My sister, my mother, and I became the pawns of a beautiful and powerful woman—my grandmother—who found in us an acceptable rationale for continuing to live in a house and in a style which she clung to for reasons of her own. I lived with auras and essences and intimations that I only half understood. I picked up tastes, prejudices, turns of phrase that belonged to the two or three earlier generations who had lived in my grandmother's house and in the other family houses nearby. Auras and tastes which lingered on with the same long half-life of old photographs, old records, old coats and canes in the closets of country houses, old toys in top floor playrooms. Treasures if there is enough going on and if there is not, as there was not for me, then a complex burden, not unlike the burden of foreign parentage, beloved and yet rejected because it appears an impediment to defining oneself in a new land or, as in my case, in one's own time.

I saw no one my own age except my sister all summer and no adults except family. I learned no sports, no crafts. I had a few tennis lessons and a few riding lessons with ludicrous results (it seems improbable that I could have ended up clinging upside down to the neck of a horse but this is what I recall—perhaps the whole business simply felt that way). Everything I attempted was done "cold," that is without the support of other people doing and enjoying it. Performance became synonymous with an unattainable perfection. I withdrew into what I could do—read and swim, paint watercolors. I could have gone to camp if I had wanted (yet as I write it, it seems a paltry solution) but I could least of all have dared what might have freed me. And no one prodded.

I learned to read the few people I was with minutely. Survival seemed to depend—I make it sound conscious but it wasn't—on an understanding of character and motivation. An Argus grew within me (and is with me still). On summer mornings my grandmother ate breakfast in bed and my mother until her nerves drove her out to garden sat in a chair beside the bed reading the *Times*. I, too, spent a few minutes in the room remembering the pleasure I had felt there as a small child, and feeling it no more. In the summer of 1948 I wrote in my diary:

Ga crushes Mummy and fixes everything in her mind. Exasperating but I am still detached enough to be intrigued by the patterned carpet of Ga's bedroom. Ever since the idyllic mornings that I spent crawling on the floor of her bedroom the intricate blue and purple design has fascinated me. I am still young enough to enjoy rolling the hatstand down the paths and halls of my imagination's castle on this carpet.

(I went on to write that the news was bad in the summer of 1948 and that I always read the fashion page and Billy Rose first. The news has become so bad since that I have almost ceased to read it and Billy Rose is dead.)

It was in those years of early adolescence that I think I learned to counter pain with observation, not only of people but things— carpets, plants, language, paintings—and to think even if awkwardly, pompously about my own experience. Characteristic of those years, too, is the "betweenness," the awkward position between a child's pleasures and perceptions and a more adult mode, and the sense of change and changing suggested by the repeated word "still." The first "still" points ahead to a time when I might no longer be able to bear my family situation, in fact, almost insinuates that I expect someday not to be able to bear it. The second "still" harks back to a child's enjoyment. Early adolescence brings not only a sense of change and the changing nature of experience but, perhaps as a result of an awareness of change, an altered perception of time. Time begins to move faster, summers are not as long; the more static "timeless" world of childhood is passing. Ambitious person that I am, I think I began in the twelve to sixteen years to equate the passage of time with some sort of progress. (It took a long time to shake that notion.)

My sister and I became very close; we lived in our heads, at the same time longing for involvement, action, most of all people our own age. Twenty-five years later we are still convinced that for us friends are not what they are for others: to us they still seem benefactions not at all to be taken for granted. "I must build myself a world inside myself," I wrote in a 1947 diary entry which expresses much of what we felt, "a secret place, impenetrable to all but those I love. And yet from this seclusion I love people."

My sister was my ideal. I thought it was better to have curly hair, to be very fair. I valued what she was—absolute, intense, uncompromising—and I knew I could not attain to it; beside her I felt a trimmer. I was still a Roman Catholic (my diaries are full of prayers) but I was already aware that she was more religious than I and this gave her a kind of worthiness I had an inkling I could not hope for. My passion for the events of the day (I was an avid reader of newspapers in my teens) seemed second-rate beside her passion for poetry and the natural world. She became the model for later love. I wonder how often such models grow out of the close affections of early adolescence, taking siblings or friends for models rather than parents.

But I falsify if I suggest only the negative. The longing for the companionship of peers and the chance to do things with people my own age was so overriding that I tended to underrate what I had—and even now risk doing so in writing about those years. I have written recently about my relationship with my mother and do not want to repeat it here except to say that she cared for me so much and was (is) a person of such moral passion and honesty that she gave my life a kind of guarantee.

Important, too, was the experience every summer of a large household and of an extended family of aunts, uncles, great-aunts, all living nearby. I took it so for granted that there was always someone to turn to, family or not family, that I could be bored and confined by what I had (and, true, there was no one my own age). Only later did I value as nearly priceless the sense of a world small enough to perceive it whole, the play of people above and below stairs, with and against each other, the stuff that novels used to be made of—and to continue to feel as I did inarticulately in adolescence that it was experience that fitted me to a time earlier than my own.

It was easy to live in such a world without social consciousness even in the late forties. I thought my relatives snobbish and prejudiced, but I had no concrete alternatives to their point of view beyond a vague liberalism and I would not have known where to turn for other models.

Along with the discontinuities specific to my circumstances came the discontinuities of puberty, the changes in my own body. The changes of adolescent bodies are subject matter for Goldoni or the Marx brothers, if only adolescents could feel that way. I had hips before I had breasts; it seemed cruel mismanagement. My mother, slender, erect, and a puritan in her corseting as well as in the control of her emotions, bought me a girdle. I wore it with a Carter's knit undershirt, the kind with the little string tied about level with breast bone. Cotton knit in contact with other fabrics is bound to roll itself into a little ridge. It is this ridge circumnavigating my hips which I remember above all else from the marriage ceremony of my uncle—this and the little string bow which kept popping out of the slit neck of my dress. It seemed impossible that the entire gathering, absorbed in a high nuptial mass, was not eyeing me.

Self-consciousness about my body and appearance were overwhelming for several years. I did not put it into words, or even think it, but there was always the possibility that my body, like some not quite predictable tyrant, a sort of Ubu Roi, would betray me, that something else would bulge or sweat or all at once sprout hair and so depart from the firm, predictable body of childhood.

It still strikes me as fathomless that when it came I did not recognize the menses for what it was, although it had been explained by my mother and the headmistress at school. Perhaps its gaudiness was too removed from their restrained explanations. (I see the headmistress's earnest, thin-lipped face still as she wrote the Latin derivation on the blackboard. Somehow she got through the entire talk without a single mention of sexuality. Lord knows what she might have said, given the time, the place, and her own nature, but still it seems a feat.) Perhaps it was too abrupt a discontinuity with the body I had always known. Perhaps I had expected menstruation to be accompanied with immediate radical change in the rest of me, that the little girl spending a warm September weekend at her grandmother's would be instantly transformed into an adult woman. Transformation is another, more positive way of stating the discontinuities of early adolescence. It is longed for and feared, signaling as it does changes in, if not the end of the self one knows. Perhaps the fear of transformation explains something else; after my mother's "talk" I remember weeping in a great storm of emotion as I took my before-bed shower and looked down (perhaps in fear? in memory the feeling is one of extreme mortalness) at my still childish body.

In my generation rites of passage were inadequate if there at all.

Yet when I finally did know what had happened to me I felt along with confusion at least a hint of the quiet and private immensity that I knew years later in pregnancy and after the birth of my children.

This is the point: years later. In my time and in my milieu childhood was protracted and protected; the gap between readiness and fulfillment which is characteristic of human animals was at its widest; moreover, sex and birth were remote from those around me (at least as far as I knew). Possibly these factors—extreme in my case but generally present in upper-middle-class families of my generation—added to a fear of transformation and to a longing for it, forcing the young to hold in abeyance what is vital to them, refusing to sanction a chance to assay it. It was done in the name of education and in the name of culture, or rather one kind of culture. Central to this culture is a premise that a certain male bonding is necessary to achievement whether military or intellectual. Bonding takes time—namely the adolescent years. It leaves girls with a long wait, a delayed promise, and all the consequences to development which inaction brings. The current young question the premise on which this culture is founded without entirely knowing that they do so. At the same time that they refuse to keep the sexual in abeyance they whittle away at the protracted childhood which I knew. It is not clear what consequences their behavior will have for the culture they came out of, the one that I was raised in.

Not included in the bonding of young men and denied easy access to the achievement which is the reward for delay and sublimation, yet subjected to the same or greater restraints, upper-middle-class young women of my own and earlier generations were condemned to the juggling act of pretending that they would achieve (how else could one get through a school course that aped a young man's?), acquiring a nonthreatening cultural *batterie de cuisine* ("I have no accomplishments," one diary entry reads), and longing for the encompassing love which attracted doubly, not only as the thing one's heart and body were ready for but as the only goody the culture would give with full approval.

The conflict created by this situation in someone like me was considerable, but it was largely unconscious, expressed in diary entries which now seem mutually exclusive but then did not seem the least bit contradictory. Windy talk about intellectual endeavor, worry about exams, the wish to transfer to a more stimulating school—and then passages about loneliness and the longing for love, essays on what a good mother should be, including this fine sentence which could only have been written by someone very young who had never had a child: "Develop the best in them [your children] in the best possible way and stamp out the bad without seeming aggressive about it." Only once did I record any conflict over the paths that lay open to me. I wince to quote my fifteen-year-old pomposities:

> There must be one person who works twenty-four hours a day to bring up children, even when the family has only two. This is the mother's job. If she is absolutely unfitted for it, then she must supply someone who will furnish love, culture, learning, and discipline. There are no substitutes for these, and they must be supplied one way or another. This is an awful thing for me to have to face. I will never want to surrender myself wholly to the job of home-making.

It goes without saying that the example of a relative or family friend who worked would have helped me. (The only one who did was constantly put down by my mother and grandmother for neglecting her children—and they were right about her.) Today I would feel that a woman interested in what at fifteen I airily referred to as the "life of the mind" may do better not to have children, but to judge by the passage quoted above, my character and conditioning were such that even in early adolescence this option was already closed to me.

In saying that sex was remote from my adolescent life I do not mean that I did not think about it all the time. But, inheriting a romantic (and lady-like) tradition, I would have found it impossible to admit it was sex I was thinking of. Instead I called it loneliness, or more disastrously, love (which, of course, I also wanted)—that is, the only love which would have been acceptable to me, especially with my Roman Catholic background and the example of my mother and grandmother's lives: complete, final, culminating in wedlock. This led to rampant fantasy life, designs on several unsuspecting young men, and a long involvement with the first young man who cared for me. I could think of it all as farcical if it didn't still make the palms of my hands sweat. Most of it came later than the early adolescent years. At sixteen I had been no more than kissed, hardly rumpled, although I knew myself on the basis of classmates' intimated experiences (girls in those days did not compare notes) to be backward.

It was another matter if sex was in a book and did not refer to me. I read Balzac's *Droll Stories* and Erich Remarque's *The Arch of Triumph*. There was nothing more so available. I was twenty-two before I found under the counter on the Avenue de l'Opéra all the green-bound books that are now over-the-counter all over the United States—not to mention in your neighborhood theater. My grandmother told me not to read Thornton Wilder's *The Ides of March;* I protested in my diary, "What does an historical novel accomplish if it does not make us aware that though the vestal virgins were virgins the rest of Rome was perfectly normal?"

During the twelve to sixteen years I was apt to think about sex through anxiety about myopia and fat. Puberty brought nearsightedness; all at once I could not see the numbers on the sails of boats on Long Island Sound (the trickster, unpredictable body again). I can remember weeping all the way home from the optician as a new and stronger pair of glasses made the pavement look all at once like a Dubuffet. I never stated it to myself but in fact I believed that "Men seldom make passes at girls who wear glasses." I think I also believed that they never made passes at anyone who weighed over 120 pounds. (I lived, as I still do, on the dubious frontier between gourmandise and gluttony—with a cottage cheese metabolism.) The summer I turned fifteen I lost twenty pounds. It was a ritual, I see now, of sexual eligibility.

I am bitter about the way I and others of my generation were made to feel about physical appearance. There was scarcely an ad I looked at as I was growing up which did not equate the ideal body and the possibility of acceptance by others, especially one's peers. The price in self-hatred was enormous. We were without a counterculture and yet exposed in early adolescence to a post-World War II advertising style at once more blatant and suggestive than anything our parents had known. The sexual criterion was pronounced. Moreover, the ideal was a photograph, or rather a certain photographic style or styles. Mine is a generation that doubted itself in deep ways because we were not photographs. The dieting of WASPS like me was of a piece with noses altered and hair straightened, but of course paltry in comparison. In my case the situation was exacerbated by my particular background. It is the final refinement of having plenty to leave it on your plate, and scorn for gratification can be a by-product of an ethic of control.

Inextricable from worry about fat and glasses was anxiety about social life, and in the upper-class New York milieu in which I was raised that consisted of subscription dances during Christmas and Easter vacations.

A few of my contemporaries knew boys at day school in New York, often through a brother, but I did not. Many of my Jewish classmates had (or appeared to have—I feel uncertain writing about any of this; I tended to see others through a glass, rosily) a better social life because they were part of a more cohesive society with a gregarious allegiance to each other ("Our Crowd") in which families saw to it that parties at home and membership in country clubs supplemented formal social life and brought young people together. Something like this existed in the summer life of latter-day Wharton or Jamesian WASPS but it was spotted around the map of New England. It seems to me that in the city the cohesiveness of an earlier age (my grandmother's youth) had been lost and with it a degree of confidence. The group was too big to know each other and to maintain a sense of scale. And it was no longer quite the same group. To a degree it had been infiltrated, not by robber barons and their offspring as at the turn of the century, but by what my grandmother referred to scornfully as "café society." (She herself was something of an infiltrator, but that is another story and one I had not figured out during those years.) In any case, most boys of this milieu were sent to boarding school so that for most adolescents there was no social contact at all except for the vacations. Some lucky girls knew boys they could write to—"I am writing this under the covers at night by the light of a flashlight," wrote a friend of mine in study hall. The rest relied on their luxuriant fantasy life.

Everything that has been written about the horrors of the college mixer dance could be applied to the subscription dances: the emphasis on superficial attractiveness, the encouragement of puny strategies and aggressive or defensive behavior, the fostering of feelings of inadequacy, almost inevitable at least for the awkward and shy. If anything these dances were worse than college dances because the participants were younger and generally more inept socially. Moreover, the girls had to invite the boys, thus reversing the stance which they were meanwhile learning to assume. And not only one boy but two, so that there would be a stag line.

The evenings began with dinner parties at which perhaps a dozen young people awkwardly battened into formal clothes did what they could to make conversation. One of my cousins always opened by asking girls whether or not they sat facing the drain when taking a bath. Bodies, tyrannical and unpredictable as ever, were just below the surface of the conversation. Suddenly brawny wrists which had thrust three inches in three months (it seemed) out of the sleeves of dinner jackets, Etna-like pimples monopolizing one's consciousness, and in that era of the strapless dress, breasts, too much or too little. I remember falsies, in their own antiseptic way as surreal as the *mamelles de Tiresias*, rising clear out of the bodice of a friend's dress. I admit it happened while she was dancing, but I'm sure they felt unreliable even at the dinner table.

After dinner as many as 350 young people congregated in the semi-darkness of the Plaza ballroom, there to manage as best they could for three hours. The underlying myth said that everyone knew everyone because everyone was from the same milieu. In fact, little clusters of people knew other clusters based on schools attended and summer friendships—and some knew scarcely anyone at all. (My position in relation to all this was particularly difficult since my mother's family was both of the milieu and at the same time half withdrawn from it, or in the case of my mother almost totally withdrawn from it.) There were people who had a good time but they tended to be the most aggressive of the boys and the "stars" among the girls. Myopia is one of my chief memories of those evenings; I could not possibly have considered wearing my glasses. But despite nearsightedness I remember individual dresses, faces, scenes sharply at a more than twenty year distance, so intensely was I keyed up to survive in what I had plunged myself into. I had not been forced to go (my sister refused to); I had chosen to, if one can associate choice with an unrelenting effort to succeed with peers. Conforming and succeeding were inextricable in my adolescence from the desire to overcome a feeling of isolation, half social, half sexual.

My situation, and perhaps the situation of many young adolescents, demanded the comfort of a fantasy self. Hand in hand with the plump, striving, myopic individual the world could see walked a glamorous, seductive ghost socially adept and at the same time lyrical, sensitive; a creature in love with spring rains and spring flowers. Glamor and lyricism are strange companions, but this never struck me; perhaps my unconscious model was the Cecil Beaton photos I had pored over as a child: English beauties in organdy grouped on the grass around the trunk of a stately tree and in the distance ponds, sheep, woods, sunlit mist, and plenty of sward.

It was the ghost who chose the dresses in which to brave the dances: black and green moiré or net embroidered with peacock's eyes. And it was the ghost who began to read poetry, trying with words to flesh out feeling in the most traditional adolescent way.

"Up the airy mountain,/down the rushing glen,/We daren't go a-hunting/for fear of little men." This is where I was just before the twelve to sixteen years began. This was rapidly superseded by Alfred Noyes: "There's a barrel-organ carolling across a golden street/In the City as the sun sinks low."
Or:

> Yes; as the music changes,
>   Like a prismatic glass,
> It takes the light and ranges
>   Through all the moods that pass;
> Dissects the common carnival
>   Of passions and regrets,
> And gives the world a glimpse of all
>   The colours it forgets.

Next came:

> Sabrina fair
>   Listen where thou are sitting
> Under the glassy, cool, translucent wave,
>   In twisted braids of lilies knitting
> The loose train of thy amber-dropping hair,
>   Listen for dear honor's sake,
>   Goddess of the silver Lake
>   Listen and save!

Although there was still room for:

> Over the cobbles he clattered and clashed in the
>   dark inn yard.
> He tapped with his whip on the shutter, but all
>   was locked and barred.
>   (Noyes again)

Then came quantities of Shelley, the songs of Shakespeare, fragments of Keats and Coleridge, and not a single thing from the modern period except:

> A brackish reach of shoal off Madaket—
> The sea was still breaking violently and night
> Had steamed into our North Atlantic Fleet.

I did not read even Yeats until I was in college (I would have loved him; the ghost self was Yeatsian; it stood at the edge of still brown waters and watched the flight of swans, but the water was Long Island Sound and the birds were gulls).

Others have said it, but my generation and my milieu of peers were slow to discover ourselves in our own time. We read Eliot, Pound, Yeats, and Rilke in college. I did not understand *Howl* when it first appeared. It is possible that the fare we were offered in elementary and high school had some influence on our tardiness. Literature, it was implied, had stopped somewhere around 1870. Traditional education has always operated with this sort of gap or lag and for centuries no one expected the present—or the relevant as it is called today—to be formally taught. Interested people picked it up, were part of it. I am not sure now that I believe that the present should be taught, at least in literature, and yet I am bothered by what I was taught in my early teens. Somehow it was not good enough to read three Scott novels and William Cullen Bryant in seventh and eighth grades. Now young people are starved on relevance but we were force-fed the past. Is this one reason we were so slow to put any stock in the validity of our own experience or to find our own way of seeing? Or did our adolescent years come at precisely the moment when everything that has become so apparent since was just beginning to show (the technological juggernaut, the overly rapid rate of change, political powerlessness, the substitution of symbiosis with a pop environment for a relationship with the natural world)? Were we slow because we were frozen, seeing a little and not knowing how to interpret? Whatever the answer, we started out believing that traditional tools would be adequate to interpret our experience. I think we were the last generation to believe so. When at the very end of the twelve-to-sixteen period it first occurred to me that I might try one day to be a writer, I did not question that I would write novels. I did not, for instance, consider films, as did those five or six years younger than I. (My five-year-old son, on the other hand, dictating his first story, asks, "Is it going to be a book or a show or T.V.?" And when he paints—on long pieces of shelf paper taped to the floor—he asks me to attach the paper to the cardboard tubes of paper towel rolls so that he can make a moving picture.)

For me the transformation of tools and understanding came slowly and is incomplete.

In a certain sense I feel I falsify speaking of early adolescence in terms of discontinuity and transformation, sex and sensibility. What I did was go to school. Whatever my inner sense of discontinuity and isolation, for eight months of the year there was the continuity of school and the daily contact with about twenty other girls.

My sister and I left the apartment at 8:15, walked two blocks to the Spence School and thereupon were enclosed until 3:00 and sometimes 4:00 or 4:30 in a self-contained world housed in a more or less Georgian brick building on East 91st Street. The day began with prayers and announcements (some of the prayers sounded like announcements) and ended with sports. In between came a traditional curriculum traditionally and, in the case of many of the subjects, well taught. (It is easy to denigrate the education the school then offered. There were indeed endless grammar and spelling drills, a good deal of memorization, and, of course, *Ivanhoe*, the *Talisman*, and the *Heart of Midlothian*. But perhaps it is just worth mentioning that somewhere along the line I built a model of an Erie Canal lock, wrote a play about Catherine de Medici, and twice a week painted all afternoon with an excellent teacher. The strictest teacher was the French teacher—successor to the white Russian—yet it was she who would now and then stand on her desk to act out one of La Fontaine's fabels.)

It was a lock-step day, hardly broken by lunch and the free time that followed it, yet it was in this free time and in the afternoons before the hours of homework set in that friendships were formed. It is claimed that, unlike men, women do not need or else are socialized to do without close friendship groups of their own sex. I think, however, that friendships between individual girls can be important and sometimes even durable. I, for instance, count among my closest friends two women whom I first knew in early adolescence and met at school. I notice that although I do not see them very often, I confide in them as I do not in others (and they in me) as if those early years had created a special trust. We seem to continue conversations we began twenty-five years ago.

It is perhaps only ten years since I had a nightmare that I had not done my French homework. I can still conjure up the queasy stomach which I had each morning during those palatable Episcopalian prayers. (There were Jews and Catholics in the school, but it was taken for granted that tone was at least part of what parents wanted from the place and tone was Episcopalian.) I have often wondered whether school meant to my classmates what it meant to me. I think for many it did not. For me it was an outlet for ambi-tion—the only one available to me—something I could do and suc-ceed at. At the same time there gleamed out at me from the pages of sturdy textbooks baubles of true interest which I snapped at like a bower-bird: tidbits about the Renaissance, about the structure of language and the derivation of words, English history and the struc-ture of plants.

But there was a price for succeeding, or rather a double price. Doing well set one off as a "brain," winning respect but not the ac-ceptance one craved. Moreover, it pressured one to compete with one's previous record. One mid-years I wrote a long criticism of the exam system in my diary, praising intellectual endeavor for its own sake, but when I got my marks a few days later I recorded that I was not pleased—at two B's and three A's. Pressuring myself thus I was tired by the end of the year and wrote:

> Everything is endless. The work pours in; it is only ended by nine o'clock. The weather is warmer. My head is fuzzier. I wonder what I shall remember from all this hodgepodge . . . I can't remember this year at all. I remember Christmas vacation and the Big Snow [that blanketed New York in 1947]. I can recall that my hands sweated in English class from fear and hatred of Mrs. ———. I know even now that I didn't want to go back to school in October. The winter seemed interminable. The weekends were and are full of the family and the country but al-ways accompanied by a deep down loneliness and lack of anyone to talk to my own age.

Perhaps this suggests not only the melodrama of adolescence and the depression which is the ever-present obverse of natures like mine but also at least one possible effect of a school such as the one I attended. The school was a copy of a copy of a copy—that is, it was a copy of a boy's college prep school and traditional boy's schools are copies in their picture of authority, their emphasis on competi-tion and team sports of an all-male, more or less anglophile, achieve-ment-oriented model of society. But girls were supposed *not* to do what the school prepared them to do, although they were subjected to a very similar education, minus some math and science, and an identical set of values (the Episcopalian prayers, the team sports, the scholastic honor rolls). As I said earlier only the achievement of marrying well was completely sanctioned. (In an earlier generation it would have been somewhat acceptable to achieve as long as one eschewed marriage, or at least didn't count on it, but in my adolescence, which coincided with the "feminine mystique," this course no longer had any status.) I am not sure that this situation was a source of conflict for many of my school contemporaries, but it was for me, not because I put less value on marriage—it was the only thing I was sure I wanted—but because I placed a value on school that they in many cases did not. I believed in it. In 1949 I wrote as follows (and the pomposity in this case seems in direct proportion to uncertainty):

Next year I shall have to decide about college. Certainly my opinions are not those of five years ago. At that time I thought that I would never want to go to college. Now I most probably shall. I am not sure that I want to spend four years because as in the minds of most girls my age is the idea of marriage.

It seems at least possible that I could have contemplated four years of college more positively—and not been so blue at the end of a long winter of being a good girl—if I had had at home or at school any models to lead me to believe that what I was doing had a future for me on its own terms. I think it is quite clear that I thought it was perilous to extend this future even a full four years beyond high school.

As if this situation was not enough to contend with, there was in the air both at home and at school the very WASP and very American ethos (perhaps it has something to do with a pre-sputnik era in education, too) that urged high achievers never to thrust themselves forward. It was not simply a question of being lady-like (men are as affected by this as women): it was a question of being humble and humility was not exactly or only a Christian virtue but a civic one. What's good enough for everyman is good enough for anyone who gets A's, and you're rocking the boat in an un-American way if you don't think so. It was this group of ideas that was hardest for me to accommodate myself to at fifteen and sixteen. I fancied myself an intellectual. An arrogant prig was closer to the point. Nevertheless, the following episode with the school librarian still rankles:

This morning I said something which I suppose is rather rude to Miss C. She asked what books we had gotten out of the library for the Renaissance project and I said I hadn't gotten any. Then afterwards she took me out of the library and told me a lot of things. She said that I was adolescent, having an adolescent's new discovery of brain power and the new feeling of the power of one's own ideas. She said that I was riding too high, not humble enough, and tending towards intellectual snobbery and introspection.

However well founded, it seems typical of my background that the repressive put-down came first rather than any attempt at offering the kind of freedom or challenge which would have forced me to test the wings I thought I had. Why didn't Miss C. show me the books I had been too hoity-toity to discover for myself?

The complete set of signals blipped at girls like me went something like this: achieve if you want to but remember it will set you apart from other girls and make it harder to attract boys. If you achieve prepare to interrupt your achievement at an appropriate (marriageable) age. Achieve but be cool about it; hide it if possible and above all don't claim that achievement has any prerogatives.

Needless to say I didn't articulate these signals to myself. I was not even aware of them; I just did my homework. Nevertheless, I responded to the code—by making rules for myself. There are more rules than there are prayers in my diary. When I first reread the entries before writing this piece the rules appeared ludicrous or pathetic, but I now think they represent a pretty accurate rendering of what it took to do well and at the same time be accepted in the time and the setting I grew up in. For instance:

1. Not to talk too much.
2. Not to be a fix-it.
3. To be sincere without being unwitty, stupid, or a goody-goody.
4. To be kind.
5. To avoid gossip.
6. To work hard.
7. To be friendly without being obnoxious.
8. To be sensitive without being hypersensitive.
9. To cultivate and work toward the right attitude.

Another set included these:

Placate everyone.

Strive for originality.

Early adolescents are assailed with the outer world as never before in their lives, or rather assailed with the sudden importance of succeeding in it, whether this means in work or love or friendship. In my uptight case this meant giving carte blanche to my superego. (I find the admission ignominious.) While others revolted I made rules. I had always wanted to please, not out of virtue, but because I was born cowardly about conflict. The desire to please became much more intense in adolescence and at the same time pleasing was all at once far more complicated.

Rule-making led me to distrust my own perceptions. This was its greatest drawback.

There is a cold and lonely feeling which I get living here this way [I wrote one summer about life at my grandmother's]. It creeps into me from every corner of the house, and I feel it shifting into me from each object that I touch. I sit all day building up hate for the place and the way of life in general.

But then I pulled the rug out from under myself:

This is bad because I suppose there is nothing wrong with it—the atmosphere, I mean. I am thoroughly biased at this point.

Reading old diaries is a particularly blatant form of narcissism. I am glad to say it is not one I had indulged in for many years until writing this piece. It is narcissistic because one is looking for oneself, trying to give one's present a psychic or emotional continuity in the past. I do not catch a clear reflection of myself from my adolescent diary; the elements are there but they do not have the same proportions they have now and the harping on loneliness, the lyricism, the prayers seem part of a self I have not known for a long time. I have a hunch that I might feel more of a piece with the self of childhood if I had a record of it; then I think I made fewer rules, was less ambitious and less bent on acceptance by my peers—and perhaps trusted my perceptions more. Yet if I do recognize myself in the early adolescent I once was it is in this conflict between rules and perception, a conflict which is still with me unresolved. What I perceive most of the time makes me not want to cope (it is probably significant that I use the word cope)—unless writing is coping—but the pattern is set, the sense of obligation is so strong that I can do otherwise only in spurts, and then feel guilty. One of the drawn-out, painful discoveries of adult life has been the discovery that rule-making is incompatible with the kind of writing I admire and that fantasy, the escapist reaction to too much rule-making, is almost equally incompatible. But the point I want to make here is that one's stance in relation to the outer world may be partly innate or created in childhood, but it is in a sense recreated in early adolescence and so strongly set and reinforced by a feeling of the vital importance of others that it is hard if not impossible to change. A lot of the time I am still doing my homework.

THOMAS J. COTTLE

The Connections of Adolescence

I DON'T know exactly why this particular essay has given me so much trouble. I think hard about the ages twelve to sixteen and after a time that seems so long that surely I could prime my fantasies to become twelve again, I find that I am merely thinking about thinking about that period of years. I note, too, that I must reason backward and first figure out where I was at twelve, where I lived, and with whom I traveled. School comes back; I rush at it, it rushes out to meet me, although not halfway, and girls are floating around then, and boys, lots of boys, and my sister, although I must confess I felt she ignored me a lot precisely during those years, and my parents. Of course, my parents. Sports, tremendous thoughts on sports, but even more than sports and school is the sudden swell of feelings (they're coming back now, urged forward from somewhere, no doubt, by my pen) about my body, and the public exposure of my body, like in a football uniform or in a bathing suit on a crowded beach when you could keep your shirt on as protection against the sun. Or in gym class when we used to play bombardment.

I

My God, what were we doing in that progressive school? One moment we were locked away, just the boys, with our science teacher whose legendary ways and white coat made him the only one in the world to answer our questions about the universe and about sex. We had access to a little red question box which was safeguarded by a delicate but trustworthy silver lock. Anyone could write a question, deposit it unsigned, and find out whatever he wanted to know about boys and girls together—about sex. Come to think of it, it *was* a progressive school, even though the sexes were segregated during these juicy question and answer sessions.

294

The only stipulation about, well, I suppose it was our "sex education course," was that we had to sign our questions with either the male or female signature. I never told anybody, but for years I lived with the fear that I might just slip one day and make that circle with the infamous Catholic cross beneath it, instead of that gorgeous arrow pointing upward to the stars, to achievement and unguided flight, and have my question read in the girls' closed discussion meeting. Man, how we thought about stuffing that box with gross questions and listening at the door when Mr. M. would unlock the box. As for the symbolism of the enterprise, I truthfully did not appreciate it until right this moment. Unlocking the box indeed.

The one question which I remember and how it stayed with me and how I couldn't wait to make an empirical test of it because Mr. M. said, I won't answer this, find out on your own, was: Is it normal for your heart to kind of flutter or beat unevenly (I think those were the words that someone had written) when you urinate? The problem was that it never was resolved. Was it or was it not normal? Some of the boys agreed it happened, although no one dared to speak about how foolish they looked pulling up their shirts to examine their stomachs, which meant, of course, taking their minds off their business. Some boys were so fat they actually could not discern what in fact their heart was doing during micturition. (We were learning words then that far surpassed wee-wee and tinkle.) But most important, a thought had been born, namely, that on the inside of the body extraordinary connections, some rather delicious, but most rather terrifying were becoming evident. If your heart fluttered when you urinated, then when you, oh no, that was too much to think about.

I have digressed from the game of bombardment. It was a game of rudimentary rules, merciless, cruel, and manifestly adolescent. Two teams of equal number are parted forever by the half-court line on a basketball floor. Three hard rubber balls the size of soccer balls are thrown into the middle. When you get one the object is to throw it at someone on the other side. If you hit him he's out of the game and the winner is the team that has even one player left (alive). But always you must throw hard because should your heave be caught, you, the thrower, go out of the game. I remember that unbelievable thud of the ball slamming against a guy's chest and his catching it. Raw courage.

Often it did go right down to the battle of the giants, those mammoth gladiators exploding perhaps three balls at a time, or did they take away some balls as the number of people diminished? I can't remember. During it all, the rest of us, who, I am certain, were glad to be eliminated, stood along the sidelines, some not paying attention, others screaming boyish words, rooting, and thanking God Himself that he had escaped unharmed for that one day.

I was stricken with fear during bombardment. I feared for my face, for my hands and genitals and gut. It was my back and buttocks, I prayed, that would take the punishment. I could not, however, face up to this torture, I mean literally advance head on into this salvo of cruelty and aggression. But I never told a single human being of my fright. Not one single person knew my terror, so I believed. There was nothing here of any supreme consequence, no sense of humanity or morality, no notions about proper educational ideology or appropriate conduct. I was not really discovering, but enountering the deeply internal and ultimately public display of my body, of my movement, more sexual than ever before, in social space and social time. I simply didn't want to get hurt, but I did feel strongly that if I could just bonk a few guys with that hard rubber ball, maybe even sink one of their lungs when they caught my throw, and be able to get off without retribution, I'd be in good shape. I would be a better man for it. I would, perhaps, be a man.

Gym class, aggression, and bodies presented something else too. We used to play basketball a lot, and the obvious way to differentiate teams was by one team taking off their shirts. It was known as the skins against the shirts. "All right your team is the skins. C'mon, Cottle, get those shirts and sweaters and underwear off." Why was it so embarrassing, this exposure of skin and the display of our chests and backs? Some of us had acne and that was humiliating, but I think that more than anything, it was that physically we simply were not up to the ideal stature and the ideal posture, size, and strength. The ideal was evidently present in all of our minds. Partly it was an athlete here or some great guy in the high school "above us" there, but in the main it was my father's body that I had indelibly internalized as the medical model, as the model specimen against which all future assessments and evaluations of anatomy would be made. The only part of us at age twelve which showed sufficient development was the legs, and for those whose legs were thin or whose ankles were excessively fat, or whose budding, truly incongruous leg hair was already unsightly and growing uglier by the day, there was no escape if they couldn't procure long sweat pants from the gym equipment office in the basement of the school.

As skins and shirts we played each other in basketball, expending muscular energy, expending competitive energy, for sports offered the perfect way to find out who were the best, the elite, and ultimately, who was the single heroic one. Half-dressed as we were, we might check out this ostensibly random rate of maturation, for on a jump ball, or a throw-in after an out-of-bounds play, or best of all, in the struggle of bodies for the rebound, one could get a glimpse of hair under the arms and all varieties of relative muscular development, and be able to gauge the flow of manly sweat. When the gymnasium smelled, you knew men had been in there. The girls knew it too. And you were proud to sniff, like a dog, at your very own crevices and corners, and know that you had contributed to that aroma of masculinity, that ineluctable ambience of maleness. How many millions of jokes were made about athletic supporters!

Intelligence or appearing smart was an aspect of maturation and public imagery more difficult to assess. How does one describe it? To hit a home run or score a bushel of points, even in a "choose-up" game, was an unequivocal event. It tallied up at once to fame and fortune in the going currency of adolescence. Publicly and privately it felt good. It *was* good.

Not so with intelligence. Being bright earned an equivocal acceptance, for one could always draw a dangerously thin line between brilliance and pomposity, verbal aptitude and conceit, literary acumen and snottiness. Everyone, of course, was supposed to read and abide by what they used to call the "dictionary habit." But one was not supposed to read more than what had been assigned, and certainly not use those convoluted words the dictionary seemed to treasure. One could joke about big words, like Parkie, who used to parade his favorite mouthful and spell out for us: a-n-t-i-d-i-s-e-s-t-a-b-l-i-s-h-m-e-n-t-a-r-i-a-n-i-s-m. That was safe because no one could really use that word no matter what it meant. But once in the seventh grade, we heard a kid utter the word "perfidious." He actually had the temerity to flip that word at the rest of us right in the middle of a sentence, right in the middle of English class. "Perfidious" just flew out of his mouth as naturally as anything. Two periods later on the hard dirt of the East Field we almost killed him.

Only naturally did the intelligent and informed ones seek out each other and band together as a surreptitious subculture concocting a collective ideology that would make the others even more angry and envious. While there were many talents and activities that formed the basis of groupings then, the intelligence factor, in its way, seemed to be the most special and salient. After all, this was school and the major activity, though no one dared confess it, was learning, which meant that we all valued the "smarties," despite the fact that our culture forbid us to publicly proclaim our admiration for those people. In their homes after school or on weekends when we examined the contents of their rooms and just how much of their parents' property they got to use, we could let a bit of our awe spill forth. And when we went home and made those inevitable comparisons and pledges to read at least one book a week, some of our true feelings about learning would at last break through.

By Monday morning in school, our conversations were back to the clothes and the girls and the sports. But those glimpses into the recently discovered private worlds of our friends, symbolized as they were by the artifacts of knowledge, never left us. They possessed something unique, the intelligent ones, an access perhaps to different realms with absolutely marvelous temporal and spatial parameters. They actually cared about and for years, perhaps forever, *remembered* the substance and the facts of school and books. They were able to recall for us in the eighth grade, moments and data of the sixth grade, and as they sat proudly beneath the afterglow of their magical enunciations, the rest of us angrily slumped in our chairs and muttered words like "genius" and "photographic memory."

While some of us, in other words, were fascinated, or at least not totally repulsed, by the process of knowledge—like working math problems or constructing an outline for the history of the entire Middle Ages with Roman numerals and large A's and small b's, and a fixation on where and how far in one was to make indentations and place periods—others were actually learning mathematics or being enthralled by the events we were outlining. They really liked that stuff. They were transporting themselves, moreover, into mathematics or into the Middle Ages, or making mathematics and the Middle Ages come to life all over again. At least, they were establishing wondrous and enviable connections to the abstract, to the imagined, to the memorized, and to an external something one incredible step removed from "pocketable" reality.

And so, in the mode of our growing anatomies and fascination with body parts and functions, we just called this group "the brains," and caricatured them as monsters with enormous heads and tiny bodies and limbs. Sadly, I now feel, they bought that caricature, and taken as we all were by the power of the larger group's social consciousness, they tried out for athletic teams and sought entrance into activities and clubs which might yield them the acceptance and the inclusion which each of us was teaching one another to be the most important features of adolescence.

For the most part, performance in class, in school, in the world, was devastatingly important. In fact, the seriousness with which we regarded ourselves and the dead earnestness which was, after all, the backdrop to our every experience was taken for granted and eternally expected. As we saw it, the organism which was of course our simple self was extraordinarily complex, and lovably, thankfully incomprehensible to anyone but ourselves. One of the most common expressions of the day went: "You'd never understand it," "it" being that personal, despairing, hurting, wonderful thing or feeling that had assumed a paramount stature inside us. No one else could possibly understand the experience I had just sustained; nor could they appreciate what would emerge as my inimitable description or classical analysis of it.

To be sure, one constantly explained his own behavior to himself (although I doubt that we could tell others we were doing this), but rarely was one able to look out from within or in from without and laugh about something personal. We laughed all the time, of course, if something else or, better, someone else were strange. We laughed at the "sound" of words like puberty and vagina, too. I know that has not changed. And we laughed at styles of appearance and voice, and, best of all, tangible deformity drove us into hysterics. Knowing it was dreadful of us, we nonetheless could rarely contain ourselves if we caught a buddy's eyes in class or while riding a bus. Someone would be overly fat, or tall, or dressed differently, or have long hair, or slip on a stair, or ask a bus driver in "broken" English for the location of a street, and we would look and listen intently and then, blam, we would be busting with the pains of laughter, the tears rolling down our cheeks, and grappling to catch some inner strand or throw a switch that might bring us back to normalcy. If one of us got a glare or caught a few words from an old lady there would be instantaneous composure and fright, but then, as soon as our eyes would meet across the muddied aisle of the bus, we were at it again, this time even worse than before.

Other kids, other adults often seemed strange to us, and thereby funny. There were invariably funny last names and funny fantasies about Italian or Japanese or German families. Or Russia; Russia and Russian in those days meant quite a bit. Nausea or a bitter taste in one's mouth was often described as a feeling of having had the entire Russian army tramp through your mouth and one guy left a gym shoe. Then too, many people used an expression in which one was raped by, presumably, the same Russian army. Busy people those Russians, invading our symbolic fantasies as they were. The concept of ethnicity, particularly, seemed especially peculiar. That someone could be just like oneself and yet sound so funny or obey such foolish customs was beyond description. With my chums, I would hear the very same accents I had heard in my home for years and God help us if our eyes met. But the funny thing was that when I played with a kid after school in his house and a relative of his would speak with an accent, he would giggle with me almost to let me know that his uncle or grandmother sounded just as silly to him as they must have sounded to me. And yet, both of us knew this to be a different kind of differentness. Both of us just seemed to know that here was a case of a young person simultaneously honoring his family as well as the ethics and savagery of his peer group. It was all right to laugh at a German sounding woman in the bus unable to find her way to the rear exit, but laughing at a sixty-five-year-old aunt trying hard to act kindly in an American manner just did not produce the same hilarity. The setting of a home translated the profane into the sacred. Three months later I might be thinking very hard about George's old aunt from Germany. I would smile a bit, feel more than a tinge of uneasiness, and dream for a moment of what it might be like to know my grandparents, only one of whom I barely, barely remembered.

Strange how even in that early adolescent privacy of mine I felt uncomfortable and sheepish, but probably not quite what I might yet call embarrassed. To be embarrassed meant to be rebuked or at least found guilty of something. No, it was not exactly this. It was more the feeling of not being able to carry the "whole thing" off. Your body or skin or posture or demeanor had somehow failed you. In a sense, here too was a connection with parents, since quite a good many of their demands and expectations were held in consciousness as markers on a map, if not as scripture. It was not good to feel ashamed, or to stand naked, exposed, or to defacate in a doorless stall. That was the worst!

Perhaps it is the word "connection" that describes so many of the dreams and fantasies we had then—that I had then. Like, I couldn't quite tell how I was connected to my sister, or for that matter how other relatives were connected to us in those imagined layers of kinship closeness and distantness. Moreover, I couldn't sort out exactly how my connection with parents was to proceed from this point on, as my discovery of sexuality, or what we presently call "heterosexual relationships," cast a rather cumbersome veil on what I might now be able to say or be in front of my parents.

At last the recollections of that age come storming back. I have found a key. We double-dated once, four of us, on a Saturday afternoon. Before entering the State and Lake Theater I purchased a bag of red pistachio nuts from the Morrow Nut House. Nut house indeed. Then, during the movies, I nibbled and cracked the nuts between my teeth, so that, when we emerged in the late afternoon light under the billion light bulb marquee, my lips and fingers were rouged with red. And everybody, I mean everybody in the world thought I had been necking my head off in the theater when in truth the best I could do in those two and a half hours of darkness was twice accidentally on purpose brush Susie L. in the left breast. So I was unable to connect with her, but significantly, I had added to my resources something that could not be shared with parents and would thereby make, I imagined, our family connections weaker by several important units.

When I left for camp, at age twelve, I cried. Though I tried as best I could with all of my inner strength, I just couldn't hold back the tears. All of this despite my constant recognition of the public disgrace I had become.

Throughout this uncontrollable eternity, it seemed as though I was utterly trapped between the social consciousness of later years and the childhood predisposition to exposure and exhibitionism. It was a case of being twelve and understanding how the integer twelve lies equally, albeit quite comfortably, between the integers sixteen and eight. At the time, there didn't seem to be anything like stages of development or even discontinuities about life. The sixth year of existence was part and yet not part of the twelfth year. We made inadvertent distinctions between a boy and a man, but certainly we never uttered the word adolescent, which even now sounds a bit sickly and pale.

At twelve, one was both a boy and a man and yet neither one as well. I wonder whether this makes sense to anyone? In the main, I suppose, we did things which seemed natural, even instinctive, but rarely were we able to recognize that while some of us pushed our friends and some of us pulled our friends, not too much action, really, could be said to emerge unrefined out of any dark, inner depths. Things were inside us, to be sure, but in recollection it was the scene, the visible, hearable, tasteable, touchable, and smellable that drove us. The "scene" guided us away from "sissy" action to "natural" action, as if our steps were touched by the gods and goddesses of Olympus whom we had studied all about in the fourth grade. While we felt ourselves to be propelled by inner secrets and wishes, it was, to say the very least, our partners and enemies that steered our machines as much as it was our inner cowardice and courage. The real question was how to appear special and yet perfectly at one with the commonality represented by friendships and associations, all at the same time.

Well, anyway, I cried at this my first real trip away from home, and my parents bought me a pair of sunglasses which at the very time I knew to be an exquisitely sensitive solution. For suddenly I had become a celebrity, protected by a hideout which bespoke the reservation and extreme reluctance I was feeling. It was remarkable how those glasses practically transformed my inner despair into public exhibition. I walked around that enormous train station wondering whether someone might mistake me for a famous something or other, and kept thinking about the time we had seen Elizabeth Taylor in that very same station and of the time Bill Nicholson, the right fielder of the Cubs, had signed his autograph for me on a baseball when he was in the hospital in his pajamas smoking this enormous stogie. Talk about being disconnected. The thought of big number forty-three in pajamas was enough to . . . to . . . what expression did we have then that possibly corresponds to today's frightening phrase: "blow my mind"?

As good as those glasses were, I was being separated from my parents. Public presentation and adult pretense be damned. I was crushed. And that they knew it, and that I knew they knew it, and that they knew I knew they knew it, and that we still couldn't talk about it seemed remarkable and utterly hopeless. This was the point of a momentous separation, and while I understood I would be seeing them soon enough, with but the slightest incentive I could have broken down and bawled all over the filthy, oily, concrete of the Union Station, as I did when I was really young: "I'll never see my parents again."

Now this was something: a recollection of a recollection. I truthfuly cannot say how much one thinks about earlier childhood at age twelve, especially in the absence of younger brothers or sisters. But here was an instance of a connection with still an earlier time. Probably, intense feelings of any sort brought my meager, truncated little past back to me. Anger and separation, particularly, acted as though they had charged a motion picture projector to display those intense scenes which were somehow connected with immediate experience. "Roll 'em!" And I would be splashed with the madness of episodes of three, five, and eight years before.

Of the millions of feelings I entertained about these earlier and still earlier recollections, the one that stayed on to haunt me was the notion that at twelve and thirteen years of age, a person begins to get the idea that chinks, very tiny of course at first, are being chisled out of his sense of time. Like every summer one does this, that, or the other thing. The summer without horrible school means whatever it means. Then suddenly events happen to suggest that perhaps time will not always be so predictable or loyal. Days may just not follow days exactly as they did before. I wondered, too, whether others possessed pasts like my own. That is, pasts with similar contents? And if they did, was I better or less well off than before? Was I, maybe, stranger than before? But, well, there wasn't enough time to think about things like that, and anyway, the chinks were barely noticeable to the naked eye. So let's say I thought about the prior and maybe, in weaker (and more sissy) moments, yearned a bit for the people and places, certainly the externals of a time now passed. Maybe yearn is too strong. I thought about these people and these places.

I yearned for them. But no one could possibly understand this, I would think almost always in bed before falling asleep. And besides, no one else had thoughts like I had. No one. Ever.

Something snapped in me on that first trip to camp. Simultaneously, I had thoughts of not caring whether I would be seen as a boy or a man, and thoughts of knowing that a certain engine of my childhood, however small, however insignificant, had just been shut off. For good. Does anyone understand this? Does anyone else preserve similar memories? Would anyone else appeal to such a metaphor? But do you know that on that train, in a matter literally of seconds, I was scanning the other boys, my new summer friends to be, eyes cleared of all clues of sadness, glasses in pocket, and attempting to figure out scientifically on the basis of body types and ease of muscular motion, what kid in that noisy, boy-filled Denver Zephyr coach car was going to turn out to be a better athlete than I? So quickly had my thoughts turned from separation to competition and anxiety that even I was bewildered. It was as though work had now begun; I had serious sizing up to do if I was to survive the next few months.

I picked out one guy, a big kid from Des Moines with the even bigger nickname of "Buster," as the guy who would inevitably wreck that summer. (Most everyone had nicknames, of course. Fact was, there could be no special attachments to people unless they could be renamed, reborn that is, with an appellation chosen by their chums. One accumulated nicknames with pride, for in a way, apart from the intimacy, power, and even diagnosis of character they denoted, nicknames afforded royalty and superior standing. "Champ," "Killer," "Bummy," "Mick," "Poopsie," "Whamo," "Big Jim," "Fats," "Rosie." To be called by one's first name, as teachers and parents would do, was to be mundane and invisible. A nickname or an acronym or just the last name made one stand out. Actually it allowed one to escape the commonplace worlds of family and school and ascend the mountains of friendships. Nicknames were titles. They meant inclusion.)

Anyway, my fantasies assured me that this was the kid, of all the kids in the world, who would put me to shame in baseball, basketball, and football. He would do it. Oh my God. I recognized with horror as he wrote on a postcard that he was left-handed like I. And so, in a stroke of unfortunate luck, he had not only supplanted me in status, he had robbed me of the one physical characteristic I could almost always rely on to make me unique. It was, moreover, the characteristic which connected me, of all the weird happenings, to my mother, a left-hander who had been "corrected." Southpaw, a grotesque but surely prodigious term, had actually become a rather major brace in my concept of self.

How can I ever describe the relief, the lifting of that leaden shroud, that ripple of freedom that emanated from my intestines and exploded all over my once again adored body when I saw Buster throw a baseball for the first time. One throw only. Not even a catch in return, and I knew this boy's physical capacities like an internist totally on top of a diagnosis of a duodenal ulcer. Athlete? Buster from Des Moines was a complete "spasmo." He threw a baseball like every girl I'd ever seen. The left leg with the left arm, the elbow flying in the wrong direction, the masculine beauty and specialness of that gorgeous movement absent, invisible. I was still in the running, and the summer was again a possibility.

Except, there was this other guy, a kid from Glencoe, I think. He looked to be a pretty good prospect. Really. He really did.

The notion of connection, of what we might now call integrity or integration stays on. There was a belief during all of this time that everything was properly and wisely connected, one to the other. Even school or camp schedules made some inherent sense. This went with this, that with that. While they were different to be sure, Saturdays and Sundays too had the right connection to the rest of the days in the week, the school days. A boy connected with the other boys, or some of them, and in those connections was the assessment of how one himself was faring. Height and weight told an important story. What a curse to be the shortest or the tallest of the lot. Because of the age period, one only naturally suspected that genetics had either been good to him by assuring him a projected normal height, a height equal to his dad, or had a curse upon him by leaving him five feet four in a world of giants. I'll bet we inquired about normal male heights and weights for various ages twenty times a year.

Age, too, had an incomprehensible self-assessment quality about it. The oldest and the youngest in the class had to be computed at the commencement of each new academic year. "This means you'll be seventeen and six months at graduation." To be even three days older than another or share a birthday in the same month or season meant something rather vital at the time. And he or she who entered the incomparable "teen's" first was unquestionably Godly, for despite our recognition of the artificial and commercial nature of becoming a teenager, turning thirteen was still magical and surely would bring us, in time, a sweet but essential reward.

At the very least, becoming teenagers would bring us closer together in the same narrow destiny. For the most part, we never aged or traveled alone. We moved in time and space as a swarm connected by temperature and noise and the swells of motion and sensuous delight and agony, our bodies clanging together in the halls, on the street, on the stairs, and all of us hoping for those delicious accidental-on-purpose peeks at and touches of the girls who were so awkward in their weekend clothes, stockings, and shoes, in their weekend bodies and their weekend carriage. Strange how they clearly were so awkward and we were so clearly not awkward at all.

The utter safety of those mobs still impresses me. One could control one's freedom and degrees of dependency so easily. One could stand out from the crowd, fall back in to it, shield a spindly value system, and preserve those codes of a granite morality which had grown up from nowhere to handle our spreading tendrils of sexuality. But mainly there were a billion things to talk over, with one of the most important being what to talk over with whom in order to find out if you were really going through life as it was supposed to be gone through. I mean, you knew that having pimples, though a ghastly fate, was normal, because you could see the others and maybe even surprise them once applying Acnomel, or whatever it was called, to their cheeks, forehead, and chin. But there was the morality of it all. Like, what was supposed to be happening in those houses when all the couples would assemble at 7:30 and turn off the lights and you just had to neck with her, like it or not. And you didn't know where to begin or conclude, but in the midst of accidentally-on-purpose flopping your arm down, actually rather hard, there you were, having landed on some girl's newly arrived breast.

Those were genuinely unbelievable moments. What did we say to those girls? What did they hear after that confusion and excruciating pain had subsided? How did we, like little lawyers together, arrive at the agreements that have to be agreed upon as sex unfolds? How did they ever teach us about underwear, menstruation and cramps, getting the curse, and cutting gym? And why, for that matter, did so many of us completely deny this unthinkable biological and temporal feature of the other sex? It never quite sunk in, that special event of theirs. But then again, the necessary magical words and sacred deeds, the "dirty deeds," were exchanged, and felt, and the terror undraped. Words like curse, virgin, hard on, were memorized, stored away, then dragged out and rightly applied. So too, the experiences to be experienced were, I guess, experienced. Still, at the beginning of those extraordinary days, it seemed as though (or is this only the way I deal with it now?) the experiences, like the girls themselves, and the new nights and the new days when we were thrown in with and on them, as it were, bolted by us, winked and dared us grab for what we could, given our sordid passions and puritanical insecurities.

Girls were a new connection: they were the discovery of more than a new anatomy, which was itself fantastically unbelievable. Jesus, it was so incredibly exciting. That smoothness of theirs, and those, and those, and those curves and mounds and everything. How could they keep it all from us? Why couldn't we have it all the time, from the instant we awoke even, and certainly between class periods if not in the middle of the chemistry lab? How by age fifteen could they have any doubts about it? Or how about a quick lunch and then, you know. Jesus! Don't let anybody kid you, though. We showed a miraculous sense of respect. We asked, "May I?" and "Is this all right?" and "Do you mind?" and "Does it hurt?" We also asked other things in other ways and received responses in kind. It was fantastic. And the fear? Bigger than life; bigger than her father's house with the ten couples, not all of them from your class, lying all over the place. Bigger even than the stories we had heard and the morality we had constructed in the daylight and re-drafted when it got dark.

Older kids were a part of it now, and even though we had as-suredly grown up, some of the girls were suddenly looking beyond us with a new perspective. They were dating juniors and seniors! They were dating the school's heroes, the untouchables. They were actually going to the movies with the objects of our athletic and masculine curiosities and afterward doing heaven only knows what with them. They were bringing them to our sex soirées and intro-ducing *them* to *us*. Small, weaker, and less important then we, the girls had "made it" before us. They had the chance of being as old as we and older than we at the same time, and there was nothing to do but exude jealousy and warn of the day when we would be the seniors dating the freshmen (and some of those sixth graders even now looked pretty good). Then, then we would let our female colleagues pine away for their college boyfriends. We would even let them write in their diaries on weekend nights as they waited for Thanksgiving and Christmas vacations and the return of those— how could we have ever considered them heroes?—guys!

A new anatomy, and with it a whole new social structure. Is this what years later I would learn Freud had meant? Was this the des-tiny? When I think about those years and yesterday's inability to call up memories about them! So striking then was the constant re-arrangement of values. Who knows what we called them, or whether we even knew there were words and concepts that could enclose or shape our decision to go a bit farther, or stop where we were, or effect our beliefs when with horror we discussed the fact that someone had gotten drunk or was no longer a virgin. From where did all those directives, restraints, and forms of ritual derive? What, finally, was the answer to Mr. E.'s question freshman year, "What is culture?" Discretion, discretion and valor for that matter: where did they come from? Why was it that masturbation in its hormonal privacy, and sex with a girl in its privacy were both, somehow, preparation for and enhancements of the other? In the beginning, despite what you "knew," there was no way to effect the content of the fantasies that would pound into your head. At home, in the afternoon after school you might be driven crazy by the thought of what could happen that coming Saturday night. You might even have two orgasms before dinner. But then on Saturday, with her sweater off and lying on her parents' satin-covered couch, rubbing up against her, the excitement of nothing more than bare skin touching bare skin, and wondering whether you really did or really didn't want to marry her or just leave your biochemical calling card on that maroon satin cushion, your head was literally bursting from the sights and sound of the girls from the magazines. It didn't make sense. Here was a part, finally, that didn't connect. But alas, who cared; it was Saturday and there they were together again, those inseparable partners, those twins of humanity, the spires of strength and will: her anatomy and your anxiety.

Why, I wonder, was sex so closely linked to food? There was always the same pattern acted out over and over and over again. Eat dinner—now I was about fifteen—go on a date, which meant seeing a movie which meant getting something to eat afterward. Then make out and then, believe it or not, return home and maybe have a cookie or two or the left-over chicken from dinner before going to sleep. Then awake the next morning sexually starved and dying of hunger pangs. Come to think of it, I rarely if ever ate anything in the movies except when I went with a girl. Like the time with the Morrow Nut House. A little eating, a little kissy-face, a little more eating. It's amazing that our bodies were willing to keep at it. It's amazing we survived, although I never once took seriously, I never even had the thought that I might be hurting myself. I was immortal, a guaranteed machine, though I never used the words or considered the notions. The object of delicious gratification and sickening pain, the body during those eating-sexing adventures, in terms of health, was merely going along for the ride.

There were no limitations to its capacities, no uncertainties as to its resiliency.

The theme of eating and sex, however, was prominent. In the afternoons after school, on those gray November and December days, before listening to the radio or perhaps watching a little pre-dinner television, the masturbation or play or exploration was preceded or immediately followed by a little nibbling. Graham crackers crushed in milk to make a divine slop which my mother said I could always return to when my teeth fell out which they obviously would do (and soon) because I ate this divine slop; and apple slices dipped in sugar and cinnamon, the same amounts of each, made the perfect prelude or cadenza to my bathroom concerto. Well, not really concerto. It was more like an unaccompanied fugue or partita, or even better, invention.

All of these connections: food and sex and one more thing: the attachment to someone, the attachment to a woman. My mother, an aunt in the kitchen, my date (together on a date we rarely called them girls) were the final links to this seemingly natural pattern. It was the source of life that they provided, prepared, and laid in front of me—the source of life and the opportunity for individual advancement and personal power. It was to their wells I went for the fuel and resources that, when incorporated, made me believe I was strikingly independent and utterly superior in my newly found autonomy. It was for this reason perhaps, or because of this complicated set of linkages, that at the time I came to feel that the act of sex could not be connected with anything else anywhere in the world. I was barely connected to the girl and even Friday and Saturday afternoons and soon Friday and Saturday nights as well just didn't tie in with Sunday and the rest of the week as they had just a few months before. Sex lay prone out there in space, totally removed, yet totally complicated by a rich new set of unimaginable consequences and compulsions.

Women in a way, as I think of it, were not exactly objects or goddesses. They were simultaneously both, and this "fact" made it essential that men band together and engage in public competition with them. One simply could not be dependent for anything, in any way, on a GIRL! It was almost as if the script that had been written for us by society (though edited slightly by our chums) demanded that irrespective of private needs and wants, we were publicly compelled to play warrior and carry out the battle between the sexes.

I barely recall the details of this battle, but I do remember two perhaps lesser details about it. First, I knew even at age thirteen that much of it was put on. I knew, in other words, that I wasn't feeling what I was saying and acting, and that the girls in our classroom, for there were no other girls alive yet anywhere else in the world, felt similarly about it. In fact, much of the time of those early dates was spent allying oneself, secretively of course, with some girl, which meant finding out from her what girls liked what boys and in exchange divulging to her what boys liked what girls. So the first detail was that not much of a battle was being fought at all. To the contrary. The little double agent routines with their purposeful leaking of messages like, "Don't tell Mickey that I told you that Mimi likes him," were bringing all of us together, not keeping us apart.

The second detail was that at this particular age, the war between the sexes had at last become a relatively safe series of encounters. For after years of an ignominiously diminutive status, we, that is most of the boys in our class, were finally taller than the girls. We weren't necessarily heavier, although we could out eat them. And we did out eat them in the school cafeteria and on dates, and how this again mattered so much. But we *were* taller and this meant that we could see the tops of their heads, look down on them a bit, and if we had to, crush them with our strength. In this regard anyway, we were passing them by, and that made us the winners.

Come to think of it, as we got taller the comparison of height between ourselves and the fathers of the girls we dated or just spoke to became more salient, not only for us, but for the girls as well. Boys, it seemed, according to that script, were meant to compete with as well as replace the predecessors who brought them into the world. But suddenly boys had to stand up as well against those other persons who had brought those other creatures, girls, into the world, who, in discovering their own girl sexuality and maturity, had begun to recognize just a bit of their own obligations to competition, replacement, and comparison.

Thus, at twelve and thirteen, while the strongest bonds that heaven itself might secure (the bonds connecting boys to boys and girls to girls) remained intact, an awareness was beginning to creep in past the sentries of our social engagements and then past the honor guard of our unique singularity that very soon would yield a veritable convergence of the sexes. And from this convergence would emerge a cadre or mini-generation large enough to withstand the oppressions of parents. Not just one set of parents, but all parents, or at least all the parents we at fifteen could nastily refer to, behind their backs of course, by their first names. When Mr. and Mrs. Someone or Other had become Ed and Helen, it was a sign that electricity was being transferred across male-female bonds and that a collective solidarity to be used for special purposes had been born.

Parents at age twelve: what did they do with their lives? Where did they go when they went out? What did they do with their friends? What did they do in their bedroom together, and what, for that matter, did they have in their bedroom of such significant value that made them lock their door? What did my father do in his job? I mean, how did he spend his day from the time he woke up to when he would come home for dinner? Who did he lunch with? What were his goals and ambitions? How much did he make? What drove him to pursue his profession in the first place, and how did he feel when he was doing what I presently was doing? Did he ever do what I was doing? And how come? At age twelve I cannot remember once asking these questions of myself or of anyone else. Not once!

Parents simply were. When time began, when consciousness awoke as it does with a sort of mythical hangover, parents were already there with everything settled. It's like moving into a new home. Parents put the place in shape, fix up your room, and when all arrangements have been completed they move the kids in. Even knowing the facts of my biological existence and comprehending very subtle dirty jokes like the one where one man says he's going to the buttery to make butter and the other man says he's going to the country and the joke suddenly has concluded, I never thought about my parents having sex. Well, of course I did, but I must have shoved those thoughts aside somewhere and probably because of this I never explored those other questions with them either. How many of us, I wonder, ever do?

Adulthood generally was a strange concept far removed. So was society for that matter. Even if one worked for money at real jobs, it didn't quite make one an adult. Being an adult was just, I don't know what. It wasn't anything. It was like the word adolescence which meant nothing and so was never used by us. At age twelve, adulthood meant marriage, parenthood, looking out for others, and providing. In the end, adulthood for those of us who grew up in the richer blocks of Chicago's North Side was a bit like dinner. It was there; you could count on it although you rarely had much to do with its presence. It was necessary, and in a shaggy way, relevant. You had to eat and you had to have parents. There were good and bad meals, good and bad times; times you wanted to linger and watch your father smoke his one cigar of the day after coffee, times you wanted to run off even before dessert. Dinner would just be there, with lots of discussion about food, at six usually, although a little later on dad's late nights, and that's about all there was to it. It would be there, in the dining room or in the kitchen.

They'd be there too: the family, the food, the adults and children. Very few at our age ever considered that such a daily, regular, and predictable scene would ever change. Nothing, no one could possibly transform the ceremony and the presence of it all. That's the way that I, without question, without trepidation, without affect, viewed the whole business. Food would be prepared; parents and children would assemble and everything would come together at the table: Father in his chair at the head, Mother in her chair at the "other head," sister to her right, I next to my sister and to my father's left. One long side of the table stood bare or was set for those who lived with us or dined as guests. But only rarely were we four separated or forced to alter our seating plan about the table. When this happened, there was always discussion of the rearrangement, a verbal recognition of the almost sacred constancy of our seating, and though never spoken, an eerie quiver that ramified in all of us, I am sure, about the nature of family. Not just our family, but family, all families. That is, practically all families, our sample being biased.

To a great extent, the knowledge of the existence or actual setting and place of parents and food contributed to the feeling I am certain I shared with my twelve-year-old friends, namely, that underlying the whole affair—life, that is—was a sense of permanence. No sturm, no drang. At twelve and even younger, time was nothing more than a series of endless presents, always open, and yet always delicately connected to the other presents at both ends. By fifteen this perception had been traded in, and the sense of impermanence had passed those trusted sentries. Now we learned that our present lot was indeed impermanent. While I cannot recall what we made of the idea of death, we did see the present as being unlike the future, if not cut off from it, and the future as a rather husky chunk of time demanding our strictest classroom attention.

Come to think of it, I do remember what I thought about death, or at least what I felt and did when I thought about it. First, the image that someday I just wouldn't be anymore always stung me in bed at night. Then a fright would envelope me, a physiological jolt that like an H-bomb hit every outpost in my entire body at once. Second, with knees folded up into my chest, I invariably sought to ward off the fright, employing the solution that when you're dead you cannot think about anything so it's not so bad, at least not as bad as what you're presently experiencing. Third, my warding off strategy never varied, and never worked. Fourth, I spoke about this death thing with my friends and laughed as again and again I realized that millions of kids went through the same four steps. I wonder now whether anyone else still goes through them, not regularly of course, not often, but once in a while. One, two, three, four: explosion, and death has receded for the while, just as before.

By age sixteen, society like time was pouring a new fluid into us, a new substance, a new set of "healthy" ideals. Suddenly others were confirming or disconfirming our fantasies (although we took them to be the immaculate truth) about our parents. And by this inadvertent act of consensual validation, we were readying ourselves to advance, almost as an army, outside the gates and beyond our appointed sentries who guarded the palaces constituting our golden sequestered lives. We were feeling the feelings of aging.

There is one more issue born in those years that comes to mind. I remember being with Toby, a friend of a cousin in Salt Lake City. Young and alone, we had walked together through the low foothills and caverns to the grassy ground of a public golf course. It was night and the stars had never seemed closer. We were communing, Toby and I, speaking together of the slow passage of the past and the reams and reams of time that we saw then as constituting the future: he to become a lawyer, I to become a doctor. It wasn't that the future was incongruous exactly. Nor was it, in that now overly discussed way, the fact that we were unable to articulate present activities with future accomplishments. It just seemed as though doctors and lawyers were out there somewhere, and at the appointed time, with a modicum of effort, we would be among them.

Perhaps what made the night dream there on the damp grass with the stars collared by the Utah mountains so supreme was the noiseless dissipation of the effort and energy required to "make it" in the world. It just would happen, that's all. Things would evolve irrespective of one's competencies. Experiences too would pass by and you would latch on. It was like with girls. Train loads come along, you fetch your courage, straighten your clothes, pray, take a deep breath, and jump aboard. So was it then that the connection between the present and future was overly slick, or was it that a new breed of reality rode just a few feet above the ground of an older reality? Were we being separated from our childhoods there on the golf course, Toby and I, or, as they say over and over again (and I believe them), were we suspended? I shall never know.

I do know that we were communing as best we could with a form of religion, if not with God Himself. We were ascending in that crisp western air, moving up and beyond the pedestrian hours of the daylight into some new sky decorated with the lights of dauntless abandonment and flight. If we groped about trying to recall the name of a cluster of stars (that I really never knew in the first place), or complained about ninth grade or our parents or money, or listed the names of athletes, bless them all, whose public prowess had carried us through private time, and whose performance statistics were the inroads to our own secretive imagination, we were suspended, disconnected again. We were in love with our own anatomies, fascinated by our friendship and one more silent bit of aliveness that we might share. And we were totally consumed with the belief that we probably had a damn good chance despite nature's size, despite the burdens that competitions, aspirations, and self-esteem created, and despite the fact that we could not accurately label the loneliness that fell across our narrow shoulders like a cape. The sensuous ascent toward the stars, toward a sparkling new conception of wholeness and togetherness, and with Toby lying there, barely visible, each of us moving slightly in the darkness, I felt again the tremors of my interior and thought, actually thought at the time, that inside of me there lived a silent person, a whole new organism who might fly out at any hour and either make it all seem easier and better, or wreck everything, now and forever.

I make no claims of course on generalization, but that one Salt Lake City evening brought forth the power of history and the breadth of nature, and packaged them somehow in the same vessels with religion, sexuality, career, independence, and mental health. I could practically taste the tastes of all these fruits and clamp my fingers around their images and afterglows. Moreover, I could practically see the scores upon scores of human beings who, as it was taught to me, constituted my spiritual inheritance and secular legacy. For whatever the reasons, I was, on that one night, able to call forth living visions of the ceremonies and rituals that for the most part I had always dismissed as religion. And so, in the darkness, with my communing and contemplation driving me so deeply within a soul I guess I had not ever before recognized, I touched the hand of that inner silent person and for but an instant, longed for the riches and poverty of biblical orthodoxies. Had things gone differently, I might even have consented then to be baptized or bar mitzvahed. And no one, no one anywhere that I could see anyway, had urged me toward any of this.

II

It is many years later, though only seconds beyond the time of these precious recollections. I turn to my work with others and to a more "systematic" concern with "youth culture." It is the experience and imagination now of others that I call upon. For in all my recent interviews with adolescents of ages twelve to sixteen—really, they are long discussions or what the kids call "rap sessions"—the notion of connection or integrity returns again and again. How are these new young people connecting with themselves and, as metaphorical as it sounds, with their lives? Not exactly in response to my questions, they have invented phrases like, "getting it together" and "we couldn't connect." Connection is contact is drugs; having a contact, making contact. Just recently as I listened to a thirteen-year-old girl from a wealthy family speak about her life, and how brilliantly she did, I heard the themes of connection again. People were not around with whom she might connect. Knowledge, the stuff of school, was not connecting with anything, and above all, the outside and the inside, if in fact they had ever been connected, were now brutally severed.

Jennifer is actually quite representative of this group of what we still call "well-to-do" kids. She reveals a noticeable effort to make the world she sees crumbling about her crumble even more. It is a bit like throwing artificial snow about in the midst of a cruel winter blizzard. Things for her are not bad enough. They have to be worse even. She is an extremely lovely girl and embarrassed about this fact. She is an extremely competent and bright student in a fine Boston area school, and she is embarrassed about both the quality of the school and the fact that her performance is so consistently distinctive. I suspect that as the next few years come through (that train of experiences and people), that if contemporary styles and predispositions to action persist, she will take a good shot at making herself appear unattractive and reducing her now almost immaculate grades. I don't know why I say this, but for some reason I am reluctant to call this prediction self-destructive behavior. Something about "the times" is obliging her to step out of the current and the tempo she presently would recognize as her own and attempt something radically different. She's bent on making sure that change remains a possibility.

I once told Jennifer about that other person in me. Her eyes lit up, her body lurched, and she said something about how the difference between us was not so much age as it was her willingness to take the chance to meet this other person face to face, and by this deed, preserve her childhood experiences. "Head to head confrontation" was her expression. For the first time I conceived of my own inner person as possessing a head.

The theme of connection also tended to dominate a series of discussions with eight boys from Boston, all from extremely poor families. It's almost no use any more to talk about their lot. Indeed, I have almost begun to feel that their situation may just gnaw at those of us tending to overromanticize them more than it eats away at the boys themselves. Then again, perhaps not. Our discussion one day in this group of twelve-, thirteen-, and fourteen-year-olds centered about families, girls, and best boyfriends. For one reason or another, all of them were troubled by an inability to simultaneously maintain a whole lot of friendships. There was strong agreement, moreover, that no matter where they were, or with whom they might have been running at a particular time, the action, the interest, the real life were always some place else, some place apart from them. First it was at one boy's house when his mother was away, then it was an exploit in Harvard Square. Or maybe they had hit the street every night of a particular week only to learn that the one night they had stayed home, utterly exhausted and a trifle bored with it all, was the night all the action had come to pass.

Another feeling arose from these conversations as well. It had to do with not being able to fully separate themselves from some part of their lives, or some people, and not yet be able to get close enough to other parts and other people. Their fragile attachments to parents and older siblings, and their temporary antipathy toward younger siblings for whom they were obligated to play parental roles drove this group of eight into a frenzy of angry humor and raucous laughter. Girls were not the answer in the same way they weren't the answer for the sixteen-year-old boys with whom I had met earlier that week, and for whom sex brought little more than an itchy confusion and an even greater ambivalence about independence, autonomy, and self-possession. To the younger boys, girls were almost like grades in schools: they drove you crazy and used up your energy; but in the end, if you were willing to face them, they let you know exactly where you stood, first in the tracks of personal maturation, and then relative to all the others, to all the others everywhere for that matter.

I feel myself circling around the issue that reappears in these discussions with students in schools and on playfields. The clichés of the media are sometimes just about true. There is among so many students now in junior high school if not an openness, then a thinly porous sense of self. One envisions a series of gates that make the flow of stuff from the inside to the outside and the outside to the inside more easy and swift, or so it seems. Many talk so freely, for example, of getting in touch with their heads. Much of it surely is the rhetoric which, like their politics and styles, drives young people forward from week to week over the ugly bumps of school assignments and other inexorables. But much of it, too, is a sense that the task of life is meant to be simultaneously group love and exquisite internal communion. I heard this unbelievable exchange not long ago.

First boy gruffly: "You idiot. You got your head crammed so far up your ass you can't even find it if you want it!"

Second boy: "That's right. That's right. Don't you see. You're catching on. I *am* inside. I *am* inside."

Boy one, compassionately now: "Yeah. I see what you mean."

The task which many younger adolescents have set for themselves is to keep up with all the exteriors that comprise the rest of their crowd, and at the same time not overlook the resplendent inside which often is not at all coincident with what they see to be the social life they must take as their own. When I was twelve, three other boys and I built an entire television station. CBFD were the call letters, each letter being the first initial of our last names. We went about designing sets and writing out those cards that advertise coming attractions and, "Stay tuned for the football game." We played the role of cameraman, director, announcer, and producer, and we televised events, some make-believe, some very real, like one of our mothers bringing milk and cookies to us. "She's coming up the stairs now. And . . . there's the tray." Millions of young people, surely, continue to do this now, but they have been joined by a group who wish to make the distinction between televised and originally initiated reality as fuzzy as possible. It is their head some of them want to televise, not just talk about. It is the inside of their head they want to get to know, just as we used to want to get inside some girl's clothes. More and more younger adolescents are feeling for the interior of experiences and for the ways in which these experiences spray their insides, and then speak to them from their trapped states. What we cannot make happen on the outside we often will play over and over again on the inside until it comes out "right"; until it makes, as it were, a new kind of sense or nonsense.

A major difference between our generations is that, if only I can verbalize it, today's young bring a social, external reality inside of themselves, a reality that has become overly enriched and excessively stimulated by a sizzling society that cannot any longer keep itself from hiding anything. Nothing is kept out of consciousness. As a result, a person is practically deprived of knowing just what resource now inside himself is truly his own. The question of what has been created from scratch and what has been consumed is more difficult to determine than it has ever been. Psychology, religion, politics, the media, medicine—all are producing divulgence and revelations.

Many of us, actually, are engaged in work that has as its goal the revealing of the inside of something or someone so that all can see just how it functions. But at the psychological level, there is very little difference to some between "breakthroughs" (an interesting word) in brain and drug research or open heart surgery or landing on the moon, on the one hand, and the exposure to the public of CIA files, military murders, the condition of ghettos and schools, and the corrupt lives of politicians, doctors, lawyers, judges, and professors, on the other. There is a striking similarity between getting into your head in order to see what really exists and what therefore has been there all along and breaking into a university building to get at the locked away files. It is little wonder that so many young people have now turned to meditation and employed as the relaxing stimulant for this activity a word whose sound they refuse to reveal. Personal communion is one of their goals and it remains a glorious reaction to a noisy, penetrating world "outside."

One result of this constant stress on revelation is a recognition by young people, however well codified it may be, that in fact nothing seems to make sense, and that nothing connects. What had before seemed linear, logical, rational, and importantly predictable or calculable now seems irrational, absurd, nonsensical, and irreconcilable. The pieces of one's family, of one's school and country emerge as bits of knowledge that cannot be gotten together. The illegal has become legal, the impossible possible, the incomprehensible easily comprehended, insanity acceptable and seemingly normative. As many have said, the drug-taking experience reaffirms a fundamental romanticism as the brain remains a reliable source of unbelievable and, even more significantly, unanalyzable data.

A certain preoccupation with the irrational is found among younger and younger adolescents. While I am always tempted to say that little has changed in the last few decades and that "kids are still kids," the issues of revelation and widespread drug-taking at least are strikingly new. Without elaborating these points, it seems that among many of the young people with whom I talk, what was for me as a child unknowable material—stuff that I might have suspected but could always avoid because it never was openly announced—is now blatant and irrefutable. There seems to be little hiding from anything anymore; not too many secrets remain kept in trust. The openness of the media, what we call "exposure," what we mean when we say, "the kids today know things at ten and twelve that I didn't know at fifteen," are indications, perhaps, of precocious sophistication and awareness. But the sophistication at times masks the fact that many adolescents have no desire at all to be mature, informed, and responsible, and wish instead that they might step out from behind the flats of social awareness and be allowed just to indulge in the dependencies and need for love which they are happy to speak about when someone assures them that their vulnerabilities are also human and lovely.

For sure, the evil of the sophistication is manifested by the fact that in deeply personal matters, one cannot claim ignorance or, for that matter, sweet bliss. As a result, what the drug-taking suggests is that along with the marvelous discovery of the interior, the strident, unequivocal, and terrifying messages from the interior and exterior come to be garbled, met almost with pharmaceutical noise. Thus, with the inside veritably screaming with stimulation, the outside, although in the process of being incorporated, is gathered up with the noise and wild excitement and melted down or ground up or whatever happens. And still, the experiment often fails as the use of downers and uppers reveals that personal control over the most valuable of all resources, feelings, has been lost. The connection of feelings, one to another, and then their associations with events and experiences and, most important, with people, are so disrupted in a time honoring revelation, impulse, and expression, that it is a wonder that any child can sit still long enough to make it through English or mathematics class.

But a key, I think, to understanding some of this "new generation" is that the feeling that might result from an experience or from a revelation often is not permissible. A young person cannot so easily say, I wish everything were all right. He's too sophisticated, presumably, to utter such silliness. And yet, how often does one hear a person on drugs speak of a horrible separation in his life, or an inability to differentiate between himself and another, or of a wish that by taking the drug everything will be made fine—all the voids will be filled, all the feelings properly directed and their messages received. More precisely, the incorporation of drugs for control of feelings reveals a desire for something, and hence a felt sense of a shortcoming, an inadequacy, a lack. Children "in trouble," as they say, have somehow become disconnected, set apart. It may seem that they are escaping or denying, but on closer look, a complicated series of events wittingly or unwittingly designed by equally complicated people have sequestered them and created a partial emptiness, a partial incompleteness that urges a desire to be reunited and to be enfolded. It is precisely society's stress on openness and revelation that convinces me that the young cannot escape as my generation, the one we all have now agreed upon was so silent, was able to. The best contemporary youth can do is become fugitives, runners from the law, refugees from justice, normal order, and brilliant reality, outcasts not from anything as grandiose as society, but from a few important persons.

So the kids run underground and hide, we straight ones imagine, in the bowels of the earth, and from these heave their explosive, their inflammatory, logical, and illogical language, their dirty language and dirty, "subversive" thoughts at us from secret meeting houses, underground railroad stations, and underground presses. And we can't get to them. We can neither speak to them nor arrest them. And they, many of them, are thinking the exact same thing.

Whom can they reach? With whom can they connect who might believe that they are guiltless and that a system, a couple of people, a government, a school, a nation is in fact guilty? How can they prove—what a complex word it is—their innocence? How can they free themselves of thinking they have committed criminal acts and reestablish the naiveté, the ingenuousness, and the simple unadulterated charm which got everyone of my generation—well, at least the ones with resources—out of any and all scrapes?

Maybe then those gutsy boys and girls that drove us to have sex and smoke cigarettes, the ones who dared and cajoled us, made us believe that they could unroll adulthood for us, the ones who taught us the feelings of running "head" long into the hurricane of our greatest fears, are pushing a slightly new song and dance now, the song and dance of fugitivism. We simply could not run away from a thing, or so it seemed to me. Take gym class. They'd get us one way or another and dress us up in those short pants or sweat clothes and ignore the suffering that came from the indecent obligation to expose our weakest parts. It was not only the shirts and skins business and the kid, Stevie, who had the idea that if he claimed his undershirt was a deep blue he wouldn't have to take it off. It might be something like showering with a bunch of boys and exposing your entire body, or exposing the way you washed those special parts of your body. There was of course the excitement, the supreme titillation that maybe you could get a glimpse of the insides of the girls' locker room through the air ducts, but this joking idea always reminded one that girls might (want to) get a look at *you* in *your* shower.

But this, really, was the public stuff, the anthropology of our youthfulness, an anthropology that left much of the private, psychological material untouched. That is, while public events ramified plenty in our insides, there was not, as there is today, a conscious effort to teach people about psychological development and, even more strongly, to manipulate feelings. If it is a revealing society, it is also a probing one. Seemingly nothing is inviolate; nothing is able to withstand our penetrations, our investigations, our intrusiveness. Indeed, these very words scintillate with the sexual chemistry that children far younger than twelve have come to know well. It is not surprising, therefore, that the ugly terms "defensiveness" and "paranoia" are batted about everywhere, even by twelve-year-olds who never heard of Freud or maybe anyone else in psychology for that matter. A series of factors like television, group experiences advertising sensitivity training and the like, social and psychological research, the growth of psychotherapies and their own peculiar penetration into the training of teachers, principals, and guidance counselors, and the recent stress on affective education have made it necessary for people to expose their feelings and what they themselves define as their private parts. It is almost laughable to think that taking off a shirt in our day or having your feet examined by a football coach, to which we had to submit in the sixth grade (I got a B+), could cause any anxiety at all given these more modern developments. But they did, and they still do, only the adumbrations of psychic exhibitionism presently make the anxiety even more complex.

The converging evolution of cognitive and psychological knowledge and its transposed relevance to classrooms, homes, and schoolyards has meant that younger and younger people have come to be affected by the forces of revelation. Some of them have been tyrannized by an ethic of openness and obligatory divulgence. These, incidentally, are the words used by students. Yet some of the very people who in public scream the words and music of the psychological revolution, of the "let it all hang out" rhetoric, of Charles Reich's Consciousness III, are the ones who in private confess, oftentimes, to a terror: they don't know how long they can resist their own invocations to confession and destructive expression. The drugs actually help them to keep the inside from exploding, for their histories have decided that anger or aggression and intimacy or sexuality are often emotions, among many, too frightening to express or recognize. Even their shadows cause concern. The fear, moreover, among some adolescents is that full expression yields insanity as frequently as it does liberation or catharsis; hence people of thirteen, fourteen, and fifteen have reported that the insanity or irrationality they covet, or at least produce, with hard drugs is in fact the result they fear would come about should their insides ever be revealed. Accordingly, they fail to buy the products of their own advertisements. They bypass the means and thereby jump at once to the conclusions. In this way, their secrets, ironically, are either preserved or so garbled no one could know of their import. Maybe not even they themselves.

III

The tension of this early adolescent period, then, finds some of its roots in the conflict between individual integrity and public conformity. The young person constantly seems to be scanning others to check out their equipment and skills, their talents and, in a way, the contents of their interiors. In a sense, the twelve-year-old is in the process of building up his repertoire of actions and beliefs, holding at the same time all and none of them as sacred. He can speak, for example, of future careers as all the kids I know do, but there is such an amorphous and wondrous changeability about these expectations and dreams that the futures they describe can barely be considered futures at all. They are probably better seen as luminous bubbles on the surface of the present.

A more important element found in numerous adolescent fantasies and dreams is the theme of integrity which means, in this special case, that no one must have something or be something which I couldn't have or be. There is envy of a person who travels with his parents or of someone who breaks his leg and gets to wear a cast on which people scrawl messages and signatures. There is anger when friends speak about you and you cannot locate the meaning and the import. Exclusion and rejection are hardly bearable: everyone is meant to love everyone equally, except in one's own case where the intensity of the love should be a noticeable smidgen more. This is the tension of the period, or one of the tensions. It reveals itself in schools, families, and friendships. The baseline, public and exposed, is inclusion, full-fledged membership with rights and privileges like all the rest. The extremes, however, are special status, teacher's pet, best friend, favorite child, and above it all, extraordinary performance in every endeavor. That is, for some. For others, there is the paradox of Jennifer's problem. Many students, upon recognizing that they are just "bound" to do poorly in school, constantly work at the job of doing poorly, or appearing unhappy, for as they themselves describe, the impetus to do poorly or act poorly is becoming ingrained (personally) and expected (socially), and hence a deviation would be shocking to themselves and to certain others.

But it is the notion of deviation or, more precisely, the fear of deviation that dominates the world, private and public, of the young adolescents with whom I have been speaking for the last few years. Almost everything becomes for them a topic or a piece of datum that must be applied to some magical statistical distribution. They must know where they stand; they must discover in their daily inspections of equipment and personnel that nothing has gone awry and that nothing looks like it is about to snap. I guess

I must be odd or queer, strange or bizarre, is the phrase and the words I hear over and over again as these youngest adolescents speak of their dreams or, indeed, of their regular routines. It is the thoughts kept to oneself, or more generally, the activity of the interior which requires thorough examination if not immediate exorcising.

Daydreams and nightdreams are the "variables" (I feel compelled to use this word) which differentiate two groups of young people. One group cannot know enough of these marvelous eruptions of thought and emotion. It treasures imagination, storing its contents away for ready access. Then, upon establishing intimacy of a trusted kind, the dreams are paraded forth, the emotions held up to the light, or perhaps to the darkness, for closer study and sensual gratification. The second group of students, however, announces the intent and spirit of every inner voice even before the voice is identified and the message deciphered. This second group fears the inside (is that person inside ready to escape?) almost as though it might have the very effect on the outside that these people desire but dare not confess to anyone.

Yet both of these types of students, particularly at the age in question, cannot transcend the misery that derives from their notions about deviance. At this stage anyway, being identical or pretending one is identical to someone else is precisely the "thing" that refurbishes one's resilience and makes it possible for so many days to end happily. "Identicality," therefore, fabricated from the materials one recognizes as having something to do with the social world, is part of this particular era of identity. One must look like him, sound like him, or at least know what the other is doing every second, even if the doing provokes the most unmanageable terror one has ever experienced. How many times have I heard young boys and girls confess to the sheer horror of performing an act which, while they knew it would bring acceptance and that spidery respect with its miniscule half-life of a day or two, would also garner them nights upon nights of fear and ignominious defeat. And then, how marvelous was their collective relief and commiseration when they learned others were going through the same ordeals.

Still, the deviation, the exclusion by token of differences, and the seduction by those extreme few who appear to start adult culture rolling and thereby institute the initiations of adolescents remain. So, too, does the deviation represented by those who linger "too long" in childhood remain. The human markers of time are strewn across the distribution of adolescent experiences, as the tastes of adult-hood become more enticing, and the touches of early childhood, presumably, become more taboo. Nevertheless, in the confession, in the telling, and in the embellishing lie the confirmation and legiti-mation of the experience. One must fly from the experience and break the news as soon as possible. Early sex, maybe even the earliest sex, makes one a cub reporter with a front page headline story.

The first time I ever touched a girl's breast, and there was a differentiation in those days (and in these days) between breast and "bare tit," was on a Friday night. It was one of those accidental-on-purpose jobbies, but the next afternoon at the football game I just couldn't hold out any longer in telling my friend where my left hand had been but a few hours before and where both hands were going tonight. Perhaps the daytime telling wasn't better than the touching, but it was definitely the conclusion of the night experience and the connection between the privately intimate and the publicly expressive. Kept in the connection was the affirmation of my masculine maturation and semipublic-semiprivate inclusion and cultural passage. That it was sloppy, cumbersome, and, actually, had we been able to look at ourselves from the perspective of even a few more months, rather hilarious, did not matter. Deviance has to be fourteen years old and not to have gotten bare tit. I had passed the first plateau and could rest easier now for the next couple of weeks while the grapevine carried the news I brought back from heaven itself. I might even be able to take a momentary but still well-earned vacation from sex.

The notion, indeed the motivation of something being the thing to do, scintillates for young adolescents. It is not as simple as wearing clothes you secretly have doubts about, or going to sporting events you truthfully cannot enjoy. The thing to do is the artifactual, institutional, social obligation which adolescents them-selves erect as markers for measuring maturation and assessing present capacities. How many times did we shudder from the assignments predicated on a *dare*. Having done the thing to do is like an infant gaining weight. Parents and doctor shake their heads in agreement and with profound professional satisfaction. The child is growing; nature is taking its course; progress has been made and hence the time of the child and the effort put into this time has been sanctified. "He's right where he should be," says the pediatrician or the teacher or the coach. "He's right where he should be at this point in time."

At age thirteen, on that one colossal Friday night on the North Side of Chicago overlooking Lake Shore Drive, Waveland Park, and Lake Michigan, my left hand was exactly where it should have been; connected as it was, at last, to two anatomies. I had accepted the dare, partly stated, partly implied in the colossal script, and had moved my marker a whole host of notches down the board. It was now someone else's turn to roll the dice.

As painful as they are, the initiation procedures of young adolescents provide these markers and these paramedical measurements of maturation. A twelve- and thirteen-year-old person wants constant confirmation of growth as well as endless appreciation for his growing adventures. His obsession with himself, which rarely is masked even by his obsession to keep up, belongs as a part of the schemes, dares, and desires of himself and others. It permeates his sensitive and often mercurial character. Just as he tests the fabric and particularly the seams of society, so does he eye the seams of his interior which only now does he begin to locate and accept. Gaining total and predictable control over the resources he possesses in himself alone or cohosts with his colleagues is also of prime significance. After all, he knows by now what a "bad trip" is, even without ever having experienced drugs. He knows, too, what it is to have friends turn against him, and what it means to have his body surprise him. It may be that the girl he likes adores another, and if this isn't the entrance to death's womb, then nothing is. It may turn out that a young woman might menstruate at the wrong time and be humiliated by this accursed flow that pleases her one moment but destroys her equanimity and sensuous pride the next. And a young man may be put in a perfectly hideous spot by the sudden excitation in his groin and the ascent from a social nowhere of a bulge he barely is able to look at, much less treat with control and ease. How many of us recall the jokes about blood spots, and smuggling "it" in with the baggy tweeds, or their various social class analogues.

The tension between the single self and the collective, or the control over the self and the arrangements and styles of relationships bespeaks the tension of aging and that motivation we recall only now with a certain humor to do the thing to be done. These tensions and initiations, the markers of maturation as we have called them, always imply pain, or at least the juxtaposition of exquisite pleasure and pain. They provide a paradoxical union of sexual delight and revulsion. In the few times that adolescents have spoken relatively freely about sex to me, this lingering of the great with the sickening or ugly invariably appears. To place one's fingers inside a woman or inside oneself, as in the exploration of the anus or in forcing oneself to gag, yields up revulsion along with fascination, bitter illness along with sheer delight. Touching a male body for the first time, its changeableness, its hair and hardness is utterly marvelous, utterly horrible. Boys return home from dates and choke or maybe even vomit on the curb outside her home, while she, upstairs in the darkness of her bathroom, without wishing to disturb her parents, scrubs her every crevice and fold in order to comply with an edict of anatomical hygiene as well as reject or expiate the evil smells and depressions on her skin made by his presence. Sex has made them pure, both in its cleanliness and filth. Sex, intimacy, or confession, the touching through language and fingers and bodies has brought pain and the eternal end to pain.

But all of these initiations use delicious pain and pleasure as a way of pulling people through time and over the hurdles of psychosexual experiences. Smoking is the continual nurturant; the bitterness, the sickening taste, and best of all for some, it causes vomiting from inhalation and the thwarting of the lungs. Smoking is stepped up pollution, the introduction of filth into a once fail safe purity. Now the lungs may be lined with soot as the walls of all the body's orifices are lined with oils and dirt, the mucus and ugliness of life's flow. It is the pain, the revulsion, and the fascination that rest there as a pillar to a newly found humanity. If there is no pain, people discover, it just cannot be worth the effort. If it is painful it is good. It is going without food, self-inflicted fasting, or the deadly waiting out of the hours before dinner; or the fascination with those who live somewhere who one suspects may be hungry all their lives. "Don't waste food; people are starving in . . ." The pain is also like football or a street fight. It is "losing" your virginity or getting spanked. If there is pain, there is a punishment with the social and personal arms of the law built right into the act. There must be a cost to an action.

What makes the pain especially attractive (and still repulsive) is that the age we have in mind continues to maintain the omnipotence and what some would call the secondary narcissism of childhood. In the most extreme terms, one is invincible, immortal, unstoppable. Time itself will not even get in the way, for the past won't hinder you and the future doesn't yet take you seriously enough to offer any substantial constraint or repression. But the pain factor and the control factor yank one out of this infantile modality and catapult one into distinctly new realms of reality and fantasy. The inside is growing. The transparency of culture is beginning to be seen. Groups still are important, but pairing off with that certain one must also be a part of growth; new sorts of connections must be established. There are always pockets in a day for preparation.

IV

Out of this background invariably emerge a few who symbolize for the young adolescent the experimentation with and control of pain. They are the ones who, after years of practice, discover that external reality has desecrated any and all connections they once might have made. So now, attempting to avert the reality that preoccupies them, they sucker the impressionable people who, in their natural evolution, cannot get this inside and outside appropriately together. Sure, they may be escaping, this ingenious group with their religious-medical mission of initiating others into that titillating but still sickening world of theirs. But if they are escaping, who among their frightened worshippers knows enough about origins and destinies to be able to discern the boundaries of illness and glowing health, the lovely and the normal?

That's really it. When one has not had sufficient experience with that statistical distribution, how does one know he's normal or not. How does he know, as many of the young say now, that he has his "head on straight." How does he know that all parents aren't like his parents? How does he know whether others masturbate or have wet dreams or fear the darkness, even at age fifteen, or peak through keyholes at girls? How does he know the parameters of the perverse even as he walks upon them, or falls, finally, over to the other side? He doesn't even know what he knows, which is to say that while his breadth of experience is extraordinarily wide, he nonetheless feels the homogenizing process we all observe and call conventionalism and conformity.

Furthermore, this special deviant group which may not be deviant at all—indeed the word deviant seems rather strong— has found a new way, a new organ really, and has approached him with a purpose and a contract made only by lawyers or devils or shamen. Knowing much of the right from much of the wrong, the young adolescent must still incorporate all experiences, or at least the possibility of experiencing all experiences. Experiences are the constituents of the distribution. He must experience the sense of an experience just as he comes to be increasingly conscious of his consciousness. For these tasks he necessarily must make connections within himself and between himself and society, or at least with the figures of society who represent to him the keepers of these special experiences as well as the connections that will spring from them.

The hundreds of hours spent with children allow me to recall the substance of these notions, while the writings of scholars, particularly Erik Erikson, supply the organization and comprehension of these deeply complex feelings.

The young child does pass through stages, so it seems, of learning to control the organs and orifices of his body. Not just the mouth, the anus, and the genitals, but competence with hands, fingers, and feet, too, belong among the maturational processes. He explores the body's capacities, their singular parameters, and gradually recognizes differences, differential growth, and ultimately the glory and ugliness of these capacities and their anatomical structures. The nose may have a lovely outside but an icky inside. Soon, parts of the body and many of its functions become linked to social experiences, norms, or governing rituals, as we call them, through an extraordinarily intricate association of parental, grandparental, and institutional realities and fantasies. Eventually, this part and this function get covered up, that part and that function stay forever exposed. And then, certain parts and processes will become invested with an interest and excitement that make them, in their biological place and biological time, rather significant if not wholly absorbing. Anatomy, physiology, psychology, and society become a collage of color and form no critic or researcher could ever comprehend. One comes to develop intimate relations with his hands or his legs, his genitals or his chest. Or his hair. Growth of nails and breasts, height, weight, and skin shading ramify in one's privacy as well as in the most public sunlight where everyone sees you.

Somewhere in this time of early adolescence, moreover, a person begins to assess the data of his own genetic development. He knows enough about himself now to be able to project what his adult physique and stature will be. Ultimate thickness of beard, organ size, posture are suddenly envisioned years hence and a physical model of the inevitable is alive perhaps for the first time. In the recognition on a social level of one's degree of attractiveness—because only what one's peers say counts as "parents always think their kid is gorgeous"—an understanding of this genetic business is launched. The recognition often causes the young adolescent to reconceptualize his entire life, past and future. Is this truly what he has inherited? Will he be this way forever? Is there no way out, no deviation? Is this the ordained permanency? Do his parents represent not only his prior, but the shape of his future mentality, society, and culture as well?

Young people often speak of loving to ride on busses and trolleys because they get to look at people. But also true is their love of others looking at them, and recognizing them or their new hairdo, their new clothes, or just their new age, this year's age. They tell of those inevitable expressions when stupid adults say, "I remember you when you were only that tall." It's dumb and silly, but it means they are on the track. It means they are growing in all forms, and that whatever is supposed to be happening is happening. What is supposed to be happening is life, although they don't speak of it exactly in these terms.

Quite regularly it is the shaman or bully who forces young adolescents to be preoccupied with body parts or some activity which is itself directly connected to a problematic feature of social reality. Perhaps the psychoanalysts are correct and young adolescents do recapitulate oral, anal, and phallic experiences. After all, children do teach one another the antitheses of the infantile forms of these stages. Smoking and drinking hardly produce the effect of normal food intake. Ejaculation is hardly urination, while defiance and denigration of established ritual has a quality of a not so restrained anality. The accident on the rug of infancy is now being scared shitless, calling everything that smacks of the ingenuine, bullshit, and crapping on people who get in your way. Each new form, each initiation pattern has an odor and a texture that again scintillates inside the body as well as outside one's personal boundaries.

Now, more than ever before, I think, it is this scintillation that preoccupies many adolescents. Partly this is because of the inversion of the public and the private, the intimately sacred and the pedestrian and profane. I am thinking of the erotic nature of the head, and particularly of the brain or the mind. Once I thought it a rather cute play on words the notion of a "ce-phalic stage" of psychosexual development. Now I think it is accurate. I do not understand heavy drug usage but I do know that for many students becoming high is a means of moving away from sexuality, or more accurately from genital sexuality. It is a means again of filling emptiness, completing the incomplete, satisfying the lack. True, and this fact cannot be underestimated, society's ugly parts are now being paraded in front of each of us as though life itself were a course in pathology. A new culture is trying, an older culture is whimpering but fighting back doggedly, and the certainties that I relied upon are not as visible to my young and very young friends. Let me elaborate on this.

When I first commenced having those sexual experiences which a week ago I was unable to remember, two things which helped me to relieve, well, I suppose it was the guilt about these experiences was first the chance to speak to friends and put the news on the grapevine (never thinking, of course, what it did to the girl's reputation), and second, the fact that as society generally covered up all of these "indiscretions" and adventures, maybe my parents wouldn't know what I was doing. But the important part was that I knew they knew what I was doing. It was like the sunglasses episode. Of course they knew, and without their punishment it all worked out somehow. That is, the guilt was not so bad. I guess what I mean is that there was a funny balance between the content of secrets and the right to have secrets. My public manner, my clothes and comportment told everyone what I was up to. I didn't need the calling cards. It was in the walk and in the eyes. It was like not telling people you had a cold when your nose and eyes were running a regular Niagara Falls of mucous down your face.

What I fear is that the open and highly sexualized ways of our society coupled with the stress on the public or advertised approach to intimacy tend to throw the same old action and the same old guilt into reverse, which in turn drive those young people who continue to need social approval from moral authority into and unto themselves. The interior presently is glorified, often to the exclusion of the outside. The mindless animals of my day, the chauvinists and rapists who handled their (my) fears by crashing, interestingly enough, "head long" into the fray, or rather into the more frail sex, so they thought, now turn out to be the overly mindful, the full-of-mind people of this decade. Well, that is extreme, for the animal in us and the animalistic are hardly dead. But the forms of preoccupation with mind and cerebral stimulation are in many respects quite new.

It is interesting how drugs and television simultaneously produce a stimulation of the mind along with a pernicious passivity which drape the excitement of sexuality and the erotic. Both media produce that timeless ground against which all social and cerebral connections seem feeble and effete. People are separated from people, while anatomies and even portions of single anatomies grow farther and farther apart. Yet, these are the times young people tell me they are at one with themselves. And so they are under extreme conditions, for when the drugs really work, there is not a soul and not an agent from the outside who can drop in. But the data from the young people that impress me indicate that with heavy drugs one does not need sex. Genitals, biological differences just get in the way. Thus, many junior high school students don't rush to turn out the lights on Friday nights, but leave them on and teach one another how to take that deep, marvelous drag on a joint, or slip one another pills, or whatever happens. And the competition and the sizing up momentarily recedes, and the secrets one has kept from everyone are ushered out back somewhere, hopefully, and maybe the first steps of a new society are taken. So be it.

I cannot understand the serious drug-taking that we see in this age group. Maybe I just don't want to get myself to understand it. Maybe, too, the move toward understanding and knowing is precisely what many of the young fight. But the aloneness some discover in drugs and the separation and cleavages which drive them on a particular day to take drugs suggests to me, nonetheless, that where we dove into people as a way of running from our insides, some young people now are turning their heads around or inside out, or whatever they say, in order to inflict a pain and sustain a guilt that comes from that same old connection between the inside and outside. Yes, society is sick and everyone's popping pills of one sort or another, but that does not explain the excruciating need to be totally left alone and totally cared for, the moods that inevitably result in heavy drug usage.

The inside, now in the absence of public secrets and unspoken morality, has taken over as the agent of personal communion and spiritual encounter. Where what I did made me think I would go crazy or blow my brains out, drugs do precisely this. But we're still not sure whether or not drugs merely echo the "mind blowing" experiences in which the child is caught by token of a family social pathology that anyone with the interest could detect. At thirteen and fourteen, I was the odd ball, so I thought, in a straight, predictable, square society. I was a social prude, a psychological sex maniac, and a social psychological normal. This meant that I was square, that I possessed unbelievable thoughts, but acted as I assumed everyone else acted. There was very little craziness around, very little social terror, very little deformity. Now there is a lot, or we have been taught to believe there is a lot. The script is constantly revised. I was self-destructive at twelve, naturally, but while I used expressions like going crazy or words that had to do with death, I didn't really believe yet in these consequences and eventualities.

Now kids go crazy or feel themselves to be going crazy or deal with themselves in a brutal fashion. We spoke often of castration and mutilation, which symbolically, although we never articulated it as such, were vital aspects of our prescribed initiations. Drugs seem to me to be castration of the mind or ablation of parts of it, or at least cerebral scarification. Scarification, I think, is more accurate—self-inflicted wounds, suicidal but exhilarating, and somehow bringing one in closer touch with the others still in an extended moment of immaculate separation. And everything comes to be a dance of death: the mind as the womb and the flooding out or wretched trip as the miscarriage or abortion. The child's death is seen and felt before the child's birth.

Once again I cannot tell whether I believe more strongly in the metaphoric or the scientific truths of these words. Maybe both are valid. We used to speak, for example, over and over again of genitals—like erections at the wrong time, or having intercourse and having the girl "lock on you." Everyone had a story about this. All of these stories and fantasies persist. When I mention them to the boys I see regularly they giggle confirmation. The old man's not so bad appears on their faces. But my admissions and accounts do nothing for their fears. The drug-takers seem interested in these fantasies, but their analogies having to do with the mind are far more exciting to them. A bad trip can come from out of the blue at the wrong time, and your brain can lock on you and you'll never get out from within yourself. Everything will stay crooked.

I keep coming back to the notion that mental illness and death are the painful and presumably pleasurable ways this small but enlarging group of students deal with the problems of intimacy and the knowledge of others. The certainties I knew seem to be disappearing, or at least they are not as apparent as before. Everything is doubted, including the narcissism which probably sustained and carried me and many of my generation. Much of contemporary youth's brand of self-importance is just not felt to be genuine, or maybe it offers a rather miniscule payoff. While young people shake the rattles of agony and euphoria, the satisfaction does not last. And now, sadly, even the mysterious and uncanny have begun to lose their once flavorful succulence.

V

Explanations for these complex issues remain to be articulated, but one last thought occurs to me. It has been—how does one say it —a long time and yet a short time since my own early adolescence. A continuity with years ago ties me closely, vividly to childhood, and yet I know and even sense the spirit of the distance between the now and the then. More than mere time separates me from and connects me with those days about which I just cannot keep from smiling and shaking my head. There is so much more I wanted to tell, so many more notions I had listed on an envelope for reporting.

Like a country, we are only partly now what we were. We are only partly the agents of change. Mostly, we are its victims, its objects, its consumers. We are deceived if we come to believe that alterations in present styles or circumstances excuse or negate our private family and collective cultural histories, just as we are deceived by the idea that present alterations, indeed progress, avoid bringing forth destructive if not regressive behavior. Every innovation, every novelty, every seemingly progressive step has a self-adoring, out of control, excessive, or aggrandizing quality about it. Always there are people who honestly believe they can "save the world." But even the less extreme proposals require that someone somewhere pay a price. The demanded openness of contemporary parents, the ethic to close the generation gap, the very word "gap," affective education—all are noble, marvelous, and at the same time, to me, rather scary concepts and adventures. They ask us to make more and more connections, it would seem, but for some young adolescents, they simultaneously disintegrate privacy and a mystique of cautious constraint that might somehow be needed to keep existing connections viable, if not beautiful.

In the end, I feel dreadfully uncertain about so many events and so many progressive movements which involve adolescents. I would hate to think I yearn for my own youth again but there *is* something that tells me that while I do not want the young to know the world I knew—although I suppose I do, otherwise

I never would have exposed it here—that world may have been more simple, a bit more bearable if not richer, a bit less dangerous and terrifying if not lacking somewhat in adventure than today's world, that is, the part owned by the young. Still, I suspect, though I'm not sure why, that the very actions of parents, siblings, teachers, and friends that made me especially happy or especially sad as a youngster exist today only slightly modified. I suspect, too, that the connections made and to be made at ages twelve or sixteen are very much in keeping with the connections we made.

Yet what I continue to wonder about is not exactly the limitations of retrospective research nor the inability for others to generalize from my own selected life chapters. What I wonder about is a desire to make connections between portions of one's life; to fit together the blocks of time that continue to contain hordes of people—well, large numbers of people—with whom it seems one wants to stay in touch. Family members, school chums, even ones that we didn't care for that much and ones that certainly didn't care for us, all belong, connected in funny, rather sacred places and order, and all participating in excruciatingly dreadful ceremonies which, if we could, we might not change one bit.

I wonder often why the ages twelve through sixteen have been neglected somewhat by those of us who do research on adolescence. I myself was unable to recall much of this particular time; it just didn't seem salient. It would be frightening to think that political, social, and educational realities, along with an ideology that derives from the workings of the media and the social sciences, could actually render a period of time in one's life insignificant and almost totally forgettable. And yet, is it possible that sociological processes of this nature are in fact contributing to one's fundamental conceptions of self? Does the impression made by biology fade, even at an age where it obviously is so powerfully active and determining merely because the eyes of the world in which we mature have decided to look upon two-year-olds, college students, divorced couples, the poorest, the richest, or the very, very oldest among us? Is this why we skip periods of time like early adolescence, because the problems of these periods are predictable, easily comprehended, and just as easily mastered? That, after all, is why "the brains" I knew skipped grades in school and left the rest of us forever.

But if we are abandoning entire age-groups like twelve to sixteen we are most certainly abandoning as well the ages thirty to sixty-five, for just like the government, we social scientists pick people up at retirement. Evidently some of us have a way to go before our lives again seem sufficiently interesting and worthwhile to students of the life cycle. Now, given this thought, I truthfully cannot determine whether this newly discovered disconnection causes me to feel a surge of bitter rejection and estrangement, or whether it is not a rather liberating notion, one that grants me freedom to pursue my future and do the best I can about settling the affairs of my past.

TINA DE VARON

Growing Up

Introduction by Jerome Kagan

A view of adolescence by one actively assimilating the experience should not only test the validity of more scholarly essays but also permit an appreciation of the contrasting descriptions of that period offered by the dispassionate spectator and the embroiled actor.

The introspective upper-middle-class American adolescent recognizes that sense must be made of the discrepant visceral information that is the essence of emotion, and new meanings assigned to human interaction. Sensory bombardment from heart, stomach, and hand, and invitations from and attacks by peers pose new interpretive problems, as if a set of aneisokonic lenses had suddenly made the familiar world appear askew.

For Tina deVaron, and many other adolescents, the prime emotion to tame is a special anger growing out of helplessness. The helplessness is not new, but it is now unacceptable to the ego's definition of maturity. Passivity, obedience, and retreat are appropriate for the child, but are resented and resisted by the adolescent. The threat embodied by the difference between what one is and what one wishes to be generates strong anger. There are times when Tina deVaron resembles a vocal representative of one of America's minority groups. But this should be so, for both groups share many conflicts. The adolescent's anger is directed at parents, friends, and, of course, the self for being insufficiently courageous. The realization that one must be loyal to new convictions in the face of seductions to compromise places enormous stress on American adolescents.

The adolescent is also afraid of revealing a view of self that is believed to be uninviting. The adolescent is mildly paranoiac in his belief that others will discover his frailties, and enormous psychic energy is assigned to the task of disguising what is impossible to hide. The flee to secrecy is not unlike the schizophrenic's bizarre speech, for in both instances to be understood is to be known and to be known is to be vulnerable to the mind of the knower.

Tina deVaron insightfully lists the limited set of defenses the adolescent can use to deal with these uncomfortable tensions: emotional isolation, escape from thought to sensuality—be it sex or drugs—and the shaping of a skill. The gradual development of a talent can abort guilt and anxiety by deflecting the mind from worry to work. Educational planners should heed Tina's suggestion that perfection of a competence is

337

a prime defense against the inevitable dysphoria of this period.

At the time when Spock, Ginott, and Skinner offer different recipes to parents, Tina deVaron reminds us that there is no substitute for wisdom. Parents must be sensitive diagnosticians with their enigmatic adolescents, knowing how far to let the rope out, while remaining acutely vigilant for subtle requests for tightening of the reins. Since it is impossible to give simple instructions as to how taut the rope should be, honest conversation is the best source of guidance and the best protection of harmonious relations between the generations.

The reader should note the similarities and contrasts between Tina's concepts and those of the mental health professional. Where the psychiatrist talks of repression, Tina speaks of "emotions that threaten because of their obscurity." Where the psychoanalyst promotes the affective aspect of catharsis, Tina emphasizes the rational component, "giving words [to emotions] can help to clarify the adolescent's thought." Tina helps us see that the repression of strong passion is not always driven by the fear of being overwhelmed by sexuality, but can simultaneously serve the simpler apprehension of being disavowed. In one of the most significant passages Tina notes that the feeling of total responsibility for one's problems is one of the critical defining characteristics of early adolescence. She remembers, "I kept on crying in order to prove to them and to myself that they were unable to stop my crying, that they were helpless this time and it was my problem." Perhaps it is only in Western society that the adolescent feels so obsessed with cutting psychological roots to his family and creating, as soon as possible, a completely autonomous conscience. Since it is impossible to achieve a coherent morality that is totally independent of the first dozen years of instruction, the adolescent is doomed to fight ghosts—to struggle against an immensely powerful opposition. Tina deVaron reminds us that the American sixteen-year-old does not fit the press's stereotype of the autonomous rebel. He still needs his parents to test his ideas, constrain him in time of doubt, and to be rational when he is too demanding. The editors believe that this statement from the battlefield brings freshness and perspective to the other views in this volume that are primarily the products of memory.

I was running down
　　　　　　　　you couldna tell
　　　　　　me anything
　　　　　　　　　　　　　　and as for livin its always
now when we will be going down
　　　　　　　　　　　　　　sweet lights bigger than
　　　　　sweat　love will be　cities　running in
　　　　　　　　　　light night flash flash
　　　　　　　　　　　　　　　　flash down to
　　　　　　sound singin trippin round town
　　　　　　　　　　and in the morning the room and the sheets
　　　　　　　　　　　　are naked and dirty in
　　　　　　　　　　　　　　　　the sun.

THE ADOLESCENT faces two basic conflicts: dealing with his emotions and interacting with new people and situations.

The adolescent has to handle what's inside of himself as well as what is happening around him. Sometimes the inside feelings are so strong that he must struggle to deal rationally with his reactions. He must learn not to overreact to situations despite strong emotions, and he must watch that he doesn't hurt other people's feelings.

The emotions which demand the most energy, thought, and figuring out are ambiguous and present themselves in indirect ways. They threaten because of their obscurity. For me, anger has been one of the most demanding emotions. Many times there is a direct link between anger and the outside world—she took my doll, I'm angry, I hit her and take the doll back—or, in older people, war is an expression of anger. But anger does not always have such a direct link. Often a feeling of helplessness, or of being used, comes between my angry feelings and the action or instance which caused them. When I was fourteen, I wanted to stay in the city one weekend with friends and go to a party. My parents, knowing that I had lots of homework to do, and feeling that I needed a rest from the pressure of being with my peers, wanted me to come up to the country with them for the weekend. I knew that no argument of mine could stand up to theirs because they were older and "knew what was best for me." Helpless against this strong and uncompromising reasoning, I could not fight back. My feeling of helplessness resulted in a feeling of anger: "What right have they to tie me down so; they really don't know what they are doing."

This same pattern of feelings can occur with peers—for example, when smoking grass in a large group. George, the typical fifteen-year-old of the 1970's, goes off from a party to smoke his dope with a couple of friends. On the way, four more friends latch on. They are not George's closest friends, but he likes them and would like to be thought well of by them. When they decide to smoke, George finds that these friends have no dope, and are expecting him to be hip, cosmic, and peaceful and give them some of his. George may feel that they are "using" him, but he wants them to like him and think he's cool. Although George feels that they are using him in a selfish way, he also feels helpless in terms of their position (they could tease him and spread ugly rumors about him if he wasn't generous—why not?), so he gives them some of his dope. George is angry that he has been used and forced into a helpless position, but he must watch out for his anger. He doesn't want an angry word or motion of his to prove him "uncool" in front of his peers.

From these examples you can see how strong helpless feelings can become. They can produce powerful anger. One of the components of anger is aggression; George feels like hitting those people who made him angry, or shooting off his mouth at them. The strength of his anger is threatening; he fears that it may overpower him, may take hold of his life and hurl it in the wrong direction. I have been scared many times by this kind of aggression. I fear that I won't be able to handle the results of my anger (if I let it loose) and I feel helpless.

I wrote a poem when I was angry at a girl I know for using someone:

He is winning her, with his long looks and
                his sweet smiles.
        so why do you sound so confused?
you who slapped him in the cradle of his
            of his first time.
you who slandered the night
            of his dumb virginity
and you left him hiding naked under the sheet
       left him, lonely self inside his game.
And you danced, happily martyred
        and sang the curses of the awkward night
          to all your friends.
      Some were his friends too   can friends identify
              or help
              or slander back?
    and I who have only sighed and bended to little love
        would never in any bedtime fantasies
          have done what you did.

One way to handle strong and scary emotions is to isolate them from the environment which causes them. The best way to do this is to talk about them with a close friend. Describing the emotions out loud, giving words to them, can help to clarify the adolescent's thought. If he has a close friend, he can trust the person to whom he is telling his feelings. Close friends can be relaxed with each other and don't need to be aware of their actions. Each can talk freely about emotions and show them. With each other, the two friends have a chance to see themselves wide open; they are not afraid of talking too much about themselves. One can say he likes or dislikes someone, and he knows the other won't tell. One can be in a sour mood one day and know that the other will understand. Best friends can complain to each other, and most important, they can act stupid or silly, loud or crazy with one another and understand that there is no need to feel that that silliness endangers their friendship. With other friends who are not close but who are friends nonetheless (like the people one hangs around with), the relationship is not as secure. The adolescent is easily preoccupied or dissatisfied with actions and reactions in this group. He may dislike or be angry at a person whom everyone else likes. He thinks that if he shows his anger and/or dislike other friends will not understand and will disapprove of him. (I think he is fairly correct in assuming this.) Therefore, he feels that since he is alone in disliking someone, his feelings of dislike are not justified; there is no one to back them up. So here he is with ugly, unpleasant feelings that he is not even sure he approves of. In order to keep them from causing him any more trouble, the safest thing to do is to keep them private. Now he is all the more concerned about his interaction with others because he is worried that what he does or says may betray the nasty feeling he is keeping to himself. He becomes very conscious of his actions because he fears that others may discover just as much about him as he himself knows. Sometimes he assumes that this discovery has already been made, and he believes that things which his friends have actually said and done by chance have been meant to hurt him. The difference between these friends and an intimate friend is that with an intimate one doesn't feel he has to hide ugly feelings in order to maintain the friendship. He doesn't have to contend with being self-conscious or taking his friend's acts as dangerous. He is not worried that his friend will betray him.

A friend of mine says that if she openly shows emotions, especially around boys, she feels "vulnerable." She says, "It puts you way out on a limb." I think that the adolescent can feel "vulnerable" if he shows what he regards as too much emotion.

I have just described the adolescent guarding against a feeling of vulnerability among his peers. He would have been vulnerable if he had shown his angry feelings. Friends could use their knowledge of his bad traits or nasty feelings against him. They could tease him, talk about him, and push him outside of their group. The adolescent's feeling of vulnerability, of being "put out on a limb," is one of alienation from the group, of suddenly becoming an outsider. Emotions are being taken from the private world where one is discovering and dealing with them. As he enters the world of action and people, the adolescent fears that he may lose control over his emotions. He fears that if he lets his emotions enter strongly into his interaction with others, the actions that follow will be hard to handle or disappointing.

When I love someone and want to know him better, I am afraid to tell him of my feelings for fear that his reaction will disappoint me. He may not love me back. This would shatter all the fantasies I had while loving this person before I told him. So, I may stifle my feelings of love because I don't want to handle the disappointment of being refused the real love that I would eventually ask for.

In childhood, disturbances caused by emotions can be soothed by actions from parents. When a child is sad, he is picked up and comforted. When he has nightmares, he goes and sleeps with Mom or Dad. Disturbing emotions that a child has can be taken care of by simple actions or explanations from parents.

In adolescence, parents lose their power to comfort or explain away fears, because emotions are more demanding and powerful. When he is unhappy, the adolescent himself must understand the emotions behind this unhappiness before he can be happy again. For example, if I feel crushed because a good friend has gone off to spend the weekend with another friend, I have to work this out myself so that I cease to feel abandoned and lonely. I may go out and see another friend. This shows me that I am capable of having other friends also; that I can survive without my good friend just as she can survive without me.

Also, as the adolescent grows more independent his values begin to differ sharply. Often now, I feel that I must not talk about some of my problems with my parents, because they would think of a totally different solution than one that would be appropriate for me. This would only confuse me. I must figure out for myself what I want out of the situation that presents the problem. No one can do this for me, certainly not my parents.

When I was about twelve, I was very afraid of death. I didn't see the point in living if I was going to die. I used to cry and cry for my parents' attention, but they couldn't take away this fear from me; they were helpless. The strength they had had in dissolving my childhood fears was gone. I had to come to an understanding of death on my own. Even though I knew they couldn't help, I think I kept on crying in order to prove to them and to myself that they were unable to stop my crying, that they were helpless this time and it was my problem. This loss of their power was disturbing to both my parents and me. I felt anxious; a lonely, sick feeling would come easily. I'm sure they also felt very frustrated, and for a while just did not know how to help me. This loss of power has been beneficial, in that it has forced me to search for my understanding of me and of life, independent of my parents.

Now I will make a rash and subjective statement, and say that parents of adolescents must be as clever and perceptive as possible. It is their responsibility to decide whether the child is mature enough to carry through with what he wants to do, that is, whether or not to let him do things like going out alone, staying out late, and traveling alone. If they let him do anything without questioning, he could easily feel abandoned and that nobody gives a damn. From there, he could feel that growing up is too much for him to handle, that it just is not worth all the trouble. On the other hand, if parents don't let the adolescent be on his own enough, he may feel that they are not allowing him to grow up. He is not only trapped into coming home at 10:30, but he is also trapped into not being able to explore his limits and feelings about himself. He is using someone else's limits, and he is afraid he will start feeling someone else's feelings also. Parents should try and understand this stress, and assess the amount of the child's knowledge of himself. Parents should support, by being willing listeners and not trying to measure the adolescent in their own values. This is something which I think should happen more than it does. Blaming it on "the generation gap" is stupid. An example follows in which talking with parents would have helped.

One night last year, a friend of mine smoked some dope, and drank a little too much whisky, proceeding to get very sick. The people she was with were not very sympathetic, and she spent half the night alone, in a strange bathroom, drunk and very sick. This was her first mean experience; it upset and frightened her to think that it actually happened. She would have liked to have talked with her parents about it, but she couldn't. She knew that the incident would upset them; they would get angry and make her feel stupid and wrong. She already felt stupid enough. So she came and talked with me. That's what friends are for, of course, but if the "generation gap" were shoved out of the way, and parents were more like friends, parents could be more helpful. They could also keep in better touch with their kids. Parents can also support by not being overly critical of their adolescents. In many cases, the adolescent is so critical of himself that he doesn't need more from the outside. Adolescents are finding differences between them and their parents which are hard to understand. One thing that is difficult for me to understand is that Dad is fifty years old and that his life is in a pattern which is already molded. Dad's hardly changing at all, while I am being hit with new things each day. He's not going to give in to something new as quickly as I am; he's not going to be frustrated as easily, either. It's easy for me to criticize his settled, hardened ways. From my experience, adolescents expect their parents to be perfect, and take their faults seriously. Parents must live with the resulting criticism by not taking their children's attitude (though it is at many times bitter) too personally.

Much of the confusion between me and my parents comes when I make ridiculous demands of them and they are personally offended. In the first place, I am not aware of the ridiculousness of my demand, nor of the great seriousness with which it is received. Such a demand is in accord with some of my feelings and I do not always know how it will affect others. It might even be formed in accordance with emotions of which I am unaware. Thus my demand is unsure, backed up by shaky, unfamiliar emotions. If the reaction in my parents is motivated by a feeling that they are threatened and they take my demand too seriously, I am thrown off balance. My sureness of myself is weakened because I see a reaction different from the one I meant to arouse. Furthermore, if my parents' reaction is irrational, I may wonder whether there is a tremendous lack in me which produced a demand that threatened them so. If they respond by noting a specific lack in me, I will take this too seriously, feel bad about myself, and conclude in a dramatic overreaction that I am helpless and forsaken. What I have described here is an overreaction on the part of both parents and adolescents that parents should watch out for. Parents have more control over their overreactions than children, and parents should guard against losing perspective.

Now that I'm sixteen, and can look back on much of my growing up, I see parents as valuable in two ways. I am learning how to live with others and myself at the same time, and if I have difficulties, they will not walk out on me if I get a little hard to live with. They are also my blood relations, they have known me longer and better than anyone else. Because of this, I can be sure that they, above all others, will stand behind me if I get in a bind. The love they gave me as a child has helped to reinforce this feeling, and helped me to feel how important we are to each other.

I have described some of the conflicts which confront the adolescent. In order to cope with these conflicts, the adolescent must create a device which keeps him from being hurt and from hurting himself. Subconsciously he can find a way to deal with the sources of his unpleasant emotions and vulnerability. The easiest thing for him to do is to build a wall. This can be done by maintaining a high level of cynicism or sarcasm all the time, or by pretending not to care or to take anything seriously. Anything that puts the adolescent at a distance from people also protects him from losing control, or from dependence on others. An attitude of "not caring" can put him at a distance from others. He can create another wall by becoming preoccupied in being "hopelessly messed up." This draws the attention of others (which he needs to keep from becoming lonely) and protects him from having to come out of himself or forget about himself.

By having a wall, the adolescent is exercising a tight control over himself. He cannot easily forget himself or get involved in someone or something else. He can hardly relax with the wall up. The safe distance between himself and others is too safe. His isolation leads to loneliness, when he finds himself much farther away than he need be.

Loneliness plays a large part in adolescence. When afraid of showing emotions, the safest thing for the adolescent to do is withdraw. By withdrawing he alienates himself and can easily lose perspective about his feelings, taking them too seriously. When he spends time alone, he can get into the rut of thinking bad things about himself. Part of his task is learning how to keep himself good company, to find things he likes to do. If he is bored, loneliness comes easily.

When the wall is up, the adolescent often feels tense and detached. Now the use and abuse of sex and drugs enter in. Grass can relax and give a pleasurable feeling. Like a hobby, grass provides the adolescent with a release from his tension and an escape from his problems. Dope (and liquor) can muddle his control so that he can use "being stoned" as an excuse for doing the wrong thing. He does not have to answer for what he does. Drugs can be abused if nothing else eases the tension. The adolescent can find himself depending on dope for all his relaxation. Nobody wants to be in that position.

With sex, the adolescent can keep his isolation and alienation from becoming acute and obvious. If he chooses, he can stay behind his emotional wall, and stay invulnerable. By this, I mean that the adolescent can keep sex purely physical, and remain without the hassle of becoming emotionally involved, thereby not getting hurt. The problem with using sex to ease the tension caused by loneliness is that one can hurt others without being aware of it. I think this is mostly a boy's problem. For girls, on the other hand, there is a great need for love and understanding. A girl may think that she can gain this love and understanding through sex—affection—but she may not, and may be embarrassed and hurt as a result. The adolescent becomes aware of strong sexual feelings that are exciting, new, and frightening. They frighten the adolescent because he doesn't know how he will react to them, or whether he will be able to control them.

Some new things which frighten, challenge, and excite are: sex, travel, meeting new people, doing new things, and going away from home. They are frightening because the adolescent has never confronted them before, and he is unsure of his reaction. The adolescent is gaining a new awareness of time—of past, present, and future. For me, this awareness has manifested itself in two ways. When I was thirteen and fourteen, I felt bereft of the time of my childhood. I knew that this time could never come back, that I would only get farther and farther away from it. I wanted to be little all over again. But at the same time I couldn't wait to be grown up; I was buying bras and eye makeup, and holding hands with boys. I can remember saying to myself, "You are stupid to want to be big and little at the same time." Somehow I knew that by wanting to be more grown up, I was making my precious childhood go away too fast. This mixture of feelings used to frighten me and make me sad. Now, an awareness of time manifests itself in a complete unawareness of time. By this, I mean that, although I am always fairly prompt and know the hour, I don't see any correlation between how I'm feeling and days and weeks. I can feel that I'm at peace with things for weeks, yet I also know that this feeling could last only another two hours. One minute I can feel bitter and hateful enough to spit, the next minute I could be laughing and happy enough to hug someone. The consistency of my feelings doesn't go with the consistency of time; they are two separate cycles. When I first sensed this, I was frightened, but now it rarely bothers me.

The adolescent needs a tangible escape from the conflicts of his world, and he needs a place to channel the energy and potential of which he is becoming aware. Therefore, it is important that the adolescent have a skill in which he can excel, or that he possess an interest that will provide release and impetus for work. This can be in the area of schoolwork, sport, or the arts—for example, music or photography. Whatever the area, it is most important that he can feel sure of his work, that he can look at his accomplishments and see his good points reflected in the mirror of his skill.

Even those adolescents who do not have the training or incentive to achieve tangible results have a fantasy outside themselves, produced by an instinct for survival. The danger with this fantasy is that it can be so grand that it puts current achievements at a distance from reality. Trying to perfect a skill teaches the adolescent to handle his thoughts or actions constructively. He explores his potential, his ability to work. He learns what work is, and comes closer to other people whom he sees working. By using self-discipline in his work, he finds that he has control over much of what he thinks and does; he sees more clearly his control over emotions and interactions with people. The adolescent realizes that although beliefs form a large part of his character, they are also constantly changing. A skill does not have the inconsistency of beliefs; it grows steadily in strength as work is invested in it. He learns how to deal with what is lacking in his skill, and with this experience can more easily handle his feelings of inadequacy. Hence, his achievements reinforce his good opinion of himself; the steadiness of his work helps him see the outside world with perspective, and with this interest he can keep himself good company when he wants to be alone. A skill has as much value as a best friend.

In coming out of childhood, the adolescent is asked to leave behind the simple play of toy trains, dollhouses, miniature bears, and baseball cards. He is asked to leave behind the simple diversion, amusement, and fun that had been his to enjoy for so many years, no questions asked. He has about ten years in which he must learn how to be adult. Pressures in this direction can be: high school advisers, colleges, the need for money, political action groups. Society asks him to be serious and constructive. A skill provides him with the most effective way to meet society's demand, while at the same time he can retain the sense of recreation that he had as a child.

I will end this essay with a poem I wrote, which describes how,

after all the struggle, pieces of understanding begin to slip into
place.

Long depths would fall and
                        hit me
                    against the wall
                            of my terror-room
                the walls, cement would hold me
                    fast
                            clutch freeze
                stopped me in an icy smothering
                        of choked up time.
Now the walls, warm and bloodwet   smiling
                    bounce me
            back into the middle of the room
                        they
                move me together
                        pushing
                        my liquid
                        into one
                        gently.

Notes on Contributors

JOSEPH ADELSON, born in 1925, is professor of psychology and codirector of the Psychological Clinic at the University of Michigan. He is co-author of *The Adolescent Experience* (New York, 1966) and associate editor of the *Journal of Youth and Adolescence*.

DAVID BAKAN, born in 1921, is professor of psychology at York University, Toronto. Mr. Bakan is the author of *Sigmund Freud and the Jewish Mystical Tradition* (New York, 1958), *The Duality of Human Existence: An Essay on Religion and Psychology* (Chicago, 1966), *Disease, Pain and Sacrifice: Toward a Psychology of Suffering* (Chicago, 1968), *On Method: Toward a Reconstruction of Psychological Investigation* (San Francisco, 1967), and *Slaughter of the Innocents: A Study of the Battered Child Phenomenon* (Toronto and San Francisco, 1971).

PETER BLOS, born in 1904, is a psychoanalyst in private practice. He is the author of *The Adolescent Personality* (New York, 1941), *On Adolescence, A Psychoanalytic Interpretation* (New York, 1962), and *The Young Adolescent* (New York, 1970).

ROBERT COLES, born in 1929, is research psychiatrist at the Harvard University Health Services. His publications include *Children of Crisis: A Study of Courage and Fear* (Boston, 1967), *Still Hungry in America* (New York, 1969), *The Image Is You* (Boston, 1969), *Wages of Neglect* (Chicago, 1969), *Uprooted Children: The Early Lives of Migrant Farmers* (Pittsburgh, 1970), *Drugs and Youth* (New York, 1970), *Erik H. Erikson: The Growth of His Work* (Boston, 1970), *The Middle Americans* (Boston, 1970), *The Geography of Faith: Conversations Between Daniel Berrigan, When Underground, and Robert Coles* (Boston, forthcoming 1971), *Migrants, Sharecroppers and Mountaineers* (volume II of *Children of Crisis*, Boston, 1972), and *The South Goes North* (volume III of *Children of Crisis*, Boston, 1972).

JOHN JANEWAY CONGER, born in 1921, is professor of clinical psychology at the University of Colorado School of Medicine. Mr. Conger is co-author of *Personality, Social Class, and Delinquency* (New York, 1966), *Child Development and Personality*, 3d ed. (New York, 1969), and *Readings in Child Development and Personality*, 2d ed. (New York, 1970).

THOMAS J. COTTLE, born in 1937, is a member of the Education Research Center and Medical Department of the Massachusetts Institute of Technology. He is the author of *Time's Children: Impressions of Youth* (Boston, 1971) and editor of *The Prospect of Youth: Contexts for Sociological and Psychological Inquiry* (Boston, forthcoming).

TINA DEVARON, born in 1955, is a student at the Commonwealth School in Boston.

JOHN H. GAGNON, born in 1931, is professor of sociology at the State University of New York at Stony Brook. He is the author of *Sex Offenders* (New York, 1965), *Sexual Deviance* (New York, 1967), *Sexuelle Aussenseiter* (Hamburg, 1971).

CHAD GORDON, born in 1935, is Fox Professor of Sociology at Rice University and research director of the Model Cities Evaluation Project, Southwest Center for Urban Research, Houston. Mr. Gordon is co-editor of *The Self in Social Interaction*, volume I, *Classic and Contemporary Perspectives* (New York, 1968) and author of *Looking Ahead: Self-Conceptions, Race and Family Factors as Determinants of Adolescent Achievement Orientations* (forthcoming).

JEROME KAGAN, born in 1929, is professor of human development at Harvard University. He is the author of *Birth to Maturity* (New York, 1962), *Child Development and Personality*, 3d ed. (New York, 1969), *Change and Continuity in Infancy* (New York, 1971), *Understanding Children* (New York, 1971).

LAWRENCE KOHLBERG, born in 1927, is professor of education and social psychology, Harvard University Graduate School of Education. He is coeditor of *Recent Research in Moral Development* (New York, forthcoming 1971) and author of "Stage and Sequence: The Cognitive-Developmental Approach to Socialization," in D. Goslin, ed., *Handbook of Socialization Theory and Research* (Chicago, 1969) and of "From Is to Ought: How to Commit the Naturalistic Fallacy and Get Away with It in the Study of Moral Development," in T. Mischel, ed., *Cognitive Development and Epistemology* (New York, forthcoming 1971).

PHYLLIS LA FARGE, born in 1933, is a writer. Her publications include *Keeping Going* (New York, 1971), three juvenile books published and three forthcoming, and numerous magazine articles including several on women's education. She is currently at work on a book about college undergraduate women.

EDWARD C. MARTIN, born in 1937, is staff associate at the National Council for the Social Studies, Washington, D.C. He is coauthor of *The People Make a Nation,* an inquiry and issue oriented history textbook (Boston, 1971) and editor-writer for *The Social Studies Professional,* NCSS newsletter, 1970-1971.

J. M. TANNER, born in 1920, is professor of child health and growth at the Institute of Child Health, the University of London. He is the author of *Education and Physical Growth* (London, 1961), *Growth at Adolescence,* 2d ed. (Oxford, 1962), and *The Physique of the Olympic Athlete* (London, 1964).